ecpr PRESS

Conditional Democracy

The Contemporary Debate on Political Reform in Chinese Universities

Émilie Frenkiel

ecprPRESS

The ECPR Press is the publishing imprint of the European Consortium for Political Research (ECPR), a scholarly association, which supports and encourages the training, research and cross-national co-operation of political scientists in institutions throughout Europe and beyond.

ECPR Press
Harbour House
Hythe Quay
Colchester
CO2 8JF
United Kingdom

Typeset by Lapiz Digital Services

Printed and bound by Lightning Source

British Library Cataloguing in Publication Data

A catalogue record for this book is available from the British Library

ISBN: 978-1-907-301-69-8
PDF ISBN: 978-1-910-259-50-4
EPUB ISBN: 978-1-910-259-51-1
KINDLE ISBN: 978-1-910-259-49-8

www.ecpr.eu/ecprpress

Contents

Selective Timeline of Major Historical Events

4 May 1919	Student demonstration against the Treaty of Versailles, leading to the landmark anti-imperialist cultural and political 'May Fourth movement'.
October 1949	Proclamation of the People's Republic of China.
1956–7	The 'Hundred Flowers' campaign misleads citizens, and especially intellectuals, to openly express their opinions about the communist regime.
1957–8	The 'Anti-Rightist' campaign is used by Mao to eliminate critical intellectuals.
1959–61	The 'Great Leap Forward', intended to modernise China's economy, triggers the largest famine in human history, with an estimated 14–30 million casualties.
1966–76	The 'Great Proletarian Cultural Revolution' begins.
1970–6	Mao Zedong progressively disappears from public life due to health problems. The 'Gang of Four', including Mao's wife Jiang Qing, tries to increase politcal influence by spearheading the Cultural Revolution.
September 1971	Lin Biao, Mao's heir apparent, is killed in airplane crash while fleeing after an attempted military coup.
January 1976	Death of Premier Zhou Enlai.
September 1976	Chairman Mao Zedong dies at the age of 82. The 'Gang of Four' tries to get into power.
1977	Hua Guofeng begins the 'Open Door' policy.
1977	Deng Xiaoping wins the power struggle after Mao's death; Gang of Four are arrested.
1977	After the end of the Cultural Revolution, the national unified entrance examination for universities is re-introduced.
1978–9	Deng Xiaoping introduces the 'Open and Reform' policy and stepwise economic reforms called 'The Four Modernisations'.
1978–9	The 'Democracy Wall' in Beijing displays pro-democratic posters.
1980	Special Economic Zones are created in Shenzhen, Zhuhai, Shantou (Guangdong), Xiamen (Fujian), and the entire province of Hainan.
1985–8	The 'Cultural Fever': Intellectuals identify China's alleged feudal traditions as the cause of its backwardness.
1986	Students demonstrate all over China.

January 1987	The supposedly too-liberal General Secretary of China's Communist Party, Hu Yaobang, is forced to resign.
1989	Jiang Zemin replaces Zhao Ziyang as CCP General Secretary.
April 1989	Hu Yaobang dies.
4 June 1989	Military crackdown on Tiananmen Square demonstrations.
Jan–Feb 1992	Deng Xiaoping tours southern China and accelerates market reforms to establish a 'socialist market economy'.
February 1997	Death of Deng Xiaoping.
July 1997	Hong Kong's retrocession to China from UK control.
1998	Zhu Rongji replaces Li Peng as China's Premier.
1999	Cooling of US-China relations after NATO bombs Chinese embassy in Belgrade, former Yugoslavia.
April 2001	Major diplomatic crisis after US spy plane collides with Chinese fighter jet in mid-air and is forced to land.
November 2001	After years of negotiations, China becomes a member of the World Trade Organisation.
November 2002	Hu Jintao replaces Jiang Zemin as head of the Communist Party.
March 2003	Hu Jintao is elected President by National People's Congress and Wen Jintao becomes Premier. Hu–Wen administration promotes a 'harmonious society', a 'new socialist countryside' and more 'scientific development'.
Mar–Apr 2003	SARS virus outbreak.
August 2008	Beijing hosts Olympic Games.
July 2009	China demands that new personal computers come with filtering software 'Green Dam Youth Escort'.
October 2009	Mass celebrations to mark 60 years of Communist Party rule over China.
2010	The World Expo takes place in Shanghai.
2010	Xi Jinping is appointed vice-chairman of the party's Central Military Commission.
February 2011	China overtakes Japan to become the world's second-largest economy.
January 2012	Official figures suggest city dwellers outnumber China's rural population for the first time.
March 2012	Chongqing Communist Party chief Bo Xilai is dismissed on the eve of the Party's ten-yearly leadership change.
November 2012	Seventeenth Communist Party Congress, begins transfer of power to the sixth generation of leaders. Xi Jinping takes over as party chief.

March 2013	Xi Jinping takes over as president. He launches an efficiency and anti-corruption drive.
Sept–Oct 2014	Protests against Beijing's plans to vet candidates for elections in 2017 erupt in Hong Kong.

Acknowledgements

This book derives from a PhD dissertation defended at the Ecole des Hautes Etudes en Sciences Sociales, Paris, France in June 2012. Let me first warmly thank my supervisor Pierre Rosanvallon, for his teaching, advice and encouragement, as well as for his tireless trust and support. I am very grateful for the opportunity he gave me not just to conduct this research but also to join the editorial board of *La vie des idées/ Books & Ideas* and its irreplaceable professional, intellectual and human environment.

My gratitude goes to the members of my doctoral defence committee, Yves Chevrier, Jean-Luc Domenach, Jean-Louis Rocca and Yves Sintomer, whose remarks have contributed to turning the thesis into a book. On that point, I would like to thank Dario Castiglione and Laura Pugh for their trust and patience and Deborah Savage for her excellent editing. I owe special thanks to Daniel A. Bell, Jean-Louis Rocca and Pasquale Pasquino for having commented on the whole book and fruitfully discussed it with me.

I would like to express my thanks to all those who have facilitated this research through lengthy discussions, productive remarks and stimulating contributions. I am particularly beholden to Wei Nanzhi and He Jianyu for their invaluable advice and assistance. I extend my thanks also to Liu Juanjuan, Ivan Jablonka, Florent Guénard, Emilie L'Hôte, Cristelle Terroni, Nicolas Duvoux, Ariel Suhamy, Gao Zhenhua, Jacques Marchal, Monique Marchal and Monique Frenkiel for their support and various contributions to this book.

This study was made materially possible with the help of several institutions: The Ecole Normale Supérieure de Lettres et Sciences Humaines (Lyons); The Ecole des Hautes Etudes en Sciences Sociales, Paris-Est-Créteil University; and the Collège de France, which provided a very supportive and stimulating environment for research and writing. I would also like to thank Wei Nanzhi, Wu Xia and Jean-Louis Rocca, Damien Duca, my family, my friends, colleagues and students for their priceless material and emotional support.

Finally, I owe most to the pillars of this research: my supervisor Pierre Rosanvallon and all the Chinese academics who agreed to be interviewed and without whom this study could not have been conducted.

A note on Mandarin Chinese: I have used pinyin Romanisation, except where this wouldn't make any sense to the non-Chinese reader used to other spellings such as Sun Yat-sen (Sun Zhongshan), Tu Weiming (Du Weiming), Yü Yingshih (Yu Yingshi), Peking University (Beijing University) and Tsinghua University (Qinghua University).

For Chinese names, the family name-given name order has been preserved, except for scholars long implanted in foreign countries, like Cheng Li from the Brookings Institution.

Émilie Frenkiel,
March 2015

For my son, Camille.

Introduction

Since the new generation of Chinese leaders came to power in November 2012, speculation about the policy Xi Jinping and Li Keqiang are most likely to follow has proliferated. Only a few weeks before the power transition, the *New York Times* article revealing the exceptional wealth of Prime Minister Wen Jiabao's family and the spectacular eviction of Bo Xilai – who was one of the most prominent candidates for a seat on the Political Bureau's Standing Committee – shocked both the Chinese and the world. There have been mixed assessments of Hu and Wen's record – including disappointment as regards their unfulfilled promises of a more harmonious society, better social policy, fighting corruption and rationalising and democratising governance – and these dramatic developments and the tensions within the highest Party spheres that they have disclosed are a strong incentive for the new team of leaders to make a clean break from their predecessors' policy. This break can only be formal and predictable, however, since Xi has put himself forward as a consensual leader, the son of communist veteran Xi Zhongxun, with Party apparatchik Li by his side. However, the President's manifestly strong confidence, opinions and political base lead us to think that he could, nevertheless push for a new direction. And the precise content of the reforms to be implemented by the fifth-generation leaders is, to date, hard to anticipate, except that their primary objective is bound to be to further cement the Party's hold on power.

To get an insight into the experience, worldviews and potential agenda of the fifth generation of Chinese leaders, in this book I have chosen to investigate the way in which major Chinese public intellectuals conceive democracy. It is indeed quite remarkable that most of the politically committed academics I have studied in this research belong to exactly the same generation as the current leaders: the generation whose education was upset by the Cultural Revolution. The community of experience between these famous scholars and the current leaders is all the more striking as the latter's education, training and occupations are clearly distinct from those of previous generations of leaders, which might considerably affect the nature of the policies they could implement.[1] Many of the leaders from the fifth generation studied social sciences, political science, economics or law in the same universities at the same period, whereas former leaders were all engineers. So the fifth generation of leaders may want to make their mark on these fields and discuss social and political reform in a meaningful way. In addition, the scholars approached in this work give us an insight into how this new political elite apprehends China's

---

1.   *See* Li, C. 'The Chinese Communist Party: recruiting and controlling the new elites', *Journal Of Current Chinese Affairs* 2009, 38(3), available online at http://journals.sub.uni-hamburg.de/giga/jcca/article/view/59 (last accessed 14 November 2014), p. 19; Vilfredo Pareto, *The Rise and Fall of the Elites: An application of theoretical sociology,* Totowa, NJ: Bedminster Press, 1968; and Robert D. Putnam, *The Comparative Study of Political Elites*, Englewood Cliffs, NJ: Prentice-Hall, 1968.

political future. As a result, the first objective of this book is to grasp how political reform has been approached since 1989: who takes part in discussions on that issue and makes proposals, from what point of view and with what impact?

Within the boundaries dictated by (self-)censorship, the debate on political reform in Chinese universities reveals the great diversity of the academic elites' aspirations for change. Therefore, mapping this debate enables us to understand the various conceptions of the current regime held by academics throughout China, to identify the fault lines that have materialised since the Tiananmen Square repression and to comprehend these academics' disagreements. Analysing these scholars' discussions, which have an impact on political elites and public opinion and which reflect their respective yearnings and fears even if in a distorted manner, is also an engaging angle from which to appreciate the diversity of approaches to the issue of China's democratisation.

This book focuses on the debate about political reform since the beginning of the 1990s. This date is important for two main reasons. First, it is necessary to understand the resilience of the regime, which seemed unthinkable in the wake of the Tiananmen Square repression and the collapse of the Soviet Union.[2] And it is all the more urgent as few studies have been devoted to the political reform (*zhengzhi tizhi gaige*) announced as early as 1986 by Deng Xiaoping.[3] Analysts tend to deplore its absence and to downplay the significance of reforms that are officially designed to modernise and strengthen the legitimacy of the one-party system.[4] These certainly imply no devolution of power to social groups and so far have not been accompanied by any significant calls for the active political participation of social groups. Nonetheless, the regime evolves, notably through measures supposed to boost its efficiency and accountability and introduce new forms of social control; this may help explain why various studies have shown that the regime has managed to become more legitimate to the Chinese people.[5] Chinese scholars deplore the sterility of some of the concepts and standards that have become widely accepted, such as the opposition between democracy and authoritarianism, which they consider to be a critical impediment to understanding the current regime and its evolution. This research takes these criticisms into account and explores the perspectives offered by Gunter Schubert, Thomas Heberer and Andrew Nathan, by examining the question of political reform from a different angle, namely, the discourse on the issue of the Chinese themselves.[6]

---

2. Nathan, A. 'Authoritarian resilience', *Journal of Democracy* 2003, 14(1), pp. 6–17.

3. Wong, Y. -C. *From Deng Xiaoping to Jiang Zemin: Two decades of political reform in the People's Republic of China*, Lanham, MD: University Press of America, 2005, p. 10.

4. Wong, Y. C. *From Deng Xiaoping to Jiang Zemin*; Dittmer, L. and Liu, G. (eds), *China's Deep Reform: Domestic politics in transition*, Lanham, MD: Rowman & Littlefield Publishers, 2006; Perry, E. and Goldman, M. (eds) *Grassroots Political Reform in China*, Cambridge, MA: Harvard University Press, 2007.

5. *See* Tang, W. especially *Public Opinion and Political Change in China*, Stanford, CA: Stanford University Press, 2005.

6. *See* Heberer, T. and Schubert, G. 'Political reform and regime legitimacy in contemporary China', *Asien* 99, April 2006, pp. 9–28; Nathan, A. 'China's political trajectory: what are the Chinese saying?', in Li, C (ed.) *China's Changing Political Landscape*, Washington, DC: Brookings Institution Press, 2008.

The definition of political reform still radically divides Chinese intellectuals. Some view it as a definite transition towards a democratic regime in which leaders are directly elected at fixed, regular intervals, while others have a more general take on 'political change' and assert that it cannot be limited to the mere adoption of the liberal democratic model.[7] They insist that reforms of the state, of the relationships between central and local governments, of fiscal and social policies and so on, should also be taken into account in the debate about past, present and future political reform.

Previous research has often focused on the activists who conform to a stricter definition of political reform, that is, dissident and liberal intellectual movements – as in the seminal books of Elizabeth Perry and Merle Goldman[8] – or has introduced intellectual developments in China in a very broad perspective without a particular focus on political ideas or on academics – as in Chen Yan's *L'eveil de la Chine* and Zhang Lun's *La vie intellectuelle après la mort de Mao*. My object is closer to that of Joseph Fewsmith in the second part of *China Since Tiananmen*, which is devoted to the development of neo-conservative thinking and statism in China. I also follow in the tracks of Hua Shiping, in *Scientism and Humanism: Two cultures in Post-Mao China (1978–1989)*; in this study of six 'organic' intellectuals,[9] he describes their great independence of mind, despite their perfect integration in the system, and the consequently greater impact their analyses and proposals had on the policy orientation of the 1980s.

The doctoral research which led to this book confirmed what American scholars Andrew Nathan, Hua Shiping and Tang Wenfang have claimed: it is simplistic to identify organic intellectuals simply as defenders of the *status quo*.[10] Behind official discourse and the line of argument often taken up by scholars who are close to authorities, multiple logics are at work and scholars have proven to be

---

7. Frenkiel, E. 'Political change and democracy in China. An interview with Wang Shaoguang', *Books & Ideas*, 15 July 2009. Available online at http://www.booksandideas.net/Political-change-and-democracy-in.html (last accessed 14 November 2014).

8. Goldman, M. *Sowing the Seeds of Democracy in China: Political reform in the Deng Xiaoping era*, Cambridge, MA: Harvard University Press, 1994; *From Comrade to Citizen: The struggle for political rights in China*, Cambridge, MA: Harvard University Press, 2005; and Perry, E. *Challenging the Mandate of Heaven: Social protest and state power in China*, Armonk, New York: M.E. Sharpe, 2002.

9. I use here the Gramscian concept of the organic intellectual as adapted by Zins, M. -J. in 'L'intellectuel occidentalisé indien: de l'intellectuel syncrétique à l'intellectuel organique', in Trebitsch, M. and Granjon, M. -C. (eds), *Pour une histoire comparée des intellectuels*, Paris and Bruxelles: Editions Complexe/IHTP-CNRS, 1998: 'his main function is to contribute to setting up a "legitimate problematique of politics" designed to fundamentally meet the demands of the social group he or she belongs to'.

10. Fewsmith, J. *China Since Tiananmen: The politics of transition*, Cambridge: Cambridge University Press, 2001; Hua, S. *Scientism and Humanism: Two cultures in Post-Mao China (1978–1989)*, Albany, NY: State University of New York Press, 1995; Wang, J. *Reverse Course: Political neo-conservatism and regime stability in post-Tiananmen China*, PhD dissertation, Columbia University, 2006; and Van Dongen, E. *Goodbye Radicalism, Conceptions of radicalism among Chinese intellectuals during the early 1990s*, PhD dissertation, University of Leiden, The Netherlands, 2009.

experts at using official language to advance their own objectives. Besides, the closer scholars are to power, the more opportunities they get to openly voice their opinions and the more impact their criticisms and suggestions have. This is the situation of senior researchers from the most prestigious Chinese universities or think tanks, who enjoy the chance to interact more easily with political leaders. They should therefore be considered less as organic than as reflective intellectuals, who take both a close and a distant position with regard to the system.

At first glance, Chinese scholars' academic freedom and freedom of expression seem very limited. It is difficult to imagine that an interesting debate on the question of political reform could take place in China or, given the absence of political reform, that the proposals which some engaged academics put forward in spite of everything could have an impact on public policy. My first-hand experience of prestigious Beijing universities (mainly the Peking University and Tsinghua University) encouraged me to go beyond this reticence and to study what is actually being said and happening in Chinese universities. The first interviews conducted with academics and PhD candidates in philosophy and political theory from the best universities in Beijing, and questionnaires filled in by their students, aroused my curiosity. The free tone in speaking of the academics I met and the variety of publications on democracy which were available at the Peking University library contrasted quite dramatically with my preconceptions of the censorship and the constraints imposed on the debate on the political future of China. What struck me even more was the contrast between the free spirit and conversation of researchers (no matter senior or junior) devoting their attention to the issue of democracy or China's political evolution and the guarded tone of students, academics and people from all walks of life that I encountered while living in Beijing, whenever our conversation approached political issues. This is how I sensed that studying experts – specialists in political theory and political institutions, philosophers, political scientists – would be of great interest. They, indeed, were in the eye of the storm, since they seemed to be less affected than the rest of the Chinese population by censorship and self-censorship. What also attracted my attention, regarding reflection on political change, was the constant combination of dissatisfaction with the current system, patriotic concern regarding China's future and the call for reform (often taking the form of problem-solving reflection), while the views expressed, models referred to and solutions offered varied greatly. It led me to posit that there was a lively debate on political reform in China that deserved deeper scrutiny than the existing literature offered.

Methodologically speaking, I tried to keep my distance from ideological preconceptions that have often oriented research on contemporary Chinese politics and to scrutinise actors from the whole political spectrum, from the most liberal to the most conservative, from the far left to the far right. I also assumed that I would examine what is being said and what has been going on in China for the last 25 years, rather than what has not occurred. This implies discarding the regular approach towards Chinese politics, which relies on the study, or rather criticism, of China's democratic deficit. Through reviewing the most salient publications related to the issue of political change in China, and through consulting with the first participants in the debate on political reform that I had identified, I came up with a list of about 20 prominent scholars from various universities and departments in mainland China, Hong-Kong and Singapore.[11] As a result, this book is based mainly on the study of the academic and media publications of these well known and politically committed academics, as well as on interviews that I conducted with them between 2005 and 2013. It investigates the historical, political, social and ideological context of the positions taken by some Chinese scholars in discussions on the direction that reform of the Chinese regime should take. It first presents the context in which Chinese researchers are taking a stand. This context has seen university departments in the humanities and social sciences reopen from 1978 onwards to enable and serve the Open and Reform policy, in parallel with access to higher education for a generation of students strongly marked by the Cultural Revolution and eager to discover and use the theories and research developed in American and European universities. It defines the status of Chinese researchers and academics, the outlines of academic freedom and the relationship that engaged academics have with the authorities. Divided on the ideological front but united by their patriotism, certain academics step out of their domain of expertise and take a stand, in the hope of influencing the orientation of government policies. The impact of their political interventions is often difficult to assess but the Party has opted for a strategy of promoting its legitimacy, through greater attentiveness to society's needs and adapting to social changes – even though the Party readily resorts to repression when this charm tactic does not suffice to silence the opposition. The Party ultimately needs researchers' expertise and is, in many ways, subject to their influence. Academic freedom and freedom of publication are therefore extensive, provided one does not explicitly call the supremacy of the Party into question. This taboo is a major constraint but one which is nevertheless somewhat mitigated by the new flexibility and the size of the Party (over 80 million members), as well as numerous circumventing strategies. Finally, as the sources of funding for research become increasingly diverse, researchers are gaining even more leeway.

To get a clear grasp of the prolific and multi-faceted debate on political reform in China, I have studied intellectual debates within Chinese universities and in dialogue with universities in the rest of the world. This book therefore mainly focuses on Chinese social sciences and humanities academics from major China or Hong Kong universities; and on their proposals for reform. They set the tone for new ideas in Chinese society; all the more so as they are more or less directly connected to the new generation of leaders. However, these academics can in no case be seen as representative of the whole of Chinese academia. The size and heterogeneity of the Chinese academic field are indeed colossal. On the contrary, these academics are all university professors, often honorary (*mingyu jiaoshou*) or (*tepin jiaoshou*) chair

11. In alphabetical order: Cui Zhiyuan, Deng Zhenglai, Gan Yang, He Zengke, Kang Xiaoguang, Li Qiang, Liu Dong, Liu Jiunning, Pan Wei, Ren Jiantao, Wang Shaoguang, Xiao Gongqin, Xu Jilin, Xu Youyu, Yang Guangbin, Yao Yang, Zheng Yongnian, Zhu Guanglei (and Qin Hui, Yu Keping, Hu Angang, Zhu Xueqin, Jiang Qing).

professors with administrative responsibilities. Most of them are department heads (*suozhang*), faculty deans or vice-deans (*yuanzhang, fuyuanzhang*).[12] They have had exceptional careers, which may explain their influence, against the backdrop of a technocratic regime and the great respect the Chinese tend to have for expertise and knowledge. This also accounts for the absence of any female academic in this study.[13] These academics stand out from the silent majority of their colleagues because they rely on their research and expertise to speak out beyond a strictly academic context and make proposals regarding the issue of political reform.[14] They are famous intellectuals, in the sense that these academics engage in the public sphere to provide an assessment of the most urgent 'problems' that must be solved in order 'to save China', to share their analyses and views on current matters and to defend important values.[15] The choice of these 'public intellectuals' (*gonggong zhishifenzi*) – to resort to this label designating, outside of France, intellectuals addressing an intellectual audience on political or ideological issues[16] – was motivated by their public interventions and publications on political reform; and by the potential impact of these. It is no easy task to accurately measure the scope of ideas and intellectual proposals, even though some studies have managed to document the influence of sociologists such as Anthony Giddens in Great Britain, for instance.[17] This is all the more difficult as scholars, in China and beyond, are often reluctant to answer questions regarding their relationship with power, especially when faced with counterparts who are likely to disapprove of it.

This study investigates the diversity of currents of political ideas in China, of forms of political commitment among academics and of conditions in which they work and speak out. It also explores influential views and tries to measure their impact on power and on the Chinese population. These ideas, very much like political concepts, emerge, live on and spread out in a historical, social and political context that is an essential consideration for understanding them. Conceptual historians of politics have stressed the importance of taking into account 'systems

12. It is much harder for the most explicit advocates of political liberalism, such as Xu Youyu, Qin Hui and Liu Junning, to reach such positions.

13. Women with exceptional careers are also less common in European universities but sexism is definitely stronger in China. According to a 2011 report, 24.2% of undergraduates and 47% of master's students are women: http://www.wiareport.com/2011/08/women-in-china-nearing-equality-in-higher-education-enrollments (last accessed 14 November 2014). Besides, it is well known that it is extremely hard for female PhDs to marry in China, where they are considered the 'third sex' (*disanxing*).

14. They publish their views in general intellectual reviews and journals such as *Dushu, Ershiyi Shiji, Xueren* Or *Zhanlue Yu Guanli* (shut down in September 2004) or liberal weeklies like the *Nanfang Zhoumo*, but also in blogs and on websites like *Tianya*.

15. The notion of the intellectual will be analysed more thoroughly in Chapter Three.

16. *Cf.* Posner, R. *Public Intellectuals, A study of decline*, Cambridge, MA: Harvard University Press, 2001, p. 1: 'intellectuals who opine to an educated public on questions of or inflected by a political or ideological concern'.

17. Tournadre-Plancq, J. 'Un "intellectuel consacré" dans l'espace politique: le cas d'Anthony Giddens', *Socio-logos. Revue de l'association française de sociologie* 3, 2008 Varia, available online at http://socio-logos.revues.org/1723 (last accessed 14 November 2014).

of representations in order to understand the way a generation, a country, or social groups lead their actions and consider their future'.[18] This research was inspired by the conceptual history of politics, in so far as it focuses on the systems of representation underlying the public stands the academics under scrutiny make. The involvement of contemporary Chinese intellectuals in the debate on reform is indeed conditioned by their representation of the era they have lived in and of the future of the Chinese political regime. It is more specifically conditioned by how they conceive the impact of the economic reforms (the Open and Reform policy) launched by Deng Xiaoping after the Cultural Revolution, his policy of opening to the outside world (and to western thoughts and political systems), the brutal repression of the Tiananmen Square protest movement in June 1989, China's entry into the WTO and the rise of protest movements in Chinese cities and villages for the past fifteen years.

This book, mainly devoted to the ideas and political representations of politically committed scholars, also analyses the context in which they make a stand in the debate on political reform. As a result, it comprises a sociological dimension, that is, an analysis of the status of academics, the limits of academic freedom and the relationship between politically committed scholars and authorities. It also includes a prosoprographic study, as it draws the intellectual portrait of a generation of a certain type of Chinese intellectuals. The book questions the possibility of that group tackling the crucial issue of political reform in the current Chinese context: a single Party; censorship; depoliticisation; and the restriction of political science to Marxist and Maoist studies. Their personal assessment (which is related to their field of expertise but also to their experience and ideological leaning) of the current situation and the so-called Chinese conditions (*guoqing*), their attitude towards Chinese 'tradition' (*zhongguo wenhua chuantong*) and their reception of various western theories and political models provide a valuable angle from which to approach the wide array of political trends reflected in many publications, during intellectual meetings and on the internet. The intellectuals under scrutiny belong to various tendencies. To name only a few, Xu Youyu is a philosopher from the Chinese Academy of Social Sciences. He belongs to the liberal camp. Historian Xiao Gongqin from Shanghai Normal University launched Chinese neo-authoritarianism and was the first one to theorise Chinese neo-conservatism. Political science professor Wang Shaoguang from the Chinese University of Hong Kong started the debate on state capacity that led to the emergence of the Chinese New Left. Pan Wei, from the international relations school in Peking University, is a conservative who is very critical of electoral democracy and promotes the implementation of a 'genuine rule of law'. Kang Xiaoguang, an interdisciplinary scholar from People's University, advocates reviving Confucian ideas and setting up an elitist and meritocratic regime. He Zengke, a researcher at the official Political Innovations Research Centre, is an

---

18. Rosanvallon, P. 'Pour une histoire conceptuelle du politique', *Revue de synthèse (Questions d'histoire intellectuelle)* 1–2, 1986, pp. 93–105.

adherent of the idea of a gradual 'mixed democracy'. Liu Dong is the vice-head of Tsinghua University's China studies department. He is an editor of major humanities journals and book collections. Yao Yang is the Dean of the School of National Development and Head of the Economic Research Centre of Peking University. He has focused on the economic consequences of village elections and described the Party as a 'disinterested government', playing the role of a neutral arbiter of the various interest groups that compose Chinese society.[19]

To establish the list of scholars I studied, I proceeded step by step. I first collected the names that were invariably associated with the main ideological trends constituting the majority of public intellectual debates on political reforms. As to the New Left, Wang Shaoguang, Gan Yang, Cui Zhiyuan and Wang Hui (even though the latter is a literature professor) are the most cited, no matter the format or media. The main voices of (the political brand of) liberalism are Zhu Xueqin, Xu Youyu, Qin Hui, Ren Jiantao and Liu Junning. Many economists also advocate liberal ideas but they express themselves on economic liberalism and are outside the scope of this research. Xiao Gongqin, the most famous neo-conservative theoretician, as well as Kang Xiaoguang, Pan Wei and Jiang Qing, are essential participants in the debate, famous for their explicit rejection of democratisation for China. These thirteen scholars constitute the core of the debate on political reform in China. As I went further in this research, it appeared that other scholars should be included as well. First, Yu Keping and He Zengke are also involved in the debate as political scientists in charge of the Political Innovations Research Centre. They have published lavishly on the issue of political reform, and developed institutional arrangement proposals. Economists Hu Angang and Yao Yang's involvement in the political debate has also left a strong mark. I also felt that it was necessary to interview again Liu Dong, a famous Beijing professor and editor, and Li Qiang, a political science professor – both of whom I had already met in 2005, when writing a dissertation on the introduction of Anglo-American contemporary political philosophy in Chinese universities.[20] Besides, to better comprehend the evolution of political philosophy and political science in China, the study has also included Deng Zhenglai, Yang Guangbin and Zhu Guanglei, who have also directly worked and published on that issue. Last of all, Zheng Yongnian and Daniel A. Bell have brought a more remote insight into this debate: the former as a leading scholar based abroad (first at the University of Nottingham and more recently at the National University of Singapore) and the latter for his experience as a foreign scholar working in Chinese universities and for his elaborate views as regards this debate.

Undertaking interviews with these scholars, completed with the study of their work (articles published in academic, intellectual or mainstream journals and books published in mainland China and abroad, including Hong Kong and Taiwan), as

---

19. The biographies of the main scholars under study are available in Appendix B.
20. Frenkiel, E. *Perfect Freedom: A Study of the evolution and representation of contemporary Anglo-American political philosophy in China*, MPhil dissertation, Ecole Normale Supérieure de Lyon, 2005.

well as their public interventions, allows us to explore and go beyond the imperfect categories of conservatism, New Left and liberalism: we can then grasp the diversity of points of view within these trends and also better identify thinkers expressing themselves outside the confines of the confrontation between these last two groups. Neo-conservatism (*xin baoshouzhuyi*) was theorised with precision by Xiao Gongqin to justify the necessity of an authoritarian transition so as to guarantee social stability and efficiently boost the economic development of the country. The term was later gradually used in a much broader way to qualify official discourse,[21] the general mind-set of the Chinese intelligentsia[22] and the middle classes[23] as well as of the Asian diaspora.[24] First used in an exclusively pejorative way by opponents, the New Left (*xin zuo pai*) label designates those who, contrary to the traditional or old Left, accept the principle of a market economy but endeavour to regulate it more. As to liberals (*ziyou zhuyi*), they include a wide range of defenders of political liberalism defining themselves mainly in opposition to the New Left and notably to its controversial defence of some elements of the Maoist legacy.

Research based on discourse is necessarily oriented by the status of this material. The interviews transcribed, translated and quoted in this volume, reflect the way actors narrate their trajectories and try to rationalise their positions and deeds. Besides, their discourse may vary depending on their audience and this double language is not always easy to detect.

Moreover, the role of intellectuals is not limited to influence-seeking. They inform, refer to values, theories and systems of thought, reflect on issues and events, compete, express themselves, come from different fields and opt for various directions.[25] Within the intellectual field and within the specific field of intellectuals involved in defining Chinese political reform, competition, oppositions and struggles are many and fierce. As a result, this inquiry is divided into three parts.

The first part aims at understanding the perspective from which interviewed scholars speak and on what conditions; what their status is; which experiences have marked them; and how they define themselves. Chapter One describes the dramatic evolution in their living and working conditions and the great heterogeneity of their situations. Beside censorship, which looms constantly over researchers' heads, and their lack of autonomy from the state, the academic field is more and more dependent on the market: companies, NGOs and various institutions and foundations offer the possibility of copiously supplementing the stipend academics

21. Walton Keller, W. and Rawski, T. G. *China's Rise and the Balance of Influence in Asia*, Pittsburgh, PA: University of Pittsburgh Press, 2007, p. 81.

22. In his PhD dissertation, dissident Wang, Juntao labels the whole Chinese intelligentsia neo-conservative (Wang, J. *Reverse Course*).

23. Li, C. *China's Emerging Middle Class: Beyond economic transformation*, Washington, DC: Brookings Institution Press, 2010.

24. Wu, J. Y.-S. and Chen, T. C. *Asian American Studies Now: A critical reader*, New Brunswick, NJ: Rutgers University Press, 2010, p. 2.

25. Collini, S. *Absent Minds: Intellectuals in Britain*, Oxford: Oxford University Press, 2006, p. 6.

receive, which is meagre unless they are part of the academic elite constituted by famous professors who graduated from the Chinese or international 'Ivy League' universities. The Chinese academic condition varies depending on the type of university, the researcher's subject, his years of experience and his capacity to multiply sources of funding. However, some common elements in all Chinese academics' daily practice emerge. What makes their experience distinct from their foreign counterparts' is the presence and the power of the Party in universities; resilient limitations to academic freedom and freedom of publication in particular; the process through which the Chinese social sciences have been revived and made to catch up after a 30-year clampdown; the practical role assigned to them in China's modernisation process; and the reversed conception of the role of the committed academic in this country where criticism is more effective and legitimate when it comes from within the system.

The second chapter is devoted to the itinerary of two generations of scholars. It focuses on their feeling of belonging to two unique generations, especially marked by the experience by the Cultural Revolution and the liberalisation of the 1980s, which the Tiananmen Square repression put an end to. Scholars from the so-called 'Cultural Revolution generation' or 'lost generation' are quite typically animated by pragmatism, interest in the Chinese nation's destiny and a constant reflection on history and the future of humanity. They harbour elitist feelings, which they justify by their direct experience, when they were sent to the countryside by Mao, of the low level of education and the passivity of rural populations. As a result, it is quite common to hear that the Chinese population is still too 'backward' (*luohou*) and of a too-low quality (*suzhi di*) to be trusted with the hard task of electing its leaders at all levels. Scholars from the following generation who are involved in the debate on economic and political reform strive to set themselves apart from this older generation: partly because of the latter's interrupted primary and secondary education and also because of its relative lack of specialisation, related to both their self-taught training and the broad political and disciplinary interests of some of the older scholars. However, I will show the generations have become close while studying together at university. Yet, in spite of this common background, the range of intellectual and social responses to the stimulus of historical experiences shared by members of a whole generation is very broad. The different political groups and associations that emerged during the 1980s and 1990s partly correspond to distinct interpretations of the experience these individuals had of the Cultural Revolution; but the process of ending the revolution and the subsequent decades of reform, including the trauma of the Tiananmen Square repression and the collapse of the Soviet Union, was also important in this.

The second part of the book deals with the intellectual engagement of these scholars, the different strategies they adopt to make their voices heard and their ideological divisions. Chapter Three investigates the relationship between research and power. It investigates the historical, political, social and ideological context of the positions taken by some Chinese scholars in the discussions on the direction that the reform of the Chinese regime should take.

The chapter investigates the relationship between intellectual[26] and political elites; the changing relationship between the Chinese state and Chinese society; the progressively more complex perceptions of western history, theory and experience of Chinese scholars; and the shift, from the 1990s on, to the 'indigenisation' (*bentuhua*) of thinking about reform.

Defining intellectuals narrowly as explicit critics of the establishment has the serious disadvantage of discarding a whole group of relatively independent figures and the wide array of forms of commitment they manifest, corresponding to their multifarious positioning towards power. The scholars under scrutiny must be considered as intellectuals in the sense that they leave their specific field of expertise, comforted by their cultural capital and national or even international academic accomplishment, and because they speak out and publically share their analyses and points of view. They observe the technocratic 'rules of the game' because they have given up on revolutionary breaks and give more or less credence to the official discourse on the crucial role the single Party plays in developing and maintaining stability (*weiwen*), given the insufficient 'quality' of the population. A vast market of ideas has, consequently, materialised, in which intellectual elites are at the service of political elites. It is fairly well supplied with customers and products and the variety of interests and political opinions within political circles guarantees powerful sponsors for all types of proposals academics might make – as long as they are legitimised by cultural capital and expertise. Suggestions from a committed scholar, even if first submerged in the mass of academic proposals, can, consequently, emerge, if a leader or an institution chooses to resort to them so as to legitimise or justify the ratification of an idea or policy. The methods of internal (*neibu*) communication between researchers and leaders gradually lose ground. The regime has recently promoted its greater transparency, listening, accountability and responsiveness. This implies that it pays greater attention to public opinion. State and society, far from being opposed, co-operate, and their strategic interaction benefits both sides. Chapter Four is mainly devoted to the large debates on social issues launched by committed scholars in the 1990s and 2000s and to the impact of the Open and Reform policy on the political views of intellectual elites, amongst whom different groups with varying perspectives on the potential benefits of 'tradition' for China's modernisation have emerged, as is discussed in Chapter Four. I will show that the neo-conservative and nationalist claims first made in the year 1990 triggered active introspection on the part of Chinese scholars; that these considerations have gradually spread out and affected

---

26. To refer to intellectuals from a sociological perspective in Chinese, *zhishifenzi* has been the word used for a long time. It designates a socio-cultural category whose professional occupation is directly connected to ideas or culture. The words *zhishijie* (field of knowledge) and *zhishijieji* (intelligentsia) are often used as well. From a cultural perspective, to refer to the cultural authority of an individual expressing himself or taking a stand publicly, the adjective *gonggong* is often used: *gonggong zhishifenzi* (public intellectual). The reference in studies on Chinese intellectuals is Xu Jilin, who uses precisely that phrase, which is also used in the media: *see* Xu, J. *Gonggongxing Yu Gonggong Zhishifenzi* (*The Public and Public Intellectuals*), Renmin Chubanshe, J, 2003.

the whole intellectual sphere, from the most conservative to the most liberal thinkers; and that they have led to the emergence of a third tendency: cultural nationalism.[27]

The final part of the book is devoted to the polemical discussion by academics of the 'good regime', the regime that is best suited to China. Chapter Five studies perceptions of 'western democracy' and the impact of conservatism. Chapter Six analyses the debate on the definition of the current political regime, democratisation, the right conditions to set it up and the definition of the best-suited regime. Deeply opposing views are expressed on these matters. Cultural nationalists, influential but isolated, categorically reject the possibility of democratising China and favour introducing a meritocratic regime instead. Neo-conservatives are not opposed to liberal democracy but they advocate delaying the democratisation process until the economy and Chinese society have reached a sufficient level of development. One section of the Chinese intelligentsia, dissidents included, considers that the New Left and the intellectuals who reject liberal criticism of the regime lack courage and do not dare confront the Party-emperor directly, which supposedly constrains and consequently invalidates their proposals. It finally seems that, apart from in the most conservative official and intellectual spheres, the idea that China will necessarily become a democracy prevails. However, a set of conditions is put forward as having to be imperatively fulfilled before a genuine democratic regime is set up. It can therefore be said that the democracy to be introduced in China is conceived as conditional in two respects. First, it is conditional because, as is often said, it must wait for its time to come; that is, the time when the Chinese people is ready for it, in order to ensure that democracy will solve and not exacerbate the moral, social, rural, national and procedural crises the country is going through. Democracy is also conditional because of its uncertain definition, in China as elsewhere. Chinese thinkers are taking advantage of this uncertainty to explore the idea of a distinctively Chinese conception of democracy, which may be some way away from western understandings.

---

27. This movement launched in the 1990s contrasts with the intense intellectual catching-up phase of the 1980s, when foreign theories and concepts were imported: subsequently, the Chinese intelligentsia began to cherish Chinese history and traditions more and began to develop its own thinking.

Chapter One

Horses in a Pen? The Situation of Chinese Academics

For a few years, humanities and social sciences departments in the three most prestigious universities in China – that is, Peking University, Tsinghua (Beijing) and Fudan University (Shanghai) – have been ranked among the top 50 in international rankings like Times Higher Education-QS World University. However, while these long-neglected and even censored disciplines are in the process of being normalised, the international media coverage of the more or less intense pressures academics have faced in these last few years reminds us that their working conditions differ radically from those of their European and North American counterparts. This chapter makes an assessment of their situation. It aims to understand the status currently granted to Chinese academics. In that perspective, I will rely on the example of academics engaged in political science and reflection on political change in government studies, public administration, international relations and history departments; in particular, I will focus on the trajectories of 20 or so influential academics who push for political reform proposals through their research and publications. Scrutinising the Chinese academics dedicated to such a 'sensitive' subject as political reform has the advantage of uncovering the contradictions with which they struggle while conducting their research. They are indeed torn between constraints on academic freedom, official demands, professionalisation, internationalisation, opening to the market, patriotism and political commitment.

Reopening humanities departments: 'The great leap forward' (1978–2010)

Since the reforms Deng Xiaoping launched in the wake of the Eleventh Party Congress of August 1977, the Chinese government has repeatedly underlined the importance of knowledge and expertise as the foundation of political decision-making. As a result, official hostility towards law and political science studies has gradually receded. These disciplines have become truly indispensible to the juridical reforms that have been undertaken, which are themselves vital to the opening up of the market economy. Social sciences were also publicly recognised again. The Chinese Academy of Social Sciences, the highest institution in academic research in the field of philosophy and the social sciences, was founded in 1977, to allow the government to meet the objectives established by the Four Modernisations policy.[1]

---

1. Sleeboom-Faulkner, M. *The Chinese Academy of Social Sciences: Shaping the reforms, academia and China (1997–2003)*, Leiden: Brill, 2007.

The reorganisation of departments led to the creation of 18 research institutes – in philosophy, economics, industrial and agricultural economics, finance and trade, world economics, law, literature, linguistics, history, modern history, world history, archaeology, world religion, ethnology, journalism and information. The application of social science knowledge to the setting up of policies and social programmes intensified. New disciplines such as international relations, demography, law, sociology, anthropology and political science emerged and the work of academics from these fields was encouraged: through sending academics for studying and training abroad; publishing translations of major reference books and giving academics new responsibilities. Simultaneously with the Open and Reform policy, a true charm offensive has been launched towards intellectual professions for the last 30 years. The income of academics has been increased considerably and they have recovered the prestigious status they lost during the Cultural Revolution, when Red Guards called them the 'stinking ninth category' (*chou lao jiu*), stigmatising them as of low status and their contribution to the advancement of society as insignificant. As for teachers, academics were promoted to the rank of 'soul engineers', equal to workers and peasants. Their salaries have risen and their living conditions improved, with better access to accommodation, schools for their children and the reorganisation of unions.

Consequences of the Open and Reform policy for higher education

In April 1978, a conference on national education discarded the priority given to class struggle and replaced it with modernisation as the ultimate aim of education. This decision was passed simultaneously with the return of the university entrance examination and signalled the beginning of higher education's rapid expansion. This new era was stamped by the idea, which Hu Yaobang notably emphasised, that the Four Modernisations (of agriculture, industry, national defence and science and technology) could not be achieved without the help of a large contingent of scientists and experts. Science and technology have been closely associated with China's modernisation because they are vital to the Four Modernisations and the improvement of the population's living conditions. As a result, new departments have been opened to train new scientists and technocrats.[2] People debate the inconvenience of academic politicisation in a non-democratic context, since academic freedom relies on a democratic system. As early as 1979, Li Shu wrote in an article published in *Historical Research* that an 'environment where a scientist can work without fearing and dare express his opinions' is the prior condition for the development of science and culture. He added that academic work couldn't be limited to explaining policies. Intellectuals must be allowed to make proposals and

---

2. Mathur, N. *Educational Reform in Post-Mao China*, New Delhi: APH Publishing, 2007, pp. 152–3. At that time, there were 404 universities in China. Each decade, their number has doubled, with 1,075 in 1988, more than 2,000 in 2002 and more than 4,000 nowadays. On the policy of expanding of Chinese higher education to the masses, *see* Lin Jing and Sun Xiaoyan, 'Higher education expansion and China's middle class', in Li, C. *China's Emerging Middle Class: Beyond economic transformation*, Washington, DC: Brookings Institution Press, 2010, p. 217.

bring advice regarding economic and social policies.[3] Reforming the system of the intellectual professions was officially connected to successful economic reforms in Zhao Ziyang's speech at the third plenary session of the Twelfth Central Committee in October 1984, condemning persisting forms of anti-intellectualism in China:

> In our drive for socialist modernisation we must respect knowledge and talented people. We must combat all ideas and practices that belittle science and technology, the cultivation of intellectual resources and the role of intellectuals. We must take resolute action to redress cases of discrimination against intellectuals which still exist in many localities.[4]

In the early 1980s, exchange programmes with many foreign countries were reinstated and most OECD countries launched development-aid programmes, to enhance opportunities for Chinese students to study abroad. The World Bank financed many projects aiming at encouraging training visits abroad for the higher education teaching community. It was indeed crucial at the time for Chinese universities to start catching up with other universities in the world. Under Soviet influence, the development of higher education since 1949 was supposed to 'serve economic construction, which is the foundation for any construction (whether political, cultural or of national defence)'.[5] The whole system, which was extremely centralised, was therefore structured to ensure higher education would directly contribute to the economic and social objectives of the first Five-Year Plan. The main aim was to train a disciplined elite corps of specialists in all the fields that were necessary to the new socialist state and industrialisation, which led to the decline and restructuring of social sciences and humanities. The consequences of the Cultural Revolution and the radical desire to overthrow experts and top-down policies and 'cleanse' the elitist selective system so as to open up peasants' and workers' access to education were extreme: mass primary and secondary schooling were introduced but access to higher education totally frozen.[6]

---

3. Li, S. 'Identify the essence and absorb it', *Lishi Yanjiu*, 15 November 1979, p. 35, quoted in Goldman, M. 'Hu Yaobang's intellectual network and the theory conference of 1979', *China Quarterly*, June 1991, p. 239.

4. Quoted in Simon, D. F. 'China's scientists and technologists in the post-Mao era: a retrospective and prospective glimpse', in Goldman, M. *et al.* (eds), *China's Intellectuals And The State: In search of a new relationship*, Cambridge, MA: Harvard University Press, 1987, p. 145.

5. *Renmin Ribao*, 14 June 1950, quoted in Hayhoe, R. *China's Universities, 1895–1995: A century of cultural conflict*, New York and London: Garland Publishers, 1996, p. 75; Shlapentokh, V. *Soviet Intellectuals and Political Power: The Post-Stalin era*, Princeton, NJ: Princeton University Press 1990.

6. From 1966 to 1969, no new student was admitted to Chinese universities except for short political mobilisation training. The national entrance examination was suspended in 1967. Admissions progressively started again after that date, based not on academic standards but on work-unit recommendations, according to class background and political behaviour, and on the condition that candidates had performed manual work for more than two years. As a matter of fact, the children of city cadres requalified as peasants and formed the great majority of those entering university at that time. *See* Perrolle, P. M., Reed, L. A., U.S.-China Education Clearinghouse., Committee on Scholarly Communication with the People's Republic of China (U.S.); National Association for Foreign Student Affairs, *An Introduction to Education in the People's Republic of China and U.S.-China Educational Exchanges*, Washington, DC: The Committee: The Association, 1980, pp. 24–5.

Besides, most university faculty were sent to 'May Seventh Schools' (*wu qi ganxiao*) for cadres' re-education through rural labour at that time. As a result, academics were distanced from their work for a long period of time. This can help explain why so few, among the interviewed scholars, aligned themselves with major professors who had impressed them during those years.[7]

Consequently, in the early 1980s, the task ahead was daunting: everything had to be started from scratch. In Chinese universities, that era was one of hope and promise. In 1985, the education reform officially promised more autonomy to universities in terms of curricula and textbook selection.[8] Universities became not only teaching but also research centres, in contrast to the Soviet model which had limited them to professional training and teaching. However, from the mid 1980s, disappointment and demoralisation began to creep in. Awareness that job opportunities were scarce for young graduates, who were more and more numerous, and that the top professional and bureaucratic positions had been monopolised by former graduates, enticed the most talented students to study and work abroad.

Our aim here is not to get into the details of the upheavals affecting Chinese universities since the Open and Reform policy but to understand the key features of higher-education reform: that is, reinstating research as the central mission of universities; reopening social sciences like sociology and anthropology, which had been forbidden since the 1950s; official recognition of the major contribution of 'soft sciences' and applied social sciences; questioning ultra-specialisation; and a more global approach to knowledge and greater freedom for universities to select academic curricula.

How Chinese universities operate

What makes the Chinese case singular is that any university or higher-education institution is always managed by two authorities: the Party and the administration. University presidents and Party secretaries depend on the CCP's Organisation Department (*zhongguo gongchandang zhongyang zuzhi bu*), in charge of nominating and overseeing bureaucrats. From the point of view of human resources and institutions, the organisation of Chinese universities is not so different from that of ministries. The system is highly hierarchical. All public universities are administratively ranked according to their level of excellence. The best universities are ranked as vice-ministries and their presidents as

---

7. Pan Wei is an exception. He mentions Chen Han-seng, who was among the first holders of a PhD from abroad to become a member of the Communist Party, and Pu Shan, a Harvard graduate, former Zhou Enlai Minister of Foreign Affairs and head of the World Economics and Politics Institute at the Academy of Social Sciences. For Peking University political scientists like Yu Keping, He Zengke and Liu Junning, Zhao Baoxu was a major influence: *see* Zhao, B. *In Pursuit of Harmony: An academic anthology*, Beijing: Foreign Languages Teaching and Research Press, 2008. Sociologists refer to Fei Xiaotong: *see* Arkush, D. R. *Fei Xiaotong and Sociology in Revolutionary China*, Cambridge, MA: Harvard University Press, 1981.

8. 'Decision of the CCP's Central Committee on the reform of the education system', 27 May 1985, *Foreign Broadcast Information Service* 104, 30 May 1985.

vice-ministers (*fubuzhang*).[9] There were 14 at first; by 2000 there were 31 of them. The other universities are ranked as bureaux (*ju*) and the least prestigious institutions as vice-bureaux. Debates on universities' administrative rank have discussed whether this 'bureaucratisation' is harmful to their quality. This actually signals the central role the state plays in allocating resources, recruiting the staff and ordering the hierarchy of institutions. As a result, a university president is hierarchically subordinate to the Party secretary, even though, from an administrative perspective, he or she is ranked general director or vice-minister. This structure guaranteeing the Party's domination of higher education was set up in 1949, when all private education was abolished and schools were merged into public ones. The Party therefore had authority over any education institution's political principles and orientations and over teachers' hiring. Since 1985, however, a university president has had the final say over non-political decisions; political decisions being reserved to the university's Party secretary. Defining what is political or not is subject to interpretation but a political dimension can be found in all major decisions.[10] Consequently, public universities are all under the control of regional or national public authority.[11]

From the late 1980s on, universities started to face scarce public financing and intense economic pressure, and inflation reduced the modest salaries of academics, which led the latter to look for alternative sources of income. The term '*chuangshou*', (creating income) designates very diverse lucrative activities, ranging from teaching and research activities based on academic expertise to purely commercial occupations, which individuals, departments and sometimes whole universities undertake. The benefits harvested by companies founded within universities like Tsinghua or Peking University are anything but insignificant.[12] This leads to great income inequalities between academics, disciplines and institutions, which we will later focus on.

In some universities, up to 80 per cent of academics are Party members and academic research is ruthlessly oriented by government policies and 'national subjects' (*guojia keti*). A complete political-orientation guidebook, the guidelines for national research projects (*keti zhinan*) and the subjects that are publicly funded guide social sciences researchers away from fundamental towards

---

9. For more details, *see* Zhao, L. and Zhu, J. 'China's higher education reform: what has not been changed?', *East Asian Policy* 2(4), October–December 2010, available online at http://www.eai. nus.edu.sg/Vol2No4_ZhaoLitao&ZhuJinjing.pdf (last accessed 14 November 2014).

10. Rai, S. *Resistance and Reaction: University Politics in Post-Mao China*, Hemel Hempstead: Harvester Wheatsheaf and New York: St. Martin's Press, 1991, pp. 65–70.

11. In 2008, more than 1,500 universities and higher-education institutions (out of 2,263) were administered by provincial or local authorities and 111 by central ministries (Zhao, L. and Zhu, J. 'China's higher education reform: what has not been changed?', *East Asian Policy*, 2(4), pp. 115–25).

12. According to data provided by the Education Ministry in 2005, Beida's companies made more than 27 billion yuan profit while Tsinghua made 20 billion. *See* Li, Y. , Whalley, J., Zhang, S. and Zhao, X. 'The higher educational transformations of China and its global implications', NBER working paper series, 2008, available online at http://www.nber.org/papers/w13849 (last accessed 14 November 2014).

applied research.[13] However, research is manifestly becoming more professionalised, with academics taking refuge in key universities (*zhongdian daxue*): top-rated institutions and social sciences academies subjected to strict academic norms modelled on international standards.

Limits to academic freedom

Chinese academics cannot express themselves in a totally autonomous way since censorship still exists and careers can be threatened at any time if comments or research displease some official. In this context, what is the nature of academics' freedom of action? How can they fulfil their mission of developing and spreading critical knowledge, which, *a priori*, implies the effective and strict respect of academic freedom?

As to publication, it is easier to publish in internal (*neibu*) outlets, which are less affected by censorship because they address a more select readership than mainstream journals and magazines.[14] It is also easier to publish in specialised journals than in the mass media. According to People's University Kang Xiaoguang, rules are straightforward.

An official slogan explains that research is free but publications are controlled [*yanjiu you ziyou, chuban you jilu*]. This means that you can undertake all the research you want, no one will pay heed, but if you try to publish them, especially in the mass media, things will get more complex. When you write a challenging article in *People's Daily*, you are not the one in trouble. The newspaper is. As a result, researchers are completely free to conduct their research. Academic freedom is a fact. No one is afraid of focusing on one specific issue, but the opportunities for publication are limited. For instance, my books cannot be published on the Chinese mainland. They are published in Singapore or Hong Kong and the government does not pay attention. I won't be persecuted for that. On the contrary, leaders will rather buy the book and read it. Therefore, the government, the Party and academia are in no trouble to communicate. Academic freedom is under no constraint, contrary to publications. On the other hand, purely academic research is rarely under control. For instance, specialised journals such as Sociological Studies [*shehuixue yanjiu*] and Economic Studies [*jingji yanjiu*] are never censored

---

13. Zhang, L. 'La crise de la recherche fondamentale: recherche académique, logique du marché et intervention étatique', in Rocca, J. -L. (ed.) *La société chinoise vue par ses sociologues*, Paris: Presses de Sciences Po, 2008.

14. Perry Link confirms this relative freedom of publication in academic journals: 'Censorship in intellectual matters broadly follows the same pattern. Nearly anything can be said in private, which is a big advance over the Mao years. And because academic journals have very small circulations, they are given somewhat more latitude than other publishing media. As long as scholars don't confront the top leadership head-on, they can write in scholarly journals pretty much as they choose.' Link, P. 'China: the anaconda in the chandelier', *New York Review of Books*, 11 April 2002). Publishing in English is also an effective way of circumventing censorship.

even if some articles can be quite radical. Censorship affects popular media, addressing a large public. The essential element is that if power believes one scholar is important, he will look for him and ask him what the findings of his latest research are.[15]

As a matter of fact, the standards to be met to be allowed to publish articles or books are not clearly defined. It is, in any case, impossible to criticise the current leaders or their overall policy openly in mass publications. It is also relatively difficult to publish independent research on some historical events, such as the Cultural Revolution or the Tiananmen Square repression. In the early 1990s, Wang Shaoguang and Hu Angang wrote a political economy report in Yale on the low capacity of the Chinese state. The report was eventually published in internal journals and its impact on the fiscal policy at that time is widely acknowledged. It was, however, only published in its complete form by Oxford University Press in Hong Kong.[16] Similarly, Wang Shaoguang's PhD dissertation on the rationality of the masses during the Cultural Revolution was published by Oxford University Press in Chinese in 1993 (*Rationality and Madness: Masses during the Cultural Revolution*) and in English in 1995 (*Failure of Charisma: The Cultural Revolution in Wuhan*).[17] It was finally published by the Chinese University Press in 2007. To give another example, two well known New-Left scholars, Wang Hui and Huang Ping, who had been chief editors for more than ten years of *Dushu* (*Reading*) one of the most popular intellectual journals with 60,000 to 100,000 subscribers, were let go in 2007 because Sanlian publishing house suddenly 'remembered' that chief editors should be full-time workers, which they were not.[18] The reasons behind such a dismissal can seem hard to decipher. With the new priority officially given to social justice rather than efficiency (*xiaolü youxian*) since 2004, it seemed that the New Left, which was known for constantly finding fault with the policy of prioritising efficiency, seemed to have gained traction among political leaders. However, the situation simply is more complex and some of the quality articles published in *Dushu* explicitly lambasted the economic liberalism that has nonetheless remained one of the main pillars of China's economic policy. Ren Jiantao, a liberal philosophy professor, explained that he could never publish what he considers to be his best books.

It is difficult to publish this type of observations because political research is limited like horses in a pen. Researchers are guided like horses. They can only play where they are told. As soon as they start straying from the guidelines, things go wrong. It should be allowed to research any subject, but this is not

---

15. All quotes whose reference is not indicated are extracted from personal interviews, which are detailed in the Appendix C.

16. Wang, S. and Hu, A. *Zhongguo Guojia Nengli Yanjiu Baogao*, Hong Kong: Oxford University Press, 1994 (published in English as *The Chinese Economy in Crisis: State capacity and tax reform*, Armonk, NY: M. E. Sharpe, 2001); Wang, S. and Hu, A. *Bupingdeng Fazhan De Zhengzhijingjixue*, Beijing: Beijing Jihua Chubanshe, 2000 (published in English as *The Political Economy of Uneven Development: The case of China*, Armonk, New York: Sharpe, M. E. 1999).

17. Wang S., *Failure of Charisma: The Cultural Revolution in Wuhan*, New York: Oxford University Press, 1995.

18. Zhang, Y. 'No forbidden zone in reading?', *New Left Review* 49, January–February 2008.

the case. Conducting research on universal values, the constitutional regime, the future of the CCP is not allowed on Chinese territory unless you are an amateur. As far as I am concerned, I cannot afford to. I am already a university professor. I supervise PhD students. I publish some of my research. It does not matter too much that I cannot publish it all.[19]

University professors are still at the mercy of arbitrary decisions, often made by their academic institution's Party secretary. They can be punctually prevented from getting in touch with students, as liberal philosophy professor Xu Youyu from the Chinese Academy of Social Sciences explains. During one interview, he claimed to have become aware of being blacklisted along with other liberals who are blocked from expressing themselves openly in universities in Beijing and in the mainstream media. Academics can also be suddenly transferred, which was He Weifang's case, a professor from Peking University's prestigious law school. A very influential media figure, He wrote far-reaching articles advocating judicial reforms and setting up an independent judicial system. In March 2009, after he signed the Charter 08, he was transferred – or exiled – for two years to a minor university in Shihezi, Xinjiang. Finally, academics can lose their positions, which happened to Liu Junning during the repression aimed at stifling the spread of liberalism in China in the late 1990s.[20] This brilliant political philosopher at the Political Science Institute of the Chinese Academy of Social Sciences, undoubtedly the most influential libertarian in China, was told he could no longer teach students, he would obtain no more salary increases, and would not be allowed to buy a flat or go to conferences in Hong Kong and Taiwan. In December 2010, economist Zhang Weiying was removed as the Dean of the Guanghua Management School in Peking University but remained a professor and assistant to the University President.[21] Academics can still be imprisoned, which is Liu Xiaobo's case after he drafted and signed the Charter 08. He was first dismissed from the university for his dissident activities before being sentenced to eleven years in jail on 25 December 2009. This former professor from Beijing Normal University is the president of the Chinese branch of the international anti-censorship group PEN, an independent Chinese centre associating writers 'devoted to the protection of freedom of speech and the defence of writers suffering from government repression'.

However, these manifest examples of censorship and repression do not teach us much about the conditions for producing and diffusing knowledge in China nowadays. Describing limitations to academic and publication freedom is not

19. Ren Jiantao tends to exaggerate here. A great number of studies are conducted in China on constitutionalism.

20. Liu Junning had seized the opportunity of Peking University's hundredth anniversary to publish a collection of liberal texts: Liu, J. (ed.) *Ziyouzhuyi De Xiansheng: Beida Chuantong Yu Jindai Zhongguo* (published in English as *The Beginning of Liberalism: Beida's tradition and modern China*), Beijing: Zhongguo Renshi Chubanshe, 1998.

21. Shan, H. 'Zhang Weiying dismissed from PKU post', *China.org*, 13 December 2010, available online at http://china.org.cn/business/2010-12/13/content_21533731.htm (last accessed 14 November 2014). http://www.eeo.com.cn/ens/homepage/briefs/2010/12/14/188926.shtml (last accessed 14 November 2014).

sufficient. Cannot all the major political science reference books be found both in original language and in Mandarin in the libraries of Peking University and other prestigious universities?[22] Are not the faculty from these universities, in which western political science and law are taught, invited, like foreign academics such as Jürgen Habermas or Pierre Rosanvallon, to teach at the Central Party School, which trains Chinese political elites? Finally, are not famous American political science and law professors regularly invited to give conferences in Chinese universities?[23] We must wonder why China invites them and why these visits constitute major events. This is certainly because the practice of applying social sciences to the design of policies and social programmes has intensified and because China tries to make up for its lost time through studying what takes place abroad. Every year, 15 per cent of graduates from the best Chinese universities pursue their studies abroad. To rise to excellent academic levels, Chinese universities have fully opened to internationalisation.[24] Researchers are sent abroad to train and a great number of reference books are translated into Mandarin Chinese. The tendency is such that holding a PhD degree from a foreign university has become indispensible to getting or keeping a teaching position in a major university, depending on discipline. Chinese leaders have opted for the strategy of knowing everything so as to understand the international community's suggestions and comments and, above all, to be able to reflect on and prepare for the future of the country. As a result, historical and current political systems and the theories describing ideal political models are now studied in minute detail in Chinese universities and official think tanks.

Besides, liberal ideas are widespread in China, especially in universities and Party schools. Interviewed scholars surmise that the liberal trend is the most popular one, compared to the New Left and cultural nationalism. Courses on the classics of liberalism, on John Rawls, Robert Nozick or Friedrich Hayek's theories, are taught in Party schools. The most influential economists, who have become true stars, advocate liberalism. The major liberal figures (He Weifang, Liu Junning, Qin Hui, Mao Yushi, Wu Jinglian, Xu Youyu, Zhu Xueqin and so on) can all be found in the rankings of the most influential intellectuals. The *Nanfang Zhoumo* (*Southern Weekend*), a Guangzhou liberal weekly famous for its investigative reports, designing these rankings is one of the most popular newspapers, with above 1.6 million copies sold.

---

22. Frenkiel, E. *Perfect Freedom: A Study of the evolution and representation of contemporary Anglo-American political philosophy in China*, MPhil dissertation, Ecole Normale Supérieure de Lyon, 2005.

23. Jürgen Habermas was triumphally received in April 2001. During his tour in Beijing (Academy of Social Sciences, Tsinghua and Beida), Shanghai and Nanjing, his conferences mainly focused on the 'pressure of globalisation on nation-states'. He was invited to give a speech at the Central Party School, where he also held discussions with top leaders (it was the first time a foreign philosopher had been invited to do so). The press compared his popularity to a popstar's. Jacques Derrida's visit took place the following year; Richard Rorty in summer 2004; Thomas Michael Scanlon, Thomas Nagel, Charles Taylor, Michael Walzer, Thomas Pogge and many others followed. Behind the politically correct titles of these conferences, sensitive issues were often approached.

24. Ryan, J. *China's Higher Education Reform and Internationalisation*, Abingdon, Oxon and New York: Routledge, 2011.

Obviously, the internet has created a wholly new situation, even if the government has set up a virtual army of censors. Blogs and articles from committed intellectuals like Zhang Weiying or Liu Junning, and many Chinese and international websites or forums, are devoted to the issue of political change and are accessible online. The scale of the internet in China, now home to the largest internet community in the world (632 million users in June 2014), allows only imperfect censorship because censorship is extremely difficult to enforce and is, consequently, concentrated on priority areas such as direct criticism of the government or the non-official coverage of sensitive historical events. The five liberal intellectuals whose repression has just been mentioned are among the most famous liberal thinkers in China and their blogs and articles are available online, which shows that censorship or political pressures, no matter the forms they take, are not so predictable. Besides, Liu Junning has worked for years as a researcher on social issues at the Institute of Chinese Culture of the Culture Department; he is the editor of *Res Publica*, a publication that is not officially registered as a periodical, allowing him not to depend on official certificates, and he publishes many books and articles online. He lives in comfortable conditions in Beijing, probably thanks to extra income offered by his connections with NGOs and foreign foundations such as the American libertarian CATO institute, which promote the advancement of liberalism in China. Xu Youyu publishes articles and books on a regular basis, often takes part in conferences in Oxford or Paris and taught many students until he retired. In March 2009, he met Vaclav Havel in Prague on the occasion of the Homo Homini Prize awarded to Liu Xiaobo and to Charter 08 signatories.[25] He explains that censorship is most constraining for those expressing liberal views.

> This explains why my best books were published abroad. In spite of censorship, I can make a tour outside of Beijing and give speeches in various universities. I am very popular among students. But if someone organises a conference in a university in Beijing, it cannot take place because I am blacklisted. Recently, it happened in Beijing Normal University and China University of Political Science and Law. Students informed me at the last minute that the Party committee of the university had ordered my conferences to be cancelled. I think this blacklist is only enforced in Beijing. China is a very complex country and the situation is hard to grasp. First of all, this list is shameful and therefore hidden. It cannot circulate widely. Besides, [...] the Education Department is very conservative. Local governments have actually already invited me to give conferences, in a very open manner. I could approach very sensitive issues without any problem. The situation is quite peculiar. It seems that the most conservative figures are all in Beijing.[26]

---

25. 'Remarks by Václav Havel and two members of China's Charter 08 at the ceremony for the Homo Homini Award', *New York Review of Books*, 30 April 2009.

26. This claim has to be put in a context in which the behaviour of local governments is actually very difficult to generalise about. Scholars have had contradictory experiences. The Shanghai government is often said to be more conservative than the Beijing. Jean-Louis Rocca, for instance, was censored in Shanghai for having said that China was capitalistic, which he had often said in Beijing previously.

As I am writing this book, Xu Youyu is imprisoned for having participated in a small-scale meeting commemorating the Tiananmen Square massacre.

To summarise, censorship and repression in China focus on extremely precise issues and are hardly institutionalised. The state needs the co-operation, goodwill and expertise of academics. Academic censorship and self-censorship tend therefore to be less prevalent these days. It can be noted that workers' rights and environmental issues, for instance, which used to be tricky to tackle a few years back, are now openly discussed both in academic and mainstream publications. Censorship and repression are imponderable phenomena which can, nonetheless, be circumvented. Their lack of institutionalisation is constantly mentioned in interviews. It is the cornerstone of navigating in academic territory. Their freedom being limited by fluctuating and undefined constraints, academics who are faced with censorship perceive the practice of their profession in China as a unique experience, which is radically different from that of academics in Singapore, for instance. Zheng Yongnian and Daniel A. Bell have had the opportunity to compare the two academic systems and both have noticed the difference. According to Zheng Yongnian – a political science professor born and educated in China, who has taught for many years at the University of Nottingham and now chairs the East Asian Institute, National University of Singapore – and Daniel A. Bell – a philosophy professor from Canada who first taught in Singapore before moving to Tsinghua University[27] – the sources and forms of censorship in China are manifold. Chance and subjectivity therefore play a great part, whereas in Singapore, the issues to be avoided are clearly announced and fixed in advance.

To go back to publications, which are of peculiar interest to our study, in China, censorship varies according to publishing houses. When Zheng Yongnian tried to get his book on globalisation published on the mainland, the publishers he met, whether academic or commercial, in Zhejiang, Shanghai or Beijing, were all interested in publishing the book but wanted to modify certain passages that they deemed too sensitive. Surprisingly, all the publishers identified different problematic passages. It proved much easier to get the book published by Sanlian in Hong Kong but Zheng eventually agreed to modify the manuscript for Zhejiang Publishing House.[28] He is aware that academics (and other authors) looking for a publisher often engage in an extensive tour of publishing houses to hunt out one

---

27. Interview with Daniel A. Bell, Beijing, June 2005. *See also* Bell, D. A. *China's New Confucianism: Politics and everyday life in a changing society*, Princeton, NJ: Princeton University Press, 2010, p. 129: 'In comparison, China is a paradise of academic freedom. Among colleagues, anything goes (in Singapore, most local colleagues were very guarded when dealing with foreigners). Academic publications are surprisingly free: there aren't any personal attacks on leaders or open calls for multiparty rule, but particular policies such as the household registry system, which limits internal mobility, are subject to severe criticism [...] more surprisingly, perhaps, I was not given any explicit (or implicit, as far as I could tell) guidance regarding what I could teach at Tsinghua. My course proposals have been approved as submitted.' Bell qualifies this on pp. 144–5.

28. Zheng, Y. *Shijiehua Yu Zhongguo Guojia Zhuanxing* (*Globalisation and the Chinese State's Transition*), Hangzhou: Zhejiang People's Publishing House, 2009.

that is willing to take some risk. All the publishing houses are associated with some Party official, who is more or less lenient and must give his or her approval before publication.[29] Besides, censorship can be more tightly enforced at certain times, like in 2008, 2009 and 2010 – these years were supposed to be more sensitive (*mingan*) due to the Olympic Games, the Shanghai Expo and the anniversaries of 1949 and 1989.[30] In other cases, publication is devoid of all censorship but is at the author's expense (on average 30,000 yuan or €3,500).

Zheng Yongnian, who has worked in foreign universities since 2002, is aware that he self-censors when he writes with a mainland publication in mind. Academics and students are well aware of the risks but the line not to be crossed fluctuates and can be difficult to see. This complex situation offers many opportunities to circumvent obstacles, however. Liu Dong, Tsinghua professor and editor of book collections in humanities and social sciences, gives the following summary of the situation: 'we do not enjoy total freedom, but great leeway'. One of the bestsellers of this book collection was the translation of John Rawls' *Political Liberalism*. According to Liu, the title alone was a hit in China and, in some liberal circles, displaying the book on one's bookcase is actually well thought of. Yet because of this very title, the book came close to be banned. It indeed drew the attention of a retired cadre in charge of identifying books opposed to the government and who had never heard of John Rawls. He wrote a report on the book and sent it to the Propaganda Bureau, where, fortunately, it landed in the hands of an employee whose PhD supervisor was Wan Junren himself, that is, the Tsinghua political philosophy professor who had translated the book. This anecdote uncovers how arbitrary and absurd censorship can be and why it is often possible to circumvent it.

Self-censorship and compromise

American sinologist Perry Link, himself blacklisted,[31] highlights the efficiency of 'censorship with Chinese characteristics', that is, indefinite censorship; this contrasts with the Soviet Union, where manuals listed phrases to be avoided and where an official bureaucracy specifically in charge of censorship was set up.[32] The Chinese system, like an immobile and silent anaconda in a suspended chandelier, mainly relies on the production of self-censorship.

---

29. *See* http://www.cecc.gov/pages/virtualAcad/exp/bookflow.php (last accessed 14 November 2014).

30. Bell, D. A. and his publishing house were forced to wait for several years before the Chinese version of *China's New Confucianism*, was published (as *Zhongguo Xin Rujia*, Shanghai: Sanlian Shudian, in November 2010).

31. This is a specific case. Perry Link cannot enter Chinese territory because he helped Fang Lizhi flee through the American embassy after 4 June 1989, not because of his research or publications. Besides, he angered the Chinese government when he published the *Tiananmen Papers* with Nathan, A. and Link, P. (eds), *The Tiananmen Papers*, London: Little, Brown and Company, 2001.

32. Link, P. 'China: the anaconda in the chandelier', *The New York Review of Books*, 11 April 2002. He explains that imprecise censorship can intimidate more people, who constrain themselves in a wider range of activities.

The few cases of repression mentioned above fulfil the function of diffusing fear among Chinese intellectuals, who could be cut off from their families and their hometown. It does not mean, however, that it is impossible to utter any heterodox thought. As Perry Link acknowledges, academic freedom is extensive, provided one does not openly criticise leaders. It is still extremely difficult to publish texts questioning the Party and foreign policy or presenting alternative institutional arrangements at the national level, which can explain why books from Daniel A. Bell or Jiang Qing could not be published in mainland China.

Leo Strauss's analysis of the art of writing between the lines to avoid persecution is enlightening. He insists that

> persecution [...] cannot prevent independent thinking. It cannot prevent even the expression of independent thought. [...] Persecution cannot prevent even public expression of the heterodox truth, for a man of independent thought can utter his views in public and remain unharmed, provided he moves with circumspection. He can even utter them in print without incurring any danger, provided he is capable of writing between the lines.[33]

Strauss also allows us to understand how certain forms of censorship can be acceptable. He indeed explains that 'what attitude people adopt toward freedom of public discussion depends decisively on what they think about popular education and its limits' (p. 33). Elitist thinkers who 'believed that the gulf separating "the wise" and "the vulgar" was a basic fact of human nature' accepted much more willingly that freedom of expression be limited and that only the wise could express themselves between the lines. In Europe, the relevance of censoring far-right discourse is debated but democratic pluralism forbids it: only explicit racist assertions are forbidden. In China, fear of populism and of the irrationality of the masses encourage liberals like Ren Jiantao implicitly to wish for censorship of the far-left, precluded by the Party's ideological positioning.[34]

Dissidents are defined as such because they refuse to express themselves or act in an oblique or diverted way and instead run the risk of directly 'provoking' those in power. For Xu Youyu, who has called for political reform very explicitly, this strategy is a gross strategic mistake. It is irrational to act too bravely and create an opposition party in China, for instance, he says.[35] For the sake of political efficiency, compromises must be found. He Zengke explains that his PhD

---

33. Strauss, L. *Persecution and the Art of Writing*, Chicago, IL: University of Chicago Press, 1988 [1952], pp. 23–4.

34. His wishes were fulfilled after Bo Xilai's purge. The Maoist website Utopia was then blocked.

35. *See* Zha, J. 'Enemy of the state', *New Yorker*, 17 April 2007. In this article, idealistic dissidents are associated with the penguins in the 2005 documentary 'March of the Penguins' whose determined appearance and gait are ridiculous off the water but beautiful in the water. On the founding of the China Democracy Party, *see especially* Goldman, M. *From Comrade to Citizen: The struggle for political rights in China*, Cambridge, MA: Harvard University Press, 2005, chapter 6: 'The establishment of an alternative political party: the China Democracy Party', pp. 161–82.

dissertation, which originally focused on corruption in China, then a touchy issue (right after 1989), was extended to corruption issues in developing countries as a whole, including China, so as to allow him to assuredly bring it to fruition. As for Ren Jiantao, who did not succeed in getting his best books published in Chinese publishing houses, he made the decision not to publish them in Hong Kong or Taiwan, contrary to Xiao Gongqin, Kang Xiaoguang or Xu Youyu, so as not to be identified as a dissident as such and, as a result, lose any chance of being read and listened to as a university professor.

> I have not followed the strategy of scholars like Xiao Gongqin, who publish in Taiwan. Indeed, the objective of my research is to serve political reform in China. I cannot see the use of swimming against the tide and being labelled a dissident. I have decided to publish when I can in China and not to publish elsewhere if it can bring people to question my loyalty. I strive to pursue my research on politics at an official, academic and popular [*minjian*] level.[36] It allows me to find my niche, develop my ideas freely and keep the little influence I have gained. If I decided to publish my research abroad, my loyalty could be put into question and I could lose all influence on the Chinese territory. It happened to Liu Junning. He should be more influential that I am, because his articles are brilliant and perfectly suited to journals like *Dushu* [...] Intellectuals like Zhu Xueqin and Liu Junning can write beautifully. They could compete in writing contests. They are therefore better equipped to influence society. But Zhu Xueqin has written little lately and Liu Junning is forbidden from writing in official publications. I would rather remain moderate and not feel under surveillance and hated. It does not mean I have given up on the cause. To be able to talk about politics, political elites have to accept you. This allows you to speak continuously and to have an unending influence.

These last remarks from Ren Jiantao can help us understand why so many intellectuals accept the necessity of making concessions and abide by the rule of the game imposed by the regime. Their influence and political efficacy is at stake. So as to grasp what can be legitimately perceived as dishonourable behaviour on the part of Chinese scholars, it is therefore necessary to better figure out what their status is and what role they assign themselves.

The status of Chinese academics

With reforms and opening to the outside world, intellectuals recovered their elite status in Chinese society. The rapid change and multifarious upheavals brought about by these reforms have led to a loss of bearings, however. In such a context, there is a pressing need for great figures of authority and commitment, who take

---

36. The word *minjian* cannot be easily translated. It expresses some distance taken from official circles, without implying a clear separation between state and society (Ham, C. H. and Bell, D. A. (eds), *The Politics of Affective Relations: East Asia and beyond*, Lanham, MD: Lexington Books, 2004, chapter 8.)

sides as regards the direction of public policies, point out the issues to be urgently solved and offer solutions. These media intellectuals are, consequently, very often solicited. Their status is very high and they earn a decent living. Is it necessary to recall how crucial studies and knowledge are in a country like China? Any person of knowledge, in so far as she can contribute to deciphering, correcting or improving the situation of a mutating China whose future is open, is considered an expert and asked to inform and advise leaders at different levels, in the private sector, institutions, international foundations or organisations, an enlightened public, or even the larger public. However, intellectual elites are, except for a few exceptional cases, kept at a distance from the arrangements found between political and economic elites; the impression given is of intellectuals having a limited impact on the decision-making process. This contributes to qualifying their public reputation and image, all the more so as they are among the first ones to benefit from the government's co-optation policy. Chapter Three is devoted to that issue.

The internationalisation of Chinese universities: The American transplant

To rise to academic excellence, Chinese universities have fully opened to internationalisation. According to official statistics, between 1978 to 2011, 2.25 million Chinese students and academics studied abroad, 90 per cent since 2000. This massive wave of students sent abroad corresponds to the Open and Reform policy launched by Deng Xiaoping. After the chaos of the Cultural Revolution, the priority was to put the Chinese education system back on track and to produce the labour force necessary to meet the objectives of modernisation. The Chinese leaders thought it would be faster to learn the 'secret' recipes of power and wealth from western countries, which led to the necessity of gaining a foreign PhD in order to land or keep a position in a major Chinese university.

The scholars I interviewed insisted on the great appeal of American universities, where 22 per cent of foreign students were Chinese in 2011. They mention the worship of foreign terminology, the compulsive emulation of models and the excessive use of foreign concepts, which were much written about during the debate on the reform of Peking University. The phenomenon of compulsive publication also stems from the internationalisation of Chinese universities. Like in the United States, the system of assessment and promotion of academics relies more and more on the number of publications, especially international ones.[37] The latter are better credited than national publications and entitle authors to larger bonuses. As a result, to an academic publishing an article in an international SSCI (social sciences citation index) journal, the government gives a subsidy that can reach up to 10,000 yuan (€1,200). The author's university or department then gives the same amount. Bonuses awarded for national articles are smaller but they still amount to a lot, against the backdrop of the meagre salary of young academics. The rush to publish

---

37. Li, Y. et al. 'The higher educational transformations of China and its global implications', NBER working paper series, 2008, available online at http://www.nber.org/papers/w13849 (last accessed 14 November 2014).

research findings has led to a bottleneck phenomenon: journals are overloaded with publication applications and a junior researcher is required to pay 3,000 yuan (€360) on average to publish an article in a Chinese academic journal.

The reform of *Beida*, (a common 'acronym' for Peking University), triggered an intense debate, starting in 2003, about the tenure of junior staff and the commodification and internationalisation of Chinese universities.[38] On that occasion, Gan Yang, an influential New Left scholar, contrasted that reform unfavourably with the founding mission of Chinese universities, which consists in learning from top-rated systems and successful western universities so as to reinforce the independence and self-determination of the Chinese in terms of ideology, research, culture and education. To his mind, the reform of *Beida* ran the risk of

> turning Chinese universities into dependent bastions of western universities in terms of ideological knowledge and educational research. As a matter of fact, the way to rise up to international top rank research amounts to constraining academics to use English to publish their research findings in American journals of hard and social sciences. Academia therefore runs the risk of being limited to American PhDs.[39]

The supremacy of foreign, and above all American, universities in Chinese universities and research is therefore manifest. Many academics deplore the fact that they enter a predefined academic community and discipline, where assumptions, ideas and limits were fixed without their participation. To counteract this, attempts to indigenise political, philosophical and social studies have multiplied. In the domain of reflections on political reform, Kang Xiaoguang developed a theory of political legitimacy and made proposals for a new regime based on a concept of *renzheng* (enlightened, humane government),[40] for instance. China-studies departments have recently reopened or emerged. In Tsinghua University, Liu Dong and Chen Lai are in charge of giving life back to the department reopened in November 2009. Liu is also the editor of several book collections, including

---

38. Ji, Z. 'Chine: L'amorce d'une "sphère de délibération publique"? Le débat sur la réforme de l'Université de Pékin', *La Vie des Idées*, November 2004, pp. 16–20. The debate was notably triggered by Zhang Weiying's propositions, gathered in Zhang, W. *Daxue De Luoji* (*The Logic of a University*) Beijing Daxue Chubanshe, 2004. The reform aimed at selecting the best teachers (*xuanyou he fenliu*), setting up a recruiting system based on the principle of 'up or out' (if *jiangshi* and *fu jiaoshou*, assistant and associate professors were not promoted after their three-year contracts were renewed – once in the case of *jiangshi* and twice for *fu jiaoshou* – they could not be hired again) and to open more than half of the new positions to external recruiting.

39. Gan, Y. 'Huaren daxue linian yu beida gaige' ('The conception of Chinese universities and the reform of Peking University') *Business China*, 3 May 2003; Ryan, J. *China's Higher Education Reform and Internationalisation*, Oxford: Routledge, 2011, pp. 41–3.

40. Kang, X. 'Renzheng: quanweizhuyi guojia de hefaxing lilun' ('Benevolent government: the legitimacy of the authoritarian state'), *Strategy and Management* 2, 2004; Kang, X. *Renzheng: Zhongguo Zhengzhi Fazhan (Renzheng: The Third Way For China's Political Development)*, Singapore: World Scientific Publishing Co., 2005.

Humanities and Social Sciences Translations (*Renwen Yu Shehui Yicong*), with translations of Derrida, Foucault, Berlin, Taylor, Rawls, Kojeve, Elias, Ulrick Beck, Habermas and Strauss and *China Studies Overseas* (*Haiwai Zhongguo Yanjiu Xilie Congshu*), which publishes the research of foreign sinologists. These two collections 'publish theories which can prove useful to China's reality'. Several hundred books have been published since the late 1980s, when the need to 'understand the West and enter into a dialogue with them' was strongly felt. According to Liu, there is a gap between the twentieth century, when the Chinese successively adopted entire theories or systems of thought, and the twenty-first century, even though they still need to be more pragmatic.

> I think one idea must be balanced with another one. If western society could develop until now, it necessarily is thanks to a balance between many systems which acted against, mutually improved and completed one another. The British elections take place today. Three forces compete: conservatives, liberals and the Labour party. It is not one bloc. I have recently criticized Yan Fu for having us believe that Mill's *On Liberty* encapsulated true Great Britain. As a matter of fact, it only was the Great Britain he was dreaming of. Several parties co-exist. We have taken a fictive West as a model. It was a fiction which only existed in our minds. After the October Revolution, Marxism arrived in China and people believed in it for many years. I don't think it was a pragmatic attitude. We completely adopted Marxism and nothing else seemed possible. Everyone was engrossed in deep reflection on social, historical and political issues, but not in their own way. In China, the twentieth century had nothing specific, but it will no longer be the case in the twenty-first century. What's essential in research is to balance concepts and make cultures enter into a dialogue.

Two opposed traditions of the public intellectual

Chinese academics are torn apart between two intellectual traditions. The western idea of an autonomous university, which was introduced during the Qing dynasty by Chinese officials trained abroad, conflicts with the Confucian ideal of scholars destined to become officials (*xue er you ze shi*).[41] The whole challenge of the intellectual is to strike a balance between this necessary independence as regards power and the urge to contribute to the country's future. As Lynn T. White III explained,

> Intellectuals do not crucially oppose or support any government. That is not how their work influences most politics. If they support a regime, it lasts or falls mainly because of other constituencies. If they try to oppose it alone, they

---

41. Only a minority of intellectuals passed the imperial examinations and became civil servants. Elman showed the impact of this massive failure on China's social and cultural life (Elman, B. A. 'Political, social, and cultural reproduction via civil service examinations in late imperial China', *Journal of Asian Studies* 50(1), February 1991, pp. 7–28).

are regularly repressed. Their power is longer-term, more elusive, a matter of symbols. The social task of Chinese intellectuals is to see China clearly, and to say what they see.[42]

During our interviews, the main academics involved in the field of political reform explained why they had chosen to devote themselves to political studies even though some of them were mathematicians, philosophers of language or historians of the countryside originally. They emphasised their desire to better their fellow citizens' conditions and to make their knowledge and skills serve their country. Beyond the expression of patriotism, this discourse reminds us that in China, as elsewhere but maybe even more than in other countries, knowledge tends to be assessed depending on its utility. Called upon by leaders to give their opinions and guide decision-making, intellectual elites have proven very pragmatic and academic research has been used to solve social and policy issues. This peculiar intellectual position can be associated with the history of the Chinese intelligentsia. At the turn of the twentieth century, the sole objective of spreading western knowledge was to save the country from inner decadence and imperial invasion. For more than a century, Chinese nationalism has been closely connected to the dream of a powerful China (*qiangguomeng*), whose rejection of tradition and pragmatism constitute nationalism's two main tenets. Since the late nineteenth century, successful Chinese modernisation is envisioned according to the motto: Chinese essence and western means (*zhongti xiyong*, contraction of *zhongxue weiti, xixue weiyong*). The formula is Zhang Zhidong's, a learned bureaucrat who launched the Self-Strengthening (*ziqiang*) Movement from 1861 to 1895 with Yan Fu. It was about keeping an essentially Chinese system while borrowing more efficient techniques from the West. China is supposed to protect itself through adopting its aggressor's methods (*yi yi zhi yi*), mainly science and democracy, which were deemed more useful: 'China is sick, two great western Misters should be called to China's bedside: *de xiansheng* (Mr Democracy) and *sai xiansheng* (Mr Science)' was one of the slogans of the 1919 May Fourth Movement. The movement was triggered by Chinese students' indignation, under the guidance of progressive intellectuals, in the wake of the Versailles Treaty. It signalled the emergence of new liberal elites seeking to save the country at any price, accepting the need to abandon Confucian doctrine and instigate a cultural renewal, since this was the last possible resort. This iconoclasm, materialised in Wu Yu's slogan: 'Down With the Confucian Shop' (*dadao kongjia dian*), can also be found in many campaigns later launched by the Communist regime.

The quest for power and wealth (*fuqiang*) that Yan Fu formulated has deeply marked Chinese intellectuals' conception of their vocation.[43] Faced with national crises (the Opium Wars and the collapse of empire) in the late nineteenth century,

---

42. White, L. T. III, 'Thought workers in Deng's time', in Goldman, M., Cheek, C. and Hamrin, C. L. (eds), *China's Intellectuals and the State: In search of a new relationship*, Cambridge, MA: Harvard University Press, Asia Center, 1987.

43. Schwartz, B. *In Search of Wealth and Power: Yen Fu and the West*, Cambridge, MA: The Belknap Press of Harvard University Press, 1964.

intellectuals were less eager to embrace Enlightenment ideals than to solve political, social and economic problems through a zealous iconoclasm and setting up a strong and efficient state. Chinese intellectuals made it their responsibility to find solutions to the problems the country was confronted with. This made their co-optation to and inclusion in the nationalist and communist revolutions, and consequent finding themselves in the service of power, self-evident.

The origin of this feature can also be traced back to the *literati* tradition, which is far remote from Edward Saïd or Noam Chomsky's definitions of the intellectual.[44] Tu Weiming describes Confucian *literati* as active intellectuals profoundly immersed in 'the government of the world' (*jingshi*) of the economy, society and politics. They can only act by the emperor's side. To Tu, the Confucian *literati*-official still plays a part in the psycho-cultural imagination in Far Eastern societies. However, in China in particular, the impact of this was qualified because of the watershed of the turn of the twentieth century and the Republican era as far as the forms of intellectual commitment are concerned. Besides, the Communist regime later alternated periods of expert-consultation and expert-persecution. In other words, the elitism of Chinese intellectuals is as strongly connected to the Confucian tradition of the *literati*, who were responsible for the world's wellbeing, as to the Marxist belief that real physical, psychological and social needs can be uncovered by the best-educated and -informed individuals, consequently called upon to guide society.

Besides, these two tendencies do not suffice to fully account for this elitist attitude. From this tendency also originates some unease in the relationship between intellectuals and the Party, because the latter co-opts this avant-garde as it is necessary to its modernising policy, while worrying about its subversive potential.

In the 1980s, and mostly in the early 1990s, research became more professional and the great majority of researchers focused on purely academic research. To Deng Zhenglai, a major figure of law and social sciences in China who recently passed away, this professionalism is one of the main features of scholars from his generation.

> Let us suppose we lived during the Cultural Revolution. I would have no opportunity to pursue my research. It is only possible in normal times. At the end of the Cultural Revolution, I could choose to pursue my studies and dedicate myself to research. During the Cultural Revolution, we could not study. Many books were banned. We could not buy them. We however had the opportunity to reflect. The times we now live in have no incidence on my career. Whether the country is developed or in development, it does not change much for me. I am interested in research and nothing else [...] After the Open and Reform policy of 1978, the reach of the state has started to visibly recede. The economy has become mercantile, even though it is still partially guided by the state and remains distinct from western economies. We can therefore dedicate ourselves to research, which was absolutely unthinkable during the Cultural Revolution.

---

44. According to Edward Saïd, the intellectual must speak truth to power. For Noam Chomsky, he should yearn to become a moral actor, not to serve power.

Income and research funding

For the last thirty years, academics have benefited from many advantages and received flattering proposals from the public and private sectors and the media. In this context, should we infer that Chinese scholars are subservient to power? In a study which confirms the importance of higher education in the critical attitude of Chinese citizens, Tang Wenfang remarks that intellectuals who are integrated in the system are, finally, harsher critics of it because they know the situation better and are more confident in their political efficacy.[45] As soon as they are given the institutional means to solve problems, they are more active, even though their relationship to power remains complicated. The proximity between the spheres of knowledge and of power is worrying because academic research is very much oriented by government policies and national subjects (*guojia keti*). The 1990s are often described as an era of professionalisation and co-optation (or even subordination) of intellectual elites, which are transformed into institutional advisers. Animated by a more progressive vision, the government has paid closer attention to social-development issues and constantly increased subsidies for social science research. However, a political line remains, which is a major obstacle to top-rated research. Sociologist Zhang Letian explains that a complete political orientation guidebook, the guidelines for national research projects (*keti zhinan*) and the subjects that are publicly funded guide sociologists away from fundamental research towards applied research.[46] Low salaries compel academics to create individual projects and to apply for public funding, which guarantees some degree of political control since most projects have political objectives. Applications also reduce the time spent on conducting research. Finally, it is difficult to set the right use of allocated funds and many could be accused of corruption if they were investigated. This implies another form of political control, since it makes it harder to criticise the regime from a moral point of view. Let us note that the early development of social sciences and political science in many western countries was not devoid of interaction between the governments at that time.

In China, perhaps more than in other countries, the income of scientific laboratories and researchers varies greatly depending on the prestige of the institutions they are affiliated to. Zhu Guanglei, Dean of Nankai University's Zhou Enlai School of Government, considers that state funding is a recognition only provided to the best universities, whose faculty is almost exclusively composed of PhDs. According to him, it is quite easy for a good researcher interested in a marginal subject which is not directly related to political action to obtain funding.

Most researchers pursue their own research, which they are personally interested in. But if their work is top-rated, they obtain funding. Because

45. Tang, W. *Public Opinion and Political Change in China*, Stanford, CA: Stanford University Press, 2005.

46. Zhang, L. 'La crise de la recherche fondamentale : recherche académique, logique du marché et intervention étatique', in Rocca, J. -L. (ed) *La société chinoise vue par ses sociologues*, Paris: Presses de Sciences Po, 2008.

every year, they can receive national funding for social sciences, funding from the Department of Education or from the city of Tianjin, for instance. These funding sources consider the two types of research separately. Concretely, in universities like Nankai, research on participation and political decision-making is quite common, but it is not the case in most universities.

It is undeniable that Chinese intellectual elites have sought more financial comfort since the 1980s but the state is losing its monopoly and other sources of funding and personal wealth multiply. China redefined its knowledge policy under the sharp pressure of the market economy on intellectual production. Chen Pingguan divides the history of specialised research in China into different periods: individual research in the 1940s; planned research in the 1950s; and 'market research' in the early 1980s. This means that academics have found new 'employers' and their stipend as civil servants now only represents a limited part of their income, compared to much greater resources coming from extra-curricular teaching, publications and missions for the private sector and international organisations. This income-diversification renders the influence of political authorities all the weaker. However, Chen Pingguan reminds us that 'if the market partly frees from political dependence and financial pressure, it can also impede the independence and dignity of intellectual work. And it makes it all the more difficult to resist the lure of profit than the power diktat'.[47] Zhang Letian explains that 10 billion yuan a year are devoted to training of all kinds, which encourages academics in charge of it to leave the peace and quiet of their office and laboratories to teach. The monthly stipend of the junior teaching staff in Chinese universities in 2012 is about 3,000 yuan (€360), which is insufficient to cover the basic expenses of these young academics aspiring to the middle class. NGOs and international foundations also supply Chinese researchers with generous funding for many projects related, for instance, to AIDS-prevention or village elections. To obtain such funding, sometimes reaching staggering amounts, researchers adapt to these organisations' standards; and this form of dependence, like political dependence, can threaten the autonomy of conducted research.

The gap between the prestigious status of academics and the salary they start their career with has become cruel in contemporary China, where those who have successfully risen to the happy middle classes are subjected to intense family pressure. Without owning a flat and a car, it has become virtually impossible to get married. Funding one's parents retirement and one's children's studies (private lessons, access to the best schools so as to prepare them for the highly selective university entrance examination) is extremely costly. Opportunities to complete academics' income are now so numerous and common that it has become extremely difficult to accurately assess their overall income. Basic salaries depend not only on academic status but also on discipline and, above all, on universities and departments. A professor in economics or management

---

47. Chen, P. 'Scholarship, ideas, politics', in Wang Chaohua, *One China, Many Paths*, London: Verso, 2003, p. 124.

often earns ten times more than a counterpart in political science. Besides, extra-academic consulting activities for the private sector are much more numerous and lucrative than the missions a social or a political scientist can undertake. However, even for these academics, taking part in training, commercial publishing and project-funding can multiply salaries by ten. Liu Dong explains that the additional annual income for well established professors like him, who have reached the zenith of academic recognition, can easily reach €50,000 euros thanks to the conferences they give.

The scholars I interviewed are all well known and well established and live in very comfortable conditions, even if their subjects are not the most lucrative. Liu Dong explains that he has lost his taste for travelling abroad. He is delighted to be able to supervise the translation of major Chinese scholars into English and to benefit from the recent financial prosperity of Chinese universities, which allows them to invite foreign professors and frees academics from the need to leave the exceptional comfort they now enjoy in China.

> The French must get a firmer grasp of contemporary China, which cannot be achieved through people who claim to be representative when China is so diverse. These people have no family in China, to spend so much time abroad. As to me, I feel so good at home, in my duplex, with three sound systems of 29 speakers for each. My personal library is 100m^2, with 260 sections. This can explain why I no longer feel like travelling abroad, but foreign scholars must understand China better. It is therefore necessary to calmly and scrupulously select, the central publications of the best Chinese scholars and have them translated and published.

Deng Zhenglai underlines the spectacular evolution in the living and working conditions of academics and the heterogeneity of their situations.

> The income of academics has greatly risen. It is unbelievable. Simply look around at my office, equipped with private toilet and shower, a place to have a nap. The situation is beyond comparison with former conditions. Nowadays, as far as academic freedom is concerned, all views are acceptable as long as you do not violently criticize the government, which remains the last sensitive area. […] It was utterly unthinkable, thirty years ago, to imagine living and working in such conditions. With social development, the population has become richer. Some people are extremely wealthy. Academics have also had their share. Academic life in China is relatively comfortable; it is even very enjoyable.

> As to sources of funding, research projects can be funded by the Chinese state, local governments but also private companies. My estimates are that 70 per cent of funding comes from the state, but situations vary greatly from one scholar and from one discipline to another. Academics from economics, finance, management and law enjoy incomes which are much more diversified than political scientists, historians or philosophers.

As a result, the conditions in which Chinese academics practice their activity are very complex. Liu Dong's words give the impression that they walk a fine line.

You cannot easily get rid of a Chinese government with such a development and growth rate. Many other countries like Yugoslavia or Argentina developed as well before regressing again. We therefore criticise the Chinese government. There's a phrase in China: 'a small criticism for a great help'. Each criticism contributes to progress. We are all in the same boat. The Chinese boat is moving forward but for it not to sink, we must solve this distribution problem and manage to check the power of officials. It might be too late. Intellectuals might already be too weak or bought. The CCP has launched many research projects, which you can apply to. After a few years, you finish a project and your findings can allow you to get a better position, or a better title. It's hard to resist.

Beside censorship, which looms constantly over researchers' heads, and their lack of autonomy from the state, the academic field is more and more dependent on the market, companies, NGOs, and various institutions and foundations which offer them the possibility of copiously supplementing the meagre stipend they receive, unless they are part of the academic elite constituted by famous professors who graduated from the Chinese or international 'Ivy League' universities. The Chinese academic condition varies depending on the type of universities, the researcher's subject, the length of his service and his capacity to multiply sources of funding. However, some common elements in all Chinese academics' daily practice emerge. What makes their experience distinct from their counterparts' is the presence and the power of the Party in universities, resilient limitations to academic freedom, and in particular freedom of publication, the process through which the Chinese social sciences have been revived and made to catch up after a 30-year clampdown, the practical role assigned to them in China's modernisation process and the reversed conception of the role of the committed academic, in this country where criticising is more effective and legitimate when it comes from within the system. This shift can partly explain why dissidents and marginalised intellectuals are often deemed too emotional and lack popularity in China.

Political science revived in Chinese universities

Our feet in China; our eyes on the world. (Zhao Baoxu)

The example of political science as an academic discipline allows us to flesh out this brief overview of the Chinese academic condition and to better understand the political commitment of the researchers under scrutiny. Political science departments, closed after the university reforms of 1952, progressively reopened in the 1980s, in the wake of Deng Xiaoping's exhortations to quickly catch up (*zhuajin buke*).[48] First limited to Marxist studies and completely steered by class struggle, political research opened up to the study of conflicts of interests and institutional analysis in the late 1990s.[49] Thousands of scholars returned to China at that time after being trained in foreign universities.[50] This has helped Chinese political science to catch up. According to Zhu Guanglei,

> Narrow-focused research in political science in China is uncommon, contrary to broader research. That's the reason why I think Chinese political science is not sufficiently developed as far as specialised academic and scientific research are concerned. Many very broad studies are undertaken and the researchers in charge are satisfied with their work, thinking it is political science. That's not the case. They think they are writing political science articles but it's pointless. Here's the current situation. But political science took off only in 1985. It is less than 30 years. Before 1949, there were very few studies in that field, and the level was very low. It could almost be claimed that there was no such thing as political science in China before 1985. Before 1949, there were a few famous scholars, whose works I read. They are mostly translations of western studies. They were very wise men, compared to the general illiterate population. That's a general assessment. Besides, we lack scientific method. For the last ten years or so, we have made some progress but there is still a long way to go.

To better understand the debate on the existence or not of political science in China, and when it emerged, Yu Keping makes a distinction between a broad conception of political science as the study of the causes of political phenomena and a narrow conception as an independent science, which developed in China only a century ago.[51] He explains that in 1899, the Shixue Guan, a training centre for administration cadres, was funded at the the Metropolitan University (*Jingshi Daxue Tang*), *Beida*'s former name. Between 1901 and 1904, 70 western political classics were translated into China. According to Zhao Baoxu, in 1948 more than 40 out of 100 Chinese universities had a political science department.[52] From the 1980s, after a 30-year ban, major western political science books were translated

48. Yu, K. 'Zhongguo zhengzhixue bainian huimou' ('Assessing a hundred years of Chinese political science'), Central Compilation and Translation Bureau, 15 January 2009, available online at www.chinaelections.com/newsinfo.asp?newsid=101404; Wang, S. '"Jiegui" haishi "nalai": zhengzhixue bentuhua de sikao' ('Harmonizing or bringing in: reflections on the indigenisation of political science'), *Human Sciences and Society*, 24 September 2009; Deng, Z. 'The state of the field: political science and Chinese political studies', *Journal of Chinese Political Science* 14, 2009, pp. 331–4.

49. Yang, G. *Zhengzhixue Daolun (An Introduction to Political Science)*, Beijing: Peking University Press, 2007.

50. Li, H. 'Returned students and political change in China', *Asian Perspective* 30(2), summer 2006, pp. 1–29.

51. Yu, K. 'Political science and public administration: an overview', *Democracy Is a Good Thing: Essays on politics, society, and culture in contemporary China*, Washington, DC: Brookings Institution Press, 2009, p. 7.

52. Zhao, B. *In Pursuit of Harmony: An academic anthology*, Foreign Languages Press, 2008, p. 38.

and the impact of western paradigms has been overwhelming. Simultaneously, Deng Xiaoping's Open and Reform policy and the economic reforms it includes have led to major political and institutional problems, which has encouraged the academic community to identify them, warn of their potential impact and offer ways to solve them. Zhao Baoxu, who organised the discipline and trained the first Chinese political scientists in the 1980s, claims that 'real life had brought out a series of problems that needed political scientists to study and to help solve. These problems included theoretical aspects as well as systemic and administrative ones. At present, the most important reason for restoring research in political science is to solve these problems.'[53] These pressing problems are mainly related to the system, the administration, democracy and the legal system.[54]

The commitment of interviewed academics is closely connected to the observation that the Open and Reform policy has led to intolerable geographical and social inequalities and to the will to change the situation before the country collapses. Potential flashpoints are the growing gaps between urban and rural populations,[55] between eastern and western regions and between the winners and losers of the reforms.[56] These inequalities get deeper as reforms continue; and they trigger greater instability. Official statistics for 2010 record 180,000 uprisings in 2010, a steady rise from 8,709 in 1993, 87,000 in 2005 and 90,000 in 2006.[57] Cases of corruption, power abuse, unfair expropriations, police or judicial mistakes, or environmental pollution often spark off these so-called incidents. The most common themes in Chinese political science, therefore, are social stability, conflicts of interest, distribution, defence of human rights and citizens' rights, regulation and authority, democratic institutions, rule of law and rule by law, (in)efficient policy-implementation, designing an 'honest' government and value systems.

---

53. Zhao, B. *In Pursuit of Harmony: An academic anthology,* Foreign Languages Press, 2008, p. 40. Zhao Baoxu gives a detailed introduction of the discipline's revival after 1978: the creation of the Chinese political science association, the political science research institute at the Academy of Social Sciences and political science departments in universities, as well as the emergence of training programmes for local cadres and the publication of manuals. He lists some of the foreign scholars who were invited, such as Robert Scalapino, Kenneth Waltz, David Easton, Michel Oksenberg, Lowell Ditmer, Seymour Martin Lipset, Alex Inkeles, Herbert Simon, Leslie Lipson, Martin Landau and Tang Tsou, pp. 44–52.

54. He, Z. for instance, presented the central notion of 'political development' in Chinese political science since the late 1970s: He, Z. 'Democratisation: the Chinese model and course of political development' in Yu, K. (ed.), *Democracy and Rule of Law in China*, Leiden: Brill Academic Publishers, 2010, pp. 49–76.

55. The ten coastal provinces monopolise three-quarters of international trade exchanges and 60% of wealth production.

56. Sun, L. 'Women zai kaishi miandui yige duanlie de shehui?' (Are we confronted with a fractured society?'), *Strategy and Management* 2, 2002; Sun, L. *Duanlie* [*Division*], Beijing: Kexui Wenbian Chubanshe, S. 2003; Hu, A. 'Yigeguojia sigeshijie fendiqu fazhanchaju' ('One country, four worlds'), *China Economic Times*, 4 April 2001; Wang, S. *Anbangzhidao: Guojia zhuanliede mubiao yu tujing*, Beijing: Sanlian Shudian, 2007.

57. Yu, J. 'Baozhu shehuiwending de dixian' ('Maintaining a reference level of social stability'), speech given before the assembly of Beijing lawyers, 26 December 2009, available online at http://www.chinaelections.org/Newsinfo.asp?NewsID=169507 (last accessed 14 November 2014).

Chinese political scientists are quite critical of their discipline. They deplore the fact that the domination of 'fads' for some subjects leads to repetitive publications while other major and important subjects, such as the regulation of coalmines, food safety or pharmaceutical companies, are hardly approached. It is interesting to notice that those subjects which are deemed important correspond to major practical issues that the discipline is expected to help solve.

The pragmatism and civic mission that Chinese political scientists assign themselves have no Chinese specificity. Political science in the world is known for its focus on contemporary developments. Lucien Pye claims that the discipline is characterised by our 'sensitivity to the problems and developments in the real world of public affairs'.[58] When political science emerged, first in the United States and later in the rest of the world, the discipline was intimately connected with the issue of good government. The first mission it assigned itself was to improve society. The American Political Science Association still defines scientific research in the field of political science as an undertaking serving human interests and not purely as a quest for knowledge.[59] This original mission seems all the more distant nowadays as universities have markedly forsaken this civic spirit to engage in a positivist quest for more 'objectivity'. The latter is supposed to be evidence against the accusation of excessive 'scientism' levelled against these disciplines whose utility and cost are constantly questioned. The debates about the respective advantages of quantitative and qualitative studies that regularly animate our academic communities illustrate that point. However, Claire Snyder, in an article encouraging the revival of the original civic mission of American political science, emphasises that it was mobilised during the Cold War, firmly steering itself towards democratic promotion and, accordingly, enjoyed generous funding.[60] This is the reason why Wang Shaoguang has undertaken to prove that American political science is not as 'scientific' as it claims to be. It indeed actively contributes to American politics, which explains why he objects to Chinese political scientists adopting its concepts, methods and theories to the letter and without circumspection.[61] Li Qiang offers an insightful diagnosis of the 'crisis' Chinese political science is going through.

Political science is insufficiently developed in China, for historical reasons. In 1952 disciplines were readjusted and political science as a scientific discipline was completely eliminated. The discipline disappeared in China until the 1980s. There

---

58. Pye, L. 'Political science and the crisis of authoritarianism', *American Political Science Review* 84(1), March 1990, pp. 3–19.

59. Gunnell, J. 'The founding of the American Political Science Association: Discipline, profession, political theory, and politics', *American Political Science Review* 100(4), 2006, pp. 479–86.

60. Snyder, C. 'Should political science have a civic mission? An overview of the historical evidence', *PS: Political Science and Politics*, 34(2), June 2001, pp. 301–5.

61. Wang, S. '"Jiegui" haishi "nalai": zhengzhixue bentuhua de sikao' ('Harmonising or bringing in: reflections on the indigenisation of political science'), *Human Sciences and Society* 24, September 2009.

were not many competent people to reconstruct it. I belong to the first batch of students having received disciplinary training in political science. The discipline lacked scholars with a good academic political science background. That's why, after the Open and Reform policy was launched, students like me were sent abroad to study. We later came back and now constitute the most active group of political scientists in China. But let's face it, we are a minority. Most political scientists have not benefitted from a full training. Political science needs time to develop in China. The number of qualified scholars is limited. Besides, we have been very quickly influenced by western political science, above all American. We have been affected by its scientistic influence. The discipline develops in China at a different stage. In Europe and in the United States, in the seventeenth, eighteenth and nineteenth centuries, political thinkers approached big issues like the relation between religion and society, between the state and society. They wondered why democracy was necessary and how to set up a representative regime. Nowadays, western political scientists no longer feel concerned with these big issues. They focus on very precise questions so as to help governments rule. Especially in the United States, political science has become very scientist [meaning, too scientifically orientated]. It studies who becomes president, etc. In China, we are faced with very serious problems, that political scientists have to reflect upon. We must study Chinese traditional culture, the connection between modern society and modernity. We must study the relation between state and society (family and clan) and investigate their potential impact on the creation of a democratic regime, a representative and constitutional government. There are no simple answers to these questions. I do not think western theories offer easy ready-made answers to these questions. They cannot be easily solved. The shame is, Chinese political science is not in a position to solve these problems for the time being. We cannot fulfil this function yet. Because of this 30-year break, Chinese political scientists lack academic training and experience. Some of us were sent abroad, but political science in western countries has precisely become scientist and limited to questions which are so narrow that it cannot be of use in China. It cannot help us face the problems we currently encounter. The situation is different in Japan. Political science there benefits from a longer tradition. Some Japanese political scientists understand some issues and accurately analyse the Chinese situation. The discipline is more developed in Japan. But in the United States, political scientists are too influenced by scientism. They cannot meet our needs. This can be explained by the fact that the United States has already solved basic issues. Discussing the advantages and drawbacks of democracy, its degree of desirability and so on is no longer a priority. But it's precisely what we are interested in. That's the reason why our discipline is in trouble. We have not been able yet to answer the questions society asks. That's my assessment of Chinese political science.

Chinese political science must thus meet transitional China's needs. This makes political scientists' research more concrete and likely to have an impact. It also means that the 'scientist' brand of political science which is practised in North

American universities cannot bring much to Chinese scholars. According to Yang Guangbin, great change has recently happened:

> I strongly disagree with the idea that there is no such thing as political science in China. Chinese political scientists conduct the best research on Chinese politics. We are very confident. Ten years ago, we still paid attention to the work and findings of foreign scholars. Today, it is their turn to study the research and work of Chinese scholars on China's politics and economy. The situation has changed dramatically for five to ten years. It depends on the chosen perspective and standards. If Chinese political science is assessed according to American standards, one might say there is no political science in China. Rational choice theory has not taken hold in this country. Few people find it interesting here. To my mind, this theory is only of interest when the issue of the political system is solved. It does not allow to study macroscopic issues. It belongs to an individualistic culture whereas our culture is rather collective. Besides, we have numerous macro problems to solve, such as the transition of the CCP and all sorts of issues related to the setting up of the political system. The American methods are not useful in that sense.

Yang Guangbin explains the radical differences between the processes of modernisation in China or Russia and Great Britain or the United States:

> Some academics strive to contribute to the government of the state. One concept derives from this: since Locke, we focus only on society, which is considered crucial. We only hear about human rights, freedom, individual rights. Political science focuses on those ideas. That's what it's based on. This system of thought derives from English and American history. Its other foundation stems from the German and French experiences. It corresponds to the return of the state. Theory therefore derives from lived experience. However, developing countries like Russia or China have gone through another experience of the state. In the English or American modernisation process, the role of trade was crucial. This explains why the focus is on society's power, individual rights, the market economy and so on. Then France, and Germany most of all, but also Japan, have gone through a more bureaucratic modernisation process. They tend to focus more on the role of the state and have theorised it. In Russia or China and many other countries, we realise that trade does not allow to build an organised state. Public authority is failing. In such cases, the state needs an organising force, a political Party. This is what is happening in Russia and China, where there is a need for a central political party, a need for centralism. We need a theoretical system to understand those regimes. From the perspective of comparative politics and comparative political science, these are theoretical research objects. But two questions remain central: what should China do? Which direction should it take? This is the crux of the matter. As I often say, I feel very lucky as a researcher to practise my profession precisely when China is undergoing this transition. It is only in these specific transitional times that research can

have a concrete outcome and have a true impact. American political science is no longer stimulating. The situation is similar in France. Political research on China is most exciting. This is a large country and no one knows the direction it will take. This might be the most fascinating research to be undertaken.

Zhu Guanglei, Dean of the Zhou Enlai School of Government, which opened in May 2004 in Nankai University, Tianjin, deplores the unequal development of the discipline, especially as far as comparative politics is concerned, due to the exclusive attention paid to the United States and Japan. He explains that he has found it extremely hard to hire specialists from France or Russia. His assessment of the discipline can seem contradictory. He laments the lack of scientism of Chinese political science outside the ten best Chinese universities while criticising political research for its excessive degree of abstraction. His endeavour is to identify a specific issue and to strive and solve it. According to him, political science's role is indeed to solve problems.

The mission of political science and social sciences is proclaimed loud and clear: solving some problems and thereby serving the country's development. As a matter of fact, the phrase 'solving problems' was pronounced about 40 times in the interviews. According to Xu Xianglin, policy analysis goes hand in hand with producing interpretations and suggestions intended to sway government decision-making. He refers to a traditional model of political participation and commitment consisting in voicing intellectual suggestions and 'speaking truth to power'. This mode of participation undermines the independence and objectivity of political science research, since the research framework is often affected by the will, worries and interests of leaders.[62] Zhang Yongjin attributes this tendency Chinese scholars have of influencing the direction of public policies to the history of the Chinese intelligentsia, whose members tended to feel an urge to 'save' China from the time of the emergence of the intellegentsia.[63] As already mentioned, in the late nineteenth century, diffusing western knowledge in China only served an instrumental aim: saving China from inner decay and imperialist invasion. Yang Guangbin goes even further back in Chinese history:

In Chinese culture, the relation between officials and literati, government and study, is intimate. As the saying goes, the literati are supposed to govern *[xue er you zeshi]*. This comes from Confucius. The proverb can also be turned upside down: the officials are supposed to study *[shi er you zexue]*. This is a constant feature of Chinese tradition. This is not only the case of economics and politics, which must more or less directly serve to govern the country. When conducting comparative politics research, for instance, in relation to

62. Xu, X. 'Mianxiang 21 shiji de zhongguo zhengce kexue' ('Chinese political science and the challenge of the 21st century'), *Peking University Academic Review (Philosophy and Social Sciences)*, 37(4), 2000, pp. 108–20.

63. Zhang, Y. 'Politics, culture and scholarly responsibility in China: toward a culturally sensitive analytical approach', *Asian Perspective* 31(3), 2007, pp. 103–24.

China, a scholar is bound to wonder how China should proceed and what should be done to reform the political system. This is our main activity. Of course, the rest of the time, we also focus on many other concrete problems, because practical issues can also lead to theoretical issues. This affects one part of political scientists. The other part focuses on political theory. They study John Rawls mostly. They are into pure research. They study to cultivate their minds, but also to prove that they are superior and that they read a lot. Here's what they do mainly. Just look at their research themes. In political theory or philosophy, they conduct pure research. In Chinese political science, practical research prevails. Scholars focus on governance issues and their research are supposed to be put into practice.

This can explain why some scholars who are close to power, like Yu Keping, despite his reputation as non-official adviser of Hu Jintao and his role of expert in charge of the official Bureau of Compilation and Translation, are considered major political scientists in China. The quality of Yu's academic research is fully recognised in Chinese academia. We should note that the most influential scholars belong to a peculiar generation whose strong political commitment and views were marked by their experience of the Cultural Revolution, popular movements, the opening up in the 1980s and the Tiananmen Square repression, as we will discuss in Chapter Two.

Like in other disciplines, after a frantic and necessarily incomplete absorption of concepts and theories developed in western universities, a debate emerged on the need to further 'westernise' or 'nationalise' political science. Members of the New Left, like Wang Shaoguang, a professor at the Chinese University of Hong Kong, condemn the vacuity of many analyses of the Chinese political situation. According to Wang, the preponderant usage of imprecise concepts like authoritarianism or democracy is an obstacle to the actual and relevant analysis of the regime and the political change that has (or not) taken place in China. This is the rationale behind his advocacy of an innovative spirit and curiosity for new approaches to be developed so that the understanding of Chinese politics is comprehensive.[64] Xiao Gongqin explains that a sinicisation (*hanhua*) of political science, after the input of international political science is well absorbed, allows scholars to get a better grasp of the assets and liabilities of political developments in China. For instance, a new approach should be adopted to identify and understand what Xiao calls the Sino-Vietnamese model of development, which, to his mind, political scientists have so far overlooked.[65]

64. Wang, S. "'Jiegui' haishi 'nalai' : zhengzhixue bentuhua de sikao' ('Harmonising or bringing in: reflections on the indigenization of political science'), *Human Sciences and Society*, 24 September 2009.

65. Xiao, G. 'Zhuanxing zhengzhi shiye xia de zhongguo sanshinian' ('30 years of reform through the looking glass of transitional political science'), *Leaders* 21, April 2008.

As a result, within Chinese political science, calls for indigenisation (*bentuhua*) are numerous.[66] These insist on the need for an indigenisation that is paired with an unceasing open-mindedness to international political science, resulting in both taking the features and conditions requisite for the Chinese political development into account and falling within the universal knowledge that transcends countries and societies and which allows political science to exist. In other words, Chinese political science must become a branch of international political science, develop comparative-politics research and produce categories, methods and analytical frameworks based on the Chinese experience and therefore better adapted to understanding it. Zhao Baoxu encapsulates the political scientist's desirable positioning as keeping his feet firmly on Chinese ground and keeping his eyes firmly fixed on the world.[67] Li Qiang endeavours to detail what is at stake in this debate on political science's indigenisation from a more neutral perspective:

A good political scientist cannot ignore the situation and the events taking place around him. It is impossible. When you are a political scientist in China, you must first choose which major political problem that affects the society you live in you want to focus on. In that sense, it is right to call it indigenisation or localisation. But it does not preclude some specialists from studying western countries, because their academic research is also of great interest. And a good researcher, when undertaking research, is aware that there is no ready-made solution to the social issue under study and that no solution can solve it completely. Human society is not a machine. Social sciences and political science are not hard science. Human diversity is too great. The Chinese, foreigners, the French, Americans, have different ways of thinking. For instance, the French and American regimes are very different. Anglo-Saxon societies follow their own logic while continental European societies follow theirs. For instance, the French political tradition is strongly republican. In the name of that republican tradition, France bans young girls from wearing a scarf at school. You are citizens first, religious affiliation comes second. In the United Kingdom or in the Unites States, traditions differ and from them stem significant variations in political regime. In a similar way, when political reform is discussed in China, Chinese habits and ways of thinking must be taken into account. In that sense, indigenisation is a relevant notion. However,

---

66. Several articles were devoted to that issue. *See* Jing, W. and Wang, G. 'Western political research approaches and the development of political science methodology in China', *Journal of Chinese Political Science* 14, 1999, pp. 299–315; Yu, J. 'Reflection on the development of political science and the construction of Chinese political science', *Teaching and Researching (Jiaoxue Yu Yanjiu)* 5(21) 2005; Yu, K. 'Zhongguo zhengzhixue bainian huimou' ('Assessing a hundred years of Chinese political science'), Central Compilation and Translation Bureau, 15 January 2009.

67. Zhao, B. *In Pursuit of Harmony: An academic anthology*, pp. 56–7. This phrase is reminiscent of the famous *zhongti xiyong* of intellectuals from the turn of the twentieth century.

some use the term *bentuhua* as a strategic call for action. The danger, when the concept is overused, is that it becomes the norm of what is politically correct. Only indigenisation appears acceptable. Let us suppose that an academic like me, who specialises in western political philosophy, studies western political philosophers and writes about them, only writes on China on the side. How could I apply this *bentuhua* principle? Besides, I think that we need a plural society to reflect upon China's situation. Personally, I try to promote the idea that to study China's political issues, we must focus on China's reality. But I cannot prevent someone from thinking that applying the western method to the letter in China is sufficient, that China only needs to emulate the Unites States' model. I strongly object to that but I will not resort to this label to claim that if we don't indigenise Chinese political science, this is not politically correct. This is gross intolerance. Each individual, each researcher, brings his contribution relying on his own experience and readings. Any good researcher reflects upon his surroundings, which is less the case for minor researchers. This morning, a student came and talked about a village primary school and its problems. I told him he had to go there and do some fieldwork. You cannot limit yourself to reading the papers. You must talk to people before making your mind on state investment in primary education and the fact that going to school is hard and expensive. I told him he was too ideological. When he gets to the village, he will realise that this issue is not people's priority because children have all gone to town and the village schools are empty. In such circumstances, should schools be expanded? The rural population is not faced with the problem of education cost or state investment in that domain. The most urgent issue is the gap between countryside and city schools. In that sense, a good researcher must contextualise his research subject. Each problem is embedded in a local situation. A good French political scientist, for instance, must indigenise his research to solve the problems the French government encounters. It would be unthinkable for him to claim that the American example should be followed. We learn a lot through understanding how the United States conceived their political structure. Once this process has been studied, it can be discussed in France, but to investigate the problems France faces, the French situation itself must be examined.

The tendency to indigenise and put together a so-called 'Chinese model' signals that China's intellectual and political elites are now much more self-confident. It triggers lukewarm reactions throughout the world. Without taking sides in the polemic on the potential risks of a 'Chinese model' designed to be exported and to spread to the rest of the planet, we should remember that this discourse, in the academic field of political science, mostly aims at calling for more circumspection in the use of theories and concepts originating from North American universities, and to encourage the production and not only the consumption of such analytical tools.[68] Liu Dong, who aligns himself with Republican-era thinker Chen Yinke, wants a Chinese theory to be devised once the great western thinkers have been closely studied and understood. He refers to Chen's words: 'Those who are truly able to develop their own independent system of ideas and who have creatively accomplished this, must absorb and import foreign learning on the one hand while bearing in mind the position of our nation.'[69]

---

68. According to Elizabeth Perry: '[Political science in China is] on the verge of maturing from a 'consumer field', (dependent for its analytical insights upon imports from the study of other countries) to a 'producer field' (capable of generating analyses of interest to comparatists in general)' (Perry, E. J. 'Trends in the study of Chinese politics: state-society relations', *China Quarterly* 139, September 1994, pp. 704–13).

69. Liu, D. 'Jingti renweide "yangjingbang xuefeng"', *Ershiyi Shiji* 32, 1995, revised and translated by Davies, G. and Liu, K. as 'Revisiting the perils of "designer pidgin scholarship"', in Gloria Davies, *Voicing Concerns: Contemporary Chinese critical inquiry*, Lanham, MD: Rowman & Littlefield, 2001, p. 96.

Chapter Two

Two Generations of Committed Scholars

> The Cultural Revolution remains the dominant explanatory variable (or excuse) for everything that has happened in China in the 1970s and 1980s. It continues to define Chinese understandings of what they are trying to achieve through 'reform'. [...] The impact of the Cultural Revolution obscures the continuities in ideology and social practices from the entire Mao period that continue to shape life in China today. (Timothy Cheek)[1]

Academic research on the Cultural Revolution is still relatively uncommon in China, because it is officially deemed 'sensitive'. Against this backdrop, the frequency with which scholars refer to that period in order to explain their political commitment is striking, all the more so as these references are often stereotypical and ideological.[2] The aim of this chapter is to understand how the generation of committed scholars who experienced the Cultural Revolution, despite marked differences, rely on this experience to justify their political commitment, ideological positioning and conception of a good regime. Many of the scholars who engage in the debate on political reform were born in the 1950s and the unique experience they went through – the Cultural Revolution and its wave of mobilisation and political activism; violence; pain and frustration (due to interrupted studies and transfer to countryside villages or factories) – but also the subsequent experience of liberalisation (restored university entrance examinations; China's opening to the world; the blossoming of liberal ideas and student movements in the 1980s) are the historical, social and political conditions which lead this age cohort to think of themselves as a generation, aware of their common destiny. The younger generation of scholars, also engaged in discussions on Chinese political reform, were born in the early 1960s. They define themselves as close to the previous generation in some ways – because they entered university at the same time and also experienced the liberalising 1980s – but, nonetheless, as a distinct generation that was not scarred by the Cultural Revolution in the same way as the older one.

---

1. Cheek, T. *Living With Reform: China since 1989*, Zed books, 2006, p. 59.
2. Chong, W. L. *China's Great Proletarian Cultural Revolution: Master Narratives and post-Mao Counternarratives*, Rowman & Littlefield, 2002.

The Cultural Revolution generation's main features

The concept of generation

Karl Mannheim's contribution to generational theory is a very enlightening approach to understanding the generation of scholars under scrutiny. Four notions allow him to define the concept of generation. First of all, a 'potential generation', or 'a biological generation', is defined as a group of people born in the same period. But such people form a generation from a sociological point of view only in times of social upheaval or change; it is this social background that turns them into an 'actual generation'. This common social experience triggers different forms of intellectual and social response and creates a bond between generation members, although differences in location, class, culture and so on mean that members have somewhat different perspectives on and responses to their shared historical and social experience; a generation is not completely homogenous. Mannheim nevertheless insists on the importance of common historical experiences in the formation of social generations. The former have a significant impact on the malleable minds of young people; they realise that their views on the world, society and politics differ unmistakably from their elders' and they develop a strong generational consciousness. But the members of a generation can tap into their common experience in various ways.[3] These units debate over the same issue but the solutions and ideologisations they offer vary. They are materialised in 'concrete groups'.

My approach is similar to Rudolf Heberlé's who, in line with Mannheim, develops the idea that youthful experiences have a strong impact on individuals' political attitudes. He therefore expands the concept of social generation to that of political generation. According to him,

A social generation cannot be defined in biological terms or in terms of groups of defined ages but rather in terms of common experiences, feelings and ideas linked to each other. A generation is therefore a new way of feeling and of perceiving life, in opposition with the previous way or at least different from it. A generation is a moral and mental collective phenomenon. The members of a generation feel linked by their shared points of view, beliefs, desires.[4]

A generation is thus mainly constituted by a historical event that profoundly marked a given age group and whose social reconstruction in collective memory contributes to the cultural organisation and constitution of that generation.

This study therefore focuses on the 'cohort effect'; that is, the idea that people's political beliefs are less influenced by their growing up or getting old than their socialisation, in the sense that the ideas that prevailed in society when they were

---

3.   Mannheim, K. 'The problem of generations', 1923, re-edited in Mannheim, K. and Wolff, K. -H. (eds) *From Karl Mannheim*, Transaction Publishers, 1993.

4.   Heberlé, R. *Social Movements*, New York, Appleton-Century Crofts,1951, p. 119.

young have a considerable impact on the way each individual forms her values.[5] It also focuses on the 'period effect', which is based on contemporary events and foundational experiences, such as war and disasters, to which age groups react.[6] These are momentous events that transform cohorts of youths into active political generations. In Europe, these landmark events led to the emergence of pivotal generations such as the 1914 generation, the Resistance generation or the 1968 generation. They offer opportunities to reshuffle and redefine how power is organised from a political and intellectual perspective.

The usefulness of the concept of generation of intellectuals was emphasised by Benjamin Schwartz, who insisted on the concrete experience of intellectuals in a given society and on the concrete specificities of history since

> in China, the end of the examination system in 1905, the Japanese incursion into China [...] are specific historic movements which must figure in any effort to understand the experiences and the responses of Chinese intellectuals within the time period with which we are concerned [in his case, the May Fourth Movement].[7]

In the case under study – Chinese scholars whose primary or secondary education was interrupted by the Cultural Revolution – the notion of generation is relevant because, on top of the undoubtable constitution of a specific age cohort, they have commonly experienced events that have deeply impressed them and have become representative of their generation. Besides, their group consciousness is very developed. To refer to Mannheim's theory again, this potential generation has become actual due to the strong bonds its members have created. It is striking that when scholars introduce themselves during interviews or at conferences, in the preface of article collections and so on, they spontaneously identify themselves as members of this generation, which the extraordinary intensity of the experiences they have commonly gone through has rendered unique. The different generational units and the numerous divisions within this generation can partly be explained by their diverse ways of reacting to and starting over after these events. Indeed, the range of intellectual and social responses to the stimulus of historical experiences common to all the members of a generation is very wide. The different political groups and diverse associations which formed during the 1980s and 1990s partly correspond to the diverging ways individuals interpreted the Cultural Revolution, as well as the end of the revolution and the subsequent reform years, including the trauma of the Tiananmen Square repression and the collapse of the Soviet Union.

---

5. Maggini, N. 'Voting behaviour of the young generations', intervention at the Fifth ECPR General Conference, Potsdam, 2009.

6. Braungart, R. and Braungart, M. 'Les générations politiques' in Jean Crête and Pierre Favre (eds), *Générations en politique*, Economica-Presses Universitaires de Laval, 1989, p. 25.

7. Schwartz, B. *China and Other Matters*, Cambridge, MA., Harvard University Press, 1996, p. 55.

Xu Jilin pioneered the systematic analysis of generations of Chinese intellectuals.[8] To his mind, six intellectual generations punctuated the Chinese twentieth century: the generation of the end of the Qing dynasty (born between 1865 and 1880); the generation of the May Fourth Movement (born between 1880 and 1895); the generation that followed the May Fourth Movement (born between 1895 and 1930); the 'generation of the 17 years' (born between 1930 and 1945); the generation of the Cultural Revolution (born between 1945 and 1960); and the generation that followed the Cultural Revolution (*houwenge yidai*, born after 1960). This analysis is based on the assumption that, as Michael Yahuda put it, 'as a result of the Cultural Revolution and its aftermath (1965–76) the generational issue has become one of the most important and fascinating aspects of Chinese politics'.[9] Ruth Cherrington points out that it is often hard to define the exact beginning and end of a generation;[10] this is not the case of the scholars under study here, however, who were all born between 1946 and 1957.

In an article on political generations in China,[11] Michael Yahuda explains that, for the young people designated by officials as the 'lost generation' because their education was interrupted or affected by the Cultural Revolution, 'the Cultural Revolution was perhaps the most significant political experience of their lives'. As a result of the distinctiveness of their experience of that period and the strong consciousness of belonging to a definite group that pervades its members, the definition of this specific generation of Chinese people born between 1945 and 1960 is quite consensual.

Given the importance bestowed to the specificities of this generation and its role in Chinese society and politics, the labels attached to it are manifold. It is most often labelled the 'Cultural Revolution generation', the 'Red Guard generation' or the '*Zhiqing* generation'. Zhiqing is a contraction of the phrase *zhishi qingnian*, that is, 'intellectual youth'. It is the standard phrase used to describe the urban youths who were sent to remote country or mountain villages from 1967 to 1976, officially so they would benefit from sharing the experience of local peasants and workers, which would create a 'new generation' of men and women.

This generation can also be designated the 'lost generation' (*shiluo de yidai* or *miwang de yidai*; *danwule de yidai*). Michael Yahuda explains that 'This is the term given by their elders to the generation whose education was affected by the Cultural Revolution and whose educational standards are regarded now (with some exceptions) as so low as to be less than useful.'[12] In the PhD dissertation appendix he dedicated to this issue,[13] Wang Juntao explains that

8. Xu, J. *Ershi zhongguo shiji liu dai zhishifenzi* (Six generations of Chinese intellectuals in the 20th century), Selected Works, Guangxi Normal University Press, 1999.
9. Yahuda, M. 'Political generations in China', *China Quarterly* 80, 1979, pp. 793, 794 and 802.
10. Cherrington, R. *Deng's Generation: Young intellectuals in 1980s China*, Basingstoke, Macmillan, 1997.
11. Yahuda, M. (1979) 'Political generations in China', pp. 793–805.
12. Yahuda, M. 'Political generations', p. 802.
13. Wang, J. *Reverse Course: Political Neo-Conservatism and regime stability in post-Tiananmen China*, PhD dissertation, Columbia University, 2006, pp. 156–72.

the phrase 'April 5 generation', which he chose to use in his research, was coined by He Jiaodong[14] in reference to 5 April 1976, when a million Chinese gathered on Tiananmen Square to commemorate Zhou Enlai and oppose the Gang of Four. They were finally repressed but that event was the first step in a series of political events initiated by these young demonstrators. The young people who took part in that movement were encouraged by their conviction that men make history and by the mission they had internalised. They felt that the responsibility to serve as critics of the Cultural Revolution and of its nihilism was conferred on them. They felt responsible, because of their revolutionary avant-garde experience, for the political change to come and for breaking away from the May Fourth tradition, which had erred in its unconditional and precipitate embrace of western ideas and rejection of Chinese tradition, a tendency repeated during the Cultural Revolution. Some tendencies surface at the time: some of these youths become more confident in a new national culture.[15] For the same reasons, this generation is also branded the 'political generation'.[16]

Finally, *laosanjie* is the generational concept commonly used in China to refer to members of this generation. It often describes with some nostalgia men and women who were in secondary school in 1966, 1967 and 1968 (hence the name *laosanjie*, 'the three old classes'). Academics resort to this term with caution because of its connotation. It recalls the movement of glorification of the Red Guards, launched by the opening, on 25 November 1990, of a Beijing retrospective on the *zhiqing* and confirmed by the publication of a book entitled *A Youth Without Any Regrets* (*Qingchun wuhui*) in 1993 and later by one called *Adversity and Heroism: Trajectories of laosanjie members* (*Kunnan yu fengliu – laosanjie ren de daolu*). *Laosanjie* is therefore a term which must be used with circumspection. It cannot be separated from the stereotype of the young Reds Guards coming from the best schools in town and driven by their Party loyalty, sense of sacrifice and wholehearted commitment to modernising the most remote areas of the country. This is the opposite of another stereotype demonising the Red Guards, considered as the bloody and irrational offspring of totalitarianism. The movement condemning the *sanzhong ren* ('three types of people') associated with far-leftism is an example of the desire, made explicit in the 1980s, to start with a clean slate after the Cultural Revolution. However, this movement met with strong resistance because many craved revisiting their experience, notably through

---

14. He, J. '"Women laizi hechu yu you quwang nali": Dangqian "zhongguo wenti yanjiu" de sanzhong jinlu' ('Where are we from and where will we go?' Three roads of China's problem research today), *Tribune of Social Sciences* 4, 2003.

15. Liu, X. 'Guanyu wusi yidai yu siwu yidai de shehuixue sikao zaji' (Some sociological thoughts on the April Fifth generation and the May Fourth generation), *Dushu* 5, 1989, quoted in Sausmikat, N. 'Generations, legitimacy, and political ideas in China: the end of polarization or the end of ideology?', *Asian Survey* 43(2), March 2003.

16. Sleebom-Faulkner, M. *The Chinese Academy of Social Sciences – Shaping the Reforms, Academia and China (1977–2003)*, Brill, 2007.

literature, and the formidable surge which led to creating a very extensively documented collective memory.[17]

Many among the scholars I chose to study because of their active participation to the research and debate on political reform belong to this generation and are contemporaries of the Cultural Revolution, the Lin Biao incident, the April Fifth movement, the reopening of universities, the New Enlightenment movement, the Tiananmen Square repression and Deng Xiaoping's subsequent Southern Tour. These scholars constantly emphasise the deep impression that these events made on their lives and worldviews.

Experiencing the Cultural Revolution

Let us first come back to the reasons for this sense of belonging to a distinct generation. Chinese pupils born from the late 1940s to the 1950s were repeatedly told at school that they were the 'national flowers of new China' because they were the first generation of Chinese to be entirely brought up in the new society. The Young Pioneers organisation (*zhongguo shaonian xianfengdui*) had already been set up and their education was tainted with Communist propaganda, drilling moral doctrines designed for a totalitarian society into their minds. They owed absolute loyalty to the leaders, the Party, the nation and the community and were endowed with the mission to obliterate capitalism and establish a Communist society.

As a result, Xu Youyu explains:

Before the Cultural Revolution and until the middle of that period, I was a true believer of Marxism-Leninism, Mao Zedong thought and Communist ideas in general. I was fully convinced that the CCP was an objective, extraordinary and glorious party. I thought Mao was the greatest Marxist of his time and that the Chinese system was the best one in the world. We had the responsibility to free the populations of two thirds of the planet, who suffered from the worst calamities and atrocities, including the French people. They were the victims of exploitation and oppression. We had the duty to free these people. I truly believed all that. I was not only fully convinced, I was a fanatic.

When Mao Zedong launched the Cultural Revolution in 1966, the formal education of this age cohort abruptly ended: they were given the great responsibility to help the leader reverse the tide of revisionism he detected in Chinese politics and society and to purify the Party and the country of its corrupt elements. Mao thus brutally put an end to the official education of this whole generation. He managed to set up an unexpected coalition of military, radical intellectual elites (grouped around his wife) and of Red Guards, which allowed him to circumvent the Party's direction and to impose his vision of socialism, urging people to engage in direct

---

17. Yang, G. 'Days of old are not puffs of smoke: three hypotheses on collective memories of the Cultural Revolution', *China Review* 5(2), Fall 2005, pp. 13–41; Gao, M. *The Battle for China's Past: Mao and the Cultural Revolution*, Pluto Press, 2008.

political action. Students diligently created Red Guard factions – whose role was to find, display in the streets and generally persecute people with authority (cadres, professors), whom they identified as revisionists – in their schools. As a result of the inequalities within the education system because of the importance of a person's class background (the 'bloodline theory'[18]) for university admission, the Red Guards split into radical (Mao followers) and conservative (opposed to Mao's will to destroy the *status quo*) groups. Therefore, the supposedly Great Proletarian Cultural Revolution was, ironically, carried out by the offspring of the former bourgeoisie, who had been radicalised by the unfair treatment they had suffered.

Cadres and intellectuals were the main victims of mobilised youths, who were entranced by the unlimited authority to change the face of Chinese socialism with which they had been endowed. However, the young and naïve Red Guards themselves, after experiencing an immense sense of importance and honour, were turned into villains and became scapegoats when Mao resolved to put an end to the unrest that resulted from their violent activities. He resuscitated the 'up to the mountains and down to the villages' movement (*shangshan xiaxiang yundong* ou *xiaxiang*), which was first launched in the early 1960s by Liu Shaoqi, and sent away the Red Guards who had risen up to his call; which had led to a situation close to civil war. Among urbanites born between 1947 and 1969, half experienced the *xiaoxiang* and spent an average of six years in the countryside. The *laosanjie* were the most affected. When twelve million of these young urban graduates, who, at least in the early stages of the Cultural Revolution, genuinely believed in its values, were harshly criticised in the press and exiled to remote areas, they felt manipulated and betrayed. The resulting trauma for these youths should not be underestimated. Michel Bonnin describes the repressive dimension of this rustication, which was in both the imperial tradition of banishing potentially dangerous elements and in the communist tradition of 'reform through labour' (*laodong gaizao*). He also reminds us that this policy was a quick fix for the employment and overpopulation problems of Chinese cities. Even among young people initially enthusiastic about gaining a rich experience through contact with workers and peasants, the discovery of the latter's' passive obedience to cadres undermined their excitement.[19]

Besides, after these young people experienced the same dire conditions and the harsh way of life of peasants, who, it had always previously been claimed, had greatly benefited from the communist regime, their loss of faith in the CCP and its capacity to rule the country was complete. Xu Youyu's memories illustrate this disenchantment very well.

---

18. The bloodline theory (*xuetonglun*), promoted by children of high-ranking officials in the summer of 1966, advocated that China should be ruled only by those with the purest and finest revolutionary family pedigree and led to much of Red Guard violence, which wantonly targeted people and things of 'impure' social origins.

19. Bonnin, M. *Génération perdue: le mouvement d'envoi des jeunes instruits à la campagne en Chine, 1968–1980*, Éditions de l'École des hautes études en sciences sociales, 2004. This interpretation is contested by supposedly less elitist scholars like Gao Mobo and Wang Shaoguang, as discussed below.

After the Cultural Revolution, almost all secondary-school pupils were sent to the countryside, myself included. I remained there for three years, and changed a lot during that time. Before that, I thought China was the most powerful, richest and most egalitarian country. I no longer believed in the Cultural Revolution, but I still thought our system, and our country, were the best ones. But after we were sent down to the countryside, we realised how weak the central authorities were and hardly developed the countryside was. It deeply modified our vision of the Chinese system. I think the rustication movement had a major impact on our political beliefs.

As a result, the experience of the Cultural Revolution is an exceptionally distinctive element. It profoundly marked a whole age cohort and has become an explicit element of self-definition and distinction for a whole generation of people.

A group of scholars is subsequently constituted

Autodidacts

This study specifically focuses on the most fortunate ones among this 'lost' generation, that is, those who, contrary to the experience of the vast majority, managed to educate themselves in different subjects during the years in which they were deprived of a formal education and worked in the countryside or factories. They were among the happy few who managed to pass the university entrance examination in 1977 and 1978. As the examination had stopped for ten years, selection for the first batch (*di yi pi*) of university students was the most competitive in the history of Chinese universities with only 4.7 per cent of applicants accepted.[20] According to estimates, 700,000 to 800,000 potential students were unable to benefit from the advantages of higher education during that decade.[21]

Wang Shaoguang insists that, contrary to what people usually claim, he had wide access to books during the Cultural Revolution:

Many people now have a wrong impression that during the Cultural Revolution everything is suppressed, there is no book to read. I think this is rubbish. I later always talked to young friends: 'I never lacked a book to read, always had a book to read.' And there were so many books to read that I didn't read the two most popular books of the Cultural Revolution: *Jinguang dadao* (Hao Ran, *The Golden Road*, 1972) and *Yanyang Tian* (Hao Ran, *The Sun Shines Bright*, 1964).

20. Given that the entrance examination had been stopped for ten years and the age limit of candidates was exceptionally extended to 30 years, there were 5.7 million candidates (2.8 million being sent-down youths) 270,000 of whom finally passed. 17 million young urbanites are estimated to have been sent to rural communes or production brigades or to the army by Mao.

21. Chow, G. C. *China's Economic Transformation*, Maldon, MA: Blackwell Publishing, 2000, 2007, p. 205.

In Wang Chaohua's collection of articles *One China, Many Paths*, Shanghai liberal Zhu Xueqin writes that, because of the Cultural Revolution, he enrolled in an average secondary school only in spring 1967. However, because the premises used to shelter a mission until 1949, there were books galore in the school library. The Red Guards could not possibly get rid of 40,000 books in a flash. As a result, he regularly picked original editions from the rubbish heap the books of his school library were cast into and carried piles of them home: 'It was this forbidden trove that first awoke me intellectually.'[22] Owing to the persecutions, cadres and teachers could not keep most of their books. When these were not destroyed, they were sold and book-thirsty students could find ways to retrieve them. The lucky pupil could therefore buy the principal works of Marx, Engels, Lenin and Stalin, as well as Lu Xun's complete works, in a second-hand bookstore on Fuzhou Street, Shanghai.

The Sichuanese liberal Xu Youyu explains how he managed to obtain forbidden books:[23]

Many people associate the Cultural Revolution with destruction of culture. [...] As a matter of fact, it was much easier to read then than before. I can share my experience with you. I started reading books, especially foreign books like Hugo's *Miserables*, at a very early age. I also read Flaubert and many others early. But when I was in secondary school, Mao Zedong only advocated class struggle. It made it very difficult for me to go on reading these books. Librarians would no longer allow me to borrow them, and my teachers criticised me for reading too many foreign books. It was undoubtedly harder to read before the Cultural Revolution. During the Cultural Revolution, libraries were destroyed and books landed in the hands of students. It was the opposite. In China as a whole, it might have been difficult to read books because the Cultural Revolution considered them capitalistic and feudal. But from another perspective, it was much easier to exchange and to access books than before the Cultural Revolution. Because at that time, if the Youth League cell believed you were a bad element, and if your class teacher agreed, you were under surveillance. But during the Cultural Revolution, there was no one left to deal with such things. As a result, even though the Cultural Revolution made it harder to read for some people, for people who really felt like reading, that time felt rather like a liberation. Especially in the countryside, no one kept an eye on us. I personally had many opportunities to read during the Cultural Revolution.

The prevailing narrative of the Cultural Revolution as ten years of calamity (*shinian haojie*) tends to overlook the great freedom these youths benefitted from, when rid of the strict surveillance of their teachers. The scholars from the first

---

22. Zhu, X. in 'For a Chinese liberalism', in Chaohua, W. (ed.), *One China, Many Paths*, Verso, 2003, p. 89.

23. *See also* Qin, H. 'Dividing the big family assets', *New Left Review* 20, 2003. Qin Hui explains he could easily borrow books reserved to internal communication at the local library, which, at the time, failed to shatter his faith in the regime as he then became a Party member.

batch often humbly explain that they could enter university in 1977 only because, out of sheer luck, they had access to books during the previous period. According to Xiao Gongqin, the ability of candidates to prepare for the university entrance examination entirely depended on chance:

> Exam preparations were haphazard. We all had limited access to books and we depended on friends who luckily for us accepted to lend us university manuals. I am greatly indebted to a librarian who lent me that kind of books. Reading them considerably helped me during the exam period. I was very lucky.

The historian recalls that scholars from his generation taught themselves most of what they know as they could rarely benefit from the teachings of great professors:

> Our generation and the past generation of intellectuals are different because the thinking of our professors had developed in a closed environment. On the contrary, as to our generation, our ideological development was first spontaneous, even if some of us could benefit from the help of good professors. However, in general, the latter did not have a decisive influence on our way of thinking. We studied and understood many things on our own. There is one phrase in Chinese to refer to autodidacts [*wu shi zi tong*]. The current academia is composed of that kind of academics.

The fact that academics from this generation are autodidacts, and that they define themselves as such, is crucial to understanding their personality and the nature of their academic production. Along with the impact of growing up at a time of 'liberation of thought' in the 1980s, this at least partly explains their unique propensity to think independently. As Xiao Gongqin explains,

> During the Cultural Revolution, I was 19 years old. Before that, society was very closed. We were not allowed to discuss political problems, there were no such discussions. For that reason, I used to secretly read books on western philosophy – I had read a few in secondary school – but I could not talk about it to anyone. I was very much in favour of western democracy, I loved that idea and I found it dreadful that China did not have the opportunity to set up a democracy. Then the Cultural Revolution erupted. Mao Zedong launched the movement and gave people more time to think. From that perspective, the movement differs greatly from the Anti-Rightist Movement of 1957, when everybody was to be a docile instrument of the CCP, all Chinese intellectuals included, like elephants as docile as horses. That was the 1957 Anti-Rightist Movement; the opposite took place during the Cultural Revolution. Mao Zedong encouraged liberation of thought, so as to bring the class of bureaucrats down. This gave us the opportunity to discuss politics much more often in private. I was a worker at the time and this allowed us, with my friends, to privately discuss politics on Sundays, during our leisure time. But we could not do it openly at the time.

The fact that the education of the so-called 'educated youths' (*zhiqing*) was sacrificed during the Cultural Revolution is a strong defining element for this generation. Those who now are scholars describe with emotion their frustrated thirst for knowledge. They often acknowledge with bitterness that they are academically weaker than the older and younger generations, who have benefited from a better education. Zhu Guanglei describes this frustration in vigorous terms:

I was a gifted child, but when I was eight, I could no longer go to school because there no longer were students accepted in Chinese schools in 1966 and 1967. I was supposed to enter primary school in 1967, but at the time, we only had class for two hours a day, with a half-hour study of the Little Red Book. Education was interrupted during those years. So a good student like me, who would have naturally studied sciences, ended up studying social sciences. When you often read the newspaper and you teach yourself, you naturally study social sciences. It's harder to study hard science in such conditions, isn't it? I had a natural leaning to sciences. I used to read a book collection entitled '100,000 whys'. But it was difficult to study on my own. That's how I started liking social sciences. For instance, I read Engels' *The Origin of the Family, Private Property and the State* (1884), an essential Marxism classic. I was 13 to 15 when I read Huxley's *Evidence as to Man's Place in Nature*. If my father had been a teacher or a senior cadre, I would not be where I am today. I would have a better position. At the time, no one could help me out. And that's how my taste for politics gradually led me to political science.

It should nonetheless be noted that two apparently contradictory narratives contest on that issue: some interviewed scholars declare that this generation was sacrificed and that its members will suffer for the rest of their lives from the consequences of what they lived through; others claim that the *zhiqing* generation monopolises all the current power niches in China, no matter the area (government, arts, universities, the judiciary, CEOs and so on). This contradiction is explained by the distinction between the happy few who made it and the great majority of the members of this generation who were less fortunate. Ren Jiantao, for instance, asserts that 'the Chinese elites are mainly from the Red Guards generation and they will be replaced by the Little Red Guards [the following generation]. Academics from the Red Guards generation completely monopolise key positions and have a hegemonic power'. The majority of members of the 'lost generation' did, indeed, greatly suffer from their lack of education. However, there is a tremendous difference between average people and those who later entered university, as these scholars had a significant advantage over the latter: they were blessed with an uncommon access to reading materials and with time to study by themselves. The highly select group who did get a college education now occupies the powerful niches. As Wang Juntao explains, the young graduates of 1982 greatly benefited from Deng Xiaoping's reformed personnel-recruitment system, which required cadres to be younger and better educated so they could take important positions in the fields of research, education, culture, publications and the media.[24] In universities, the urgent need to recruit teachers and to train the successive waves of students who could finally access higher education sped the recruitment process up for those from the first batch (*di yi pi*).

Besides, in the late 1970s and early 1980s, everything seems possible to young students and scholars. The Cultural Revolution, even as far as ideas are concerned, was a large-scale rampage. Zhu Xueqin explains how, in the 1980s, cultural life was revived after thirty years of repression in the context of a great void in the field of ideas. According to him, his generation did not inherit anything from anyone. To him, this is a major drawback compared to the long training years of the May Fourth generation. Those who were lucky enough to enter university were actually quite disappointed when they realised their teachers did not live up to their expectations. As a result, one of the main elements of self-definition put forward by scholars from this generation is their atypical education: their being autodidacts with strongly independent thinking. It is crucial is to keep this in mind in order to understand some of the *lacunae* in their scientific knowledge and, in particular, their partial and sometimes erroneous understanding of western and Chinese thinkers and academics.[25]

Sceptics

This age cohort inherited idealism and enthusiasm from the unique role they were given to play in Chinese history. The climate of the Cultural Revolution is often described as romantic. In contrast, their subsequent virtual banishment led to an extreme kind of disillusionment that deeply marked them. As a result, the scholars who belong to this generation describe themselves as independent thinkers, who are wary of the state and its manipulative tendencies. However, this depends on the deeds they were led to perform when they were Red Guards and on the depth of their disillusionment. This subject dominates very noticeably in any testimony of the victims of the Cultural Revolution.[26]

Scholars often recall the massive impact the Lin Biao incident[27] had on the minds of his generation. In 1971, they completely lost their trust in authority. Zhu Xueqin

---

24. Wang, J. *Reverse Course: Political Neo-Conservatism and regime stability in post-Tiananmen China*, PhD dissertation, Columbia University, 2006, p. 170.

25. Yan, X. *Ancient Chinese Thought, Modern Chinese Power*, Princeton University Press, 2011, p. 251: 'I have two serious shortcomings in my knowledge. The first is that, because of the Cultural Revolution, I did not receive a proper secondary education, with the result that my knowledge of the natural sciences is very poor [...] Second, because the May Fourth movement denied traditional culture and because in the 1950s China promoted simplified characters and educational reform, people of my generation are very poor in their knowledge of classical works [...] hence, I cannot hope to achieve great academic success.'

26. *See* Tsou, T. *The Cultural Revolution and Post-Mao Reforms: A historical perspective*, University of Chicago Press, 1986 and, in particular, the chapter entitled 'I don't believe', referring to the poem-manifesto (*wo bu xiangxin*) Dao, B. wrote in 1988. Xu, B. *Disenchanted Democracy: Chinese cultural criticism after 1989*, University of Michigan Press, 1999.

27. Lin Biao was Mao's expected successor, who died in a plane crash in his attempt to flee to the Soviet Union on 13 September 1971; subsequently, a political campaign was initiated to destroy his reputation.

explains that after he was sent to work in a chemical factory in 1972, he took part in lively evening debates among young workers with a rebellious streak, like his. 'My experience during these years set the direction for my future thinking.' To him, his undisciplined character stems from the experience of studying on his own and of these evening debates. His way of thinking is supposedly distinct from that of younger scholars, in the sense that 'we cared about ideas for their own sake, with no thought of personal advantage or career gain – unlike our typical academics today'.[28]

He admits he never understood why Mao allowed books destined to be published for internal circulation (reserved to Party cadres) to be re-published in 1974 and gave more permissive guidelines for recent novels and political theory from the Soviet Union and western countries to be translated and published, with devastating results. According to Zhu Xueqin, those who read these translations were further disabused. To him, the first breakthrough of the New Enlightenment movement taking place in the 1980s, which we will further consider in Chapter Four, dates from 1974, when these books were first released. The historian thus acquired 16 volumes of selected articles on western bourgeois philosophy and sociology published by Shanghai People's Press, along with the 23 volumes of Soviet revisionist philosophy, in which he could read Sartre and Sidney Hook's *Marx and the Marxists – The Ambiguous Legacy* for the first time.[29] Scholars from this generation describe themselves as deeply engrained with scepticism. Precocious disappointment supposedly immunised them against any ideological obliviousness and endowed them with the great independence of mind that characterises their political engagement. This claim must, however, be qualified: in fact, this generation was brought up in absolute faith and, despite the successive disappointments they went through, has a tendency to look for ways to fill the resulting void by seeking to remedy the problems they encounter through diverse western theories.

Politically committed youths

The various attempts at describing the main features defining this generation of scholars therefore tend to focus on their undisciplined character as sceptical autodidacts completely disabused by their early indoctrination. They learnt to think on their own and to rebel. The authorities realised they were able to elaborate political conceptions that could undermine the regime's foundations and, consequently, decided to send them far away from the cities.

Scholars from this 'political generation' all explain that the Cultural Revolution gave them the opportunity to better explore and debate various political issues. Xiao Gongqin recalls the vividness and freedom of the political discussions organised by small private groups in factories or villages. These scholars explicitly

---

28. Zhu, X. 'For a Chinese liberalism', in Chaohua, W. (ed.), *One China, Many Paths*, Verso, 2003, p. 88.

29. *See also* Qin, H. 'Dividing the big family assets', *New Left Review*, April 2003, sect. 3.

highlight the impact this experience had on their future orientation. Zhu Xueqin believes that his experience as a Red Guard and as a worker for ten years 'has steered his way of thinking forever'. Liang Shuming wrote that 'to those who later became intellectuals [among members of that generation], the questions they raised around 1968 condition their perception of things forever and even define the outcome of their thoughts.'

Wang Juntao describes the Cultural Revolution as 'The first benchmark in their political experience [leading to] their independence from the authority of the government or party'.[30] These youths developed independent ideas as a result of Mao's demands to doubt all political authority except his, the mass chaos that ensued from it, and their being turned into counter-revolutionary youths needing re-education in the countryside. The Lin Biao incident led most Chinese to cease to regard Mao's authority as unchallengeable and therefore had a tremendous impact on this generation of scholars. When Red Guard organisations were dissolved in late 1968, free political discussions were expected to stop. But quickly, former Red Guards launched informal groupings. Wang Shaoguang thus recalls:

I graduated from secondary school in 1972 and then I and some of my classmates and friends formed some sort of informal grouping. We would meet almost every week, during the weekend. [...] my friends, some of my old classmates, and I, met almost every week and discussed everything. Most importantly politics, nothing else. And also literature, and poetry and many interesting subjects. [...] my friends and classmates read those stuff and we discussed issues. By 1975–6 we were very much against the Ultra Leftists. The tendency represented by the Gang of Four at that time. I remember in 1975, Zhang Chunqiao, one of the members of the Gang of Four, published one of his most important piece in his entire career, entitled dui *zichanjieji de quanmian zhuanzheng* ('On exercising all-round dictatorship over the bourgeoisie').

We didn't like the idea. So, my friends and I, we went back to Marx, Lenin, Mao and tried to find out how those people talked about the proletarian dictatorship. To find out how Marx's ideas are different from Zhang Chunqiao's. So we come up with a collection of the phrases from Marx, Engels and Lenin, which was meant to be a critique of Zhang Chunqiao's book. We even published it. We didn't publish it openly. At the time, it was pretty much primitive, even though we didn't copy it by hand. [We used the stencil technique]. You write on wax paper and then you can use the wax sheet on the printing machine to print many copies. Probably a hundred copies. So we did that during Spring Festival. It was quite secretive. We could get in big trouble if this was discovered. So we distributed our small booklet among our friends.

---

30. Wang, J. *Reverse Course*, p. 163.

The profusion of semi-official and underground cultural activities is one of the least documented aspects of the Cultural Revolution, even though some estimate that more than 10,000 newspapers and pamphlets were published at the time, including 900 in Beijing.[31] After their graduation from China's most prestigious universities, as these scholars entered the official institutions, they maintained their work within the personal informal networks that they had gradually built during the Cultural Revolution, after Lin Biao's death and in the wake of the April 5 incident.[32] This is Wang Shaoguang's case, for instance:

At Beida from early 1978 to 1982 I spent four years in Beijing. That was a most exciting period, I think. There was the Democracy Wall. There were many publications on the wall at the time. And many underground publications like *Beijing Spring* and *Today*, not quite underground because it was already published, put on the wall. I think in 1978–1979 almost every night I rode my bicycle to Xidan (about 10 km) to read the Democracy Wall (*minzhu qiang*). We didn't like Wei Jingshen too much. We believed his ideas were too radical. His ideas were not so much for the Chinese. He was trying to speak to foreigners rather than to a Chinese audience. But in any case, it was a period when you could access anything, for discussion. The first thing I did, after I arrived at Beida, was to write an essay talking about the necessity to assess objectively Chairman Mao's contribution. This was before the third preliminary meeting of the Eleventh Party Congress. One of my classmates and I wrote that essay and tried to get it published in *Zhongguo Qingnian Bao* because another classmate at Beida knew the Party Secretary, no not the Party Secretary but the First Secretary of the Communist Youth League. We tried to go to his channel to get the piece published. But we didn't, because at the time, it was kind of taboo to talk about objectively assessing Chairman Mao's contribution and mistakes. So I would say I was among the first group of Chinese trying to do that even though the piece was never published. About a year ago, I went over my diary again. My wife found out I was always labelled as a rightist, a liberal during the Beida period. Many teachers believed I was a little too unorthodox [...] I believe I was a Marxist, a socialist. But they believed my point of view was different from theirs. So I got into a little bit of trouble at Beida. Academically, I performed very well, but politically, they believed somehow I was not fit.

Interviewed scholars recount how this generation was steeped in politics from a very early age and how the least political events and decisions were part and parcel of their lives. They grew up with a sense of the collective, which led to two

---

31. Some of these publications even attracted the leaders' attention and were published in the *People's Daily: see* Chen, D. and Du, P. (eds) *Zhonghua Renmin Gongheguo shilu* [Chronicles of the People's Republic of China], Jilin renmin chubanshe, 1994 quoted in Gao, M. *The Battle for China's Past*. Wang Shaoguang collected such a large number of these publications that they constituted the main sources for the PhD dissertation he wrote in Cornell.

32. Wang, J. *Reverse course: Political Neo-Conservatism and regime stability in post-Tiananmen China*, PhD dissertation, Columbia University, 2006, pp. 166–168. *See* chapter 4.

radically opposed attitudes: on the one hand, a strong and unremitting political engagement justifying labelling them the 'political generation;'[33] on the other hand, the total rejection of politics and the glorification of the individual.[34] To Xu Jilin, the backdrop against which this generation of scholars grew up led them to focus most of all on politics: 'the interest people from my generation have in politics dates back to their youth and its context. We grew up in the 1960s. All the intellectuals from my generation are extremely interested in politics. It is by far the subject we are the most interested in.' Deng Zhenglai gives a precise report of in what this constant steeping in politics consisted:

> I was a kid when the Cultural Revolution started. A teenager, I was sent to the factory for eight years, from 1970 to 1978. These years as a worker left a deep mark on me. I used to listen to the radio almost every night and I attentively followed Chairman Mao's new guidelines, new editorials and the last news. Many major events happened those years: the Lin Biao incident; Deng Xiaoping's comeback and fall; Zhou Enlai, Zhu De and finally Mao's deaths. With the unique mode of popular mobilisation of the Cultural Revolution, all these events truly were part of our lives. We organised collective meetings to study together. I was overjoyed when the Gang of Four was neutralised. It was all an integral part of my life. It was a collective movement. Everything we saw, heard, and participated in was collective. Individuals did not exist. We were part of a whole.

They also describe themselves as engaged in idealistic pursuits, as they felt they had a role to play for the betterment of Chinese society. They were driven by a strong sense of political responsibility:

> In their early education, they nurtured a strong consciousness about their personal or individual responsibility to the nation and the society. Although they began to embrace individualism in the late 1980s, they continued to be concerned about the public interest and the crises facing Chinese society.[35]

The image scholars from the following generation have of the generation of the Cultural Revolution or Red Guards (*hong wei bing*) confirms the distinctiveness of that earlier generation. Ren Jiantao, who, like Pan Wei, was among the first batch of students who entered university, in 1978, calls his generation the 'generation of the Small Red Guards' (*hong xiao bing*). He thinks scholars from his generation are very different from those from the previous generation, even though they were immensely influenced by their elders and the way they narrated their experience of the Cultural Revolution at university.

---

33. Sleebom-Faulkner, M. *The Chinese Academy of Social Sciences – Shaping the Reforms, Academia and China (1977–2003)*, Brill, 2007.

34. Li Qiang also mentions this rejection, which explains why so few students wanted to study politics at the end of the Cultural Revolution.

35. Wang, J. *Reverse Course*, p. 171.

The approach of intellectuals such as Xu Youyu, Zhu Xueqin, Qin Hui and Xiao Gongqin is much more political than ours, and their academic research is less rigorous and systematic. Those born in the 1960s tend to reconcile politics and scientific rigour. We have not experienced the political enthusiasm and the hardship of the Cultural Revolution. When I became aware of the world I was living in, the Cultural Revolution was already over. I only have blurred childhood memories of that period. Intellectuals from the previous generation are well-educated. They are Sartrian intellectuals: very well-educated and very passionate. But it is not passion China most needs nowadays. [...] There is something unique that binds them together: they are distinctly concerned by the fate of the Chinese nation. From the CCP they have inherited the need to reflect on history and the future of humankind. Contrary to the following generations, who are able to focus their research on one book or one person, they still often resort to grand narratives. We focus on general issues. This is our fate and what mainly binds our two generations. What makes us different is political passion and past suffering.

Academics from this generation are considered by their younger colleagues unique in the sense that their research is mainly driven by a patriotic will to contribute to the Chinese nation's advancement, a topic to which we will return in the next chapter.

The end of the revolution and pragmatism

While younger scholars describe them as engaged in idealist pursuits, scholars from this generation, and most notably Xiao Gongqin, nonetheless claim that, in the 1990s, their political romanticism died.[36] The events of June 1989 and the collapse of the Soviet Union shattered any remnants of faith in revolution and revolutionary methods that had survived from their radical upbringing. Xu Youyu describes this disenchanting and de-fanaticising process:

The Cultural Revolution deeply transformed me. It made me first lose faith in the Cultural Revolution. Then I completely lost faith in Mao. Most people from my generation went through the same process because the Cultural Revolution has been an extremely painful experience for us. I nonetheless believe I am more serious than average. I have reflected and gone further in my reflection than most people. I have tried to comprehend how the Cultural Revolution could take place and why there could purportedly be a new China. Then I went on: how could the revolution of the CCP leaders be victorious? It forced me to wonder why a Communist movement took place worldwide in the previous century. Consequently, without the Cultural Revolution, I would probably have remained a fervent Communist, convinced by Marxist-Leninist and Maoist theories. The Cultural Revolution totally changed my political views.

---

36. *See* Chapters Four and Five.

When consulted on the painful experiences they went through, these scholars insist on the fact that they came out stronger and more mature. They boast that the years they spent tilling the land or working in factories before they could enter university taught them lessons no other generation of scholars can pride themselves on knowing. Going against the mainstream narrative, Gan Yang thus claims that:

> Chinese students do not acquire any practical knowledge. They have no experience, unlike my generation. This is the reason why some go as far as to say that Mao's sent-down policy was not such a bad thing. This policy had a major impact because it allowed us to meet all sorts of people whom we would never have met if remaining in town for all our lives. [...] When I departed from Hangzhou station for a six-day trip to China's far north, to the Great Xing'an Mountains, I was made to understand what the concept of class meant. As a matter of fact, my fellow travellers mostly came from working-class families. I was among the last ones to leave in my entourage. As a result I was alone with these working-class people I did not know. We all had completed our primary school studies. We all had the same education but the family we had grown up in manifestly played a great part. We were from different backgrounds. This is the reason why people who were sent down to the countryside at that time constitute a deeply marked generation. No sent-down youth ever regretted having made that experience because despite the terrible hardship they went through, people from my generation have managed to learn and benefit from that experience. It only happened in China. It is a unique experience.

From these hardships and humiliating experiences, these scholars claim they have gained in endurance, adaptability and humility. They boast a sense of reality as they have a unique insight into Chinese economic, social and political realities that academics spending all their time in their city laboratories could never have. This generation of scholars thus defines itself and is defined by younger generations as branded by its precocious political activism – which led them to develop the wide-ranging political skills that they mobilised in the 1980s – and by deep feelings of disillusionment and betrayal. On the professional level, this experience translates into research guided more by political than academic incentives and therefore less scientific than pragmatic and interdisciplinary,[37] and even heterogeneous. In Liang Shuming's words, the Cultural Revolution generation is a pragmatic, 'problem-engaging generation'; it is not a 'scholarship generation'. 'For those who became intellectuals, the issues posed around 1968 always shaped their outlook and even determined the outcome of their thought.' These scholars put forward their rejection of dogmatism, presented as stemming from their independent minds, scepticism and past sufferings. As a result of

---

37. This is Hu Angang's case, who does not hesitate to mix economics, political science, environment studies and demographics so as to analyse China's development as accurately as possible. Hu, A. *China in 2020*, Brookings, 2011.

such loss of faith in their former Communist beliefs, members of this generation accepted new theories and ideologies with open minds. 'They did not believe that any general principle or ideal was unchallengeable. Everything was up for grabs. Free of any state-mandated doctrines, their minds remained completely liberated and questioning.'[38] Chapter Four will show that this rejection of dogmatism was not easy to put into practice for this generation. However, they underscore the fact that the shock of the Tiananmen Square movement and repression compelled them to gradually stop relying on all-encompassing theories. Liu Dong defines himself as a liberal aware that each theory emerges in a specific context and no theory can solve all problems. He criticises his colleague Qin Hui, who trusts in the market to entice people to reduce climate change and further protect the environment. After an excessive faith in one unique theory, which Liu identifies as the greatest problem of the twentieth century, the time has come for theoretical patchwork, a pragmatic attitude of cherry-picking useful elements from various theories emanating from different cultures. He advocates the path to follow – distrust in dogmatism – but he implies that it is hard to enforce and that all scholars have not adopted it yet. Whether among liberals fully convinced that the undesirable side-effects of economic reforms (greater corruption, inequalities, unemployment and so on) are mainly due to the fact that the introduction of the market economy in China is incomplete and that free trade would solve most of them; or among New Left sympathisers whom, according to Liu Dong and others, American Marxists convinced that the Cultural Revolution was the Chinese version of May 1968, the priorities of pluralism and rejection of dogmatism do not prevail. However, distrust in grand theories and volontarist policies predominates, as does a consensus on the most suitable method for reform – which some try to develop into a 'Chinese model' – that is, trial and error, local experimenting and gradually expanding such reformed practices when successful.[39]

How the Cultural Revolution affected this generation's vision of the regime

A crucial aspect of experiencing the Cultural Revolution for rusticated youths came from the opportunity given to them to leave their daily lives and circle of friends and to discover the diversity of situations in China, depending on people's homelands and social backgrounds. For large numbers, the early years of the Cultural Revolution offered the first opportunity to travel widely in China, to connect with people from all over the country and to compare their conditions. This incredible opportunity is often mentioned by people who express nostalgic feelings about that period, including the New Left. As a result, memories of the Cultural Revolution are of two main types. There are memories of fanaticism and manipulation leading to violence and to cruelty for some, but which overlap, for other actors, with memories of freedom – of exchange, travels, expression,

---

38. Wang, J. *op. cit.*, p. 171.
39. We will focus on this consensus in the last two chapters of this book.

reflection – related to the 'big democracy'[40] (*da minzhu*), which encouraged the 'masses' to freely publish big-character posters (*dazibao*), organise large-scale debates and exchange their revolutionary experiences as much as possible.

Acutely aware of inequalities and calling for more justice

Witnessing the dire poverty – seen as intolerable by young privileged city dwellers – of the peasants living in the least developed areas as a result of the *xiaxiang* movement, these scholars also claim to be acutely aware of the discrepancy between propaganda and reality and to deeply resent situations of poverty and inequality. Strong resentment towards a regime which did not fulfil its promises stems from their recognition of the existence of such a shocking gap. But the principles of equality that were drilled into the minds of this generation left a strong imprint, so that the experience of the Cultural Revolution generated strong antipathy to unequal situations, especially for left-wing scholars. That's the case of economist Hu Angang, a 16-year-old high school pupil sent to work, in 1969, on a collective farm in the desert Heilongjiang region.[41] He claims that these seven years spent at the farm, and a few more months of manual labour for a team of geologists, allowed him to understand what was life like in the poorest regions and sparked his interest in economic, regional and urban/rural inequalities. Having lived part of their youth in remote villages or worked in factories is indeed an invaluable experience for left-wing intellectuals. It seems that the realisation that solid inequalities existed allowed some of them to understand Mao Zedong's wariness towards the polarisation and corruption of the bureaucratic class.

For other intellectuals, the Cultural Revolution rather conjures up memories of the unthinkable violence they took part in or were the victims of, along with memories of their compulsory rustication and subsequent loss of their privileged urban living conditions. As a result, they find it unconvincing that the memory of the Cultural Revolution can be used to derive egalitarian principles, which they identify as the root of the totalitarian downward spiral of that era. Xu Youyu thus deplores the distorted conception of some former Red Guards that educated youths volunteered to share the lives of peasants and the claim this was an irreplaceable experience of toughening up.[42] This liberal philosopher dismisses any attempt to heroise the memory of the Red Guards. According to him, their actions were not motivated

---

40. Promoting 'big democracy' (*da minzhu*) dates back to the Cultural Revolution, when the masses were encouraged to freely make large-character posters (*dazibao*), convene large-scale debates and exchange their revolutionary experience as much as possible (mainly through travelling across the country. *See*, for instance, Lin Biao's call for the Red Guards to implement 'big democracy' in the *People's Daily* (*Renmin ribao*), 4 November 1966.

41. Hu, A. *China in 2020*, Brookings, 2011, Introduction, by Li, C. p. xxi.

42. Xu, Y. 'Lishi yanjiu bu neng liuxia kongbai, guanyu hongweibing yu wenge' [Historical research cannot leave a blank space on the Red Guards and the Cultural Revolution], in Li, H. and Ying, H. (eds), *Shiji zhi wen* (Questions of the Century), Zhengzhou, Daxiang chubanshe, 1999, pp. 229–58; *Zhimian lishi* (Confronting History), Peking, Zhongguo wenlian chubanshe, 1999, quoted in Froissart, C. 'Xu Youyu, or how to write the history of the Cultural Revolution so as to set China on the right future path', *China Perspectives* 42, July–August 2002.

by revolutionary altruistic ideals, and to say so is a reconstruction of memory, contaminated by western studies of the Cultural Revolution insisting on the 'social contradictions' which supposedly encouraged the actions of the Red Guards.

Suspicious of arbitrary power

The turmoil of the Cultural Revolution exposed a party that was more concerned with political differences and factional infighting than the welfare of the masses. These young intellectuals lost all trust in a Party that had proved unable to prevent one man from taking rash decisions and plunging the country into anarchy. There was a general huge loss of faith in the CCP among those who had devoted most of their lives to politics during the Cultural Revolution and led them to question whether the party was still fit to run the country at all. To liberals, the Cultural Revolution is the apotheosis of totalitarianism. According to Xu Youyu, there was no such thing as autonomy from power in society and the Red Guards were totally manipulated by powerful political leaders. The idea that their becoming aware of this made the rule of law popular circulates widely among Chinese elites. When Deng Xiaoping became leader, he launched a set of institutional reforms explicitly designed to preclude the possibility of any leader ruling the country alone and arbitrarily. The notion of 'monistic leadership' (*yiyuan hua lingdao*) was challenged and the need to set up a supervising system started to be accepted.[43] Since the mass mobilisation of the Cultural Revolution was associated with 'big democracy' (*da minzhu*), the democratic regime, despite its remoteness from the reality of the political participation of the masses, was officially condemned as simply not well suited to China. Democracy tends to be less popular among this generation of scholars than the rule of law, which guarantees the control of leaders, whom they tend to view with circumspection. Interestingly enough, a scholar from the following generation but who entered university simultaneously with and was greatly influenced by his elders, Pan Wei, is the epitome of this way of thinking, with his explicit defence of the rule of law independently from democracy.[44] The institutional arrangement which he advocates features an elitism justifying a meritocratic rather than democratic regime, which we will discuss below at greater length.

Suspicious of the people

Their first-hand experience of the irrationality and the cynicism of the masses in moments of extreme violence and when sheer survival was at stake is often brandished as justification of intellectuals' elitist tendencies. It is interesting to note that the critics of the 'official' memory of the Cultural Revolution tend to focus on its elitism. The period indeed tends to be portrayed from the point of

---

43. Tsou, T. *The Cultural Revolution and Post-Mao Reforms*, chapter 7: 'Political change and reform'.

44. Zhao, S. *Debating Political Reform in China: Rule of Law vs. Democratisation*, Sharpe, 2006.

view of elites, who pretend to be representative of the experience of the whole Chinese population and neglect the point of view of ordinary citizens. Gao Mobo has published a book devoted to that issue, *The Battle for China's Past*, under the influence of Wang Shaoguang's works, according to which the attitudes of masses during that era cannot be reduced to irrationality and sheer fanaticism.[45]

Besides, the poor level of education and the passivity of the rural populations with whom these scholars were made to live with during long months can partly explain the widespread argument that the Chinese population is too 'backward' (*luohou*) and its quality too low (*suzhi di*) to be entrusted with the difficult task of electing its leaders at all levels of government. Studies of the 1989 students' movement have unveiled connections between the mild support it received from intellectuals from that generation and their common suspicion of popular movements. Wang Juntao considers them as

> [...] negative realists. They have experienced moments of horror and despair and have witnessed political schemes and the chaos that enfolded in their wake, so that they regard human behaviour from a simultaneously realistic and negative perspective – all the more so in a chaotic context. They perceive all democratic games in a Hobbesian context.[46]

One of the reproaches the Chinese New Left makes to liberals is that they can be so elitist that they limit their defence of democratisation to setting up a representative democracy without any form of direct democracy. To them, the Cultural Revolution's experience of direct democracy was a partial success and some 'innovations' introduced by Mao in the political system (*zhidu chuangxin*) could be updated so as to fight against the downward spiral of inequality that is happening under the current regime. On the contrary side, neo-conservatives believe that the Chinese people is not mature enough for democracy. According to Xiao Gongqin, neo-conservatism advocates that a benevolent leader or regime becomes the 'visible hand' of China's modernisation.[47]

The Little Red Guards generation

Members of the next generation of Chinese scholars, who were born in the 1960s, such as Cui Zhiyuan, Kang Xiaoguang, Liu Junning, Yang Guangbin or Yao Yang, emphasise the distinctiveness of their generation from the previous ones, because they have benefited from an uninterrupted education and have only childhood memories of the Cultural Revolution. Nonetheless, depending on individual experience and personal maturity, the line dividing the two generations

---

45. In his PhD dissertation, whose English version is entitled *Failure of Charisma*, Wang Shaoguang resorts to game theory to show that most participants in the Cultural Revolution were not fanatics but rational individuals trying to maximise their interests, even though they deeply respected Mao Zedong, Wang S., *Failure of Charisma: The Cultural Revolution in Wuhan*, New York: Oxford University Press, 1995.

46. Wang, J. *Reverse Course*, p. 171.

47. Xiao, G. *Fansi de niandai* (The era of reflection), Shanghai, Fudan University Press, 2010, p. 19.

can sometimes be blurred. Pan Wei, for instance, promptly evokes the suffering he was made to endure during that period despite his young age (he was born in 1964). On the contrary, Xu Jilin, who was born in 1957, minimises the impact of the period on him, insisting that he was too young to be more than a distant witness of its events. It is very interesting to compare the incentives these scholars have to position themselves strategically as part of one generation or the other. However, it should be noted that parents' class background, hometown and so on are crucial for understanding the fate of their families and, as a result, the impression and the seriousness of the scars left by these events. Xiao Gongqin, who had a former Kuomintang general in his family, spent twelve years in a factory as a result, before finally being admitted to university. Pan Wei's family – his father was an academic at Beijing's geoscience university – was persecuted, which encourages him to consider himself as a full member of the Cultural Revolution generation.

In general, members from the following generation, even though they also belong to the first batch of students entering university after the Cultural Revolution, explicitly define themselves in contrast to the previous generation. This urge to distinguish themselves generationally is striking in Ren Jiantao's words:

> The difference between these two generations resides in the fact that the Red Guards had the time to be indoctrinated by the principles of the Cultural Revolution; that is the theory of permanent revolution under the dictatorship of the working class. We were too young to understand what it was about while they were in high school, even if they did not understand it all. [...] My generation only has childhood memories of that period. The essential element to understand my generation is that we entered university in 1978, at the same time as the previous generation. We are very different. At the time when they formed their political convictions, revolutionary thinking prevailed; and they had an impact on us. However, when the time came for us to form our own convictions, China had already opened, so that my generation could compare and choose.

Pan Wei being an exception, scholars from the following generation tend to distinguish themselves strongly. They have, like Mannheim, the feeling that the experiences they have in common (entering university, the liberating 1980s, the Tiananmen Square repression) did not have the same impact on them as on the older generation; even though they acknowledge that, at the time, major political and social upheavals took place and any student or academic could not but be interested in these changes. Yang Guangbin, People's University, thus considers these two generations as clearly distinct:

> I was a child during the Cultural Revolution. I don't remember anything. It is only when I started my studies that I learnt what the Cultural Revolution was about. I had no idea. I could pursue my studies uninterrupted. I entered primary school in 1971. It was the Cultural Revolution at the time but I did not know what it was. I could later enter high school and university [...] [Those who were ten years older] were sent to the countryside. People who were born like me in the 1960s do

not have any memory of the Cultural Revolution. We tend to envisage the future more optimistically. They have gone through much harder times. These are general remarks of course. This is not everybody's case. Experiences are diverse.

However, even if this generation was not formed solely by direct experience of the Cultural Revolution, it cannot be seen as completely distinct. Indeed, scholars belonging to that generation of the Little Red Guards (*xiao hongbing*) were considerably influenced by the generation of the Cultural Revolution because they entered universities at the same time. The first batch of students entering university in 1977–8 also included students from the previous generation as the age limit was exceptionally delayed to thirty years so as to offer older ones the opportunity to get a higher education. Besides, it was no longer compulsory to have worked for two years before sitting the entrance examination, so high school pupils could apply directly after their high school graduation.[48] For scholars like Pan Wei, these students, despite their age difference, formed a group ('we') whose members had much in common:

We learnt how to be idealistic during that time. Then later, in 1967–8, some of them who are older than me were disillusioned. For me, it was a time of formation of ideals. And when a kid experiences hardship, I guess a kid wouldn't feel that bad. But then we all wanted a liberation of mind. Around 1978, when I entered University.

I roughly entered University at the same time as all of them, that you have listed, like Wang Shaoguang and so on. Because I entered college earlier and I was mature somehow earlier than my middle school classmates.

The 14-year-old Pan Wei indeed was accepted by Peking University because the 'maturity' he apparently displayed during the exams impressed his examiners. He was, consequently, among the youngest students; but his fellow students were still united by similar experience, even though it was lived differently. And the older students told the younger ones what they had gone through and shared their feelings:

It's because they had from 5 to 10 years of work experience in factory, in the countryside, in the military. Many of them had shattered illusions toward the revolution. It was a shock to me. I learnt a lot from them. But as to their experience, I wasn't feeling so fresh. But I wasn't that old. When you are in the countryside at the age of 20, you feel hopeless. But I was there at the age of 10. I wasn't feeling that bad. It was just hard.

These elder students, often ten years older, influenced the younger ones, which may explain why the following generation defines itself in relation to the Cultural Revolution generation, as its name suggests ('the generation that follows the Cultural Revolution', *houwenge yidai*). Pan Wei thus deems that belonging to the

48. Mathur, N. *Educational Reform in post-Mao China*, APH Publishing, 2007.

first batch of students was an opportunity, despite the hardship of being in constant competition with students twice as old as him:

> It was bad. It was hard. Because I was with fellow students who were at least five years my senior, sometimes ten. I had less experience just by a matter of age. I could not be a student leader or anything. I wanted to but I couldn't get it. I learnt a lot from these older fellow students. But now, when I think of it, I am glad I was among the first group of students who entered college after the Cultural Revolution, together with those guys.

Pan Wei's feeling of belonging to the Cultural Revolution generation is unique, but it still reveals the proximity between the two generations, especially for those who went to university together. Besides, it seems that what makes these two generations so close is the numerous upheavals of the social and political context and their direct impact on the education, higher education, professional careers and living conditions of their members. Moreover, all the scholars I interviewed, no matter their generation, emphasised that they had been steeped in a highly politicised environment. And for those scholars – whom I have studied precisely because of their political commitment, contrary to others who followed diametrally opposed careers, notably because they were driven by disgust with politics – from this highly politicised context originates their research focus on political issues. It also explains their vocation and political commitment. As a result, the idea that the generation of the Cultural Revolution is more passionate, and idealistic and less scientific and rigorous than the following generation prevails in Chinese universities. However, the nature of this political commitment must be qualified according to generations and above all individuals.

Consequently, the two generations to which the interviewed scholars belong are primarily distinct because they define themselves as such, even though, as we have mentioned, experiences and perceptions vary from one individual to the next. However, it is interesting to approach them simultaneously as they constantly compare themselves and they share some traits and experiences; and · because some scholars make use of these for various purposes. Pan Wei, who partially rationalises his rejection of the principles of the democratic regime and his defence of an elitist meritocratic regime through his mistrust of the masses, stemming from his experience of the Cultural Revolution,[49] is a fine illustration. One of the crucial factors for understanding divisions between scholars is the date of their entrance to university, rather than their date of birth.

In that sense, for scholars like Yao Yang, the powerful experience of the 1980s was shared by both generations and the true division is between those who went to college before 1989 and those who studied afterwards:

> People from my generation lived the 1980s. That's the decade of my twenties. I started university in 1982. With hindsight, the 1980s were a very special period, a time of thought liberation. All currents of ideas co-existed. We spent

---

49. Zhao, S. (ed.) *Debating Political Reform in China.*

our time reading, especially western books such as Sartre or Marcuse. We read anything we could find, including Kant's *Critique of Pure Reason*. Moreover, we also participated to the reform process. Students conducted several practical investigations at that time. Two research institutes prevailed: the Institute for Reform [*tigaisuo*] and the Institute for Development [*fazhansuo*]. They were composed of junior researchers, who had experienced the Cultural Revolution. They were recent PhDs but they were all above thirty. Associated to younger students like me, they were discovering the reality of China and the western thinking. This two-fold discovery conditioned people from my generation. The dividing line is very clear between those who studied before 1989 and those who started their studies after that date. The difference is blatant. Those who went to university after 1989 are not as familiar with the actual situation, including many junior staff at Peking University. It seems that they do not know exactly what happened in China. They lack an in-depth understanding. Students in the 1980s have a more intimate knowledge of realities. They have studied the concrete problems China faces. These generations are very different.

All of the scholars under scrutiny correspond to this criterion. They indeed all entered university between 1978 and 1982, as this chart shows.

Table 2.1: Scholars' years of birth and entrance to universities

Names and dates of birth	Years of entrance to university
Xiao Gongqin 萧功秦 1946	Master's degree started in 1978
Xu Youyu 徐友渔 1947	1977–8
Gan Yang 甘阳 1952	1977–8
Zhu Xueqin 朱学勤 1952	Master's degree started in 1982
Jiang Qing 蒋庆 1953	1977–8
Li Qiang 李强 1953	1977–8
Qin Hui 秦晖 1953	Master's degree started in 1978
Hu Angang 胡鞍钢 1953	1977–8
Liu Dong 刘东 1955	1977–8
Wang Shaoguang 王绍光 1954	1977–8
Deng Zhenglai 邓正来 1956	1977–8
Xu Jilin 许纪霖 1957	1977–8
Yu Keping 俞可平 1959	1977–8
Wang Hui 汪晖 1959	1977–8
Zhu Guanglei 朱光磊 1959	1980
Liu Jiunning 刘军宁 1961	1978
Zheng Yongnian 郑永年 1962	1981
Kang Xiaoguang 康晓光 1963	1982
Cui Zhiyuan 崔之元 1963	1981
Ren Jiantao 任剑涛 1963	1977–8
Yang Guangbin, 杨光斌 1963	1981
Pan Wei 潘维 1964	1977–8
Yao Yang 姚洋 1964	1982
He Zengke 何增科 1965	1981

Two generations divided over the Cultural Revolution

To use Karl Mannheim's terminology again, these two potential generations of Chinese born in the 1950s and 1960s were actualised – especially as far as scholars among these age cohorts are concerned – by the significant social and political upheavals they lived through. Scholars from these two effective generations are close – and in our study, all the more so as they were all selected because of their reflection on China's political reform. The initial problem which encouraged them in their choice of career, research and commitment was their urge to understand what the Cultural Revolution was, its origins and its excesses and, for most of them, how to prevent such an event happening again in China. However, their more or less directly endured experience of the Cultural Revolution led to a broad range of interpretations of events and solutions. As a result, 'concrete groups' correspond to the expression of these contrasted views of the Cultural Revolution and of the world as a whole.

From this common experience emerged a strong group consciousness reinforced by the 'solidarity of the marginalized' as described by Michel Bonnin. Common features, a common legacy, are claimed by scholars from this generation. However, the lives, principles and commitments that the scholars from this generation built vary infinitely and condition the narratives, interpretations and reinventions of that period. In interviews and articles, scholars recall a quite large degree of consensus on the reforms in the 1980s connected to this general background and to a broad aspiration to leave the Cultural Revolution behind, to prevent its reoccurrence, to reform the Party and to open up to the world and modernity. They describe themselves as yearning for an ideal regime in which leaders could not act whimsically without constraint, in which decisions were taken in a rational and scientific manner and in which individual liberties were respected. The Chinese intelligentsia started to split when the first side effects of the reforms became blatant, such as the phenomena of corruption, rising unemployment and inflation. Students and scholars' observations and condemnation of the widening inequalities, growing corruption, rising unemployment, inflation and so on converged. But the reasons they detected for these differed. Chapter Four is more generally devoted to the fragmentation of Chinese intellectual elites. Our aim here is to underline that these divisions are not only frames used by intellectuals as diverging answers to the problems that emerged in the wake of the launch and subsequent intensification of the Open and Reform policy, but are also connected to their individual positions as regards the Cultural Revolution. During the interviews, when I asked these scholars to which intellectual tendency they belonged and with which other scholars they got along best, it clearly came out that these comings-together and disagreements were gradually exacerbated by their different interpretations of the Cultural Revolution. For instance, all scholars outside the New Left, whether close or not to that group, indicated that their distinguishing feature, at the core of their disagreement with New Left scholars, was their assessment of the Cultural Revolution. It is especially the case of Xiao Gongqin, Yao Yang, Liu Dong, Yang Guangbin. Disagreements on that subject are often attributed to age difference, hometown, or class background – elements which are supposed to explain gaps in the perception of these events, since they determine whether the scholar was one of the persecutors, one of the victims or one of happy few who only witnessed events from afar.[50] It is therefore very common to hear one scholar accusing another of having a superficial understanding of the Cultural Revolution and disqualifying his view on that period because of his young age.[51]

Some scholars claim that the conflict between Red Guards factions (Rebels *versus* Loyalists or radicals *versus* conservatives) has surfaced again and led to the divisions between the New Left, conservatives and liberals.[52] To Australian political scientist He Baogang, all the current liberals are former Rebels. However, these labels describe the Red Guards inaccurately since within the Rebels themselves, divisions emerged as well. Xiao Gongqin thus describes the different factions within the Rebel camp as thugs, Rebel Red Guards, average workers and factory intellectuals. He identifies himself as a respectable Rebel who was 'educated, able to write good articles and connected to university Rebels'.[53] To his mind, what western analyses of the Chinese intelligentsia today lack is a fine understanding of its complexity and the complexity of its different facets. According to Xiao Gongqin, the experience of the Cultural Revolution is insufficient to explain the current divisions among Chinese intellectuals:

> Each thought comes out of the necessity to solve problems. A problem arises, it has to be resolved. Hence the great plurality of ideas. I therefore believe that the analysis of different currents of thought should not necessarily be based on the experience of the Cultural Revolution. What matters is to observe how a multiplicity of experiences can lead to the same thought while a similar experience can lead to different thoughts.

The Cultural Revolution was experienced in multiple ways but, in the last two decades, its most violent and traumatic manifestations are the most constantly referred to. Indeed, the Party controls research on that period as much as possible and the 'official' version, established by the leaders responsible for launching reforms – those who were most intensely persecuted and who denounce the Cultural Revolution altogether – has therefore prevailed.[54] To name only Deng Xiaoping, his family was targeted by Red Guards. His son Deng Pufang was so terrified when he was attacked that he jumped through a fourth-floor window and

---

50. Xu Youyu believes Wang Shaoguang to be a serious scholar on the Cultural Revolution who, however, did not 'truly' experience the Cultural Revolution.

51. The idea that 'it must be experienced to be grasped' is quite widespread. Liberals like Xu Youyu often use this argument to discard Cui Zhiyuan's discourse and research.

52. Sausmikat, N. 'Generations, legitimacy, and political ideas in China', pp. 376–7.

53. Xiao, G. 'Gongchang zaofanpaide liangzhong leixing' (Two types of rebel in the factories), *China News Digest*, Luntan, Z. (débat libre), August 8, 2000, quoted in Sausmikat, N. 'Generations, legitimacy, and political ideas in China'.

54. Many have questioned this so-called elitist interpretation of the Cultural Revolution over the years, especially online.

has been paraplegic ever since. The necessity of full condemnation (*chedi fouding*)[55] of the Cultural Revolution was self-evident to the new leaders. But condemnation of the whole Mao era in which they had played a role had to be qualified, so leaders could appear as legitimate to the population. As a result, it was officially claimed that Mao's legacy was 70 per cent good and 30 per cent bad. Complete rejection of the Cultural Revolution, central in the 1981 Sixth Plenary Session of the Eleventh Central Committee, focused less on giving justice to victims within the population and on questioning the regime's foundations than on reasserting the latter while breaking away from the theory that contradictions still exist under the socialist regime, which had allowed Mao to justify resorting to mass mobilisation. Besides, many authors of works in the 'scar' literature,[56] a major corpus of testimonies of that time, come from families of cadres and intellectual elites, who were the Red Guards' first victims. The outcome is that those who did not participate or even witness the most tragic manifestations of that period – their number remains to be defined – and who express some nostalgia for that time regarding the freedom of expression of that era and the opportunity they had to travel through the country, meeting and debating everything with other youths, dirtying their hands working in the fields or in factories before pursuing their studies, are not 'politically correct' at all.[57] Such scholars claim to present the views of the common people, not of the elites. Liu Dong believes they are insincere arrivistes:

All those who experienced the Cultural Revolution do not agree to say it was a bad thing or a good experience. What is the variable in this matter? Western theory. Around us, there is a group of people whose body tells them the Cultural Revolution was wrong while their soul, or the theories they have read, tells them that is was a good thing. This is all the more the case as they realise that

---

55. Resolution taken at the Sixth Plenary Session of the Eleventh Central Committee in 1981, 'Guanyu jiangguo yilai dang de ruogan lishi wenti de jueyi' (Resolution concerning some questions in the history of our Party since the founding of the PRC), chapter '"Wenhua dageming" de shi nian' (Ten Years of 'Cultural Revolution'), in Tan, H. and Jian, S. (eds), *1895–1995 Shiji dang'an* (Archives of the century), Beijing: Dang'an Zhongguo chubanshe, 1995, pp. 571–8.

56. The 'scar' literature, which describes the tragic sufferings of cadres and intellectuals as they experienced the Cultural Revolution, emerged after Mao's death. Even today, a great number of novels and movies, such as Zhang Yimou's 'To Live', Chen Kaige's 'Farewell My Concubine', Yu Hua's *Brothers* or Dai Sijie's *Balzac and the Little Chinese Seamstress*, narrate these persecutions. *See also* Xu, B. *Disenchanted Democracy.*

57. Quite a number of studies have however explained the reasons for this 'freedom' and confirmed the existence of a real power vacuum during the insurrectional period of the Revolution, the danger some radical organisations such as the Central Group for the Cultural Revolution presented, and the skilful resort to Central rhetorics by the Red Guards: Madarès, H., Wang, G., Redon, E., Nguyen, K. and Xi, X. *Révo. cul. dans la Chine pop., Anthologie de la presse des gardes rouges*, Union générale d'éditions, coll.10–18, Bibliothèque asiatique, 1974; Hua, L. *Les Années rouges*, Le Seuil, 1987; Song, Y. 'The end of innocence, heterodox thought on human rights and political reform during the Cultural Revolution', *Human Rights Forum* Spring 2001, pp. 18–22 ; Wang, S. 'Qunzhong yu Wenhua dageming' (Masses and the Great Proletarian Cultural Revolution), in Li, S. (ed,) *Dalu zhishifenzi lun zhengzhi, shehui, jingji*, Taipei, Guiguan tushu gufen youxian gongsi, 1991, pp. 90–4.

saying that the Cultural Revolution was a good thing draws a lot of attention abroad. And they think they can claim to be big professors. This happened to many of my classmates. They have gone through the Cultural Revolution. They know what it is but they strive not to speak of it that way.

Liu Dong's criticism is not very objective but it is striking to note how he implicitly manages to aim the accusation of being bankrolled by the West at scholars like Wang Hui or Cui Zhiyuan who refuse to reject the Mao legacy altogether, including the Cultural Revolution. This is a reversal of the usual situation in which the left and nationalists often accuse liberal dissidents of being bankrolled by the West. This criticism crossfire reveals the disastrous consequences of officially blocking academic research on the Cultural Revolution. It has paved the way for its partisan reinterpretation and ideological reinvention, which are far from stimulating. Studies like Wang Shaoguang's or Xu Youyu's cannot go beyond that limited debate because they are too limited in number and also quite subjective. The Cultural Revolution, nonetheless, is a landmark period that each intellectual trend refers to: neo-conservatives and elites close to power insist on the chaos to which mass mobilisation led and they justify delaying China's democratisation for this reason, as long as the rule of law advances in the country so as to avoid abuses and excesses on the part of leaders; the New Left refers to the positive legacy of the egalitarian institutional innovations of the popular revolution; finally, the massive scale of the totalitarian excesses of the Cultural Revolution encourages liberals to reject the revolutionary legacy altogether.

Chapter Three

Ideas - A Market or a Battle?

The first chapter endeavoured to grasp the scope and limits of Chinese academics' freedom of expression, which has expanded even if some rules must be obeyed and research is partly oriented by authorities. Let us now distinguish between the different types of political commitment that the academics I studied opt for. I focus on so-called intellectuals, committed scholars adopting one of the postures described by Liang Shuming: the scholar completely 'engrossed in learning' and knowledge, working at most indirectly for the transformation of society and the regime; or the scholar 'engrossed in issues', accepting political functions in the hope of having a direct impact on political decisions.

Intellectuals and patriotism

Intellectuals?

In order to understand the array of intellectual postures which academics can opt for, specific attention should be paid to the different types of audience they target, which can be defined as academia, the leadership and/or society. Intellectual production therefore oscillates between specialised academic forms and widely accessible generalist ones, depending on the targeted audience(s). French sociologist Raymond Boudon distinguishes between three 'markets', which obey different writing rules: the type I market, the scholarly market of the scientific community of peers; the type II market, which reaches out to a wider educated audience, comprising peers and specialists who are not sociologists but who are directly concerned with the themes sociologists tackle; and the type III market, which is less clearly defined and corresponds to all citizens (the audience of public conferences, for instance).[1] To this typology should be added the market of official publications, in which experts and technocrats are involved as well. Academics, as well as senior cadres, may work and publish under the command of public authorities, referring to publications on the primary market which they adapt and popularise. They could be assimilated to the academic type that Gérard Noiriel describes as 'the government intellectual' (*l'intellectuel de gouvernement*), who shouldn't be confused with 'specific intellectuals' (*intellectuels spécifiques*) or 'revolutionary intellectuals' (*intellectuels révolutionnaires*).[2] The primary

---

1.   Boudon, R. 'L'intellectuel et ses publics: les singularités françaises', in Reynaud, J. D. and Grafmeyer, Y. (eds) *Français qui êtes-vous? Des essais et des chiffres*, Paris: La Documentation Française, 1981, pp. 465–80.

2.   Noiriel, G. *Les Fils maudits de la République. L'avenir des intellectuels en France*, Paris: Fayard, 2005.

function of the government intellectual is to bridge the gap between scholarship and political leadership as he accepts the way current problems are raised by politicians and mobilises his expertise in his attempt to resolve them. Noiriel insists on the ambiguous nature of such a position, in contradistinction to the image of the intellectual as a spokesperson for the oppressed.

This matrix can help us understand the similarities and discrepancies between committed academics in China and in Europe or in the United States. In France, government intellectuals are looked down upon because they are deemed too close to power to fulfil their role as Sartrian intellectuals. But elsewhere, the situation is quite different[3] and all the more so in China. Since, in the current situation, a narrow definition of intellectuals understood as explicit critics can only describe dissidents, such a definition excludes a whole set of relatively independent figures and the wide array of types of political commitment corresponding to their various stances as regards power.

The set of well known academics involved in the debate on political reform that I have studied in this research doesn't correspond to the definition of intellectuals directly opposing power. They are animated much less by the 'adversarial culture' that Lionel Trilling describes as the tendency of scholars, artists or writers to ceaselessly attack the *status quo*[4] than by a sense of 'social responsibility' as regards the development of the Chinese nation.[5] These scholars should, however, be seen as intellectuals in so far as they go beyond their field of expertise, emboldened by their cultural capital and their national and international achievements; and because they have become involved in the public sphere, in order to share their analyses and views on burning issues and to defend values. The positions they take and their publications on political reform, as well as their impact, make it particularly relevant to describe them as 'public intellectuals'.

According to Amitai Etzioni, what the different approaches used by public intellectuals have in common is the idea that these academics express themselves publicly on a wide array of issues; are generalists rather than specialists; focus on problems affecting a large public; and don't keep their

---

3.   In *Absent Minds*, Oxford, Oxford University Press, 2006, Stefan Collini studies the denial that such a thing as 'true' intellectuals exist in Great Britain, which considers itself as a unique case. Even in France, intellectuals are said to be an endangered species, which is the explicit title of Etzioni, A. and Bowditch, A. *Public Intellectuals: An endangered species?* Lanham, MD: Rowman & Littlefield, 2006.

4.   Trilling, L. *Beyond Culture: Essays on literature and learning*, New York: Viking Press, 1965; to Trilling, this culture of contestation ran the risk of becoming a new diktat.

5.   Hayhoe, R. *China's Universities, 1895–1995: A century of cultural conflict*, New York: Garland Publishers, 1996, pp. 115, 117, 125. 'Social responsibility' is also the concept used in Zhang, Y. 'Politics, culture, and scholarly responsibility in China: toward a culturally sensitive analytical approach', *Asian Perspective* 31(3), 2007, pp. 103–24. *See also* Hao, Z. *Whither Taiwan and Mainland China: National identity, the state, and intellectuals*, Hong Kong: Hong Kong University Press, 2010.

judgments and opinions to themselves.[6] These 'specific intellectuals'[7] go beyond their particular field of expertise to make statements on general-interest issues, in the name of ethical or moral universal values, which can be associated with particular regime forms or forms of political organisation that supposedly embody them. Tony Judt refers to this definition when he calls Raymond Aron a 'peripheral insider'.[8] Richard Posner highlights the fact that these intellectuals address an intellectual public on political and ideological issues in an accessible way.[9] Russel Jacoby insists on the public dimension of their commitment, which is not only professional and private.[10] A major component of being a public intellectual is the public reception of one's ideas. To be a public intellectual, on top of expressing oneself publicly, a scholar must find an audience: mainly an educated audience and sometimes a highly educated one, limited to intellectual and political spheres, but which thereafter spread the ideas more widely. This means that even if the number of people who are truly familiar with the work and ideas of a public intellectual is very limited, the public impact of them should not be underestimated since the

---

6.   Bowditch, A. and Etzioni, A. *Public Intellectuals*, p. 1.

7.   Foucault, M. 'La fonction politique de l'intellectuel' (The political function of the intellectual), *Dits et écrits II, 1976–1988*, Paris: Gallimard, 2001, p. 109: 'For a long time the "left" intellectual spoke and was acknowledged to have the right of speaking in the capacity of master of truth and justice. He was heard, or purported to make himself heard, as the representative of the universal. To be an intellectual meant to be, a little, the consciousness/conscience of everyone. I think we encounter here an idea transposed from Marxism, from a faded Marxism indeed: just as the proletariat, through the necessity of its historical position, is the hearer of the universal (but its immediate, unreflected bearer, scarcely conscious of itself as such), so the intellectual, by his moral, theoretical and political choice, aspires to be the bearer of this universality in its conscious, elaborated form. The intellectual is supposed to be the clear, individual figure of a universality of which the proletariat is the obscure, collective form. For some time now, the intellectual has no longer been called upon to play this role. A new mode of "connection between theory and practice" has been established, intellectuals have become accustomed to working not in the character of the "universal", the "exemplary", the "just-and-true for all", but in specific sectors, at precise points where they are situated either by their professional conditions of work or their conditions of life (housing, the hospital, the asylum, the laboratory, the university, familial and sexual relations). Through this they have undoubtedly gained a much more concrete awareness of struggles. They have also thereby encountered problems which are specific, "non-universal", often different from those of the proletariat and the masses. And yet, I believe that they have really come closer to the proletariat, for two reasons: because it has been a matter of real, material, everyday struggles, and because they often came up, even though in a different form, against the same adversary as the proletariat, the peasants and the masses, namely the multinational corporations, the judicial and police apparatuses, property speculators, etc. This is what I would call the "specific" intellectual as opposed to the "universal" intellectual.'

8.   Tony Judt about Raymond Aron: 'he took an active lifelong interest in public matters beyond his sphere of professional expertise.' *See* Tony Judt, 'The peripheral insider: Raymond Aron and the wages of reason', in Melzer, A. Weinberger, J. and Zinman, R. (eds) *The Public Intellectual: Between philosophy and politics*, Lanham MD: Rowman & Littlefield, p. 142.

9.   Posner, R. *Public Intellectuals, A study of decline*, Cambridge, MA: Harvard University Press, 2001, p. 1.

10. Jacoby, R. *The Last Intellectuals: American culture in the age of academe*, New York: Basic Books, 1987, p. 235.

concepts, ideas and values which the public intellectual espouses can influence a much larger public. Conversely, in some cases, the great popularity of an intellectual leads political elites to take his point of view into consideration.

The most contested aspect in the definition of public intellectuals is related to their positioning as regards power. According to Epstein, Saïd or Wright Mills,[11] one can be called a public intellectual only when one criticises power relentlessly, which, in the case of China would lead us to discard all but dissidents. This research relies, on the contrary, on the idea that expressing direct criticism of power is not a criterion for assessing political commitment and determining whether a scholar is an intellectual; in this understanding, the well established university professors under scrutiny here can be considered intellectuals.[12] They enjoy enough academic recognition and job security to be able to express themselves on major social issues. However, they walk a fine line since criticising power openly and radically can lead to repression and falling into dissidence. Besides, the conception of intellectual commitment has evolved. The hopes which were kindled by the liberalising 1980s led to more direct forms of criticism, which the post-Tiananmen 1989 repression and the fears that arose from the collapse of the former Soviet Union soon made impossible.[13] In her study of the Chinese Academy of Social Sciences, Margaret Sleeboom-Faulkner evokes the shift, which took place among scholars from the 1980s to 2000s, from practices of blunt criticism to recognition that accepting an instrumental role to the state can help change it from the inside.[14]

Scholars who belong to the generation of the Cultural Revolution, because of the incomplete education they received, because they often taught themselves and because it is rare for them to specialise in a narrow field of study (they tend to work on a large set of political and academic subjects), form a group of intellectuals involved in the debate on economic and political reform. Unlike Roosevelt's Brains Trust – law professors such as Rexford G. Tugwell and A. A. Berle and unofficial ministries of economists, professors, lawyers and social workers, who used their expertise in the fight against the Great Depression of the 1930s – the intellectuals under my scrutiny are not just experts convinced

11. Epstein, J. 'Intellectuals - Public and otherwise', Commentary, May 2000; Saïd, E., 'The Reith Lectures: Speaking truth to power', The Independent, 22 July 1993; Wright Mills, C., Power, politics and people: the collected essays, NY: Oxford University Press, 1963.

12. Li, C. 'Introduction', in Hu, A. China in 2020: A new type of superpower, Washington DC: Brookings Institution Press, 2011, p. xxv. Cheng Li describes the attitude – which American observers find difficult to understand – of well established professors in Chinese universities who are both close to some leaders and very critical, yet without being dissidents at all. Their arguments and views can be extremely diverse. Cheng Li refers to Cai Fang, Yu Yongding, Xu Xiaonian, Sun Liping, Zi Zhongyun and Hu Angang. My aim in this chapter is to describe similar forms of political commitment.

13. This watershed can also be sensed in the artistic field. Marc Abélès explains that 'most artists gave up the idealism characterising the avant garde group "the Stars" from 1979 on. After the repression of Tiananmen Square, they no longer hoped to change the regime and were more down to earth. Fang Lijun and his friends said that they could not be fooled by ideals and shunted about by illusions forever.' Abélès, M. Pékin 798, Paris: S-tock, 2011, p. 188. See also Chapter Four.

14. Sleeboom-Faulkner, M. The Chinese Academy of Social Sciences (CASS): Shaping the Reforms, Academia and China (1977–2003), Leiden: Brill, 2007.

that universities should serve the state and that research can be applied to solve the problems that affect its citizens. Neither can they be compared to French *enarques* (alumni of the prestigious National School of Administration or ENA), because they weren't trained in schools of administration and do not belong to the Chinese administration. Moreover, they should not be confused with specialists, who forgo a large audience and address a limited number of counterparts and colleagues through inaccessible and technical publications in scholarly journals.[15] They rather remind us of the American sociologists who answered Robert King Merton's call for an incremental science and who benefitted from the funding of the Rockefeller Foundation's Social Science Research Council (which actively promoted sociology as a policy science) as well as from the federal and state governments. The latter, indeed, welcomed sociologists, who were asked to study social problems to inform and guide political leaders in the fields of social security, education, health, criminal justice and so on. According to Aronowitz, the Cold War played a crucial role at this turning point for American sociology because it forced scholars to side with the West if they wanted to avoid marginalisation or even professional annihilation.[16]

Patriots

These Chinese intellectuals are driven by patriotism, in the name of which they give up pure research. They want to take part in the common effort and even feel responsible for the proper modernisation of their country. In that sense, they are perfectly in line with China's first intellectuals, looking for national wealth and power (*fuqiang*) but trying to play their part as guides of the Chinese nation in a more or less independent manner. According to Wang Juntao, who belongs to this generation of intellectuals, 'they replaced the officially established intellectuals [...]. They caused the intellectual community to become more independent – they independently manipulated the officially established institutions to produce and distribute their ideas'.[17] Scholars such as Kang Xiaoguang openly express their patriotism, which does not necessarily mean they support the regime on everything. Kang denounces its lack of legitimacy, legality and social security, insufficient regulation of capital and excessive control of workers' unions. But Kang does not fear repression because the criticisms he makes do not aim at undermining or at overthrowing the current government at all. On the contrary, they aim at helping

---

15. *See* Joffe, J. 'The decline of the public intellectual and the rise of the pundit', in Melzer, A. Weinberger, J. and Zinman, R. (eds) *The Public Intellectual*, p. 109. Joffe describes the idiosyncratic specialisation of the American academia: 50 years ago, there were five disciplines in American political science while there are now 104.

16. Aronowitz, S. 'Comments on Michael Burawoy's "The critical turn to public sociology"', *Critical Sociology* 31(3), May 2005, pp. 333–8.

17. Wang, J. *Reverse Course: Political Neo-Conservatism and regime stability in post-Tiananmen China*, PhD dissertation, Columbia University, 2006, p. 97.

it reform and improve.[18] Because of his patriotism and utilitarianism and the fact that his research's starting point is problems to solve rather than principles or knowledge, he is thoroughly different from other thinkers like Jiang Qing, who also advocates a return to Confucianism:[19]

> What makes me different from most scholars is that my first concern is the nation's interest. China's status in my mind is immense and surpasses my individual interest. My approach resultantly is general interest, national interest, and it guides my take on development and everything else. My colleagues who advocate a liberal democracy certainly believe that freedom of association and the freedom to set up opposition parties are fundamental liberties, which we cannot live without. To me, the national interest comes first. I have mentioned this example so as to show that options vary according to one's position. We could mention the labour law: cadres and workers are satisfied while capitalists complain. My point is that no matter what we talk about, an absolute judgement cannot be expressed. What is decisive is the place where we stand to judge. This is the reason why I believe the gap between liberals' views and mine is less due to our personal opinions than our different positions and starting points. I think these intellectuals are all concerned with the country's future, they are patriots who only wish the best for their country. Even though our viewpoints are opposed, we share a similar goal: we want our country to thrive, to be more harmonious, stable and powerful.

---

18. Kang, X. 'Hezuozhuyiguojia: ziyouzhuyi, shehuizhuyi zhiwaide disandaolu' ('Co-operationism: liberalism, socialism and the third way'), available online at http://www.aisixiang.com/data/11511.html (last accessed 14 November 2014). Kang proposes that the current regime must become co-operationist. The pluralisation and strengthening of social groups, co-operation and sharing will allow to reduce pressure and resistance and therefore help maintain growth, which is a *sine qua non* condition for elites to support the regime. According to Kang, capitalists are the ones who fear democracy the most, contrary to the people, intellectuals or leaders. He advocates relaxing the control over intellectual elites to persuade them to co-operate; strengthening co-operation between the masses and the government; developing the welfare state; and popular supervision of capital before it controls the government itself. *See* Yan Xuetong, *Ancient Chinese Thought, Modern Chinese Power*, Princeton NJ: Princeton University Press, 2011, pp. 249–50: 'Giving advice on policy is the responsibility of the intelligentsia to society. I think that if we were to revive the personal legal assistant system and establish a system of think tanks it would enable policymaking to be more scientific. I want to be both a scholar and a policy advisor myself. The term intelligentsia means someone who has received an education in the humanities, has a sense of responsibility to society, and undertakes criticism of the government [...] The use of the term in China tends to obscure the true nature of the intelligentsia, because it refers merely to people who can read. Moreover, the genuine intelligentsia are not just critical of the government; they also tell the government what to do and how to do it.'

19. *See* Kang Xiaoguang's interview in 2004 with Wang Dasan, 'Wo shi ruhe zouxiang rujia' ('How I became a Confucian') in *Zhexue Zhuanye Wangzhan*, available online at http://phi.ruc.edu.cn/pol/html/03/t-14903.html (last accessed 14 November 2014). in which Kang explains that the aim of any political scientist is to play the role of the broker between the pure scholar and the statesman, who is unfamiliar with Confucian values of righteousness and benevolence. The latter could not achieve these values in his policy without the help of a political scientist, who not only explains Confucian ideals and principles but turns them into a system and into policies, so that political leaders pay attention to them.

While Kang is one of the scholars who expose their nationalism openly, others tend to express their concern,[20] their sense that China is going through a major crisis that they should help to solve. This crisis mind-set (*youhuan yishi*) is a defining element for Chinese intellectuals, which Gloria Davis' book, *Worrying About China*, has explicitly emphasised.[21] This mindset has been a powerful driver of their attempts to identify and solve the problems threatening their country. Timothy Cheek mentions the 'historical pragmatism' of historians, who refer to the past as if it were 'a storehouse of human experience', which they tap into to solve current problems.[22] It's indeed the approach that historians like Xiao Gongqin or Zhu Xueqin openly claim to have. Similarly, Yan Xuetong, Dean of Tsinghua University's Institute of Modern International Relations and Chief Editor of Oxford University Press's *Chinese Journal of International Politics*, explicitly introduces his approach as the study of pre-Qin thinkers aimed at drawing practical lessons for China's current foreign policy.[23] He actually tries to convince the government of the importance of defining great principles, selecting quality leaders and building sufficient moral authority to guide the country's future. His research is entirely oriented towards this pragmatic goal.[24] Another example is Gan Yang, one of the main scholars of the New Left, who is currently devoted to educational reform. He explains that he left the Chinese University of Hong Kong for Zhongshan University in Guangzhou mainly because he was given the opportunity to put his educational reform proposals into practice there.

Researchers

The scholars chosen in this research define themselves as academics first. They hold positions in the most prestigious higher-education institutions: Peking University, Tsinghua, People's University, Fudan, Nankai and so on. They publish for Chinese and foreign scholarly journals and publishing houses. They all are members of the editorial boards of major scholarly journals. Their works are reference points in their fields and sometimes seem to have monopolies in those areas. Apart from those holding political positions, like Yu Keping, Zhu Guanglei or He Zengke, they insist upon their role as researchers from civil society (*minjian*). Hu Angang, director of an influential think tank whose political advocacy has often been well received by the government, nevertheless defines himself as an independent researcher and refuses to be called a government advisor. He rejected the political career offered to

---

20. Link, P. *Evening Chats in Beijing*, London and New York: Norton, 1992, p. 249.

21. Davies, G. *Worrying About China: The language of Chinese critical inquiry*, Cambridge, MA: Harvard University Press, 2007, pp. 5–8, 15

22. Cheek, T. 'Historians as public intellectuals', in Edward Gu and Merle Goldman (eds), *Chinese Intellectuals Between State and Market*, London and New York: RoutledgeCurzon, 2004, p. 209.

23. Yan, X. *Ancient Chinese Thought, Modern Chinese Power* Princeton NJ: Princeton, Princeton University Press, 2011.

24. Hu Angang also insists on his patriotic motivations: 'This book represents my efforts to observe China as an insider, to understand China as a researcher, to forecast China's future as a participant in its evolution, and as a scholar of the era following Deng Xiaoping to help construct China.', *China in 2020: A new type of superpower*, Washington DC: Brookings Institution Press, 2011, p. 20.

him in 1993, following the example of Paul Samuelson, the Nobel-prize-winning American economist who refused to become a White House advisor and whom he sees as a role model.[25] Hu Angang claims that 'speaking for the least advantaged is the highest principle of my professional career'.[26] To take up the metaphor Marc Abélès uses regarding Chinese contemporary art, these researchers, 'while staying close to the centre, nonetheless remain outside, on the other side of the fence',[27] while keeping open the possibility of jumping periodically from one side to the other. This barrier between government and civil society is absolutely porous and has become all the more so as exchanges between the two sides are now multitudinous.

Technocracy and the market of ideas

In this section, I shall try to understand the forms that political commitment and soft protest can take in Chinese universities. Chinese scholars' positions and modes of intervention are numerous and ever-changing, partly because of the lack of institutionalisation of censorship and repression. But this diversity is also fuelled by the heterogeneous ideological stances of academics and CCP senior members. Moreover, the regime has become very technocratic. The legitimacy of the Party is mainly based on its economic and social efficiency (economic development and growth, improved living conditions, stability and so on): so much so that consulting experts has become a crucial element of the current regime's legitimacy-building. As a result, between the Sixteenth and Seventeenth PCC Congresses (from 2002 to 2007), the Political Bureau of the Central Committee organised 44 official meetings dedicated to collective study, at which experts and researchers were invited to give conferences to leaders. Economists, sociologists and political scientists have taken part and have competed to attract and keep the attention of leaders. Some have thereafter proudly claimed to have had an effect on the political decision-making process.

The dominance of technocrats in the regime

According to Kang Xiaoguang, political participation is currently expanding in China and the central government can no longer make decisions all by itself.[28] Local governments, among others, put pressure on the central authority. Besides, websites, hotlines and polling, on top of the *xinfang* system,[29] are set up

---

25. Hu, A. *China in 2020*, p. xxv.

26. Hu, A. *Zhongguo Fazhan Qianjing (The Future of China's Development)*, Hangzhou: Zhejiang Renmin Chubanshe, 1999, p. 6.

27. Abélès, M. *Pékin 798*, Paris: Stock, 2011, p. 166. Marc Abélès describes the famous spontaneous Exhibition of the Stars that Huang Rui and Ma Desheng organised on 27 September 1979, in the park of the National Gallery.

28. Kang, X. 'Jianshe minzhu fazhi: chongjian hefaxing jichu de changqi xingdong' ('Building a democratic rule of law: the long process of reconstructing legitimate foundations'), *Aisixiang* 30, October 2006, available online at http://www.aisixiang.com (last accessed 14 November 2014).

29. The Administration of Letters and Visits currently receives more than 13 million complaints a year (Thireau, I. and Hua, L. *Les ruses de la démocratie: Protester en Chine*, Paris: Le Seuil, 2010).

to allow people to express themselves. These devices are decisive governing tools because they help the central government to be directly informed of the mistakes and misappropriations of local governments. The government strives to be seen as more responsive and transparent but, since that does not solve problems, much more radical ways are often adopted for the population to voice its demands. Kang Xiaoguang explains that intellectual elites have a unique way of intervening. They pick key moments to make suggestions. The government pays attention to them and their suggestions are often adopted by official institutions, especially those emanating from scholars specialised in economics and economic stability, who are encouraged by the government and have the possibility of becoming officials themselves. They play the role of advisers. Some make suggestions before major congresses and try to influence government decisions.

In an article on 'The rise of technocrats', Xiao Gongqin describes how, in the late 1990s, new technocrats strengthened their power, which was entirely focused on pragmatic modernisation, thanks to public policy.[30] The role of the authoritarian state apparatus was then to facilitate a fast transition to a market economy rather than to communist egalitarianism. Some pluralism was adopted. Leaders, who were mostly trained as engineers, adopted a functional and pragmatic approach towards 'democracy'. Limited democratisation was proposed, not in the name of lofty democratic ideals but for pragmatic reasons. Technocrats have been guided by four criteria: utility; security (can democratic innovation overthrow the current political order?); feasibility (can it work without causing some structural conflict?); and legitimacy (can the new democratic measure be justified by some Marxist principle so as to silence the marginalised left?). Xiao Gongqin evokes the government's pressing need for expertise:[31]

Recently, sociologists like Yu Jianrong have attracted the government's attention to research on social issues. Their research questions and findings are very solid and the government now needs to benefit from their knowledge. They consequently have had the opportunity to take part in political decisions. Specialists of ethical questions have also been called upon. Scholars specialised in politics can contribute to politics in many ways. The government needs think tanks and people reflecting on some issues. As a result, it is fairly easy to get into one of these research groups.[32]

It can be thought that if Chinese scholars get involved in the technocratic game, it might be because they have given up revolutionary change and more or less

---

30. Xiao, G. 'The rise of technocrats', *Journal of Democracy* 14(1), 2003, pp. 60–5.

31. Jean-Louis Rocca believes Chinese sociologists have been more politically committed since the 2000s: Rocca, J. -L. (ed.) *La société chinoise vue par ses sociologues*, Paris: Presses de Sciences Po, 2008, pp. 28–9. Yu Jianrong put up a 10-year plan for political and social reform on his microblog: Bandurski, D. 'Scholar posts 10-year plan for social and political reform', *China Media Project*, 26 March 2012, available online at http://cmp.hku.hk/2012/03/26/20910/ (last accessed 14 November 2014).

32. Xiao, G. 'The rise of technocrats'.

support the official discourse on the leading role the Party plays in developing the country and maintaining stability (*weiwen*), given the insufficient 'quality' (*suzhi*) of the population. This perspective is enlightening as regards their compliance with the system and their willingness to offer to help in the market of ideas submitted to the leaders' attention.

A market of ideas

A vast market of ideas exists wherein intellectual elites make their ideas available to political elites. The market has plenty of both products and customers and the variety of interests and political opinions among political elites guarantees powerful sponsors for all types of proposals academics make, if these are legitimised by the latters' cultural capital and expertise. Consequently, a politically committed researcher's proposals, even if first submerged in the great mass of academic proposals, can eventually emerge if a leader or a leading group chooses to use them to legitimise the implementation of preferred ideas or policies. Gan Yang believes that the complexity of the decisions leaders must make justifies their interaction with academics:

> As far as the relationship between intellectuals and the government is concerned, I think we must go beyond the idea that it necessarily is a conflicting relationship. Concerning social policy, for instance, and education issues, the role of the state is crucial. This is the reason why, if a scholar has some interesting thought to share, and that the government is willing to listen to his proposal, it is evidence that the government is actually doing what it has to do. These examples should not be denounced. This is the problem democratic regimes face, where one cannot but criticise the government. No one dares to support government policy. This is not a proper thing to do in places like Hong Kong or Taiwan. The result is people are confused as regards what is right or wrong, and what they should expect from the government. I think we must be honest. We should denounce what goes wrong, but also praise a satisfactory policy. Criticising for the sake of criticising is pointless. Some government decisions are too complex for the whole population to exactly understand what they are about.

Intellectual and political elites naturally have to meet and join forces to navigate through troubled waters. Kang Xiaoguang, who tends to generalise from his own personal experience, therefore calls for less censorship so that intellectual elites (he is not so interested in the freedom of speech of the whole population) can express themselves freely.

> Censorship affects the mainstream media, addressing a large public. What truly matters is that, if leaders consider an academic important, they will come to him and ask for his last research findings. Besides, when strategic decisions are debated, consultation meetings are organised and scholars are encouraged to attend and make suggestions. This is especially the case for legislation. In the law-drafting process, the opinion of many experts and scholars is asked.

Besides, let us not forget the internal reference system and the people in charge of collecting relevant information in mainstream, internal, international publications so as to transmit full reports to all leaders.

Communication is easy and common between academics and power, especially between well known scholars and institutions. Ministries and specialised commissions can attentively follow the work of some researchers and contact them. Some connections are institutionalised and scholars become members of consultative political conferences [*zhongguo renmin zhengzhi xieshang huiyi*] and are in close connection with the government and members of the People's Assembly. As far as I am concerned, I am part of a group of intellectuals from outside the Party, which is officially connected to the Central Committee's United Front Department. I am also a participant in regular meetings. If I have some idea, I can easily make it known. It is not hard to have leaders listen to you these days. Obviously, truly influential scholars are not countless. Any researcher who is eager to give suggestions to the government is not certain to be successful. A few hundreds of us are in a position to express ourselves and be heard. This obviously does not mean that our suggestions are bound to be accepted and adopted. The government has the final say. But they know what we think and if we have something to say, it's easy to communicate with them.

The role of academics is to help the government understand a problematic situation and the criticisms being targeted at it, whether from China or elsewhere, and to help the government remedy deficiencies. Historical and current political systems as well as theories describing ideal political models are therefore now studied in the most minute detail in Chinese universities and official think tanks, partly because leaders have opted for the strategy of knowing everything, so as to better understand the suggestions and comments of the international community, but more importantly to reflect on and prepare for the future. Hence the lectures on liberal democracy delivered by political philosophy professors from major Beijing universities at the Central Party School. For instance, in an article on different models of participation in the political agenda, Wang Shaoguang mentions the special relationship leaders of the Hu–Wen era – leaders claiming to rule in a more democratic and scientific way than their predecessors – have with some scholars. Since December 2002, one seminar a month on average has been organised for philosophers, legal experts, scientists and social scientists to present their research.[33] It is often said that among academics, economists, legal

---

33. In the Ministry of Foreign Affairs, according to one official, a 'conservative' like Yan Xuetong, a 'liberal' and a 'centrist' like Wang Jisi are regularly invited to discuss a policy or a specific issue. This process was chosen in order for the ministry to benefit from the confrontation of contradictory viewpoints and policy recommendations. It is remarkable that even Confucians like Jiang Qing, who has not been able to publish all his writings and proposals in China, have been invited several times to meet senior leaders. *See also* Bell, D. A. *China's New Confucianism*, Princeton, NJ: Princeton University Press, 2008, p. 12.

experts and sociologists are the most often called upon to share their expertise with Chinese leaders. More rarely, the research findings of political scientists can also lead to policy re-orientation. Zhu Guanglei, who is both an academic and a political official, considers that it is extremely common for leaders to listen to the suggestions of academics, to exchange and be influenced by them when making political decisions:

> Our research group interacts with decision-makers in many ways. For instance, China currently insists upon the notion that government is at the service of the people and implements our administration and institutional reform proposals. In almost all fields, there are scholars involved. This involvement is relatively intense. On the one hand, some scholars publish their ideas in journals and reviews so as to influence political decisions. On the other hand, some actively participate in decision-making. It should not be inferred from this that the scholar decides on his own, but that he is consulted, that a dialogue and exchanges take place, through the reports he helps produce, even though they may not be published. Many scholars play that role. Our research group is very active in that field.

> [...] Sometimes, researchers are invited to meetings and conferences to exchange ideas. At other times, they are asked to write research reports. But scholars also spontaneously express themselves in journals and in the press because they have reflected on a specific issue and think that they have found out something interesting, which might be useful. If the case arises, they are then invited to take part in political action. All sorts of situation arise. For instance, within the central government and the CCP, there are many different ministries and commissions, which all offer research topics that can easily be found on their website. A fourth scenario is when they encourage some scholars to accept missions or positions so as to undertake some study. I for instance am an adviser of the Advisory Committee of the Ministry of Civil Affairs. I am also the vice-director of the Chinese research institute on institutional reform, related to the State Commission Office for Public Sector Reform.

Most academics, however, think, like Yang Guangbin, that scholars are consulted only occasionally and individually, especially in the political field:

> From a general perspective, there is not really such a thing as relationships between academics and the government. The Chinese culture is quite curious in that sense. Even though academics as a group do not interact with the government in politics, law, economics, they often participate in an indirect – sometimes direct – way in political decision-making. But on an individual basis. It sometimes happens that a ministry (or a State Council Commissions) finds your point of view interesting and invites you to become a consultant. Academics are often invited to intervene on an individual basis.

The scale of this market of ideas, in such a vast country with an army of researchers, makes the identification of the ideas which are adopted and the assessment of their influence all the more difficult as researchers can discreetly publish work in internal (*neibu*) journals or reports or be invited to introduce their ideas behind closed doors.

We should recall that the technocratic system, which wants to be seen as more rational and legitimate, is designed to help maintain the one-party system. Shanghai historian Xu Jilin therefore draws a clear distinction between western-style technocracy and the current Chinese one. He also draws our attention to one crucial element: the scholars are exploited:

> Technocracy is a government of rationalisation. This rationalisation is instrumental, in Max Weber's words. What matters is to know which choice is the most efficient, not to define the value of such or such objective or to know if the ultimate aim of this choice is good or bad. That's not the technocracy's priority. But who reflects on these problems? Leaders. And whether these leaders, when deciding on a moral aim, are controlled or not is decisive. Whether they act in a democratic system or not is crucial. Are they submitted to other kinds of control? In China there is no such thing. The first supervision is that of public opinion, but it is controlled. Current China has therefore become a bureaucratic government and its mode of government is more and more rational, bureaucratised. But what is the government at the service of? Authoritarianism. It has actually reinforced it while making it more formally rational even though less rational in essential terms. This is the reason why I disagree with some Chinese political scientists who say that China's reform is gradually more rational. Rationality is a neutral word, with no meaning of its own, which means that technocracy is not necessarily a good thing [...] because an expert does not have a brain or a soul, and their technical management is bureaucratic. We should have a complete vision of this issue in China instead of praising the system. This is also the issue with many political experts who are only administration specialists. A political scientist should ultimately be concerned with the reasonableness of the underlying values and goal of policies. However, these days, many Chinese political scientists [...] do not reflect on the rationality of political activities but on efficiency issues. This is the reason why I left political studies. I could not stand this trend.

Xu Jilin draws our attention to an essential point: political leaders exploiting scholars. The technocratic system relies on unsaid things, which scholars are aware of when they make proposals with a political dimension. As a matter of fact, their expertise serves as a justification, which liberals like Xu Youyu and more conservative figures like Kang Xiaoguang alike suggest:

> Many scholars like to show off and say which of their ideas were accepted by the government. This is groundless. The central Government may have had that idea before the scholar expressed it. It is completely absurd to claim the government

entirely adopted one's idea. Even when the government accepts a suggestion, it does not mean that it will follow it and leaders will never explicitly say that a new policy directly derives from it. This explains why I cannot answer your question [concerning the elements of his research which had attracted the attention of leaders] precisely. I can only say that I have observed some concrete change after having made some suggestions. I cannot say more about that. I don't know the causal relation which led to the implementation of this or that suggestion. It might be a coincidence. I have, for instance, campaigned for the CCP to accept and institutionalise Confucian culture. It finally happened. I advocated more focus on Confucian philosophy, its intensified teaching in the Party schools, and instituting Confucian-style standards in the public-sector entrance examination. All these measures have been enforced. I have also suggested that some Confucian principles should be used to guide the country's development; that happened too. More precisely, I suggested that NGOs worked for the diffusion of Confucian culture in the world and this measure materialised when Confucius Institutes opened all over the world. There are several hundreds of them. The slogan of harmonious society also refers to the key Confucian concept of harmony. This has nothing to do with Marxism, which advocates class struggle. This neither is a liberal principle. I made these proposals in 2001–2002 and they have now all been realised.

According to Xiao Gongqin, scholars who can speak the same language as leaders have a greater influence on policies. Depending on their favoured field, their degree of optimism and how they assess their political efficacy, they adopt different attitudes as regards power.

A typology of political intervention types

Given the nature of the regime, ways to make an impact on the political agenda vary greatly. Being technocratic, the system encourages scholars who wish to express themselves to use their connections to directly and discreetly get in touch with leaders. This method is, nonetheless, adopted less and less by independent scholars, as it is well known that academic production is reviewed and that the government is systematically told about research results which may be of interest.[34] Moreover, as already mentioned, the leadership wants to be seen as more responsive, which translates into a growing attention to public opinion. State and society, far from being opposed, work together and their strategic interaction can benefit both sides.[35] This helps explain why, in the event of conflict, the main

---

34. Wang, S. 'Changing models of China's policy agenda setting', *Modern China* 34(1), 2008, pp. 56–87.
35. Zheng, Y. *Technological Empowerment: The internet, state, and society in China*, Stanford, CA: Stanford University Press, 2008, p. 135. *See also* Zhao, Y. and Sun, W. 'Public opinion supervision: the role of the media in constraining local officials', in Perry, E. and Goldman, M. (eds), *Grassroots Political Reform in China*, Cambridge, MA: Harvard University Press, 2007, pp. 300–24.

targets of uprisings are local actors and central authorities are often seen as acting as an outside arbitrator. Academics like Sun Liping have publicly called for the recognition of protest as a natural social phenomenon that cannot be dispensed with in a healthy society. He also called for the opening of new channels of expression, allowing the identification and solution of more problems.[36] Simultaneously, the government has multiplied official commitments to becoming more transparent and attentive to the 'wisdom of the people'.[37] The central government tries to increase its means for becoming informed about what is going on throughout the vast Chinese territory. Among other methods, it encourages people to petition and inform it of cases of injustice and corruption from local governments, which the Chinese population tends to do more and more willingly.[38] This is a powerful tool for boosting central government's legitimacy and improving governance. It also leads to an ever-increasing number of intellectuals willing to express themselves in the public media and thus indirectly impact the orientation of public policies.[39] Ren Jiantao distinguishes three possible types of influence.

Academics can be influential in three ways. They can first inform political leaders that several options of political reform are available. [...] We can participate in some way or another, and we mostly expect more rationality from the part of leaders. They cannot reject our ideas or methods on the pretext that they are not theirs or, worse, accuse us of being counter-revolutionaries, like in Mao's time. We expect more influence in that sense. Given the fact that new leaders are university graduates, they view political scientists completely differently from the violent revolutionaries of the Mao era, when political science was completely suppressed. This is absolutely impossible nowadays. As a matter of fact, the CCP, on the contrary, reinforces and encourages research in political science, which shows how much it needs it. [...] To my mind, the second type of influence – on society – is more important because the current development of Chinese society

36. Sun, L. 'Maodun, chongtu benlai jiu shi shehui changtai' ('It is inevitable that contradictions and conflicts arise in our society'), *Zhongguo Jiangxi Wang*, 27 March 2009, available online at http://news.163.com/09/0327/09/55DDGSC400012Q9L.html (last accessed 14 November 2014).

37. 'Hu Jintao talks to netizens via People's Daily Online', *People's Daily*, 20 June 2008; 'People have right to criticize government, says Chinese Premier Wen', *China View*, 28 February 2009; Qian, G. 'Guidance/supervision/reform/freedom: looking at Chinese media through the media buzzword', *China Media Project*, 13 July 2005.

38. Beside *xinfang*, 'public opinion supervision' and 'public opinion leadership' are conceived as governance instruments.

39. Yan Xuetong insists that the impact of scholars like him is bound to be indirect, unlike European or American think tanks, which benefit from institutionalised communication channels with leaders: 'I do not think that I myself have any direct impact on China's policy-makers. I just reckon that my articles have some influence on a few people who work in the relevant government departments. Maybe they have an indirect influence on policy, I do not have a direct influence. The influence of a scholar comes through his published articles.' Yan, X. *Ancient Chinese Thought, Modern Chinese Power*, p. 249. It is indeed relatively common to see a policy launched after a leader reads an academic article. It happened to Wang Shaoguang, with his publications on the budget, and to Cui Zhiyuan, as related in Bell, D. A. *China's New Confucianism*, p. 193, note 5.

is very unfair. The cost of development is too high and society too unequal and divided [*fenlie*]. Economic development is apparently vigorous but internal contradictions have accumulated since 1989, a development through force and violence, so as to stifle conflicts. Such a society is actually very dangerous, because each stratum wonders what the next step is. This is the reason why political science researchers can help the Chinese people, intellectuals included, to understand institutional reform proposals, the advantages of western political thought and research on the history of traditional political thinking. Nowadays, when we put forward some political principles, people who are interested can train themselves, compare, understand and choose. This is the direction China can take. The influence of public opinion could finally surpass the influence of political scientists on political practice; because their political leeway is too limited. We cannot rely yet on public opinion, the media, the public sphere. We therefore need an efficient means to influence politics and society. However, we can transmit and make our ideas public by way of our research, our lectures, the opinion pieces and books we publish, encounters with the media, including debates on television. This is the role of intellectuals in the French sense of the term. The third type of influence corresponds to the progressive building up of an intellectual atmosphere and sphere.

Through our critical articles, and diverse work, we produce new points of view on society and we can criticise all political leaders, including the President and the Prime Minister or other conservative leaders, from the far right (even though they cannot express themselves in China) to the far left. We can criticise everything related to the political process, and this could make politics less mysterious. Everyone can discuss it and have their own ideas on politics. This could solve a historical predicament: in China, only political elites can discuss political reform. How to explain the predicament of political reform in China? Well, until recently, only top leaders were allowed to discuss it. Now everyone can discuss it and some political tensions should vanish.

As a result, we benefit from three ways of influencing the political process. This indeed does not mean I can undertake an institutional reform project today, and it will be implemented next year. This is absolutely impossible. This is pure fantasy.

A typology can be proposed of the different types of intellectual interventions, starting with the scholars who position themselves the closest to power.

Think tanks

Most Chinese NGOs are created by official administrations and organs, hence their appellation GONGO (government-organised non-governmental organisations). Truly autonomous organisations actually tend to have less impact. Similarly, Chinese think tanks strive less to emancipate themselves from government than to come as close as possible to it.[40] They are called upon more frequently to allow better-informed and more thoughtful decisions. Many academic think tanks affiliated to major universities conduct academic research while also looking for political solutions to current problems of general interest. The researchers who belong to these think tanks can interact more easily with official cadres.[41] Their trajectories and political stances are reassuring to authorities. They may depend less upon a senior mentor to express themselves openly and they master the ins and outs of the political decision-making process. According to Hua Shiping and Tang Wenfang, the more organic[42] intellectuals are, in the sense that they accept to comply with the discipline of an official organisation or institution, the more likely they are to express themselves openly and their criticisms and suggestions are to have some impact.[43] Let us recall, however, that the object of this study is not researchers like Wang Huning, who are now fully organic and have disappeared from academic circles while integrating official spheres.

The Centre for China Government Innovations (*Zhongguo Zhengfu Chuangxin Yanjiu Zhongxin*), affiliated both to Peking University and the Central Compilation and Translation Bureau (*Zhonggong Zhongyang Bianyi Ju Bijiao Zhengzhi Yu Jingji Yanjiu Zhongxin*), is an interesting think tank to study. Combining academic research and policy-aimed expertise, it has set up a research and award programme rewarding innovation and excellence in Chinese local governance. The innovations which researchers identify and reward are closely investigated and later experimentally implemented, with the government's approval, in other places; in the best-case scenario, they can be extended to a whole region or to the whole country if the results are convincing. Frequent and thorough fieldwork and interviews with local cadres have convinced the researchers from this think tank that extending elections to higher levels is one of the key measures that could give political leaders the legitimacy and motivation they need to rule the country properly. Thanks to their proximity to government, these researchers have had the

---

40. Li, C. 'China's new think tanks', *China Leadership Monitor* 31, 2008, available online at http://www.brookings.edu/research/articles/2009/08/summer-china-li (last accessed 14 November 2014). Zhu, X. 'Government advisors or public advocates? Roles of think tanks in China from the perspective of regional variations', *China Quarterly* 207, 2011, pp. 668–86.

41. These Chinese think tanks do not exactly tally with European or American think tanks because their degree of institutionalisation is not comparable (Yan, X. *Ancient Chinese Thought, Modern Chinese Power*, p. 249).

42. The concept of the organic intellectual is used by Gramsci to define the new functions of intellectuals from the proletariat. I rather draw from Max-Jean Zins in 'L'intellectuel occidentalisé indien: de l'intellectuel syncrétique à l'intellectuel organique', in Michel Trebitsch and Marie-Christine Granjon (eds), *Pour une histoire comparée des intellectuels*, Brussels: Editions Complexe/IHTP-CNRS, 1998: 'His main role is to contribute to setting up a "legitimate reflection [*problématique*] on politics" aimed at fundamentally meeting the expectations of the social group he belongs to.'

43. Hua, S. *Scientism and Humanism: Two cultures in Post-Mao China (1978–1989)*, Albany, NY: State University of New York Press, 1995; Tang, W. *Public Opinion and Political Change in China*, Stanford, CA: Stanford University Press, 2005. Hao, Z. also resorts to this concept in his *Intellectuals at a Crossroads: The changing politics of China's knowledge workers*, Albany, NY: State University of New York Press, 2003.

opportunity to share their conclusions with political leaders, telling them about local Party secretaries who spontaneously wished to be elected to enjoy the same legitimacy as village committees; that is, not only the Party's support but that of their constituents as well.

Yu Keping, who is the head of this think tank, is a liberal political scientist whose political status does not allow to express himself as explicitly as other liberals, but, in compensation, guarantees him a hearing by local and central leaders.[44] With other academics who have opted for a political career, like Xia Yong and Wang Jisi,[45] he took part in elaborating Hu Jintao's domestic and foreign policy, including the following concepts: 'people-centered growth' (*yirenweiben*); 'CCP's governing capacity' (*dang de zhizheng nengli*); and China's 'peaceful rise' (*heping jueqi*). From within the liberal camp, only economics and legal academics usually reach such a degree of proximity to top leaders, whom they endeavour to convince of the benefits of progressive liberalisation.

Researchers from this think tank are not the only ones to rely on the government's pragmatic, experimental approach, implementing their reform proposals first at a local scale, in the hope that this could eventually and surreptitiously lead to the democratisation of the regime. The New Left has theorised this experimental approach to sketch a Chinese model of development. Wang Shaoguang thus described the small-scale, controlled experimental approach launched in the 1980s to identify practicable policies and the means to solve serious problems.[46] Precisely this approach is used by other researchers to give more weight to their theoretical reform proposals; either they participate in small-scale implementation of their proposals so as to convince government of their fruitfulness; or they identify promising existing experiments that make the principles they abstractly devised more convincing. Resistance to political change is often less radical among local governments since local leaders are no longer only assessed by their hierarchy based on their results in terms of economic growth. They are also expected to find new means to establish their legitimacy among all the social groups in their constituencies so as to maintain social stability, which has become absolutely crucial to gaining traction

---

44. Kang Xiaoguang about Yu Keping: 'He is a liberal. His interests and position do not allow him to express himself in a fully free way but he is profoundly liberal. There is not doubt about this. He is not like Liu Xiaobo or Chen Zimin, who openly say what they think. Neither is he a regular researcher, who can conduct research without drawing attention. He is a senior Party cadre, with a deputy director rank. He must be careful about what he says, which does not mean he is not a liberal.'

45. Xia Yong used to be the director of the National Administration for the Protection of State Secrets (2005–13). He is now the Deputy Director of the Legislative Affairs Office of the State Council. Wang Jisi is Dean of the School of International Studies and Director of the Centre for International and Strategic Studies, Peking University. He has been a member of the Foreign Policy Advisory Committee of the Foreign Ministry of China since October 2008.

46. Wang, S. 'Xuexi jizhi yu sheyingnengli: zhongguo nongcun hezuo yiliao tizhi bianqian de qishi', *Chinese Social Sciences*, June 2008; published in English as 'Adapting by learning: the evolution of China's rural health care financing', *Modern China* 35 (4), July 2009, pp. 370–404. A German political scientist, Heilmann, S. has a similar approach in 'From local experiments to national policy: the origins of China's distinctive policy process', *China Journal* 59, January 2008, pp. 1–30.

and being promoted. They therefore look for efficient institutional innovations. This widespread concept was developed by Tsinghua New Left Professor Cui Zhiyuan fifteen years ago. In the late 2000s, he found in Chongqing some practical terrain to test his technical proposals – long marginalised in Beijing – of developing collective ownership and economic democracy.

Another think tank, China's Academy of Science and Tsinghua University's Centre for China studies (*Guoqing Yanjiusuo*), with which Hu Angang and Kang Xiaoguang are associated, also deserves some attention. In the 1990s, while Hu Angang successively held various positions in foreign universities, this economist realised that sinology was actually more developed abroad than in China, both in terms of theoretical paradigms and of empirical research. It convinced him that China should become the new centre of China studies, which would guarantee its 'authentic right to speak' (*huayu quan*). In 2000, therefore, he founded the China Studies Centre he still runs. The Centre rapidly became an influential think tank and Hu has written and edited more than 900 reports (*guoqing baogao*) which mainly circulate among provincial leaders, ministers and top leaders. According to Cheng Li, 'the centre's policy reports have become one of the best-known sources of policy analysis for the Chinese government'. Between 2007 and 2010, 37 reports were submitted to the State Council (*guowuyuan*) and were commented on by senior leaders 39 times.[47] For instance, the Centre issued more than 30 reports during the 2003 SARS epidemic. They provided policy recommendations on media coverage, public opinion, foreign reactions, health budget, the impact of the crisis on the economy and tourism and so on. Hu Angang was personally invited to take part in two discussions organised by the State Council and chaired by Wen Jiabao. Moreover, the report he drafted in 2004 on insecurity in health (*jiankang bu'anquan*), which he considered the most daunting challenge for the safety and development of the country,[48] received extensive media coverage. Some of Hu Angang's proposals led to public policies.[49] His repeated calls since 1988 for adopting a healthy and efficient energy policy and a green GDP growth indicator (*lüse GDP*)[50] were undoubtedly influential, even though they led to official policy change only from 2005 on and though he was far from the only advocate of such reforms. Moreover, his joint call for fiscal reform with Wang Shaoguang took only a year to be implemented (*see* page 101). In 1994, with Wang and Kang Xiaoguang,

---

47. Li, C. 'Introduction', in Hu Angang, *China in 2020*, pp. xvii and xxiv.

48. Hu, A. *Toushi SARS: Jiankang Yu Fazhan* (*Perspective on SARS: Health and Development*), Beijing: Qinghua Daxue Chubanshe, 2003; Hu, A. 'Zhongguo renlei buanquan de zuida tiaozhan–jiankang buanquan' ('Health insecurity: the greatest challenge for China's safety'), *Guoqing Baogao* 653, December 10, 2004.

49. Li, C. 'Introduction', in Hu, A. *China in 2020*, pp. xxv–xxvi.

50. Hu, A. 'Shishi lüse fazhan zhanlüe shi zhongguo de bixuan zhi lu'), *Lü ye* (*Green Leaf*) 6(15) 2003, published in English as 'Implementing a green development strategy is the only option for China', available online at http://www.chinadialogue.net/article/show/single/en/134-Green-development-the-inevitable-choice-for-China-part-one (last accessed 14 November 2014). Hu, A. 'Zhongguo: lüse fazhan yu lüse GDP (1970–2001)' ('China: green development and green GDP (1970–2001)'), *Zhongguo Kexue Jijin* (*Chinese Science Foundation Bulletin*) 2, 2005.

he pointed out the risks of authorising the Chinese army to boost its income by commercial activities. A reform was finally enforced in 1998. In 1999, the Go West policy was launched after Hu and Wang published policy recommendations in a 1995 report. The list of his interventions is still longer as Hu Angang also played some role in the adoption of an employment-centred economic development policy, the abolition of agricultural taxes, the reinforced health system and so on.

The example of Hu and his think tank is in no way representative of all Chinese researchers and think tanks. It is, nonetheless, a particularly enlightening case for understanding how a small number of researchers position themselves. They are close to power but independent, 'on the other side of the fence' but ready to cross over it at any time. Hu belongs to the group of academics who could have crossed over permanently if they had accepted official functions but who instead cherish the balance they have found between the status and image of an independent scholar and privileged access to decision-makers.

Hu Angang's case differs from Wang Huning's or Cao Jianming's, political scientists who opted for a political career when they returned from the United States.[51] Wang Huning has been credited with Jiang Zemin's theory of the Three Represents. He then became Hu Jintao's adviser and entered the Politburo in 2007, with seven other 'rising stars' also holding social sciences degrees (Xi Jinping and Li Yuanchao in law; Li Keqiang in economics; Wang Qishan in history; Wang Yang in management; Bo Xilai in journalism; Ling Jihua in business management; and Wang Huning in political science). Hu's case also differs from Yu Keping and Zhu Guanglei, who combine academic and official positions.

Different profiles can therefore be found within Chinese think tanks, depending on the political positions of researchers. However, one feature researchers have in common is that they have all spent long periods of time in major Anglo-American universities, which allows think tanks to foster connections between the Chinese government and international academia as well as with Chinese intellectuals. It also confers more legitimacy on Chinese leaders and the policies they decide upon. He Zengke, who works with Yu Keping, distinguishes two levels of influence among researchers in his think tank:

The first level is that of discourse. To give an example, my colleagues and I introduced the concept of civil society [*gongmin shehui*] in China in 1993,

---

51. Wang Huning is a former neo-conservative political scientist of Fudan University, who was an invited scholar at Oxford, UC Berkeley and the University of Michigan and Director of the Policy Research Office of the Central Committee from 2002 and is now a member of the Central Committee. Cao Jianming, who was an invited scholar at San Francisco State University and Gente University in Belgium, has become the Procurator-General of the Supreme People's Procuratorate. Both scholars played a big role by Jiang Zemin's side in domains such as ideological evolution, tensions with Taiwan and legal issues to be solved when China entered the WTO. (Kuhn, R. *How China's Leaders Think: The inside story of China's reform and what this means for the future*, Singapore: John Wiley and Sons, 2009, p. 108; David Shambaugh, *China's Communist Party: Atrophy and adaptation*, Berkeley, CA: University of California Press, 2009, p. 111).

which was quite early. We also introduced the concepts of governance and good governance, and human rights. In the beginning, these concepts had nothing to do with official language or ideology. Now, they are part and parcel of official discourse. They have been officially accepted. From that point of view, academic discourse undeniably has a direct influence on political development. We now realise that all the research we have conducted so far has had an impact. The second level is that of public policy. Have our proposals been accepted by leaders? We must acknowledge that our influence is lesser in that regard. Why is that? It is probable that for the time being, economists have the most influence on Chinese leaders. For instance, if economists suggest interest rates should be raised or lowered, leaders are likely to attentively listen to what they have to say. To be honest, I think public policy is mostly beyond the control of political scientists. I would like to mention an example directly related to my experience: with my colleagues, we have called for years for a reform extending village elections to higher administrative levels like townships [xiang] and districts [xian]. This has remained nothing more than a suggestion:

He Zengke here qualifies the influence of think tanks on the political decision-making process in China. He explains that the field of expertise of researchers is more decisive than their belonging to think tanks as far as political impact is concerned.

Specific intellectuals

Scientific experts or 'specific intellectuals' conceptualised by Michel Foucault as opposed to 'total intellectuals' such as Camus, Sartre and Mirbeau, claim to have specific skills and expertise that they put to use in service of their political commitment.[52] As already mentioned, the specific skills of Chinese economists, legal specialists and sociologists are the most valuable to the government, economic elites and public opinion. It should be noted that Chinese scholars, who tend to be quite elitist, are quite remote from the strict definition Foucault gives of the specialist, who allows people to see (*donne à voir*) but has completely given up the role of advisor of the prince, or of the people, for that matter. Peking University economist Yao Yang, on the contrary, highlights Chinese scholars' explicit quest for influence and predicts that political scientists will soon hold greater sway:

The context is such that the government is mainly concerned with economic issues. Besides [...], our government produces a lot but redistributes little. And

---

52. Foucault, M. 'La fonction politique de l'intellectuel', *Dits et écrits II, 1976–1988*, Paris: Gallimard, 2001, p. 109, *See also* Mouchard, D. 'Intellectuel spécifique', in Fillieule, O., Mathieu, L. and Péchu, C. (eds) *Dictionnaire des mouvements sociaux*, Paris: Presses de Sciences Po, 2009 and Fassin, E. '"L'intellectuel spécifique" et le PaCS: politiques des savoirs', *Mouvements* 7, January–February 2000, pp. 68–76.

when little is redistributed, there is no great need for political scientists' advice. However, when a state redistributes a lot, it needs political scientists to guide it and tell it how to do so. Redistribution is currently very limited. A great part of the budget is devoted to the bailout of the economy. This is the reason why the government, which hopes for profitable investments, is particularly attentive to the suggestions economists make. However, this situation will not last forever. The government is undergoing a transition. Leaders themselves have started to claim that they now know how to manage the economy and that the next step consists in managing society. The role of sociologists and political scientists will therefore be reinforced. Xi Jinping and Li Keqiang have respectively studied politics, economics and law. This means that their way of governing could be very different from the previous leaders, who were engineers. I am looking forward to seeing what they will do. We should watch them closely because they were trained in social sciences. I am looking forward to seeing how they reflect on the current society. We have a very exciting future ahead of us. The only thing I know for sure, is that there won't be as many projects. Gone projects 985 and 211.[53] I anticipate the end of projects, whom engineers cherished so much.

The method adopted by Chinese intellectuals mainly consists in putting a message in a bottle, even if the practice of restricted (*neibu*) circulation through connections has not disappeared. They throw their proposals into the market of ideas with the hope of convincing and having an impact:

All scholars hope their research can influence the government. [...] In the academic and intellectual spheres, when somebody writes an article, the government reads it. The government is truly interested in what scholars say. Let us take the example of the government's assessment of the potentiality of a second economic downturn. In fact, this idea is quite widespread. This is a point of view economists share. The government refers to the economists' suggestions that the American recovery may only be temporary and that the United States face a new downturn. The government's policy is decided on the basis of academic research. However, it is virtually impossible to precisely identify which researcher has specifically influenced the government. The reason the government has adopted such an idea is that 60 to 70 per cent of economists defend it. It follows academics' mainstream suggestions. If many people say the same thing, the government pays attention. For instance, when we all raised the issue of the *hukou* system,[54] and the issue of demographic control, the government resultantly decided to reform them. Scholars have a voice.

---

53. These are two government projects aiming at transforming Chinese top universities into world-class universities. For further details, *see* http://www.chinaeducenter.com/en/cedu/ceduproject211.php (last accessed 14 November 2014).

54. The *hukou* is a family residential permit delivered by the Chinese government. All the Chinese have a *hukou* attached to their residence. Even though it is less crucial than it used to be, it still determines access to education, health care and public services.

Given the growing influence of public opinion on political decision-making and the frustrations of specific intellectuals in terms of direct impact, they nowadays try to influence their students and society in general. Li Qiang deplores the still limited impact of political scientists, beyond their role in administrative reform:

> We are not often called up to take part in the decision-making process. We mainly have an impact on students and public opinion. We have political influence because some of our ideas are crucial, even though they are not directly implemented. We have a global impact on society, but our lesser political influence is due to the fact that some questions cannot be discussed entirely freely. We can nonetheless discuss issues with great leeway. [...] To mention administrative reforms, Chinese political scientists regularly present their analyses on some issues and make reform proposals. For the reasons mentioned above, we are not capable, as an academic discipline, to fully meet the expectations of society and solve issues. [...] In that sense, political scientists are neither so useful nor is society ready to listen to them. [...] But the administrative reform we actively take part in proves to be an immense contribution. Besides, as far as the economy is concerned, theoretical discussions on social justice are a major contribution. They have had an impact on policies. But we must acknowledge that our influence is not sufficient enough.

Given the growing influence of public opinion on political decision-making and academics' frustrated aspirations to have direct influence, most of all, specific intellectuals nowadays endeavour to influence their students and society in general.

Some researchers do not satisfy themselves with the role of experts in China's economic and administrative reform which their specific knowledge confers on them. They strive to make their political proposals heard as well.

Political intellectuals

The difference between those I call political intellectuals and specific intellectuals is the voluntarist strategy of influence-seeking that the former opt for. They are also closer to the conception of public intellectuals, since they are active outside their area of expertise in making larger political proposals. This positioning does not come without risk because these reform proposals often stem from criticism of a specific policy or of the current political orientation. But the discourse of these intellectuals can seem quite confusing at first sight: indeed, they tend to introduce themselves as politically committed scholars, patriots who worry about their country and their fellow citizens, so as to prove that their critical approach is both healthy and legitimate. Besides, they willingly accept spontaneous co-optation if it is a one-time and short-term experience, which leads many observers to question their independence. Some scholars, like Wang Shaoguang and Hu Angang in the 1990s, having gained confidence from the decisive contribution to policy their research had made in the past, spontaneously intervened in policy-discussions among decision-makers and mobilised their inside networks (of connections and publications) so as to regain traction.

Some academics bid for national research projects; exploiting leaders' political failures and their fears related to stability and legitimacy, they put forward reforms that they claim are more relevant and efficient. As a result, despite dull article headlines and book titles explicitly deriving from officially controlled calls for bids (for example: building a harmonious society; reviewing 30 years of the Open and Reform policy; building a Chinese model of development; good governance; and democratisation with Chinese characteristics), the reader may come across vehement criticism and bold proposals for political reform.

Wang Shaoguang's trajectory illustrates this type of commitment perfectly. In a major article, which was labelled 'neo-conservative' but which signalled the beginning of the Chinese New Left,[55] Wang deplored the mighty power of local governments, who could pursue vested interests and harm national coherence and justice. He called for establishing a strong democratic government able to fulfil three main tasks: economic growth; social justice; and environmental balance. According to him, a modern state should be able to allocate and redistribute resources and maintain stability. Otherwise, the state loses its legitimacy.

At our first meeting, Wang explained how he came to elaborate his state-reform proposal. After reading law at Peking University and political science at Cornell, where he completed a PhD, he was recruited by Wuhan University. He accepted the job on June 4 1989, the exact day the repression of the student movement began, which made him give up his plans to go back to China. He taught for a year at Cornell and ten in Yale's political science department. With his colleagues, he elaborated a 500-day transition plan for Russia; and he visited the country in 1990 and 1991 to help the Russians set up a democratic system and a market economy. When he discovered the actual situation, which appeared even worse than during the worst hours of the Cultural Revolution and Great Leap Forward, he was led to focus on the issue of state capacity and democratic state-building. To Wang's mind, analysing a country's democratisation only through institutionalised elections is pointless. The efficiency and capacity of state institutions constitute an essential condition for democratisation. He is therefore considered as a conservative scholar calling for a strong state to get reforms underway. The objective of his constant

55. Wang, S. 'Jianli yige qiang youli de minzhu guojia–taolun "zhengquan xingshi" yu "guojia nengli" de qubie' ('Building a strong democratic state: regime types and state capacity'), *Contemporary China Research Center* 4, February 1991; Gan, Y. 'Zhongguo ziyou zuopai de youlai' ('Origins of the Chinese New Left'), Conference of 28–9 September 2000 at Hong-Kong University http://www.douban.com/group/topic/1601360/ (last accessed 14 November 2014). Fang, N. 'Yingxiang dangdai Zhongguo de sanda shehui sichao' ('The three main ideological tendencies in contemporary China'), *Fudan Political Review* 4, 2006.

criticism and reform proposals has been to build a sustainable, stable, fair and equitable democratic regime.[56]

After reading Wang's articles on state capacity in the early 1990s, economist Hu Angang, then a postdoc at Yale, collaborated with Wang on a report. Hu mobilised his connections and organised a press conference in his work unit, the Academy of Social Sciences. Their aim was to make an impact on government policy and introduce their theory of democratic transition through strengthening and improving public institutions, so as to avoid democratisation characterised by blind abolition of authority. They both forcefully criticised the process that Mao Zedong launched to fight against bureaucratism and that Deng Xiaoping continued in order to put an end to the planned economy and introduce the free market. The report rejected de-regulating neo-classical economic theory, according to which a free market and economic growth would naturally lead to reduction of inequalities in regional revenues. They described the unfair imbalance between regions in detail and called for public policies designed to solve these problems. They also warned against the conception of a totalitarian, monolithic state and explained that the central state's withdrawal from regions, which made it dependent on local governments to collect taxes, only strengthened governments at lower levels. The report was immediately published in various internal (neibu)[57] journals. The Director of the research institute of the Finance Ministry, who was invited to the press conference, introduced the report to the Minister, who invited the two scholars to present it in person. According to Wang Shaoguang, who is aware of the instrumental and justificatory role that researchers can play for politicians, the ministry's staff had been devising a fiscal reform since 1986 and were looking for a trigger for launching it, which may explain the report's impact. The report underscored the urgency of the situation in tones calculated to alarm officials, whereas the ministry had only approached fiscal reform from a technical perspective and was finding it difficult to silence internal opposition to it. The report, which highlighted the political significance of the reform, enabled the process to speed up. The reform setting up the way central and local governments shared fiscal revenues was launched in 1994 and was the first step in institutionalising financial relations between central and local governments so as to regulate complex fiscal policies and put an end to endless negotiations

---

56. Wang, S. 'Jianli yi ge qiang youlide minzhu guojia: yu Wang Shaoguang de duihua' ('Building a strong democratic state: a dialogue with Wang Shaoguang'), in Ma, Y. *Zhanlue Gaodu: Zhongguo sixiangjie fangtan lu (Strategic Distance: Discussions with the Chinese intellectual world)*, Beijing: Sanlian Shudian, 2008; Hu, A. Wang, S. Zhou, J. (eds) *Dierci Zhuanxing: Guojia zhidu jianshe (The Second Transformation: State-building)*, Beijing: Tsinghua Editions, 2009; Wang, S. *Minzhu Sijiang (Four Lessons On Democracy)*, Beijing: Sanlian 2008.

57. *Neibu* publications are sealed so as to signify that their circulation is restructed, mostly to senior cadres (*lingdao ganbu cankao*). Access to domestic policy or social issues can be restricted. It is easier to publish in *neibu* publications than in mass publications. They are less subject to censorship due to their select readership and articles are published more rapidly. Articles which could harm the Party or the government's image or compromise social stability and unity are more likely to be published in *neibu* than in traditional media.

between various levels of governance.[58] The publication of the *Report on State Capacity*[59] constitutes a landmark for the political doctrine advocating a strong central government.

Wang Shaoguang's political economy and Hu Angang's economics research and collaboration led them to focus on growing regional inequalities. *The Political Economy of Uneven Development: The case of China* is a crucial report because, at that time, most scholars and political leaders were convinced that the gap between regions was reducing.[60] The two scholars showed, on the contrary, that inequalities had started to grow from 1990 on and voiced their concern about this. The idea that coastal regions could and must develop first was then the consensus. The two scholars criticised Deng Xiaoping's proposal to 'let a few people get rich first' (*rang yibufen ren xian fuqilai*) and described the political consequences of the growing gap between eastern and western regions, all the more serious as the West was mainly populated with national minorities.[61] In September 1995, the Fifth Plenary Session of the Central Committee reversed its regional policy favouring coastal areas so as to provide better support and investment to the economic development of central and western China. A few years after the publication of the three books Wang and Hu devoted to the issue, the government launched the Go West policy (*xibu da kaifa*) in 1999.[62]

In the 1990s, Wang ceaselessly publicised his concerns, seeking to compel the government to react. Once the redistribution issue was back on the political agenda, he focused on the supervision of resource spending. He wrote on budget expectations and published an essay entitled 'Lessons from the Progressive Era in the US',[63] in which he argued that there could not be a full democracy without a budget because the way the state functions could not then be supervised. He suggested that the first step for any political reform should be introducing budgetary transparency. The article attracted the attention of the Deputy Premier and the Finance Minister, who quoted him at a conference

---

58. Tang, T. 'Hu Wen's efforts to strengthen governance: regulating central–local relations', *East Asian Institute Background Brief No. 356*, 6 November 2007, available online at http://www.eai. nus.edu.sg/BB356.pdf (last accessed 14 November 2014).

59. Hu, A. and Wang, S. *Zhongguo Guojia Nengli Yanjiu Baogao (Report on State Capacity)*, Hong Kong: Oxford University Press, 1994; *The Chinese Economy in Crisis: State capacity and tax reform*, Armonk, New York: East Gate Books, M. E. Sharpe, 2001.

60. Jeffrey Sachs (Harvard) is said to rely on outdated data collected up to 1990 and publishes 'Trends in Regional Inequality in China', in collaboration with Tianlun, J. and Warner, A. NBER *Working Paper Series* no. 5412, January 1996, and *China Economic Review* 7(1), 1996, pp. 1–21.

61. Hu, A. and Wang, S. *Bupingdeng Fazhan De Zhengzhijingjixue*, Beijing: Beijing Jihua Chubanshe, 2000; *The Political Economy of Uneven Development: The case of China*, Armonk, NY: M. E. Sharpe, 1999.

62. This policy mainly encouraged investments in China's western regions through developing infrastructures and communication with neighbouring countries and between various regions.

63. Wang, S. 'Meiguo 'jinbushidai' de qishi' ('Lessons from the Progressive Era in the US'), *Dushu* 8, 2001.

on fiscal issues. He then asked Wang to edit a book on the issue.[64] According to Wang, since 2000, when there was no such thing as a budget, advances have been swift.

Wang Shaoguang explicitly recognises that his research is intimately guided by his perception of Chinese policy and his desire to impact the orientation of reform.[65] His research until the 2000s was therefore devoted to demonstrating the connection between social justice and instability;[66] subsequently, official discourse and policies seemed to address his concerns and steer to the left. Wang cannot be credited with a direct role in this new orientation but his reports and critical publications as a consultant for the Chinese government – and also international institutions such as the UN and the World Bank – have undoubtedly contributed to internal debates and to reassessment of the priorities of the reform.[67] His more recent publications reflect the Hu-Wen policy re-orientation. They are less critical and rather endeavour to encourage the recently launched social policy.[68] In 'China's health system: from crisis to opportunity',[69] Wang tries to escape what he calls the myth of economic growth and the market economy. Economic growth is only a means to an end: social justice. The market cannot improve the efficiency of the Chinese healthcare system; on the contrary. Wang describes the great waste which took place when healthcare opened to the market economy. General statistics on the level of equipment of hospitals are very good but, as a matter of fact, major cities are so over-equipped that very costly material tends to be under-used while rural areas are deprived of basic medical equipment. Wang refers to Hu Angang's 'One Country, Four Worlds' further discussed in Chapter Four of this book, to underline inequalities.[70] He underscores the gap between cities and the countryside. In 1998, each urbanite received about 130 yuan in government subsidies for medical care while rural dwellers received only 10.7 yuan, in spite of the government discourse in the

64. Wang, S. *Meiguo 'Jinbushidai' De Qishi* (*Lessons from the Progressive Era in the US*), Beijing: Public Finance Press, 2002.

65. Frenkiel, E. 'Political change and democracy in China. An interview with Wang Shaoguang', *La Vie des Idées*, 15 July 2009, available online at http://laviedesidees.fr/Political-change-and-democracy-in.html (last accessed 14 November 2014).

66. His most representative articles can be found in Wang Shaoguang, *Anbangzhidao: Guojia Zhuanliede Mubiao Yu Tujing*, Beijing: Sanlian Shudian, 2007.

67. Ma, Y. 'HuWen gaige: xin de gongshi xin de zouxiang' ('Hu Jintao and Wen Jiabao's reform: new consensus, new reform'), *Fenghuang Zhoukan* (*Phoenix Review*), April 2007.

68. Wang, S. 'Dazhuanxing: 1980 niandai yilai zhongguo de shuangxiang yun', *Zhongguo Shehui Keshui* 1, 2008; published in English as 'The great transformation: the double movement in China', *Boundary 2*, 35(2), Summer 2008, pp. 15–47; Wang, S. 'Xuexi jizhi yu sheying nengli: Zhongguo nongcun hezuo yiliao tizhi bianqian de qishi', *Zhongguo Shehui Kexue* (*Academy of Social Sciences Journal*) 6, 2008; published in English as 'Adapting by learning: the evolution of China's rural health care financing', *Modern China* 35(4), 2009, pp. 370–404.

69. Wang, S. 'Zhongguo gonggong weisheng de weiji yu zhuanji', *Bijiao* (*Comparative Economics, Sociology and Politics Review*) 7, 2003; published in English as 'China's health system: from crisis to opportunity', *The Yale–China Health Journal* 3, pp. 1–47.

70. Hu, A. *Diqu yu fazhan: xibu kaifa xinzhanlüe*, Beijing: Zhongguo Jihua Chubanshe, 2001.

1990s on the return of the Cooperative Medical System Mao set up 1965. Wang describes the devastating effect of applying principles of efficiency and profit to the medical domain: one third of patients go without healthcare lest they should be unable to pay hospital fees. A veritable cycle of poverty deriving from disease has re-emerged in China. Opening to the market has not led to greater efficiency, since the rate of bed-occupation has not reached 60 per cent in Chinese hospitals, even though the countryside lacks hospital beds. Government policy has, however, evolved since the SARS epidemics of 2003, which made leaders aware of the massive economic loss triggered by sanitary crises hitting major cities as a result of interaction between the rural and urban populations. Wang Shaoguang also reminds his audience that access to healthcare is a basic human right and that the market is unable to regulate the healthcare system in so far as the unequal access to information between doctors and patients leads to deceit and corruption.

In another article that is fairly representative of his research, 'Regulating death in coalmines: changing mode of governance in China',[71] Wang Shaoguang associates the greater attention given to mine incidents partly with more frequent media coverage (due to the more open regime and press and the way the government uses the press to put pressure on the managers of dangerous mines); and partly to the incompetence of local governments, which are supposed to regulate small-scale mines but sacrifice safety rules to the economic interest of their constituency and sometimes to their own personal interests. Work inspections were, until a recent date, very uncommon and quite inefficient under the oversight of local governments. The scholar describes how the regulation system that emerged in the mid 1990s had matured by 2004. New laws, the State Council's oversight of institutions responsible for working conditions, the institutionalisation of procedures and the rationalisation of small mines (more than 60,000 were shut down between 1997 and 2004) and better enforcement of laws and sanctions have finally made an impact. Indeed, a regime defining itself as modern needs to regulate and protect individuals on a large scale. As detailed in the final chapter of this book, Wang Shaoguang refers to Karl Polanyi's theory that a de-regulated market economy can lead to the worst situation,[72] with the aim of introducing alternative western theories to contest simplistic interpretations of liberal theories such as Hayek's.[73]

We should note that political intellectuals, in the sense that they accept the rules of game as they are imposed by the Party, take up the official discourse and undertake a strategic, Machiavellian rapprochement with power. They tend to be

71. Wang, S. 'Meikuang anquan shengchan jianguan: zhongguo zhili moshi de zhuanbian', *Bijiao* 13, 2004; published in English as 'Regulating death at coalmines: changing mode of governance in China', *Journal of Contemporary China* 15(46), 2006, pp. 1–30.

72. Polanyi, K. *The Great Transformation: The political and economic origins of our time*, Boston, MA: Beacon Press, 1944.

73. Pankaj, P. 'China's New Left calls for a social alternative', *International Herald Tribune*, 13 October 2006. In the following article, Wang Shaoguang criticises the concept of civil society: 'Jinqian yu ziyou: shichang shehui mianlin de liang nan jingdi', *Kaifang Shibao*, March 2002; published in English as 'Money and autonomy: patterns of civil society finance and their implications', *Studies in Comparative International Development* (SCID) 40(4), 2006, pp. 3–29.

less radically opposed to government and less repressed by it than liberals, who rather pose as media intellectuals or committed professors who stand more at a distance from power.

Media intellectuals

Other forms of political commitment are defined by their greater distance from power. Media intellectuals and committed professors stand further away from the fence, in Abélès' metaphor. Unlike researchers also holding political positions in some think tanks and universities, and specific and political intellectuals, they do not try to have a direct impact on leaders or policies. Media intellectuals address public opinion above all. A liberal Guangzhou press group offered a ranking of 'the most influential intellectuals' in 2004, assessing their popularity in public opinion. The academics who appear in the rankings, amid artists, writers, journalists or lawyers, are mostly liberal figures like Liu Junning, Xu Youyu, Xu Jilin, Zhu Xueqin and Qin Hui, as well as a great number of famous liberal economists.[74] Another ranking based on different criteria was published in 2007 and it is interesting to compare its results. It identifies the most politically influential figures and claims that Wang Shaoguang then had more influence than his university roommate and Prime-Minister-to-be Li Keqiang. He was followed by Wang Hui, and Hu Angang, who was deemed more influential than Xi Jinping. The earlier generation of leaders led the ranking, followed by some artists and Wang Huning, whose influence was deemed greater than Jiang Zemin's.[75] Wang Shaoguang was ranked below the official researcher Wang Huning and Zheng Bijian, the ideologue who contributed to devising the concept of 'peaceful rise' (*heping jueqi*). This ranking does not place as much emphasis on liberal thinkers, even though the economist Wu Jinglian (nicknamed 'Wu *Shichang*' or 'Market Wu') and the journalist Hu Shuli are ranked. The following explanations given by Xu Youyu allow us to understand how liberals have been led to focus on society rather than leaders:

> I don't express my ideas for the government or the Party but for the Chinese, and for students in particular. I think that even if it does not change China's situation directly, it is still very relevant. Due to traditional Chinese thinking, most scholars try to have an impact. I have personally totally given up. I think that having an impact on higher levels, if it remains possible, is absolutely crucial. But it has become impossible. This is why I now focus on lower levels. We are many to think this way. It is hopeless to try to have an impact on leaders.

---

74. Mao Yushi, Wu Jinglian, Wen Tiejun, Zhang Wuchang, Wang Dingding can be found in the September 2004 *Nanfang Renwu Zhoukan* (*Southern People Weekly*), a popular Guangdong liberal magazine.

75. This ranking is available on the following webpage: http://www.opendemocracy.net/home/chinapower/china.jsp (last accessed 14 November 2014).

According to Xu Youyu, liberals have not chosen to keep their distance from power. They have had no choice. They do not condemn the practice of involvement with power as such but believe it is hopeless as far as the current Chinese leaders are concerned. The influence that liberals can have on political elites can only be as a result of the great popularity of liberal ideas in Chinese society and among Party members.[76] Some retired cadres, like Li Rui, Hu Jiwei, Zhu Houze and He Jiaodong, have indeed regulalrly expressed their support for more liberal reforms.

According to Kang Xiaoguang, liberalism and the New Left are two popular movements that influence different social classes:

> Liberals mostly influence Party cadres, capitalists and intellectuals while the New Left influences some cadres, workers and peasants. For the time being, Confucianism is less impactful. However, from a more dynamic point of view, liberalism is losing ground. It used to be the most popular ideology in the 1980s and it has continuously lost traction since the 1990s, whereas Confucianism, our native traditional culture, is becoming more attractive, especially since the late 1990s. A survey would confirm that liberalism is still the most widespread ideology. However, its slowing pace should be taken into account. The article of one of the most influential liberals, Yu Keping, is evidence of this phenomenon: he felt constrained to write a book entitled *Democracy Is a Good Thing*. From the perspective of the liberals, this is absolutely tragic. It means that it has become necessary to explain, justify and prove that democracy is a good thing. It has become a slogan. The era when it was not even necessary to explain why democracy was a good thing is over. The idea no longer is consensual.

The political regime, its workings and Chinese society have evolved greatly and this indirect influence strategy is now seen by many as the most effective. New-Left scholar Wang Shaoguang is also aware of this tendency, which he has theorised,[77] and he has recently rather become a media intellectual. His trajectory is evidence of the idea that this typology is not exclusive and that intellectuals, depending on the stage of their careers, can navigate from one type of public intervention to the other and also combine them:

> Many researchers, me included, were wrong about the way to influence the decision-making process. Many of us believed that it was easier to mobilise hidden channels to communicate with leaders and to impact their decisions. In the 1990s, I used to believe that. But now I think that what matters is to influence

---

76. Chen, Y. 'Liberalism in contemporary China: ten years after its "resurface"', *Journal of Contemporary China* 17(55), May 2008, pp. 383–400 and Feng Chongyi, 'The Chinese liberal camp in Post-June 4th China', *China Perspective,* 2, 2009, available online at http://chinaperspectives.revues.org/4803 (last accessed 14 November 2014). Liu Dong explained when we met a second time in June 2005 that among political philosophy books he had published, John Rawls' *Political Liberalism* was the best-selling translation and had been reissued twice. According to him, the title of this difficult book as well as the popularity of liberalism in China can explain its popularity.

77. Wang, S. 'Changing models of China's policy agenda setting'.

public opinion. When I am eager to have some impact on the orientation the country is taking, I talk to the public. When you discuss inequalities in the health system, people realise that inequalities exist and start complaining and pressurising the decision-making process. This is manifest. In an article, I offer to compare recently implemented reforms with discussions taking place on the web a few years ago. A connection can be established. A few years ago, web-users discussed the health system, and it has recently been reformed. We discussed issues related to the education system and some measures have been undertaken. We discussed the accommodation issue and the accommodation policy was modified in 2006. Public opinion has visibly gained influence over the years. This is the reason why I now prefer to publish my research in newspapers, magazines and reviews which are accessible to all rather than in restricted publications. They seem less relevant and I am almost certain leaders no longer have the time to read these.

The growing importance of public opinion for leaders, who want to be seen as more responsive to it so as to guarantee their legitimacy, transforms scholars' strategies of political commitment and intervention, which the more liberal Shanghai historian Xu Jilin confirms here:

Researchers can have some impact on political decision-making but it should not be overemphasised because leaders are open to some types of proposals experts make, but they are themselves checked by their own interests and those of some groups. As a result, experts have an undeniable influence but it is limited. Personally, I have hardly ever been invited to discuss with leaders, and I usually refuse to do so. I don't think it is my responsibility to do so. My true mission lies elsewhere: I must influence public opinion, but not political leaders. Having an impact on public opinion, at least an impact on its ideas. I am convinced to be a member of the generation of the Enlightenment. I think that ideas are extremely important because history comes down to choices and initiatives taken by men and all driven by ideas. These choices are conditioned by some conceptions. As a result, I have never focused on short-term national policy imperatives such as facing the financial crisis and so on. I mainly focus on the elites' point of view and on China's fate in 10 or 20 years. Current China's battlefield is no longer the political but the cultural field.

The difference between these media intellectuals, trying to have an impact on public opinion with the explicit aim of having an influence on the political orientation of the regime, and politically-committed professors is quite nebulous.

Politically committed professors

What makes politically committed professors stand out is mainly their reluctance to use publications and interviews in the general media to make an impact on society. These intellectuals mainly count on their charisma to influence their students and peers. University professors like Liu Dong also count on the influence they can have on the new generation of leaders. It is very interesting to notice how contradictory their claim to do 'pure research', associated with their eagerness to influence leaders, is:

> The benefit of the long term is that a scholar can express himself relatively freely and it is not necessary to directly address leaders [as he trains the next generation]. The downside is that the status of a researcher is weak. The government does not give him great responsibilities. [...] On the other hand, I think there are two categories of intellectuals in the world. Those who constantly talk to government and political elites [and thinkers]. This happens. At least they can take part in operations. For instance, I don't know who inspired Hu Jintao's idea of social harmony but it is much preferable to class struggle. It is similar as regards environment policy. Scholars have obviously given the President these ideas. Personally, this is not what I am interested in. [...] I try to avoid direct contact with power but I have translated and written many books, given many conferences and influenced a whole generation of students, who are going to get ahead. I hope this could help change things. [...] Alexander the Great or Napoleon do not matter as much as Voltaire and Rousseau. Chinese intellectuals are far from perfect but there are a few exceptions. Qin Hui, for instance, constantly criticises politics. They are not many like him. I personally do not dare. I have a research institute, book collections, an academic journal, and three state-funded positions as university professor. They help me reach a higher objective. Indeed, everyone can criticise, and you teach no one anything when you do so. You can claim that we need a multi-party system, a democracy. Everybody knows it and repeating it is pointless. To my mind, the objective is to build the framework of the next culture. The greatest French or German thinkers, like Kant, Hegel or Heidegger, could never have reached such an influence if they had spent their days in the emperor's office.

Liu Dong expresses great hope of seeing ideas produced by academics taken up on the long term and on a large scale. With a similar mindset, and with as many contradictions, Deng Zhenglai and Xu Jilin minimise the importance of pragmatic research and insist on how crucial fundamental research and thorough academic works are to 'change the leaders' way of thinking' and guide the long-term evolution of the country:

> **Xu Jilin**: Too many people focus on political decisions and try to help the political decision-making process while too few devote themselves to abstract research, so that Chinese reform has lost the values which used to guide it. It lacks deep and large-scale reflection. This is related to the fact that the Chinese and Chinese intellectuals used to be influenced by a very pragmatic government tradition which valued practice. Theoretical production from the part of Chinese intellectuals is rather limited. But today, what matters is fundamental research.

Deng Zhenglai: The direction China takes is hard to guess. It ceaselessly changes and adapts without a final definition of its orientation. It experiments, errs and tries something else. I think this is a positive thing. Chinese people are overall satisfied and the government needs people's support. It cannot really follow one theoretical orientation to its end. The only certainties are the resilience of the one-party system and the attempts to fight against corruption, ensure a stable economic development, as well as security and order in the country. This is already something for the Chinese people. We may wish the development of political philosophy in China bears fruit in the long run if leaders read our publications. The issue is not to give up political science or research on politics, but to change the leaders' mind-set. Some academics strive to change policies. They yearn for direct influence on political change, but researchers like me rather try to change the mind-sets of political leaders and young generations. I personally try to make them know about the Chinese people's wisdom. Discovering this Chinese political wisdom again rather than copying the western model is crucial.

Deng Zhenglai, who recently passed away, tried, like Liu Dong and Xu Jilin, to distinguish himself from media intellectuals as well as from other liberals – like Zhu Xueqin, Qin Hui, Liu Junning and Xu Youyu – whose role in spreading liberal ideas he acknowledged but whom he did not find rigorous enough from a theoretical point of view:

These intellectuals who you refer to are all my friends, but I don't think they focus on theory. China needs people like them. But these passionate people are not interested in theory. Some things are not very convincing. They are slogans. I see them more as intellectuals than as scholars. I get along with both left and right because I do something different. They all think I am a liberal. That's nonsense. I am extremely critical of both liberal intellectuals and the New Left. I am different. I refuse to belong to any clan.

Deng Zhenglai chose a different mode of intervention as a result:

Last year [2009], at the heart of the financial crisis, I published Hayek's work and started a new seminar. People asked me why I did that now that neo-liberalism had collapsed with the credit crunch. I told them that it was exactly the reason why I had to publish that book. On the one hand, at the time of the New Deal, President Roosevelt had relied on Keynesianism. Only Hayek had expressed himself against statism. No one else did. But he was radically opposed to it. In 1974, he was awarded the Nobel Prize. He was an independent researcher following his own ideas. On the other hand, in China, with the financial crisis people have become convinced that this is the end of liberalism and statism is coming back. No independent voice rises against this general consensus. However, academics can only think independently.

They cannot follow collective movements. To each scholar his own convictions and judgements. He or she has to make a stand. This is the reason why I published Hayek's work just then. I wanted to show academia that we have not fully liberated ourselves from the Cultural Revolution's collective movements. We still produce collective discourses. I remain distant from all this.

As already mentioned, committed scholars can opt for different strategies of political influence. These are in no case exclusive but belonging to the liberal camp is bound to put more limits on the array of possibilities scholars can choose from, unless they accept and manage, like Yu Keping and He Zengke, to make their proposals in a moderate way that adapts to the official discourse and aims.

Wang Shaoguang's example shows that committed scholars can opt for various strategies of political influence. They are not exclusive, even though belonging to the liberal camp strongly restricts the array of possibilities, unless scholars accept like Yu Keping and He Zengke to voice their proposals in a moderate way adapted to official discourse and objectives. However, another factor than ideological leaning can intervene: scholars' geographical location. Of course, Beijing scholars are closer to power and have more opportunities to meet central leaders. Besides, they are more in touch with politics, are more interested in politics and are more concerned with national issues. Their concerns are broader, as Deng Zhenglai explains:

Beijing scholars think China belongs to them while Shanghai scholars are rarely concerned with general issues. They are interested in the Yangzi Delta, in Shanghai, in abroad. Besides, political influence is less strong in Shanghai. Many things happen in Beijing. Anything political takes place in Beijing so scholars there are more reactive. They follow the news on a daily basis and are engrossed in them. Shanghai does not matter to them. Shanghai-based scholars conduct their research more serenely while Beijing scholars are more active. There are benefits in Beijing, but in Shanghai, we can take more distance. Our reactions are more measured. Beijingers know everything that happens but they are too close to events. They are part of what takes place while we enjoy staying apart. In Beijing, it is impossible to avoid meetings and social events. If you turn down an invitation, you are marginalised. In Shanghai, people understand that we can be busy. I am currently very busy writing. Everyone supports me here while in Beijing, people get angry if you turn down invitations. Shanghai is more westernised. People respect each other's privacy more than in Beijing.

According to Xiao Gongqin, another Shanghai scholar, outside Beijing, research is freer. It is easier to conduct thorough research and focus on fundamental subjects than in Beijing:

Shanghai researchers have less opportunity to directly influence the government and be influenced by it. We are freer. Our networks are more limited and connected to our academic position. We are rather tolerant and try to avoid controversy and debates. It might be due to the traditional culture of the city. Shanghai has been influenced by western culture and pluralism for a long time. However, Shanghai intellectuals have focused less and less on political issues because they have less opportunity to take part in politics, contrary to Beijing intellectuals who belong to many networks, are connected to the government in many ways and can easily interact with it. Besides, Shanghai's local government is not interested in this. They would rather not deal with political issues, which they think is a central government prerogative [...] In this peculiar context, Shanghai intellectuals do not focus much on politics but they can conduct thorough research, in a slow and progressive manner. In Beijing, it is extremely uncommon to hear someone say it took him 14 years to write a book.

Beijing academics such as Kang Xiaoguang naturally deem the best scholars are all in Beijing.[78] Yang Guangbin, from People's University, explains why he refused to transfer to Fudan in Shanghai:

Last year, Fudan University asked me to join them. They offered to double my current salary but I finally decided not to go. When you conduct research in political science in China, you had better be located as close as possible to the political centre. This is crucial. Most resources are concentrated in Beijing, but conducting fundamental research is easier outside Beijing. For instance, Xu Yong from Central China Normal University in Wuhan conducts quality research on rural policy and village elections.

Ren Jiantao, whose transfer to People's University is fairly recent, qualifies these differences, which the Open and Reform policy is supposed to have alleviated, even though he acknowledges that 'a scholar's location has a definite impact on the nature and scope of his research':

The difference is not so great because of the Open and Reform policy. It transformed the intellectual field, which parcelled out in opposed kingdoms with their own sphere of influence. Before this policy, talented scholars were roughly all located in Beijing. But after the reform, debates also took place in Shanghai, Wuhan, Guangzhou, Nanjing, Xiamen or Chengdu. All these cities had their own research groups who discussed together and made suggestions. For instance, when the liberals and the New Left publicised their proposals, I was in Guangzhou, which is a liberal bastion where famous liberal newspapers like the *Southern Weekend* or the *Southern Weekly* are published. In Sun Yat-sen University's politics and public administration department, we were a major platform for liberal activities. These issues were discussed simultaneously in Beijing. Beijing often started the discussion and Guangzhou followed. Beijing scholars often say we helped opening up the debate. While the gap between liberals and the New Left was growing deeper in Beijing,

---

78. To the extent that Kang advised me not to waste my time interviewing scholars outside Beijing.

they still all published articles in *Dushu*, and organised conferences together. Guangzhou scholars suddenly declared that the rift between the two sides was too extensive and appearance of unity had become unsustainable. As a result, I would say that scholars outside Beijing focus on the same issues, discuss the same issues and constitute clans. However, differences cannot be denied. Even though I transferred to Beijing only six months ago [in 2009–2010], I have realised that local experience clearly affects the way scholars outside Beijing examine an issue. As far as I am concerned, I am interested in the Guangdong reform, which is rarely the case among Beijing scholars. I precisely consider the Chinese reform through the looking glass of the Guangdong reform, which is the opposite of what is done in Beijing. Scholars discard local policies and only focus on the way central policies evolve. Some analysts consider that the capital breeds imperialist reasonings. Beijing allegedly represents the world and China. The starting point for Beijing scholars is to examine issues affecting the whole country. They therefore dismiss some local experiences in Shanghai, Guangdong or Sichuan. Besides, as it is easier for them to interact with foreign scholars, their concepts and analyses are more easily exported even though Guangdong scholars also benefit from some opportunities offered by long-term co-operation with American or French scholars like Jean-Philippe Béja. However, contrary to a Beijing scholar, a Guangdong scholar does not claim his research indicates new national directions. Beijing scholars consider provincial research only relevant from a local point of view.

Conclusions

To conclude, the research and commitment of Chinese academics are still constrained by the Party and resilient forms of censorship. However, the technocratic and pragmatic nature of the Chinese system as well as the great diversity of viewpoints within political elites make it possible to voice criticisms and suggestions, and to experiment with reform proposals on different scales, among which institutional ones. Chinese academics' involvement in the public sphere, as in the rest of the world, is expected to comply with the standards of rigour, disinterestedness and open-mindedness that academia holds dear. However, Chinese academics' patriotism sets them apart from their western counterparts. They address a public which is not addressed in France or in the United States, the country, and they are still yearning for official recognition. Academics who do not fear losing their independence or are convinced that being closer to power brings them legitimacy and political clout, which makes up for the disruption of their lives as researchers, eventually accept official functions. Within Chinese think tanks, official researchers, specific intellectuals playing the role of experts advising leaders, and political intellectuals like Hu Angang, Kang Xiaoguang and Wang Shaoguang – intellectual originators of policy proposals who could be assimilated to Gérard Noiriel's 'government intellectuals' – can be found. The last two categories of intellectuals have been willing to co-operate actively, but occasionally, with authorities. They have been given some leeway for criticism since their political proposals stem from criticisms of the *status quo* and of certain policies. As to liberals, the liberal critique of the regime is hardly compatible with official discourse and they are, consequently, limited to the last two positions: that of the media intellectual or the politically committed professor, whose political influence is indirect. However, with the rising importance of public opinion in the decision-making process, contrasts between all these different strategies – which some scholars do not hesitate to combine or alternate – are tending to recede. Two factors tend to reduce academics' possible range of actions: their geographical position, especially when far from Beijing, and their ideological leanings. The next chapter analyses the evolution of the Chinese intelligentsia and its relationship to power through various debates, events which deeply marked it and the divisions triggered by these events.

Chapter Four

Assessment of the Reforms and Reawakening of the Intelligentsia

This chapter approaches the overall evolution of the Chinese intelligentsia, with a focus on the academics involved in the debate on political reform. We will discuss the fact that after 1978, intellectuals taking part in the 'New Enlightenment' – a major 1980s movement consisting in liberation of thought and aiming to re-examine existing socialism – supplanted the Old Left, faithful to orthodox Marxist-Leninist and Maoist principles. In the late 1980s, within this modernising intelligentsia, a series of schisms took place. First, neo-authoritarians, advocating economic liberalisation under the care of a strong monopolistic central power, emerged. The 1989 repression and the collapse of the Soviet Union were the main factors leading to a second schism related to emerging nationalism and a desire to prioritise national security. Among Enlightenment intellectuals driven by the principles of universalism and opening to the West, a significant debate took place in the second half of the 1990s between the New Left and those then labelled the Chinese liberals. This progressive fragmentation of the Chinese intellectual sphere was also characterised by a deeper and deeper reflection on the benefits of 'tradition' for China's modernisation. We can observe that this form of introspection among Chinese intellectuals stems from the neo-conservative and nationalist contentions at the turn of the 1990s. This movement then gradually affected the whole intellectual spectrum, from the most conservative to the most liberal intellectuals, and led to the emergence of a third tendency: cultural nationalism. Therefore, while the 1980s constituted an intellectual catching-up phase, when foreign books, theories and concepts were imported, introduced and translated on a massive scale, the 1990s were a turning point: the Chinese intellectual community began to experience the urge to develop its own thinking.

The liberating 1980s: A response to the Cultural Revolution

Deng Xiaoping managed to take power by way of presenting himself skilfully both as Mao's rightful successor and as a reforming leader who had himself suffered from the excesses of Mao's policy and would never let disasters like the Great Leap Forward or the Cultural Revolution happen again. In December 1978, during the Third Plenary Session of the Eleventh Central Committee of the CCP, the leadership adopted economic reform policies labelled the Four Modernisations (of agriculture, industry, national defence and science and technology, in reference to the programme launched by Zhou Enlai in 1975). The decision which was made in this plenary session to speed up the pace of legal reform and to build a modern, industrialised nation through 'socialism with Chinese characteristics' had a direct impact on intellectual life. Indeed, the flourishing cultural and intellectual activity and lively intellectual debates were encouraged by the Open and Reform policy, by the hope the latter triggered after the Cultural Revolution, and by the reopening of social science, political science and law departments in universities (*see* Chapter One), due to the official need for social scientists to advise and guide the Four Modernisations.

Greater academic freedom for the sake of better reform

Hu Yaobang was one of the landmark figures of the liberalisation subsequent to the Cultural Revolution. Locked in a stable for two years and a half during the Cultural Revolution, he returned to favour along with his mentor Deng Xiaoping, on the side of whom he had fought against the Guomindang to establish the authority of the Party in Sichuan and in south-West China. After new purges in 1976, he became the vice-president of the Central Party School before his election to the Central Committee. Despite strong opposition, he then exculpated people purged during the Cultural Revolution and the Anti-Rightist Movement.[1] According to Merle Goldman's estimations, about three million civil servants, scientists, intellectuals and skilled workers then came back to public life. The pejorative labels of 'landowners', 'rich peasants' and 'reactionaries' created under Mao were suppressed. Hu Yaobang's action was very much based on the idea that the Four Modernisations could not be achieved without the help of a large contingent of scientists and technicians. This led to a debate on the drawbacks of academic politicisation in a non-academic context, since academic freedom is guaranteed by a democratic system.[2]

As early as 1979, Li Shu wrote, in an article published in *Historical Research*, that 'an atmosphere in which a scientist can work in freedom from fear and dares freely to express views' is a prerequisite for the development of science and culture. He added that academic endeavour should not be limited to explaining policies. Intellectuals should be responsible for proposing and advising as far as economic and social policies are concerned.[3]

Since the reforms launched by Deng Xiaoping in the wake of the Eleventh Party Congress in August 1977, the government had ceaselessly highlighted the importance of knowledge as the foundation of political decision-making. Reforming the administration of the intellectual professions was officially connected to the success of economic reform in the speech Zhao Ziyang delivered at the Third Plenary Session of the Twelfth Central Committee in October 1984, which denounced surviving manifestations of anti-intellectualism in China: 'In our

---

1. The Anti-Rightist Movement (*fanyou yundong*), a series of purges of supposed rightists from the CCP and outside, took place from 1957 to 1959.
2. Goldman, M. 'Hu Yaobang's intellectual network and the theory conference of 1979', *China Quarterly* 126, June 1991, pp. 219–42.
3. Li, S. 'Identify the essence and absorb it', *Lishi Yanjiu*, 15 November 1979, p. 35, quoted in Goldman, M. 'Hu Yaobang's intellectual network and the theory conference of 1979', p. 239.

drive for socialist modernisation, we must respect knowledge and talented people. We must combat all ideas and practices that belittle science and technology, the cultivation of intellectual resources and the role of intellectuals.'[4]

This can be explained by the facts that the Party leadership itself – not only the Chinese population – had gone through the trauma of the Cultural Revolution and that it was also driven by a thorough urge for reform. In *Scientism and Humanism*, Hua Shiping hints at a psychological response to the Cultural Revolution. In parallel, for about a decade, a network of intellectuals and democratic elites organised around Hu Yaobang had fuelled a debate on the necessity of thoroughly modifying the political system so as to avoid a new Cultural Revolution.

Intellectuals awaken

The 1980s are often presented as the renaissance of intellectual debates in China, a moment of accelerated thawing during which possibilities were limitless. The scholars under scrutiny were then in college as students, young researchers or teachers. Pan Wei describes the euphoria then prevailing in Peking University:

In 1978 most students felt hope. Disillusionment was felt at the end of the Cultural Revolution: from 1974, or from 1971 to 1976. But after 1976, everyone was feeling hopeful. There was a restoration of a new romanticism. We could see a great and brilliant future because we were the happy few who could enter college. And at the time, we were studying hard. Especially in my department, everybody was studying English very hard. We would listen to VOA every night and we felt we knew a lot, and the world was going to know us. And then in 1979, it was the restoration of diplomatic relationships with America, and everybody in this department of international politics was so happy. We all jumped out and said we could go to America. We studied America, and we were fighting so-called 'hegemonic' Soviet Union at the time. So everybody felt hope that the future would be in our hands. That was the new romanticism.

The outlook of a liberal like Ren Jiantao on that period is not so remote from Pan's. They both describe a moment of effervescence and intense hope. However, Ren's overall assessment of the 1980s is much more positive. He indeed deplores the current apathy, contrasting with the activism of that time:

I wrote an article entitled 'The disastrous consequences of violence against an apathetic society and their democratic remedy.' Chinese society currently lacks energy. The only thing which can rid it of its torpor is the unfair distribution of wealth. People rebel when they compare the size of their apartments with others', or their salaries. This is the only thing which angers

---

4. Quoted in Simon, D. F. 'China's scientists and technologists in the post-Mao era: a retrospective and prospective glimpse', in Goldman, M. (ed.), *China's Intellectuals and the State: In search of a new relationship*, Cambridge, MA: Harvard University Press, 1987, p. 145.

them and drives them to act. During Deng Xiaoping's reform in the 1980s, people were very active. You should read Li Xingmin, *The Excited Age: Physical Revolution at the Turn of the Century*.[5] We then thought reform was possible, a student movement could be launched, we could hold elections, we could start companies and discuss political issues again. Comparatively speaking, today's China is extremely apathetic, exhausted. Leaders also seem to be exhausted.

Let us briefly retrace the various steps of the end of Maoism.[6] When reformers from within the system initiated the ideological and political debate related to the 'criterion of truth' in 1978, they launched a post-communist transition process which put an end to the domination of Maoist ideology, which was deeply deconstructed, and moved away from traditional Marxist thought.[7] The 'Beijing Spring' allowed people and intellectuals to free themselves from ideological discourse and to open a new public sphere in which they could express themselves freely. They were encouraged by Deng Xiaoping for a while, as he was in the process of strengthening his hold on power. The movement's most famous manifestation was the Democracy Wall, which was covered with *dazibao* in the Xidan neighbourhood.[8] The debate on 'humanist Marxism' (*rendaozhuyide makesizhuyi*) aimed at rethinking Marxism so as to question the Maoist ideology of modernisation and offering a theoretical foundation to the socialist reform movement launched by Deng Xiaoping.[9] The main feature of the 'cultural fever' (*wenhua re*) which rocked the 1980s was the Chinese intellectual community's obsession with the word 'culture' (*wenhua*), then more fashionable than science. To briefly summarise, the point was to promote the Enlightenment and to compare Chinese culture to western culture, to criticise traditional Chinese culture and reflect on its role in the nation's modernisation. The TV series *Heshang* (The River Elegy) produced by a group of former Red Guards considerably furthered the debate in 1988 when it broadcast on Central Television the message that without opening to the West and radical change, Chinese civilisation was doomed to disappear.[10] An article from Gan Yang, in which he wondered 'after the 20th century, could Chinese cultural "tradition" still be symbolized and represented by Confucianism? We reject this possibility', is quite representative of that

5. Li, X. *Jidong Renxin De Niandai*, Chengdu, Sichuan: People's Press, 1983.

6. The different steps of the end of Maoism are minutely detailed by Chen, Y. in *L'éveil de la Chine: les bouleversements intellectuels après Mao, 1976–2002*, Paris: Éditions de l'Aube, 2002, p. 109; and by Zhang, L. in *La Vie intellectuelle en Chine après la mort de Mao*, Paris: Fayard, 2003.

7. Zhang, L. *La Vie intellectuelle en Chine*, p. 88.

8. Chen, Y. *L'éveil de la Chine*, chapter 2; Zhang Lun, *La Vie intellectuelle en Chine*, pp. 96–104.

9. In *Scientism and Humanism*, Hua Shiping details the three humanist versions introduced by Wang Ruoshui, Li Zehou and Gan Yang. Hua, S. *Scientism and Humanism: Two Cultures in Post-Mao China (1978–1989)*, Albany, NY: State University of New York Press, 1995.

10. Goldman, M. 'A new relationship between the intellectuals and the state in the post-Mao period', in Fairbank, J. and Goldman, M. (eds), *An Intellectual History of Modern China*, Cambridge: Cambridge University Press, 2002, p. 514.

tendency, which saw Confucianism as passé and predicted its extinction.[11] The 'New Enlightenment' movement, which referred to the May Fourth movement, prolonged the 'cultural fever'. It designates an extremely heterogeneous line of thought which was animated by one aim: re-examining existing socialism. This movement is often presented as epitomising the 1980s mindset because 'many intellectuals then united under the banner of the Enlightenment to break ideological taboos.'[12] The liberal movement claims to be the 'spiritual heir' of the New Enlightenment movement, which embodied new modern culture as opposed to socialist tradition and Maoist dogma in the 1980s.

As the Open and Reform policy had failed to eradicate the problems of the former system and because it created new ones, a neo-authoritarian movement (*xin quanweizhuyi*) emerged as a response to the need for ideological renewal. Its appearance can be seen as the first sign of a split in the Chinese intelligentsia, between those who considered democracy as a requisite condition for the country's modernisation and neo-authoritarians who considered that democracy could not be efficiently introduced in China without a prior authoritarian transition. The debate stemmed from reflections by economics, sociology and political science researchers who were looking for a means other than liberalism and immediate democratisation to ensure a smooth and peaceful transition. The neo-authoritarian theory first gained traction when a conference on the reform strategy was organised in Peking University in 1986. At the time, these conferences were more propitious to the expression of dissenting voices than publications, which were heavily controlled. Some scholars seized the opportunity to develop the idea that a strong government was necessary to guide reform. They referred to the theory of civic culture, which emphasises the indispensible supporting factors of a functioning democracy. Only when relevant social and economic conditions are met can the transitional regime introduce a balance of power and make room for democratic institutions. This modern dictatorial governmental power could defy both conservative resistance to the introduction of the market economy and the democrats' simultaneous over-ambitious demands; and it could efficiently implement economic reform in the stable context without which economic development cannot take place. It would also enable the rise of a middle class, which was thought to be one main pillar of a country's democratisation.

Wang Huning, a former political scientist of Fudan University now a member of the Central Committee, director of the Policy Research Office of the Central Committee and one of Xi Jinping's main advisors, and Xiao Gongqin, a Shanghai Normal University historian, were the two main figures of neo-authoritarianism, which intellectuals close to Zhao Ziyang vigorously endorsed.[13] The debate was structured around Samuel Huntington's emphasis on efficient governance and political order in the modernisation process and around the idea that Chinese

---

11. Gan, Y. 'Chuantong, shijianxing yu weilai' ('Tradition, temporality and future'), *Dushu* 2, 1986; Chen, L. 'Liberalism and neo-leftism at the turn of the century', *China Perspectives* 55, September–October 2004, available online at http://chinaperspectives.revues.org/417.

12. Chen, L. 'Liberalism and Neo-Leftism at the turn of the century', *China Perspectives* 55. September–October 2004'.

13. Chen, Y. *L'éveil de la Chine: les bouleversements intellectuels après Mao, 1976–2002*, p. 109.

reform should take inspiration from the authoritarian development model of the Four Asian Tigers (Taiwan, South Korea, Singapore and Hong Kong). It is important to note that scholars sparked off the debate and the central political leadership did not guide it but resorted to the ideas that it found instrumental. To Zhao Ziyang, this trend of thought could indeed help launch new reforms.

An emerging generation of intellectuals

Following the founding of the People's Republic in 1949, the early 1950s – and the 1952 reform of universities in particular – mark the brutal decline of the autonomy of intellectuals. In a totalitarian context, the intellectual community is integrated with the government apparatus. To put it simply, we could say that the disappointments and sufferings of the Cultural Revolution acted like an electric shock and awakened the independent spirit of some intellectuals. As many scholars like Hua Shiping and Tang Wenfang have mentioned, the most influential intellectuals with liberal and intellectual ideas belonged to the system. They suffered from the limitations of their exclusively Marxist training and failed to produce theories effectively able to solve the problems China faced as it modernised. Fewsmith asserts that 'intellectuals were, to an overwhelming degree, "establishment intellectuals"' but he immediately adds that the situation evolves as early as the mid 1980s, 'as intellectuals, frustrated by the lack of political reform, began to carve out an autonomous realm from which they could push for cultural reform'.[14] According to Wang Juntao, who belongs to this generation of intellectuals, 'they replaced the officially-established intellectuals to dominate the Chinese intellectual community in the 1990s and they developed new ideologies, including neo-conservatism.'[15]

A public sphere emerges

Historian of ideas Xu Jilin describes the 1980s as the era when a public sphere, in the sense Jürgen Habermas[16] gave to the term, emerged. It revolved around a core of public intellectuals, composed of different groups: 'scientists', humanities scholars and defenders of a fusion of cultures, represented by the Chinese Academy of Social Sciences. Numerous journals, allowing intense debates to take place, flourished, among which were the famous *Dushu* (*Reading*); *Zouxiang Weilai* (*Toward the Future*), representing intellectuals from various scientific disciplines; and *Wenhua: Zhongguo Yu Shijie* (*Culture: China and the World*) in Beijing; the reference social science journal *Wenhui Yuekan* (*Wenhui Monthly*) and *Shulin* (*Book Forest*) in Shanghai; and *Qingnian Luntan* (*Youth Forum*) in Wuhan.

14. Fewsmith, J. *China since Tiananmen*, Cambridge, MA: Cambridge University Press, 2001, p. 11.

15. Wang, J. *Reverse Course: Political neo-conservatism and regime stability in post-Tiananmen China*, PhD dissertation, Columbia University, 2006, p. 97.

16. Xu, J. 'What future for public intellectuals?', *China Perspectives* 52, March–April 2004 Varia, available online at http://chinaperspectives.revues.org/799; Habermas, J. *The Structural Transformation of the Public Sphere: An inquiry into a category of bourgeois society*, Cambridge, MA: The MIT Press, 1989.

Toward the Future is the first journal that managed to circumvent the strict control of the Party and sell a few hundred thousand copies. The informal group of intellectuals constituting the editorship of *Culture: China and the World* focused on introducing western scholarship in China. Between 1985 and 1989, three major book collections were launched with that aim: 'Series of Contemporary western Academic Works' (*Xiandai Xifang Xueshu Wenku*), 'New Knowledge Series' (*Xinzhi Wenku*) and 'Collection of Research in Humanities' (*Renwen Yanjiu Congshu*), which still publishes books under the supervision of Liu Dong. The two first book series publish original translations of classic western works by such thinkers as Freud, Weber, Nietzsche, Sartre, Derrida, Foucault, Ricoeur, Habermas, Popper, Benedict and Toynbee.

From 1984 to 1987, 1,500 book series were released, among which 200 specialised in culture, philosophy, social sciences and political and economic theories. Chen Yan describes what he calls the greatest systematic effort to introduce western ideas in China since the May Fourth Movement. This craving for publishing and reading can be explained by the intellectual and spiritual void subsequent to the Cultural Revolution. Official statistics unveil the collapse of publications during that period, with 27,000 in 1957; 14,000 in 1965; 3,000 in 1967; and 8,000 a year on average between 1966 and 1976. The number of periodicals fell from 600 in 1957 to 20 in the late 1960s. This new wave of publications can also be explained by the crucial need for new ideas and by the failed Campaign against Spiritual Pollution in 1983.[17]

The dense network of interaction between active intellectuals and the publicity these journals and book collections gave to their debates, with several million readers, constituted a public sphere endowed with a well developed critical spirit as regarded the authorities.[18] These groupings and networks often originated in Red Guards groups that had been dissolved at the end of the Cultural Revolution but whose underground activities had never truly stopped. Some associate this moment of freedom with the nomination of Zhu Houze, who was close to Hu Yaobang, as head of the Propaganda Bureau in 1985. In 1986, Zhu launched the slogan of the three *kuan* (*kuansong, kuanrong, kuanhou*): 'extending flexibility, tolerance and leniency'.

In and out of the system

In that context, intellectuals who had been excluded from official circles when they began their careers gradually integrated with the system, because they contributed to defining the problems, conditions and strategic options for

17. The Campaign against Spiritual Pollution (*Qingchu jingshen wuran yundong*) was a political campaign led by conservative factions in the CCP in the autumn of 1983, to rein in the introduction of imported liberal ideas in Chinese society.

18. Su Shaozhi and Cheng Yingxiang recall the immense editorial success of *Towards the Future* among students in the 1980s: 'students fought over these books. They were in a frenzy. For some titles a million copies were published and they rapidly sold out.' Cheng, Y. *Dégel de l'intelligence en Chine: 1976–1989*, Paris: Gallimard, 2004, p. 425.

developing China. They simultaneously relied on the knowledge, experience and skills they had accumulated to grasp the Chinese trajectory of development as accurately as possible. Wang Juntao develops the idea that these independent figures monopolised the system, 'to institutionalize their independence by developing independent institutions as the reforms deepened in the late 1980s. Finally, they achieved political and social bases for their independence in the 1990s when they took positions in the official system.'[19] There was a fine line between intellectuals who belonged to the system and those who didn't. Indeed, who could be truly outside, apart from those who had been completely excluded, like Wei Jingsheng and Fang Lizhi (after 1989)? In an interview given to Cheng Yingxiang and published in *Dégel de l'Intelligence* (*Thawing of Intelligence*),[20] economist, political scientist and Marxist theoretician Su Shaozhi – who had first coined the concept of China's 'first stage of socialism' (*shehui zhuyi de diji jieduan*), argues that people's professional situation is not a valid criterion for making that distinction. He reminds us that publications which exclusively emanated from civil society had been banned after the Democracy Wall episode in spring 1979, with only a few exceptions:[21]

> The dividing line between the two groups was in most cases very hard to locate, given that even intellectuals who were mentally out of the system were also to some extent part of the system and could not refuse to be unless they accepted to be deprived of their rice bowl and completely marginalized. [...] To put it simply, let us say that in general, in the 1980s, the 'new brand' of Chinese intelligentsia was made of people who were involved in digging two simultaneous channels: the practical channel of economic and social transformation; and the channel of culture and thought or theory revival. And whether they dug the latter or the former, they basically followed the same inspiration and took the same direction, and they were more or less part of the system, even when they aspired to get rid of it.[22]

After intellectuals were exculpated, some were absorbed by the networks of Hu Yaobang and Zhao Ziyang and went on to lead research institutes, newspapers and professional guilds, which did not prevent them from posing as spokespersons of the people to the leaders and criticising public policies. According to Merle Goldman, however, it is only after the powerful shock of the Tiananmen Square repression receded that two new classes of intellectuals,

---

19. Wang, J. *Reverse Course*, p. 99.

20. Cheng, Y. *Dégel de l'intelligence en Chine.*

21. Such was the case of Wang Juntao and Chen Ziming, who founded the journal *Beijing Spring* after the April Fifth incident (1976) and published it on the Democracy Wall. They were among the only ones who dared set up a *minjian* (non-official) research institute on economics and society and a journal, *Jingjixue Zhoubao* (*Economics Weekly*). Goldman, M. *From Comrade to Citizen: The struggle for political rights in China*, Cambridge, MA: Harvard University Press, 2005, chapter 2, pp. 51–67.

22. Cheng, Y. *Dégel de l'intelligence en Chine*, pp. 420–1, p. 424.

with less ambiguous positions, emerged: disestablished and critical established intellectuals.[23] The following remarks by Su Shaozhi's allow us to get a better grasp of their subtle positions:

First, they altogether represented an extremely thin layer of the whole mainland intelligentsia back then. Second, most of them were not aware of being in or out of the system, whatever the position they actually held. Third, for most, their political views remained highly indefinite. Even when they lambasted the Communist Party, almost all of them still did it unconsciously the way Mao had taught them to during the Cultural Revolution. And almost most of them still thought that the Communist Party was still legitimate![24]

Post-Tiananmen mutism

It was precisely because the Chinese system became less tyrannical and because oppression and totalitarianism were receding that it came under perceptible or implicit attack in the 1980s. According to Lucien Bianco, the new visibility which was given to the failures of the Chinese system and the growing awareness that at least some sections of Chinese society had of these were less crucial than the retreating of totalitarianism.[25] However, these developments cannot be seen as a zero-sum game in which the opposition wins what power loses. Indeed, as resistance grew, these debates nourished the Party and reinforced its stand.

Innumerable tensions emerged with the upheavals triggered by the reform process and the absence of a genuine debate on potential solutions to the new problems caused by the reform process. Long used to strict egalitarianism, despite Deng Xiaoping's determination, people found it difficult to accept to let some get rich first (*rang yibufen ren xian fuqilai*). One fourth of the rural population migrated to cities to look for jobs. Both in city and countryside, corruption became more blatant. In the winter of 1986–7, student agitation spread from Hefei to Beijing in protest against rising prices and worsening salaries and employment conditions, and asking for more reforms. The Campaign against Bourgeois Liberalism prompted Hu Yaobang to resign; Zhu Houze was dismissed and three intellectuals were expelled from the Party.

The intense academic debates with scholars from abroad and the continuous flux of information brought fresh ideas to intellectuals and students and radically modified their perception of China. The situation appeared intolerable to them: the demographic explosion seemed uncontrollable; the education system elementary; the 'resilient' culture that quickened the destruction of the environment appeared backward. Finally, the incomplete and sketchy opening to the market economy had calamitous side

---

23. Goldman, M. *From Comrade to Citizen*, pp. 6–7.
24. Cheng, Y. *Dégel de l'intelligence en Chine*, p. 426.
25. Bianco, L. preface to Bergère, M. -C. Bianco, L. and Domes, J. (eds), *La Chine au XXe siècle: de 1949 à aujourd'hui*, Paris: Fayard, 1990, p. vii.

effects.[26] Within the Party, two groups fought: conservatives with Chen Yuan and Li Peng at their head and reformists represented by by Hu Yaobang and Zhao Ziyang. When Hu suddenly died in April 1989, student demonstrations started again and intensified, leading to the June Fourth massacre in Tiananmen Square.

The bloody June Fourth repression marked a watershed in the way Chinese scholars intervened in the public sphere. Their sudden stifling has been frequently described.[27] Even if repression was less fierce than expected, mainly because of passive resistance to mass campaigns, many critical intellectuals were in trouble. Some were jailed. Others opted for exile. Political attacks targeted think tanks and Zhao Ziyang and Hu Yaobang's neo-authoritarian and liberal advisers. Publications that had permitted intellectuals to advocate democratic reforms openly were purged. Editorial committees like that of *Towards the Future* were dissolved.

Journalists, intellectuals and students were compelled to report to the Party all their actions during the student movement and to write self-criticism. While intellectuals were individually condemned, students, in the arts especially, as they were more exposed to 'western thinking', were collectively punished. New Master's students at the Chinese Academy of Social Sciences were sent to Shaanxi for ten months to 'work'. A military training session before classes started was imposed on all the students of Peking University. Cheng Yingxiang describes in bitter terms the large-scale impact of the repression: 'one may say that, as early as the end of the summer 1989, the Chinese intelligentsia no longer existed, but in exile, where it ran the risk of gradually drying up; it was stunned, forced to silence, blackmailed to dumbness while the multiple body of basic Chinese intellectuals was placed under tight surveillance.'[28]

The leadership of the Academy of Social Sciences was blamed for the participation of researchers and students in the 1989 demonstrations.[29] Investigations were conducted at each institute but the solidarity which prevailed offered some protection. Out of 2,000 employees of the Academy who were involved in the demonstrating, petition-signing and sit-ins on Tiananmen Square, 120 were sanctioned by disciplinary measures; that is, official statements, compulsory self-criticism sessions, dismissals and incarceration. Each research institute was forced to organise a Party committee in charge of ideological control, so as to allow the Academy to recover its role as political advisor of the CCP's Central Committee and the State Council in building 'socialism with Chinese characteristics'. Worse, the authoritarian modernisation system was now in question, with conservatives and the Old Left back in power. From 1989 to late 1991, conservatism prevailed in the official media. Academics were no

---

26. Cheng, Y. *Dégel de l'intelligence en Chine*, pp. 434–5

27. Among others, *see* Béja, J. -P. *À la recherche d'une ombre chinoise*, Paris: Seuil, 2004, pp. 193–5; Hao, Z. *Intellectuals at a Crossroads*, Albany, NY: State University of New York Press, 2003, pp. 120–1.

28. Cheng, Y. *Dégel de l'intelligence en Chine*, p. 530.

29. Sleebom-Faulkner, M. *The Chinese Academy of Social Sciences (CASS): Shaping the reforms, academia and China (1977–2003)*, Leiden: Brill, 2007, pp. 119–44.

longer encouraged to guide and explain the reform policy but, on the contrary, to criticise 'bourgeois liberalisation' and 'peaceful evolution'. Deng expressed himself on several occasions against the questioning of reforms by the left, claiming that the market was not specific to capitalist countries nor planning to socialist countries. But the reform policy was only definitively confirmed and deepened after his Southern Tour in January 1992.

There was a 'Tiananmen effect' in academia.[30] The two-year repression encouraged academics to take refuge in their laboratories and to professionalise, and even 'modernise'. They no longer focused on large social issues but on their specific fields of expertise. According to historian Xu Jilin, the first breach in the unity of the Chinese intelligentsia in the 1990s can be located in the difference between thought (*sixiang*) and academic research (*xueshu*). The rejection of 1980s radicalism and engagement, now deemed excessive, led to withdrawal from the public sphere. In an article entitled 'What future for public intellectuals?', Xu Jilin introduced the debate on the history of science and its norms, which explains an 'important change in the conception intellectuals had of their role. The space occupied by intellectuals was no longer the public square, but rather a specialised sphere and a field of competences'.

This debate was situated in the context and spirit of post-1989: the intellectuals were seized with uncertainty, and everyone was wondering bitterly what should be done, and what it was possible to do. Some of the intellectuals, engaged in a reflection on cultural life in the 1980s, called for a return to science and a reconstruction of its norms. Chen Pingyuan, one of the main writers of the journal *Xueren*, is representative of this position: if the 1980s 'were a period filled with enthusiasm and imagination,' the questions of the intellectuals were steeped in a scientific atmosphere which was 'light' and 'dispersed'. They 'introduced many [new ideas] but did little research, their creativity was great but their connection with reality was weak.' In his view, 'the decade of the 1990s may have a greater need for constraining scientific norms which, through a series of scarcely poetic procedural operations, will attempt to transform 'the spark of thought' previously produced into scientific results. This trend towards growing specialisation will be a tough test for those in the university who lack the academic training necessary, base themselves only on common sense, and ask questions wherever their inspiration carries them.[31]

These two years of silence imposed on intellectuals gave them the opportunity to reflect on their relationship with power and their (in)capacity to reform society. Scholars were no longer called for. They no longer had access to the

---

30. Domenach, J. -L. and Richer, P. *La Chine*, vol. 2, Paris: Points Seuil, 1995, p. 581.
31. Xu, J. 'What future for public intellectuals?', *China Perspectives*, 52 March–April 2004, available online at http://chinaperspectives.revues.org/799, p. 20; Chen, P. 'Xueshu shi yanjiu suixiang' ('On the current of research on the history of academic life'), *Xueren*, vol.1, Jiangsu Wenyi Chubanshe, 1991, p. 3.

decision-making process, or to the framing of ideological justifications and political aims. Besides, some intellectuals sought refuge in the market. Chen Yan describes how the 1980s intelligentsia, who believed it played a central role in Chinese society, 'once repressed by the regime, suddenly found itself in lamentable and despicable material poverty'. According to official figures, in 1992, the average yearly salary of teachers was below the national average salary. The salary of an aspiring researcher was lower than that of the toilet attendant on Beijing's Chang'an avenue.[32] As a result, a significant number of intellectual professionals 'jumped into the sea' (*xiahai*) and ventured in business and trade. The new opportunities offered by the market and China's international opening made intellectuals less dependent on the state, all the more so after 1992. Some resigned from their teaching or research positions while others took a second, trade-related job. The popular saying that 'Out of a billion Chinese, nine-tenths are entrepreneurs' was ironically turned into 'Out of ten scholars, nine are amateur entrepreneurs. As for the last tenth, they are thinking about it.' Scientists tended to start new technology companies, economists consulting firms and language teachers language courses. Besides, education services commercialised as schools were encouraged to diversify their funding since the 1980s. The resulting financial autonomy had considerably modified the relationship between intellectual professions and the state but it often went hand in hand with depoliticisation and dwindling involvement in public life and debates. Therefore, in the wake of the repression of the 1989 student movement, the freezing of the 1980s intellectual debates, the collapse of the Soviet Union and the steady renewal of economic reforms in the 1990s, the Chinese intellectual landscape was forever transformed. This brief period was seen as a landmark both by Chinese intellectuals and foreign analysts.[33]

From consensus on reform to the first fragmentation of the intelligentsia

From 1993 on, intellectual debates florished and diversified again. Independent intellectual journals such as *Dongfang* (*Orient*) and the *Chinese Social Sciences Review* emerged. They registered in Hong Kong. Some level of intellectual independence was recovered. The Party clearly indicated the topics which could not be approached. They were encapsulated in the 'three Ts': Tiananmen, and Tibet. Sensitive political issues were avoided and direct criticism of the system was impossible. Journalists, writers and academics were under surveillance, even if the range of issues they could approach openly expanded considerably.

---

32. Chen, Y. *L'éveil de la Chine*, p. 135.

33. Publications with titles including the words 'after Tiananmen' can be found galore. For instance, Fewsmith, J. *China Since Tiananmen: The politics of transition*, Cambridge, MA: Cambridge University Press, 2001; Cheng, J. Y. S. *Whither China's Democracy? Democratisation in China since the Tiananmen incident*, Hong Kong: City University of Hong Kong Press.

Neo-conservatism and fears of division

Rising nationalism

To understand the great transformation the Chinese intelligentsia underwent in the 1990s and 2000s, the rise of nationalism at the time must be scrutinised. With Deng Xiaoping, pragmatic nationalism made the *zhongti xiyong* formula back in vogue.[34] More than one century after its creation, it indicated that any means to remedy the country's backwardness and to make it powerful again (*fuqiang*) became acceptable, as the famous slogan derived from an old Sichuan proverb signalled: 'No matter if the cat is black or white as long as it catches mice' (*buguan baimao heimao zhuazhao laoshu jiushi haomao*).[35] Economic growth became the leaders' absolute priority, as they were well aware that their ability to improve the lot of the Chinese people was the key to maintaining their power. This performance-based legitimacy was conjured up to explain the Communist collapse in Eastern Europe and in the Soviet Union, and to highlight China's specificity, which would prevent it from going the same way.

In official propaganda, patriotism – which is defined as loyalty to and love of the motherland (*zuguo*), as opposed to nationalism, defined by the CCP since the 1930s as reactionary and in the service of the bourgeoisie – now overtook socialism and came first. Patriotic education campaigns explicitly aimed at 'exalting the national spirit, reinforcing national cohesion, forging national confidence and pride [...] so as to guide and unite the masses' patriotic enthusiasm towards the great task of building socialism with Chinese characteristics and reuniting the motherland' but also to 'contribute to its wealth, prosperity and power [*fuqiang*]'.[36]

How to explain the apparent success of such official propaganda, destined to fill the ideological void and guarantee a minimum of solidarity and unity within a population fragmented by economic reforms? How to explain why – as well as the great majority of Chinese people – Chinese expatriates, including dissidents, who are supposed to be immune to official propaganda, have also proven very receptive to patriotic discourse? First of all, they share a deeply engrained feeling of humiliation and many common sufferings. Moreover, phenomenal economic growth has allowed for the pride and emotional connection Chinese people feel for the motherland to be restored and strengthened. A popular and spontaneous – and sometimes critical of government policy – type of nationalism is dominant in the Chinese population. It is dramatically manifest in the reaction to international events that are perceived as insulting to national dignity. The popularity of bestsellers

---

34. *See* Chapter One. Since the late nineteenth century, successful Chinese modernisation is envisioned according to the motto 'Chinese essence and western means', which advocates keeping an essentially Chinese system while borrowing more efficient techniques from the West.

35. This is a Sichuan proverb. *See* He, H. *Dictionary of the Political Thought of the People's Republic of China*, Armonk, New York: M. E. Sharpe, 2001, p. 24.

36. Quoted in Billeter, T. *L'Empereur jaune*, Paris: Les Indes savantes, 2007, p. 295.

like *China Can Say No*[37] also discloses the scale and virulence of nationalism since the mid 1990s. Due to limited official tolerance of demonstrations, online forums nowadays convey in a virtual but definite manner the anger of patriots who are indignant at foreign 'provocations,' such as the incidents which took place in Paris during the Olympic Torch relay. Despite the diversity of triggering events occurring during that period, we should recall that in the aftermath of 1989, China was heavily criticised and subjected to sanctions by the international community and the Chinese people felt weakened and disregarded, not to say humiliated, again. This reactive nationalism (*yingji zhiwei xing*) is prevalent among most of the population, from political and intellectual elites to middle classes and less privileged strata, who all harbour fears of a collapsing empire and of chaos. However, 'the nation intercedes between the people and the state [...] Each group, class, party has its own idea of the nation. This rallying object is also a subject of dispute.'[38] And indeed, leaders accused of lacking firmness on national issues such as Taiwan or Tibet expose themselves to harsh criticism.

The rise of nationalism is one of the most striking features of the 1990s. It is intensely studied and it significantly affects Chinese intellectuals and their political commitment. Xu Jilin connects nationalism with the quest for modernity. He therefore stands out from the unilateral rejection of nationalism by Chinese liberals, even if he denounces xenophobic manifestations of nationalism, like all the scholars under study here:

> In Shanghai, the liberal Zhu Xueqin considers nationalism as a form of resistance to progress, as an evil thing. I do not agree with this interpretation. Nationalism is one of the aims of the quest for modernity. It all depends on the form of nationalism we want. What kind of a nation-state do we want to become? This problem cannot be solved by classic liberalism. Liberals only see the state as a tool, a means to protect our welfare. Each state follows its own path and ideas, so that the position of a republican like me consists in trying to strike a balance between liberalism and nationalism. He must respond to nationalist demands, which have become so intense these days that young people could finally abandon great liberal demands. Conversely, the nationalist movement which emphasises the glory of the Chinese civilisation, culture and race is absolutely scary.

Popular neo-conservative thought and fears of partitioning

Fear of the country's partitioning is not only manifest among political elites. It prevails among intellectual elites as well, all the more so as the collapse of the Soviet Union has thoroughly marked them. In that context, the neo-conservative movement emerged and found a larger audience than neo-authoritarianism did

37. Qiao, B., Zhang, Z., Song, Q. *Zhongguo Keyi Shuo Bu,* Beijing: Zhonghua Gongshang Lianhe Chubanshe, 1996. The book was a collection of impassioned essays decrying western disdain for China, and the importance of China being able to defend its interests against western attempts at containment.

38. Delannoi, G. *Sociologie de la nation,* Paris: Armand Colin, 1999, p. 95.

in the late 1980s. Shanghai historian Xiao Gongqin resorted to the word 'neo-conservative' for the first time at a conference organised in December 1990 on 'Chinese tradition and socialist modernisation', where he made great impression on many official and intellectual figures. His speech was published two months later in the *Youth Daily*. His main point was that Yan Fu (1854–1921) (famous for translating Spencer, Mill, Montesquieu and Huxley) contrary to radical modernisers like Kang Youwei and Liang Qichao, advocated a gradual modernisation process in which traditional values and culture would not be seen as obstacles but rather as indispensible media (*meijie*) and levers (*ganggan*).[39] To Xiao Gongqin, like Kang Xiaoguang, tradition is instrumental in reinforcing political cohesion and legitimacy, which are absolutely requisite in transitional times. In that sense, tradition is most valuable and guarantees a certain level of loyalty towards the nation.[40]

In responses to the questions the reform has raised, Xiao Gongqin offers to 'remain prudent at each step, procede gradually and wait for opportunities to rise' (*bubu weiying, wenda wezha, xunxu jianjin, huanjin daiji*).[41] He promotes a different method – a gradual and temporarily authoritarian method – for achieving the same final objective as the 1980s reformers, that is, modernisation and democracy. Indeed, to him, a benevolent authoritarian government is the best way to launch economic reform but also to maintain the stability without which any attempt at democratising would fail. Xiao Gongqin was far from the only advocate of an anti-radical perspective. The defense of reform over revolution, incrementalism over radicalism, stability over sudden change and authority over spontaneity is in vogue. Yü Ying-shih's assessment finds a large receptive public in China.[42] He predicts a dark future for China in the twenty-first century because 'the wrongdoings Chinese people had inflicted upon themselves during the twentieth century had been too serious.'[43] To Yü, that period had been the darkest period of all over the course of Chinese history as, throughout its succeeding revolutions, 'the old had been destroyed in order to found the new' (*pojiu lixin*).

---

39. Xiao, G. 'Yan Fu dui zhongguo xiandaihua de sikao jiqi qishi' ('Yan Fu and reflection on modernisation and the Enlightenment'), *Zhongguo Qingnianbao* 3, 6 February 1991. The reference on Yan Fu is in Schwartz, B., *In Search of Wealth and Power: Yen Fu and the West*, Cambridge, MA: The Belknap Press of Harvard University Press, 1964. Timothy Cheek mentions the 'historical pragmatism' of historians, who refer to the past as if it were 'a storehouse of human experience', which they tap into to solve current problems. Cheek, T. 'Historians as public intellectuals' in Gu, E. and Goldman, M. (eds) *Chinese Intellectuals Between State and Market*, London, New York: Routledge Curzon, 2004, p. 209.

40. Xiao, G. 'Minzu zhuyi yu Zhongguo zhuanxing shiqi de yishi xingtai' ('Nationalism and ideology during China's transition period'), *Xiao Gongqinji*, pp. 350–8.

41. Xiao, G. *Fansi De Niandai* (*The Era of Reflection*), Shanghai: Fudan University Press, 2010, p. 17.

42. Yü Ying-shih was born in Tianjin but he lived in Hong Kong from 1950 on and studied at the New Asia College. He then did a PhD at Harvard and taught at Yale, Princeton and Harvard.

43. Yü, Y. 'Dai congtou, shoushi jiu shanhe' ('Putting pieces back together for a fresh start'), *Ershiyi Shiji* (*21st Century*) 2, December 1990, pp. 5–7.

He calls for Chinese intellectuals to restore a Confucian moral order and save China from the radicalisation intellectuals launched at the turn of the twentieth century, when favouring the western democratic path over the Confucian path.

Many intellectuals and the 'Princelings' (*taizi dang*, the descendants of senior CCP leaders) concur with Xiao Gongqin and Yü Ying-shih's defense of conservatism and rejection of radicalism. In a policy paper entitled 'Realistic responses and strategic options for China after the Soviet coup', intended to identify what China must do to avoid the fate of the former Soviet Union, the offspring of Party leaders resort to the term 'neo-conservatism' to designate the promotion of rational, orderly and gradual modernisation. They associate radicalism with irrational and utopian advocacy of political liberalisation as well as with socialism, whose revolutionary tendencies have become outdated. To assess the ambiguous connections between neo-conservative intellectuals and the more or less official discourse of the Princelings, Ben Xu coined the term 'rivalry-complicity relationship'.[44] The former are complicit with the latter in their rejection of immediate democratisation and common insistence on political stability and cultural nationalism. They are rivalrous insofar as rejection of revolution and promoting cultural tradition go against the Party's interests. It is therefore essential to understand that one cannot infer from overlapping official and intellectual conceptions that intellectual activity in the 1990s was orchestrated by the Party. Such an overlap results from a series of concerns, a sense of crisis, which official and intellectual circles share. Moreover, the official ideology and intellectual discourse were crafted in the same conditions; that is in reaction to the radicalism of the Cultural Revolution and the collapse of the Soviet Union.

Gradualism and the end of anti-traditionalism: A thought revolution

In the early 1990s, the debate on rewriting Chinese modern history signalled that a new conception of social change and Chinese modernity was emerging. This advocacy of historical continuity, a renewed assessment of Chinese tradition in positive terms, and support for gradual and pragmatic reform went against a Marxist conception of change as a revolution stemming from the struggle of two opposed sides. Xiao Gongqin pragmatically defended the idea of historical continuity as necessary to social stability, which a country cannot develop without. The Shanghai historian undertook a surprising fusion of Huntington, Burke (denouncing radicalism; criticising rationalism and natural right), Hayek (spontaneous growth; comparison between two liberal traditions – the French one, revolutionary, and the British one, evolutionary; will to create a market economy and civil society) and social Darwinism, which Yan Fu introduced to China.

As a result, in the early 1990s, mainly with the intermediary of Xiao Gongqin and his emphasis on the indispensible emergence of the middle class for the sake of democratisation, the heterogeneous brand of Chinese neo-conservatism cannot be simply categorised as anti-liberal. This can explain why the term became so popular,

---

44. Xu, B. *Disenchanted Democracy: Chinese cultural criticism after 1989*, Ann Arbor, MI: University of Michigan Press, 1999, pp. 183–4.

starting from 1992 and Deng Xiaoping's Southern Tour and intensified Open and Reform policy. First, conservatism is not without connection to the 'farewell to revolution' made explicit by the release of Li Zehou and Liu Zaifu's book of that title[45]– and which became an ubiquitous theme of the mid 1990s. This book is the first direct criticism of revolution, understood as a brutal toppling of the system and the incumbent authorities through mass violence and drastic methods. It is also worth noticing how the word 'conservatism' evolved and how Hayek's idea that only the French brand of liberalism should be considered radical, as opposed to British liberalism, more acceptable, because conservative became influential. Xu Jilin thus claims that the popularity of liberal thinkers like Isaiah Berlin, Karl Popper and Friedrich Hayek in the early 1990s shows that 'the word "liberalism" itself had achieved a cultural cachet previously enjoyed by such terms as democracy and science, even a certain inviolability'.[46] Els Van Dongen, in a doctoral thesis on Chinese conservatism, therefore chooses to categorise this criticism of radicalism as 'conservative liberalism', since it advocates a liberalism that is to be achieved gradually.[47] This may explain why, in 1998, one of the most libertarian intellectuals in Chinese academia, Liu Junning, then still a researcher at the Academy of Social Sciences and editor of the liberal journal *Gonggong Luncong* (*Res Publica*), published a book entitled *Conservatism*. To his mind, without liberalism, conservatism leads to authoritarianism while, without conservatism, liberalism leads to rationalism and radicalism.[48] This liberal conception of conservatism goes as far as defining Hayek as a conservative liberal, even though he explicitly rejected that label in the Afterword of *Constitution of Liberty*. Xu Jilin associates this urge for Chinese intellectuals to connect liberalism with gradual reform and to favour conservative British liberalism over the French revolutionary and utopian path[49] with several publications that were widely read and commented on: mainly, translations of Hayek's *Road to Serfdom* and *Constitution of Liberty*; Gan Yang's article on these two types of liberalism,[50] in which he explains why liberalism is connected to gradualism even before the early 1990s; and Gu Zhun's posthumous works.[51]

---

45. Liu, Z. and Li, Z. *Gaobie Geming: Huiwang Ershi Shiji Zhongguo* (*Farewell to Revolution: Reflecting on the Chinese 20th century*), Hong Kong: Tiandi Tushu Youxian Gongsi (Cosmos books), 1995.

46. Xu, J. 'The fate of an Enlightenment: twenty years in the Chinese intellectual sphere (1978–1998)', in Gu, E. and Goldman, M. (eds), *Chinese Intellectuals Between State and Market*, London and New York: RoutledgeCurzon, 2004, p. 197.

47. Van Dongen, E. *Goodbye Radicalism, Conceptions of radicalism among Chinese intellectuals during the early 1990s*, Leiden: University of Leiden Press, 2009, p. 165ff

48. Liu, J. *Baoshou Zhuyi* (*Conservatism*), Beijing: Zhongguo Shehui Kexue Chuban, 1998, pp. 9, 14, 264.

49. Xu, J. 'The fate of an Enlightenment', p. 198.

50. Gan, Y. 'Fanminzhu de ziyou zhuyi haishi minzhu de ziyou zhuyi?' ('Anti-democratic or democratic liberalism?') *Ershiyi Shiji* 39, 1997, pp. 4–17.

51. Gu Zhun (1915–1974) famously criticised the Cultural Revolution. He is often described as a liberal and an advocate of individualism. Some of his ideas become popular among liberals in the 1990s. Gu, Z. *Gu Zhun Wenji*, Guizhou Renmin Chubanshe, 1994; Zhun, G. *Gu Zhun Riji*, Beijing: Jingji Ribao Chubanshe, 1997. *See* Davies, G. *Worrying about China*, p. 157.

Denouncing radical methods amounted to turning the page and blaming previous revolutionary practices so as to abandon them in the future, which leads us to wonder about the new sources of legitimacy the Party could count upon. Breaking away from the past no longer simply meant breaking away from the 'traditional' past, as in the early twentieth century, but from the socialist and revolutionary past. The Party was, consequently, called to undertake a gradual reform in conformity with Chinese tradition, which was supposed to make the whole process easier.

That the advocates of a strong state, who form part of the Chinese New Left, but also the most anarchist liberals like Liu Junning all explicitly called for a gradual anti-radical reform is a major break in the history of Chinese thought since the term 'conservatism' had first been pejoratively used for decades by Marxist and liberals to impugn anti-progressives. This historical reversal has been allowed by the association of conservatism with progress and modernisation, which were no longer opposed. The end of what Tu Weiming calls the 'tradition of anti-traditionism', which prevailed for about 150 years in China, has made it possible for Chinese tradition to become popular again. The cultural fever of the 1980s and the views of Chinese scholars living abroad such as Yü Ying-shih and Tu Weiming, as well as the 'Asian values' and 'Confucian capitalism' arguments advocated in Singapore in the 1980s, have greatly contributed to it.

'Tradition' is back

We have explained that, from the 1990s, Chinese academics were no longer satisfied with the western 'toolkit' for investigating China, contrary to the 1980s, a period of enthusiastic adhesion to the theories they discovered in new translations of western works. To transcend the limitations of a western reading of China's past, present and future, a nativist movement surfaced. Many publications and re-opened university departments signalled the emergence of China studies (*guoxue*) and a revival of Confucian tradition(s). The latter is extremely varied, since it comprises elitist, populist, authoritarian and democratic trends, among others,[52] and it encompasses both specialists (Jiang Qing, Chen Lai, and so on) and non-specialists (such as Qin Hui and Liu Xiaofeng). This 'China studies fever' did not originate in universities but from popular demand, which the immense success of Yu Dan's TV show and book on Confucius uncovered. However, this fever rapidly spread in universities, which encountered difficulties in applying western methods and concepts to studying China. Liu Dong thus explains that, at first, Chinese historians tried to adopt the methods used by western historians. Then they realised that they were not always well adapted and that Chinese methods had some benefits too. When I first met him in 2005, he was a professor in Peking University's Chinese literature

---

52. Billioud S. and Thoraval, J. 'Jiaohua: the Confucian revival today as an educative project,' *China Perspectives* 4 (2007),pp. 4–20, available online at http://chinaperspectives.revues.org/2483; Ji, Z. 'Confucius, les libéraux et le Parti: Le renouveau du confucianisme politique', *La Vie des Idées*, May 2005, pp. 9–20.

department. When we met in 2010, he was delighted to have transferred to Tsinghua's China studies department, which had reopened in November 2009 with Chen Lai as its head, and where he no longer faced the problematic inadequacy of western academic methods in studying Chinese literature. To him, total rejection of western academic research is not possible. What is at stake is putting an end to the tendency to systematically renounce – which eventually proved superficial and ineffective – the contribution of China studies, under the pretext that there was no other way to modernise China and Chinese universities:

> The books of western political thinkers have helped me a lot. But after finishing reading them all, I thought that none could help solve China's problems. [...] I think that to fix these problems, the solution is not to read some books from a unique culture but rather interculturality, dialogue between cultures.

Liu Dong thus justifies the renewed interest in China studies for the sake of interculturality, rather than a nationalist temptation of the country. He advocates selection rather than full adhesion to western studies. The fact that his arguments converge with those of his arch-enemy Wang Hui in emphasising the fact that the great principles now erected into universal principles emerged in specific contexts, especially in Europe, proves that this point of view prevails. Some less moderate scholars, like Pan Wei, express themselves even more explicitly:

> I am standing in the China school. Russia had three schools: the western school, the Communist school and the Russian school. I am standing with the Chinese school. The leftist's, rightist's, and China's stand. I stay with the camp that defends China's own ideas and resources. Number one: beneath our feet, is 60 years of Communist practice – Chinese Communist practice – and ideas, and below that is deep, profound sources of Chinese ideas, traditional China. And then, absorbed and digested ideas from the West. I don't refuse western ideas, I select ideas. So I would say I belong to the China school.

It can easily be understood why the Party does not object to this tendency, now that it has renounced its revolutionary paraphernalia to become a governing party (*zhizheng dang*) striving for legitimacy.

We have focused on the consensus that emerged in the 1990s within the Chinese intellectual community on the neo-conservative idea of necessarily gradual reform and the rejection of iconoclastic anti-traditionalism. This landmark evolution took place among political elites too. The revolution paradigm was put on the back burner and the point no longer was to renounce the resources Chinese tradition could bring. What was at stake was, on the contrary, to draw from such resources so as to balance out the limits of western theories and allow for a careful and successful modernising reform. The dividing line could no longer be located between modernisers and conservatives since it had been blurred, but – given the serious problems originating from the Open and Reform policy – needed to be drawn between the advocates of a market economy and the champions of a strong regulating and distributing state.

Divisions over the roles of the state and the market

Inequalities and nationalism

A new statist tendency, stemming from the fear of China's implosion, gave birth to a grouping of intellectuals labelled the New Left. Beside the problems faced in the margins of the Chinese empire, several other potential cracks in the social structure come from rising inequalities between urban and rural areas, western and eastern regions, and between those who lose and those who benefit from the reforms. These inequalities, which deepen as reforms intensify, trigger a greater instability. Sociologist Sun Liping has warned of the dangers of a 'fractured' (*duanlie*) society in which fellow citizens live in different technological ages.[53] Economist Hu Angang developed the idea that four worlds coexist in China. As far as income levels and the UN Human Development Index are concerned, Beijing, Shanghai and Shenzhen are similar to developed countries; coastal provinces are above the world average while central regions are closer to average developing countries. Finally, inner provinces such as Tibet and Guizhou are as poor as the poorest countries in the world.[54] The growing social instability in these parts of China is to be connected to these serious inequalities. Chinese scholars like Wang Shaoguang have openly blamed the decentralising policy that Mao Zedong launched and Deng Xiaoping intensified. In the early 1990s, when the report Wang wrote with Hu Angang on state capacity and efficiency convinced leaders to reconsider the special treatment granted to coastal provinces and Special Economic Zones and to start re-centralising the decision-making process and fiscal policy, the central state only received 38 per cent of public revenue and was therefore unable to provide sufficient funding to the army and to civil servants. Awareness of the weakness of the Chinese state allows us to understand how some localist, sometimes corrupt practices thrive. Moreover, the central government no longer has the means to compensate the losses of those who do not, or no longer, benefit from the Reform policy. Nationalist propaganda providentially allows the government both to dissimulate the state's weakness and to boost loyalty to the national cause among those who lean towards regionalism.

Nationalism can also help achieve some necessary conditions for China to democratise. To the New Left, the ideal of nationalism, as expressed in a well defined nation with a shared identity, is a necessary condition of a well functioning democratic regime. The latter cannot flourish if the majority of its citizens does not first develop a deep feeling of belonging to a community. Indeed, a democratic regime cannot be efficient without the will and consent of the great majority of

---

53. Sun, L. 'Women zai kaishi miandui yige duanlie de shehui?' ('Are we facing a fractured society?'), *Zhanlue Yu uganli* 2, 2002; Sun, L. *Duanlie (Fracture)*, Beijing: Shehui Kexui Wenbian Chubanshe, 2003.

54. Hu, A. 'Yigeguojia sigeshijie fendiqu fazhanchaju' ('One country, four worlds'), in *Zhongguo Jingjishibao (China Economic Times)* 4 April 2001; Hu, A. 'Equality and efficiency', in Chaohua, W. *op. cit.*, p. 219–224.

citizens.[55] The state-building process on which national unity partly depends leads to strengthened solidarity and the sense of belonging to a community. An efficient state apparatus (*youxiao*) constitutes a major foundation without which democratisation cannot be fully achieved. Besides, society's politicisation, along with its 'nationalisation', has proven to be a necessary step for the political engagement of the citizens of a democratic nation. As far as spontaneous popular nationalism is concerned, which can be extremist and dangerous, the mobilisation and hypersensitivity of the Chinese people regarding the fate of the nation has compelled leaders to be more responsive, transparent and reactive.

The end of the consensus on reform

Scholars from the Cultural Revolution generation, who were gathered in the universities in the 1980s, claim to share some features and a common heritage. However, the careers, principles and engagements they developed on this common heritage are multitudinous. In the early years of the Open and Reform policy, a degree of consensus prevailed over the need to move away from the Cultural Revolution and revolution in general, and to progressively open up to the world and modernity. The ideal of a regime in which leaders could not make decisions with full impunity, without being held accountable for their consequences, a regime in which decisions were made in a collective, rational and scientific manner and where individual liberties were respected, was widely shared. However, Chinese intellectual elites started to fragment as the first side effects of the reforms appeared. Students and academics agreed to acknowledge and condemn the existence of rising inequalities, corruption, unemployment and inflation. What they quarrelled about was the analysis of the causes of and solutions to these emerging problems, which was reinforced by the uncertainties brought about by the neo-conservative realisation that anti-traditionalism and full adhesion to western theories would not fix all the problems. Kang Xiaoguang's memories of that period give us an insight not only into the context of the change of mindset which took place in the wake of the Tiananmen repression and the collapse of the Soviet Union but also into the way it has been reconstructed:

> I have always been a nationalist, in the sense that I feel concerned by the fate of my country. I believe that through the transition process of these former socialist countries, individuals have gained more freedom but social justice, economic efficacy, political leaders' integrity and the countries' unity have tremendously deteriorated. We hoped that reform and democratisation would contribute to China's economic development, more social equality, the country's strengthening but instead what happened was its division, the weakest groups getting poorer, the privileged getting richer, and corruption becoming

---

55. Wang, S. 'minzuzhuyi yu minzhu' (nationalism and democracy) in Wang, S. *Anbangzhidao: guojia zhuanliede mubiao yu tujing*, Beijing: Sanlian shudian, 2007.

commonplace. As a result, we have gradually stopped blindly believing in full westernisation, a multi-party system, universal suffrage and an independent judiciary. We were totally convinced that reform would lead us to the best results in the first place. Then we gradually realised that such a reform would actually cause many problems too.

In the mid 1990s, the social consequences of the intensification of the Open and Reform policy that took place in the wake of the 1989 repression precipitated fierce discussions in the Chinese intellectual sphere. It marked the end of the broad consensus on liberalism and democracy of the 1980s. A variety of groups emerged, roughly divided into anti-welfare Hayekian liberals – generally labelled as (market) liberals – and political liberals advocating some kind of social democracy; these latter were called New Leftists, as they did not question the need for a market economy, contrary to the Chinese Old Left.

Xu Youyu, one of the leading Chinese liberals, describes the discussion between these two tendencies as 'a phenomenon rarely seen among mainland Chinese intellectuals since 1949', in the sense that 'they are large-scale, spontaneous debates without official manipulation or ideological constraint.'[56] He efficiently encapsulates these debates in seven bones of contention. We should, however, note that each group tends to caricature the other (which is accused of not being democratic, simplifying western theories and wrongly adapting them to China and so on) and to exaggerate their differences. Disagreements are, nonetheless, real, in terms of the assessment of the revolutionary era; their respective preferences for the French or Anglo-Saxon brand of liberal tradition; and the idea of democracy as antithetical to aristocracy for the New Left, referring to Tocqueville; while the liberals consider democracy as antithetical to despotism.[57]

When intervening publicly, the New Left raises the alarm and succeeds in placing the issue of inequality and the evil effects of reform at the top of the agenda. In that sense, the New Left's assessment is relevant and plays a major role in reflection on economic reform. The liberal scholar Ren Jiantao thus explains that the 'ideological schism which takes place in the late 1990s Chinese society' is not related to the analysis of the reform but to the proposals which are made with the aim of solving the problems which are identified:

[Members of the New Left] have started pointing at the mistakes made by the CCP's reform. The economy had successfully developed, but in a very unfair way. We did not focus enough on the least privileged groups and the reform had to take a new direction. These criticisms were indeed completely justified. The current Chinese reform is responsible for this deplorable social situation where the gap between the rich and the poor is ginormous. However,

56. Xu, Y. 'The *Debates between Liberalism* and the New Left in China since the 1990s', *Contemporary Chinese Thought*, Vol.34, No. 3, 2003 p. 6.
57. Gan, Y. 'A Critique of Chinese Conservatism in the 1990s', *Social Text* No. 55, Summer, 1998, pp. 45–66.

to my mind, their analysis is flawed. Indeed, the Communist Party's reform is correct; but due to the interests of the Party, the reform is incomplete. The Party is definitely not willing to share its power.

In an interview entitled 'For a Chinese liberalism', Zhu Xueqin, one of the leading figures of the liberal movement, describes the liberal position very explicitly: 'Economically, liberals press for further market-oriented reforms.' To his mind,

> Twenty years of economic reforms have failed to establish the political checks necessary to control and balance it, and so problems of social justice have become steadily worse. These can only be resolved by reform of the political system to establish the rule of law in a constitutional democracy, rather than by returning to the kind of mass mobilisation which occurred in the past.

Because 'an all too "visible foot" is often stamping on the "invisible hand" of the market, and in China today the social injustices our New Left friends condemn, including the collusion between money and power they pillory, should be attributed more to the violent "foot" than the dirty "hand".'[58]

The New Left emerged in this very context of questioning the 'consensus on reform'. It was first composed of young academics who studied or taught in American universities for many years, read post-modern writers like Foucault and Lyotard, the Frankfurt School, or neo-Marxists like John E. Roemer. They have been inspired by western social sciences, which they view in a more nuanced way than those who have never or hardly left Chinese universities, and who rely more on translations published in China. The New Left denounces the reform's undesirable effects and blames the neo-liberal principles which have prevailed and guided the economic reform in a partly concealed way. The rise of nationalism and neo-conservatism, as well as the questioning of the iconoclastic radicalism inherited from the May Fourth movement in protest against western imperialism and calls for China's 'full westernisation' – the undisputed adhesion to the principles of classical liberalism and transitology – provide ammunition for this movement, aiming at reintroducing systematically but partially liberal theory in China after a 50-year eviction. The New Left does not purport to oppose the whole of liberal theory. Wang Hui, Wang Shaoguang, Gan Yang and Cui Zhiyuan all define themselves as liberals who draw from other resources than the 'neo-liberal' Hayekian defence of the market.

Chinese liberals, united against the New Left, nevertheless exhibit myriad ideological tendencies: some support Hayek and Berlin's 'negative liberty' while others favour Rawls' theory of justice. Deng Zhenglai, who considerably contributed to the introduction of liberal ideas in China through his translation work, explained why liberal and individualist theories are received with such enthusiasm in China.

---

58. Zhu, X. 'For a Chinese liberalism', in Chaohua, W. (ed.), *One China, Many Paths*, London: Verso, 2003, pp. 106–7.

In primary school, my teachers used to say we were the first generation to be the first pure product of China's new society. Before 1949, the former society was atrocious. Children were sent to factories to work, we were so lucky to be sent to school. And suddenly, I turn 14 and they send me to a factory. I was stunned. How could this happen in the new society? Children could not possibly be sent to work in a good society. I did not understand. I was completely lost [...] I wondered how someone could become so powerful as to make the decision to inflict this on young generations and how he could justify that decision. To find answers to this question, I read many western theories. Many thinkers answer this question. However, I think that liberal theory most specifically answers it. And the most crucial and representative liberal thinker of the twentieth century is Friedrich Hayek. Other major liberals obviously deserve all our attention: John Rawls, Robert Nozick and many others. Reading their books provides some answer. I wanted to find a satisfactory answer thanks to their work. [...] I therefore studied liberal theory and Hayek in the 1980s I also commented and criticised his work, and translated many of his books – more than 200,000 Chinese characters altogether. I devoted the whole 1980s to that thinker.

In the translations of Burke, Hayek, Rawls, Berlin, Nozick or Dworkin which have been published since the early 1980s, Chinese intellectuals look for the right formula to cure the country of its past excesses and its current woes. Liberalism, whose principles had been successfully introduced in the country at the turn of the twentieth century, has progressively recovered its status and Hu Shi and Gu Zhun's ideas have been rehabilitated.

What Gan Yang, Wang Shaoguang, and the other forerunners of the movement – which was called the 'New Left' so as damage its credibility at a time when any reference to the left was pejorative, since it was associated with the former system and with Maoism – wanted to show was that if the reform maintained its neo-liberal course, contrary to what liberals who condemned an incomplete reform pretended, the adverse effects of reform would not recede but worsen. To Gan Yang, this last division of the Chinese intellectual community amounts to the emergence of Chinese right and left wings:

Until the 1980s, even if China reformed and opened to the market, we were still far from an open market economy. It is only in the 1990s that the system started to truly change. The major division of the 1990s is the surfacing of a left and a right wing, which originated in opposed views on capitalism. Right-wing people think that capitalism is preferable no matter what to the former system. Even if it creates some difficulties, they consider that it is the price to pay, a necessary evil. They go as far as defending a number of horrendous things, including corruption. For the sake of liberty, they accept the former system to be overthrown. They tolerate inequalities, which they consider inevitable, whereas until recently, they did not tolerate them. For the sake of the market, the great iron rice bowl[59] and full egalitarianism had to be destroyed. This scission took place in the 1990s.

Gan Yang thus evokes his personal trajectory and the brutality of this fragmentation. His own experience corroborates the idea that New Left and liberal thinkers both come from the 'Enlightenment camp', which split in two when the former realised 'they had gone too far'. To prove that people can have a passionate interest in politics in China, and that debates are now widespread and free, he refers to his sudden break with Xu Youyu, his very close friend in the 1980s, when they both belonged to the same influential editorial board of the journal *Wenhua: Zhongguo Yu Shijie* (*Culture: China and the World*).[60]

I have observed lately that one of the main characteristics of this country is that people all over China debate. So much so that friends sometimes argue and become enemies. Personally, I have lost some very old friends that way, which makes me very sad. We no longer get along. They are indignant that I can now think what I think. It happened very fast. We had been friends for over 20 years. It happened with Xu Youyu, for instance. It's a typical case. Discussing became impossible. He belongs to the far right while I consider myself one of the most moderate members of the New Left. But to him, my position is intolerable. Xu Youyu is a very radical man. I deem his right-wing positions utterly intolerable. But from a less personal point of view, this is not a bad thing at all. It shows that everybody reflects and feels concerned about major issues. Everybody cares.

Gan Yang's testimony indicates that oppositions are fierce between the two camps, which interviewed scholars all confirmed in the last part of the interviews, when dealing with their sociability and networks. Exchanges between the two camps are uncommon, apart from articles addressing or attacking one another, unless they share some common interest, like Xu Youyu and Wang Shaoguang who both strive to open up reflection and research on the Cultural Revolution, each in his own way.

As to Cui Zhiyuan, his views are located even further to the left. He is one of the most controversial researchers in the eyes of both liberals and neo-conservatives. His articles have triggered fierce reactions among liberals such as Zhu Xueqin, Xu Youyu and Qin Hui, who belong to an older generation and whose political views

---

59. The iron rice bowl (*tie fan wan*) designates the system that guaranteed job security, a stable income and social benefits.

60. *Culture: China and the World*, a central group in the Culture Fever of the 1980s, was published by the Joint Bookstore. For more on the *Culture: China and the World* editorial board, *see* Gu, E. X., 'Cultural intellectuals,' and Fong-Ching, C. 'Popular cultural movement of the 1980s' in Davies G. (ed.), *Voicing Concerns: Contemporary Chinese critical inquiry*, Lanham, MD: Rowman & Littlefield, 2001, pp. 78–79.

are closely connected to their bitter experience of the Cultural Revolution. Indeed, Cui is among the only scholars in China who have dared talk of some positive elements in the legacy of Mao Zedong's era, from which, he thinks, institutional innovation can stem. In an article on the Angang constitution,[61] the internal charter written in the 1950s by the Anshan Steel Company in China's north-east region, Cui claims that its principles – *liangcan* ('Two Participations': executives of the company have to participate in productive labour and workers have to participate in the management of the company); *yigai* ('One Reform': reform unreasonable regulation in the workplace); *sanjiehe* ('Three Combinations': the alliance of workers and engineers should be combined and so on) – prove that the ideas of co-decision-making and economic democracy are not new to China and could be further developed. This political economy and political philosophy scholar from the School of Public Policy and Management at the prestigious Tsinghua University is commonly categorised as a New Leftist but prefers to be called a liberal socialist, after John Stuart Mill and James Meade. Mill developed the concept of liberal socialism in the chapter, 'On the probable futurity of the labouring classes' of his *Principles of Political Economy*,[62] in which he significantly qualified private property rights in means of production and recommended a market economy dominated by decentralised democratic co-operative firms. James Meade was a British Keynesian economist who won a joint Memorial Nobel Prize in Economics in 1977 with Bertil Ohlin. Cui Zhiyuan is an explicit admirer of his efforts to reconcile economic efficiency and a fair distribution of income.[63]

After completing his PhD on soft budget constraint[64] under the supervision of Jon Elster, Adam Przeworski and Lester Telser at the University of Chicago in 1995, Cui taught political science at MIT for six years, where he became acquainted with Charles Sabel, the leading American specialist of post-Fordist production who co-wrote *The Second Industrial Divide*.[65] At the Harvard Law

61. Cui, Z. 'Anshan xianfa he hou Futezhuyi' ('The Angang constitution and post-Fordism'), *Dushu (Reading)* 1, 1996. Cui Zhiyuan is also known for advocating the importance of Dazhai, a star commune in Mao's time, and even of the Cultural Revolution.

62. Mill, J. S. *The Principles of Political Economy: With some of their application to social philosophy*, 2 vols, Toronto: University of Toronto Press, 1996.

63. Meade designed labour-capital partnerships, where outside shareholders own Capital Share Certificates and inside workers own Labour Share Certificates, and social dividends to replace the demand for job tenure by an enhancement of the resources and capabilities of the individual citizen. Cui, Z. 'Liberal socialism and the future of china: a petty bourgeoisie manifesto', in Cao, T. (ed.), *China's Model for Modern Development*, London: Routledge, 2005.

64. János Kornai, a Hungarian economist, first observed the Soft Budget Constraint phenomenon in the Hungarian economy of the 1970s, a socialist economy experimenting with the introduction of market reforms. 'Although state-owned enterprises were vested with a moral and financial interest in maximizing their profits, the chronic loss-makers among them were not allowed to fail. They were always bailed out with financial subsidies or other instruments. Firms could count on surviving even after chronic losses, and this expectation left its mark on their behavior.' (Kornai, J., Maskin, E. and Roland, G. 'Understanding the Soft Budget Constraint', *Journal of Economic Literature*, American Economic Association 41(4), 2003), pp. 1095–1136.

65. Diore M. J. and Sabel, C. F. *The Second Industrial Divide: Possibilities for prosperity*, New York: Basic Books, 1984.

School, he also met Roberto Unger, who took leave from his position at Harvard from 2007 to 2009 to serve in Lula's[66] government as minister of Strategic Affairs. Cui's research focuses on the issue of economic democracy. To him, 'China and worldwide exploration of institutional and theoretical innovation are closely connected.' It is one of the reasons why he finally decided to go back to China, where 'there is more plasticity and things are not so fixed'.

These New Left/liberal labels are still relevant even though the left/right label is increasingly used; and the debates around them are still very intense. It is interesting to note that the labels have appeared more openly in official debates, especially through the different models of economic and political models that were put forward before the Eighteenth Congress in 2012, by two members of the Central Committee Politburo who eventually failed to become permanent members of the Politburo Standing Committee: Bo Xilai, the now-imprisoned former Party Secretary of Chongqing municipality, and Wang Yang, former Party Secretary of Guangdong province. China's relative decentralisation had allowed each camp to choose its champion and to start implementing its theoretical proposals. Wang Yang and Bo Xilai's political ambitions drove them to stray from Communist leaders' conventional austere style. They both used the media to gain popularity and hoped to get a seat on the Standing Committee, which had the merit of publicly revealing that political debates and that some form of competition for power were taking place within the Party. Before Bo Xilai's spectacular downfall, the New Left used the socio-economic policies implemented in Chongqing and described as the 'Chongqing experience' (*Chongqing jingyan*) to advance that the policy defended by the liberal right had to be fully put into question. The municipality of Chongqing became the ideal platform to promote its political suggestions. Cui Zhiyuan, a great admiror of Mayor Huang Qifan, agreed to work for him for several months.[67] As to Wang Shaoguang, he coined the name 'socialism 3.0' to describe the various experiments which had been launched in China. Chongqing's policy received intense local, national and international media coverage but it focused on very different policies, such as the large-scale campaign against local corruption or the revival of old revolutionary songs led by Bo Xilai. Chongqin's policy has been reduced to nostalgia for the revolutionary era, ambiguously received by central authorities. However, the procession of high dignitaries of the regime visiting the municipality before Bo Xilai's downfall – Xi Jinping in December 2010, the majority of the members of the Standing Committee – makes Beijing's attentiveness to the policy led in Chongqing manifest. Let us note that the dramatic fall of Bo Xilai and his wife has not led to a major policy reorientation in Chongqing, where Mayor Huang Qifan has kept his position.

We have shown how, within the Chinese intelligentsia, the political cohesion of the 1980s deteriorated after 1989 and how the intensification of the Open and Reform policy and its impact on Chinese society divided intellectuals into various camps, opposing each other in fierce debates. We can establish a connection between

---

66. Luiz Inàcio Lula da Silva, president of Brazil 2002–11.

67. Frenkiel, E. 'From scholar to official. Cui Zhiyuan and Chongqing City's local experimental policy', *Books & Ideas*, 6 December 2010, available online at http://www.booksandideas.net/IMG/pdf/20101206_Cui_Zhiyuan_EN.pdf.

the Chinese case and Vladimir Shlapentokh's analysis of Soviet intellectuals in the post-Stalin era. To his mind;

> The intellectuals' political cohesiveness is directly proportional to the extent of the repression in their society and the unity of the dominant class. In a society ruled by mass terror, the intellectuals as a group almost entirely cease to exist. They resuscitate only when society enters a period of milder and more selective repressions. Then, with the nightmare behind them, they tend to unite strongly in their hatred of the party and of the state and begin, almost unanimously, to support liberal ideology. The situation changes yet again if the regime makes progress toward liberalisation and if the dominant class breaks into factions offering different programmes for coping with society's crises. In this case, intellectuals begin to lose their unity and split into warring camps.[68]

The hypothesis that the cohesion of intellectuals is proportional to the degree of social repression and to the unity of the dominating class seems confirmed by the way the Chinese intelligentsia evolved, harbouring escalating divisions and conflicts.

Cultural nationalism: A new trend or a new consensus?

One last tendency, deriving from the growing importance, as mentioned above, of nationalism and the idea that resources can be found in the 'Chinese tradition' to reform China, has gained strength since the early 2000s. The career development of a political philosopher like Deng Zhenglai is quite telling. In the 1980s, he contributed to passing on liberal theories, which his translations made accessible in China. After discovering classic liberalism and John Rawls' theory of justice, Deng Zhenglai, and the rest of the liberal camp, who were looking for answers to the issues raised by the Cultural Revolution and the means to avoid the reoccurrence of its totalitarian excesses, explored libertarian and communitarian criticisms of liberalism. Thus, Canadian philosopher Charles Taylor has regularly been invited to visit philosophy and political science departments in Chinese universities to present his communitarian critique of liberalism. Even if these theories offer a wealth of information, Deng Zhenglai claimed he had not found all the answers he was looking for. He also railed against the New Left, which 'tries to modify the western model to improve it. They want to modify what is not adapted to China. This is not my take on all this.' This is the reason why Deng devoted the last few years before his death to Chinese philosophy.

The renewed confidence in the contribution of Chinese history, 'culture' (*wenhua*), 'tradition' (*chuantong*) and 'civilisation' (*wenming*), which are no longer considered as obstacles to but as assets for China's modernisation, is concomitant with China's rising to rank among the most powerful economies of the planet and

---

68. Shlapentokh, V. *Soviet Intellectuals and Political Power: The post-Stalin era*, London and New York: I. B.Tauris, 1990, pp. 5–6.

becoming a major international player. This movement of appropriating native resources also affects other academic disciplines, such as international relations. The research of Yan Xuetong, who is the Dean of Tsinghua University's Modern International Relations Institute and chief editor of Oxford University Press's *Chinese Journal of International Politics*, is explicitly geared to that aim. The first book he published in English, *Ancient Chinese Thought, Modern Chinese Power*, is a collection of articles on pre-Qin (770–476 BC) thinkers and on the Warring States Period, preceding China's unification by the first emperor Qin Shihuang in 221 BC.[69] In Yan Xuetong's theory, the quality of political leaders is highlighted as playing not only a key role in the nation's power but also an even more crucial role than the will of leaders to exert economic and military power, because leaders act according to moral norms. Yan explains that the political situation at that time in China's history – when many small kingdom-states were independent, sovereign and separated by precise borders even though they all owed allegiance to the King of Zhou – is such that it is more comparable to the current international system than to imperial China. Moreover, these states were striving to develop and improve their mutual relationship as well as their relationship with the royal court, so that that era was propitious for a very practical brand of political philosophy of international relations to flourish.[70]

As regards the New Left, this renaissance of 'Chinese civilisation' has implied a rejection of a western modernity, whose universal claims seem to condemn societies following alternative paths to backwardness. As a result, to Wang Hui

> 'Modern' is a temporal concept used discriminatingly to cast other periods out of the modern; in this sense, 'modern' is a discriminatory concept, rejecting all other elements present in the same space–time, and having established a 'hegemonic hierarchical structure'.[71]

Gan Yang thus proposes to give up using the concept of modernity altogether and to resort to 'civilisation' instead, which allows for pluralism and multiculturalism:

> The usual take on what is modern and modernity precludes any kind of pluralism. But why couldn't an alternative be found in the Third World, outside of the West? Well, this way of approaching modernity forbids us to think that way. This results in the development of capitalism here too, since this is the only thing we are offered and it cannot be eluded. We should not let ourselves be caught in that logic though. It is not impossible for China to opt for a different path, and to adopt another attitude. This possibility does exist and it cannot be proscribed. I believe the concept of civilisation is pivotal for a new beginning.

69. Yan, X. *Ancient Chinese Thought, Modern Chinese Power*, Princeton, NJ: Princeton University Press, 2011.
70. Yan, X. *Ancient Chinese Thought, Modern Chinese Power*.
71. Wang Hui, "Zhongguo zhizao' yu lingleide xiandaixing' ('Made in China and another modernity'), *Zhuangshi Zazhi (Ornament)* 181, May 2008.

For liberal scholars who take less active part in these debates, such as Xu Jilin, a specialist in China's contemporary intellectual history, the New Left proved instrumental in historicising and spacialising the universal project of modernity; but the shift in studies of modernity from Europe and North America to Asia must first be interpreted as a 'provocation against western universalism' and sometimes goes too far. Xu Jilin thus rejects the proposal Gan Yang makes in a political article entitled 'From "nation-state" to "civilization-state"':

> The 'model country' he wishes for is not a civilization enriched with the universal values but 'de-westernized'. To illustrate that point with modern Turkey, he deems that a country which emulates the West and destroys the cultural tradition of its own nation constitutes a 'modernity which emasculated itself'; the only thing it can eventually be is 'a country which torn itself apart.' Gan Yang believes that 'China is to choose the path of "a modernisation which does not amount to westernization". China is no minor country. The long history of the Chinese civilization has made it a great country with a 'drive to civilization'. This is a great country endowed with its own 'civilizational assets'.[72]

Gan Yang's career path can seem convoluted. As previously mentioned, he used to be one of the main members (the head) of the board of *Culture: China and the World*, vocal advocates of the introduction of liberalism in China and critics of China's tradition in the 1980s, before he joined the New Left in the 1990s. From 2000 on, he has devoted himself to the Confucian renaissance. In an article translated into French, he goes as far as singing the praises of a Confucian socialist republic.[73]

> From 2000 on, I have started delving into the issue of culture and people's soul. Few left-wing intellectuals were interested in these issues. People give me many labels. I am often associated with conservatism and the New Left. But in the 1980s, I was a leading liberal figure. And still, I haven't changed a bit. My concerns are exactly the same. This is because society itself has deeply changed so that the questions cannot be raised the same way.

As Jean-Louis Rocca[74] and Xu Jilin think, among others, conservative thinkers like Pan Wei and designers of a 'China model' emphasising the nationalist priority given to power and wealth go too far.

---

72. Gan, Y. 'Cong "Minzu guojia" zouxiang "wenming guojia"' ('From "nation-state" to "civilization-state"'), in *21 Shiji Jingji Baodao* (*21st Century Economic Report*), 29 December 2003 quoted in Xu, J. 'Valeurs universelles ou valeurs chinoises? Le courant de pensée de l'historicisme dans la Chine contemporaine', *Rue Descartes* 72, 2011/2012, pp. 56, 62–3.

73. Gan Yang, 'Prendre en compte la continuité historique pour penser le politique aujourd'hui', in Sébastien Billioud and Joël Thoraval (eds), *Regards sur le politique en Chine aujourd'hui*, *Extrême-Orient, Extrême-Occident*, 31, 2009, pp. 125–39.

74. Rocca, J. -L. 'Pourquoi nous ne comprenons pas la Chine', in Frenkiel E. and Rocca, J. -L. (eds), *La Chine en mouvements*, Paris: Presses Universitaires de France, 2013.

In the first place, supposed 'universal' values should be deconstructed and denounced as the 'Emperor's new clothes'. The absurdity of one panacea solving a hundred ills should be unveiled. Second, an accurate and complete assessment of our Chinese ways of existing is needed, so as to give theoretical explanations and presentations of the 'Chinese way' and the 'China model' which can convince the intellectual community.[75]

2008 was a unique year for China, with the Beijing Olympics and the prospect of its becoming the third greatest economic power, ahead of Germany (it rose to the second rank in 2010). While the country celebrated the 30-year anniversary of the Open and Reform policy and prepared the 60-year anniversary of the People's Republic, it was quite popular among academics to offer assessments and to venture hypotheses explaining such achievement. In a matter of months, the number of articles and public interventions on the 'China model' exploded, as an article detailing the evolution of the occurrences of the term from 2003 to 2010 on the Chinese search engine Baidu showed.[76]

Kang Xiaoguang claims to have coined the concept with his 2004 book *Zhongguo De Daolu* (*The Chinese Way*).[77] His reasoning is crystal clear: the Chinese pragmatic reform is beneficial from an economic point of view, but from a social and cultural perspective, the worst is to be expected if the Party does not accept the necessity of filling the current ideological void by fully embracing Confucianism. The latter is to serve as a philosophy of government, ensuring the leaders' morality and benevolence, and it should be imposed as a state religion. In the early 2000s, in prophetic terms, Kang therefore advocates a full Confucian renaissance, comprising its introduction in school curricula and public-service examinations, state support to guarantee Confucianism legal protection and a salary paid to Confucianists. Only then would the 'Chinese way', founded on a solid economic structure and a complete and adapted political and social structure, take on its full meaning.

Kang, contrary to a liberal thinker like Qin Hui, does not condemn what he theorised as 'the alliance of elites', since this allows social stability. Political elites gradually fulfil economic and intellectual elites' claims for extended 'democratic' rights – extended liberties, private property rights, protection of the market, rule of law and so on – so as to ensure their support for the government and stable economic growth. Jiang Zemin's theory of the 'Three Represents' (*sange daibiao*) should

---

75. Pan, W. 'Gan yu xifang zhankai zhengzhi guannian douzheng' ('Let us dare challenge the West on political concepts'), *Huanqiu Shibao* (*Global Times*), 28 January 2008, quoted in Xu, J. 'Valeurs universelles ou valeurs chinoises? Le courant de pensée de l'historicisme dans la Chine contemporaine', *Rue Descartes* 72, 2011/2012, pp. 58–9.

76. Qian, G. 'How should we read China's "discourse of greatness"?', *China Media Project*, 23 February 2010, available online at http://cmp.hku.hk/2010/02/23/4565/.

77. This book is mainly known under the title: Kang, X. *Renzheng*, Singapore: World Scientific Press, 2005.

be understood in that context.[78] Political elites pay for the support of academics, who now enjoy more comfort and significant investments in research and control students more than they did in the 1980s. This stability, combined with a large market and cheap and unlimited manpower, boosts economic development, which benefits both elites and popular classes in a 'bigger cake, bigger share' logic. This has encouraged rising nationalist (and sometimes arrogant) feelings, which are nevertheless instrumental ensuring social cohesion, as transitory substitutes for a more 'mature' nationalist sentiment. Indeed, a blossoming state needs to have a great plan for the future. And the ideal of *xiaokang* (moderate prosperity), that is, the promise of better living conditions, is not sufficient. China has no ideal plan. There is no definition of what a good society is, of what is good and fair there. This is the reason why Kang Xiaoguang advocates cultural nationalism.[79] He explains that if he had not studied the Falungong,[80] read Huntington as well as Weber and Gramsci's works on culture and personally experienced the American reaction to 9/11 when in Washington, he would not have developed an acute understanding that the absence of a convincing ideology is China's greatest challenge. He would not have grasped that cultural nationalism is indispensable to rebuilding the Chinese way of thinking, without which the nation could thrive neither internally nor internationally. Kang thus proposes to combine Chinese traditional culture, egalitarian culture based on Marxism and liberal democracy, while emphasising the fundamental role of Confucianism, which can help the whole structure hold together and last.

The liberal camp denounces cultural nationalism and discussions on the 'Chinese way' and the 'China model' as inopportune and unjustified manifestations of arrogance on the part of Chinese academics. It believes they are not credible. Ren Jiantao considers that 'market Leninism'[81] cannot be considered a model in the ameliorative sense of the term since 'China's high economic growth does not necessarily mean that the Chinese political institutions are good'.

---

78. This does not mean that Kang Xiaoguang is fully satisfied with the system as it is. He criticises its limited power, lack of legitimacy, its excessive control of intellectual elites, its lack of legality, stifling of labour union expression and lack of social security. Besides, the alliance of elites can fail if capitalists finally rule over leaders, as only the supervision of the masses and the welfare state can rein them in. Consequently, Kang Xiaoguang's defence of authoritarianism does not amount to a simply apology for the existing system. He calls for a market economy combined with a co-operative and authoritarian welfare state, where all social classes benefit from the co-operation. An authoritarian power is needed to protect the market and correct injustices. Kang Xiaoguang, *Renzheng*, Singapore: World Scientific Press, 2005. For a good summary in English, *see* Ownby, D. 'Kang Xiaoguang: social science, civil society, and Confucian religion', *China Perspectives*, 2009/4, available online at http://chinaperspectives.revues.org/4928.

79. Kang, X. 'Shi nian bu bian: shichang jingji, jinying lianmeng, quanwei zhengzhi' ('Market economy, alliance of elites and authoritarianism'), interview by Haiying, L. in *Xueshu Zhongguo*, April 2004.

80. Kang, X. 'Falungong wenti de zhengzhi xiaoying' ('The political impact of the Falun Gong issue'), *Zhongguo Shehui Daokan* 33, 2000.

81. According to his analyses, China is a Leninist state power and microeconomically free-market economy, without a proper right to property.

I don't see it as a compliment when western countries talk about the China model: 'We enjoy liberal democracy, the western model, while you live in an authoritarian regime called the China model.' As a matter of fact, there is nothing positive in that concept. I therefore believe that most Chinese academics have not fully grasped the situation [...] So as to entirely focus on building the economy, we have renounced the principles of class struggle, Mao's thought and Marxism. But the CCP still refuses to renounce its power. Apart from this very issue, we can discuss everything: how the CCP wants to maintain its power, how it does it. [...] It is impossible to precisely define what the China model is, what its underlying ideas are. It seems to be an evolving governmental principle in a transforming society. That's the best definition we can reach for now. But if the China model [*zhongguo moshi*] is seen as a model to emulate [*zhongguo dianfan*], this is a third definition, which to my mind does not exist. On the contrary, to end on a negative note, if the current Chinese development model, which is purely utilitarian, was to become a model for the world, it would be a disaster for humankind. Indeed, we rely on a destructive use of the environment, on the degradation of human institutions as well as on wealth accumulation through highly unfair means.

Liberal scholars associate discussions on the 'China model' with a nationalist strategy of rejecting the West and justifying an authoritarian policy.

We address the West and claim with self-righteous confidence: 'stop coming to China and lecturing us on universal values! China has its own democracy and specific constitutional government; it has its made-in-China modernity!'[82]

Xu Jilin and the liberals deplore that, with the aim of attacking the West, 'Chinese historicism' targets the values of the Enlightenment and liberal democracy: 'the punitive expedition undertaken against western modernity turns the rejection it can trigger on its head: it amounts to rejecting the values of civilization which constrain the will to power and to keeping the most terrifying Machiavelism.' The heirs of the Enlightenment camp now nonetheless denounce the rediscovery of the Chinese tradition less violently than they used to, as they have finally forsworn the iconoclasm of the May Fourth movement and the 1980s. To Xu Jilin, those he labels 'classicists' of the 2000s are looking for 'a new civilisation discovered in China but having global universal values'.[83] Social-democrat Qin Hui is one of the liberals most inclined toward this undertaking. In an article entitled 'Traditional culture today: the duty of taking stock to reflect on politics', his aim is to demonstrate that 'there is no necessary contradiction between what we now call "tradition" and "radical" progressivism'. He describes

---

82. Xu, J. 'Valeurs universelles ou valeurs chinoises?', p. 60.
83. Xu, J. 'Valeurs universelles ou valeurs chinoises?', pp. 63–5.

'the mistakes of the 20th century Chinese Enlightenment cultural movement'.[84] As Joël Thoraval and Sébastien Billoud have shown, 'to his liberal friends now condemning Confucianism, Qin Hui responds that they should no longer pick the wrong fight [...] The proper adversary is the centralized community which oppresses the individual, not Confucianism',[85] which, when rid of its 'legist-daoist' distortions – the omnipresent centralised power and interest groups' pressure for *laissez-faire* – could constitute 'an indigenous resource modernisation China could rely on'.[86]

Conclusions

We have studied how a nationalist and gradualist conservative thought has surfaced and advocated a modernisation which is not severed from the 'Chinese tradition' but, on the contrary, draws on its resources as well as on western theories. This trend of thought stands in opposition to iconoclastic intellectual trends deriving from the 1980s, which called for full westernisation of the economy, society and regime. Its various elements, however, simultaneously and abundantly rely on foreign references. Furthermore, this conservative way of thinking goes well beyond ideological rifts and a back-to-tradition paradigm has prevailed among the whole Chinese intelligentsia in the 1990s and especially the 2000s. Gan Yang's stance signals the New Left's openness towards tradition and, even among liberals, criticising Confucianism is nowadays less common. Consequently, there is now a consensus on not relegating imperial and revolutionary history and philosophy to the past, as was the case after the Cultural Revolution, but considering the Chinese cultural legacy as an asset for the country's future. China's future appears, as a result, more uncertain, since the country is no longer envisaged as merely converging with developed countries, as the two following chapters, devoted to the debate on China's democratisation, will show.

---

84. Qin, H. 'La culture traditionnelle aujourd'hui: un devoir d'inventaire pour penser le politique', in Sébastien Billioud and Joël Thoraval (eds), *Regards sur le politique en Chine aujourd'hui, Extrême-Orient, Extrême-Occident* 31, 2009, p. 78 and p. 80.

85. Billioud, S. and Thoraval, J. *Regards sur le politique en Chine aujourd'hui*, p. 10.

86. Qin, H. 'La culture traditionnelle aujourd'hui', p. 92.

Chapter Five

Which Model of Democratisation is Best for China? The Debate

Even if the concepts of democratisation and the rule of law entered the official repertoire years ago, defining the meaning of notions of democracy and democratisation is a source of great tension in the highest spheres in China, where the direction of an expected political reform is intensely debated. The debate on the best government for China can easily be found in official discourse, the media and society, albeit in a bowdlerised form: the best regime, even for China, is a democracy[1] but with Chinese characteristics (*zhongguo tese minzhu*) and it should be implemented progressively so as to maintain the country's order and unity by any means. From 2002 to 2012, the Hu–Wen government regularly expressed its will to rule in a more 'scientific' way. One of the main slogans of Hu Jintao's mandate was the 'concept of scientific development' (*kexue fazhanguan*) of the Party in its quest for a 'socialist harmonious society' (*shehuizhuyide hexie shehui*). The two notions, which were first used in 2003 so as to distinguish Hu's political orientation from that of his predecessor, Jiang Zemin, formed an inseparable dyad in the official rhetoric. Hu thus posed as a man closer to the common people, wishing for a 'scientific' and technocratic approach, in contrast with Jiang Zemin's excessive focus on growth and the GDP.[2] According to Zheng Yongnian, the reference to Sun Yat-sen should not be missed. Hu insisted upon '*lidang wei gong*' ('Building the Party For All'), 'meaning that the CCP does not have its own interests, it is for the interests of all people', which is reminiscent of the signature slogan '*tianxia wei gong*' ('All Under Heaven Belongs To All'), 'meaning that politics was for the common interest', which ornaments Sun Yat-sen's mausoleum in Nanjing.[3] To Hu, what was at stake was certainly not a change of direction. The aim was still economic development, but it had to be sustainable. The 'concept of scientific development' was to be the foundation stone of the edifice of 'Hu Jintao thought', revealing an urge for balance and long-term thinking. The benefits of growth were to be better shared among regions and social groups and economic, juridical and political rights had to be respected. This approach also translated into greater efforts to institutionalise

---

1. Yu, K. 'Democracy is a good thing', *Beijing News*, 23 October 2006.
2. Fewsmith, J. 'Promoting the scientific development concept', *China Leadership Monitor* 11, July 2004, available online at http://www.hoover.org/sites/default/files/uploads/documents/clm11_jf.pdf (last accessed 14 November 2014).
3. Zheng, Y. *The Chinese Communist Party as Organizational Emperor: Culture, reproduction and transformation*, New York: Routledge, 2010, p. 85.

various anti-corruption procedures and attempts to reduce corruption in the Party,[4] an endeavour that Xi Jinping rapidly took up at the beginning of his mandate in 2012. More transparency in government organisations and popular participation in decision-making have thus been promoted, though without institutionalising direct elections at higher levels than villages.[5]

This chapter explores the debate on democratisation in Chinese universities, whose sociological and historical context the previous chapters introduced. Mapping this debate, which gives an insight into the aspirations for change of academic elites in their diversity – within the limits of censorship, even though this affects academic debates less heavily than the mass media and publications – will allow us to grasp academics' different conceptions of the current regime; to identify the rifts which have materialised since the Tiananmen repression; and to make their disagreements explicit. Deciphering official discourse and editorials in official media like the *People's Daily* is a highly complex matter and its utility has not been proved; while analysing the academic debate on political reform, because such debate has some definite impact on political elites and public opinion and simultaneously reflects their respective yearnings and fears – even though in a potentially deformed way – is an interesting perspective from which to appreciate the diversity of approaches to the issue of democratisation in China.

This study was driven by my conviction that understanding this debate is crucial. Indeed, for more than 30 years, Chinese intellectuals and their abundant debates, publications, translations, meetings and so on, have ceaselessly contributed to open and diversify ways of thinking. 'Society has become more porous, the culture more diversified and tolerant, and people's consciousness about their rights and the value of democracy has been rising steadily.'[6] Zha Jianying thus calls for a change of perspective to help understand what is at stake in this movement: 'while the states have been busy building these gleaming airports and bullet trains, which change the face of China, this public intellectuals' work has been quietly changing the cultural soil', acting like a fine rain, 'a secret agent for change', which stealthily moisturises the soil. The point is to show that, as far as political reform is concerned, the situation is not so different from that of emerging economies' access to new technologies – with advances by leaps and bounds, when mobile phones are introduced simultaneously with or even before landlines, for instance. The scholarly debate on democratisation in China includes both 'pre-democratic' and 'post-democratic elements: pre-democratic reticence towards regime democratisation – with references to the insufficient capacity, education and

---

4. Zheng, Y. *The Chinese Communist Party as Organizational Emperor*, pp. 71–97.

5. In 1987, the People's Assembly passed the organic law on elections to village committees. Qin, H. 'Dividing the big family assets', *New Left Review*, April 2003, sect. 3; Schubert, G. 'Stability through more participation? Local direct elections and their impact on communist rule in present-day China', *Asien* 84, 2002, pp. 47–55.

6. Paper given by Zha Jianying at the conference Intellectuals Divided: The Growing Political and Ideological Debate in China, Brookings Institution, Washington DC, 14 September 2011.

'quality' (*suzhi*)[7] of Chinese citizens, which necessitates delaying the introduction of universal suffrage, that are specific to debates preceding the introduction of democratic institutions and procedures; and up-to-the-minute 'post-democratic' or 'counter-democratic' calls for a more complex and complete form of democracy, one that is not only electoral but also social, participative and responsive.

The 'catch-up effect' theory describes how emerging economies tend to have a superior growth rate compared to already developed economies, so that all economies tend to converge in terms of *per capita* income. Their accelerated growth can partly be explained by the fact that emerging countries take advantage of the advances of developed countries with regard to production methods, technologies and institutions. As to the Chinese debate on democratisation, there is no obvious convergence of China with democratic regimes, contrary to the expectations of transition studies. However, academic reflection on the future of the Chinese regime references both past and contemporary debates in now-democratic countries on the definition, benefits and drawbacks of democracy. The scholarly debate combines 'pre-democratic' earnestness and reserve towards democratisation with very recent 'post-democratic' (in the sense of democracy beyond elections) deliberation, doubts and criticisms; calls for the reinvention, completion and democratisation of democracy are idiosyncratic to the recent post-democratic deliberation. These have emerged from the practice of democracy, from the awareness of its tensions and difficulties, and from the desire to perfect it. They can somehow be related to recent technological breakthroughs that allow emerging economies to converge faster with developed countries. In the case of China this telescoping could help delay the much-expected democratic convergence as easily as it could help progress it; in the best-case scenario, however, it could eventually enable China's democratisation process to skip over some stages, benefiting from institutional innovations and avoiding some of the doubts and difficulties that currently undermine existing democratic regimes.[8]

A Chinese transition towards a western-style democracy?

A democratic horizon for China, but on what condition(s)?

To intellectual elites, apart from paternalistic and elitist exceptions like Pan Wei, Kang Xiaoguang or Jiang Qing, the political horizon of China amounts to its regime and society's democratisation (*minzhuhua*). Despite deep disagreements, liberals deploring the freezing of political reform and the New Left prioritising social reform all call for the democratisation that will finally complete the opening to the market launched in 1978. Therefore, to Yang Guangbin, a political scientist

---

7. Discourse on the necessary improvement of the quality of the population is ubiquitous in China. *See* Kipnis, A. 'Suzhi: a keyword approach', *China Quarterly* 186(1), 2006, pp. 295–313.

8. Rosanvallon, P. *La contre-démocratie, la politique à l'âge de la défiance*, Paris: Le Seuil, 2006; Rosanvallon, P. *La légitimité démocratique, impartialité, reflexivité, proximité*, Paris: Le Seuil, 2008.

from People's University, 'China's future will undoubtedly be democratic'. The economist from Peking University, Yao Yang, confirms this assessment when he explains his lassitude when discussing with liberals:

> When I interact with members of the Chinese right, I do not learn anything new because they keep on repeating western proposals we have heard hundreds of times. They want a constitutional democracy. What is the point in repeating this? This is obvious to everyone. The crucial point is to find the way to cross the river. It is impossible to assert for sure that everyone will precisely land there. We had better study China's history and its current conditions before deciding which bridge is adequate to reach the other side.

Constitutional democracy imposes itself as the future of the Chinese regime, 'This is obvious to everyone.' The fault line between intellectual stands is the question of how to find the right way to cross the river Deng Xiaoping famously referred to (*mozhe shitou guo he*: 'crossing the river by groping for stones'). The passage to the other side corresponds to the country's modernisation and opening to the world and to the necessary destination of joining the community of developed nations. To the vice-director of Tsinghua's China studies department, Liu Dong, China must shoulder its responsibilities if it wants to become a great international power.

> China is both a great power and a small country, in terms of consumption for instance; both a great country for sports in terms of Olympic gold medals and a small country in terms of sports practice; a great country in terms of political party, production, demographics, economy, but not as regards public opinion, resources or culture. I have written in newspapers that a great power should have some moral significance. In traditional China, greatness was a moral concept. Let us take the example of becoming a grown-up. To be given a crown and a hat when you are 20 does not make you an adult. In other words, to become a great power, China must take its responsibilities and distinguish itself from Iran or North Korea. The atmosphere must change. Otherwise, this great power could bring war to the world. I also wrote about an agenda. The Academy of Sciences has an agenda; I think the Academy of Social Sciences should also have one. In 2020, we should be told at what level elections will be introduced. In 2050, direct elections should be scheduled. Everybody would be satisfied; the Chinese population too. There would be less conflicts. I have deliberately written this in the central government newspaper and nobody criticised it. The article focused on benevolent rule [*wangdao*] and rule by force [*badao*], two traditional concepts.[9] The benevolent rule is moral while autocracy is completely arbitrary. I insist on the necessity of a benevolent rule.

---

9. Liu, D. 'Daguo zhi "da"– yi wangdao haizhi badao?' ('The meaning of "great" in a great power: benevolent rule or rule by force?'), first published in *Zhongguo Qingnian Bao* (*China Youth Daily*), and in Liu, D. *Daoshu Yu Tianxia*, Beijing: Peking University Press, 2011.

Liu Dong resorts to the traditional concept of *wangdao* to legitimise China's democratisation, which is presented as indispensible for its turning into a great international power. He suggests that Chinese traditional thinking, also mentioned by Yao Yang, has a major role to play in comprehending what is at stake in China's democratisation.

According to Xiao Gongqin, who theorised the neo-authoritarian movement of the 1980s and the neo-conservative movement of the 1990s, liberal democracy is the best regime for China. For China's democratisation to succeed and last, a number of conditions – roughly matching the conditions established by western theorists of modernisation – must apply, namely, a relatively high level of economic development,[10] a dynamic,[11] and a strong civic culture.[12] The authoritarian transition he advocates is only a temporary, necessary evil. Xiao, indeed, explains that he belongs to the generation of scholars who directly experienced the Cultural Revolution, that he 'deeply resents the despotism of that time' and that he ardently yearns for a democracy to be introduced in China.

> Intellectuals who have had such an experience as mine obviously want a free and democratic China. But the issues we focus on are more complex than in the case of most intellectuals: China does not have middle classes and the foundations of economic development. As a result, democracy could turn into. Ambitious individuals could take advantage of the popular vote to assuage their ambitions. The people's capacity to judge is not sufficient yet. This is the reason why I am particularly wary with the idea that a democracy should be immediately implemented. To put it simply, I think that after more than 30 years of economic development, we still need 30 years for civil society to develop, for social organisations, workers' unions and rural co-operatives to progressively develop and gradually become true social organisations which can unify the population through negotiation. Only after 30 years of social development could we start reflecting on democracy. Some people must deem my views are too conservative, since I do not expect to see a democratic China before I die, but for a country like China which has gone through 2,000

---

10. Lipset, S. M. 'Some social requisites of democracy: economic development and political legitimacy', *American Political Science Review* 53, 1959, pp. 69–105; Fukuyama, F. 'Capitalism and democracy: the missing link', *Dialogue 2*, 1993, pp. 2–7; Barro, R. 'Determinants of democracy' *Journal of Political Economy* 107(6), 1999, pp. 158–83; Alvarez, M., Cheibub, J. Limongi, F. and Przeworski, A. (eds), *Democracy and Development: Political institutions and well-being in the world, 1950–1990*, Cambridge: Cambridge University Press, 2000.

11. Putnam, R. D. *Making Democracy Work: Civic traditions in modern Italy*, Princeton, NJ: Princeton University Press, 1993; Linz, J. J. and Stepan, A. C. *Problems of Democratic Transition and Consolidation in Southern Europe, South America, and Post-Communist Europe*, Baltimore: Johns Hopkins University Press, 1996.

12. Almond, G. and Verba, S. (eds) *The Civic Culture: Political attitudes and democracy in five nations*, Princeton, NJ: Princeton University Press, 1963; Diamond, L. *Developing Democracy Toward Consolidation*, Baltimore, MD: Johns Hopkins University Press, 1999; Inglehart, R. *Modernization and Postmodernization: Culture, economic, and political change in 43 societies*, Princeton, NJ: Princeton University Press, 1997.

years of despotic culture, to turn into a democracy in 100 years or at least 50–60 years would not be such an extremely quick process.

Xiao Gongqin therefore introduces himself as a careful advocate of economic liberalism and liberal democracy. Like Sun Yat-sen before him,[13] he is convinced that an authoritarian transition period is necessary to guarantee social cohesion and political stability, without which reforms cannot go on.[14] To him, a certain level of economic development seems necessary to justify the deferred realisation of democracy. Otherwise, voters could vote for bad populist leaders. The elitism Xiao Gongqin proclaims without concealment can nowadays be found among a great many intellectuals and their arguments are reminiscent of those favouring a neo-dictatorship in the 1930s.[15] Xiao resorts to Huntington's arguments about the 'third wave' of democratisation and the importance of economic growth in the 1960s as factors of transition.[16] After in-depth study of Yuan Shikai and Porfirio Diaz's policy in Mexico, he fully embraced modernisation theory.[17] Without the

13. Bergère, M. -C. 'Les problèmes de la transition: tutelle et dictature', in *Sun Yat-sen*, Paris: Fayard, 1994, p. 430.

14. In the Triple Demism theory described by Marie-Claire Bergère (*Sun Yat-sen*, chapter 10, pp. 400–5), Sun Yat-sen distinguishes between three types of citizens: those who 'see and understand before others'; those who 'see after others and understand with them' and those who 'neither see nor understand a thing'. He thus differentiates between party leaders, cadres and activists, and the common people. John Stuart Mill's thought, especially his later defence of the rights of society over an individual's freedoms, inspired Sun Yat-sen. *See* Metzger, T. A. 'Did Sun Yat-sen understand the idea of democracy? The conceptualization of democracy in the Three Principles of the People and in Mill, J. S., *On Liberty*', *American Asian Review* 10(1), 1992, pp. 1–41. This does not mean that elitism has prevailed in the history of Chinese intellectuals, as Edmund Fung and Christine Vidal remind us, with the opposition to the Guomingdang dictatorship by progressive intellectuals in the 1930s. Fung, E. S. K. *In Search of Chinese Democracy: Civil opposition in Nationalist China, 1929–1949*, Cambridge: Cambridge University Press, 2000, pp. 114ff; Vidal, C. 'À l'épreuve du politique: les intellectuels non communiste chinois et l'émergence du pouvoir maoïste dans la première moitié du XXe siècle', PhD dissertation, 2006, EHESS.

15. *See* Fung, E. S. K. *In Search of Chinese Democracy*, pp. 98ff.

16. Wang Hui implicitly associates the theory developed by Xiao Gongqin to that of the Taiwanese liberals in the 1980s. *See* his interview entitled 'Fire at the castle gate', in Mulhern, F. (ed.) *Lives on the Left*, New York: Verso, 2012, p. 314: 'after the June Fourth movement was suppressed, many concluded that radicalism had undone it, and there had to be some other way to democracy. The answer would lie in the gradual emergence of civil society from the development of the market economy. For marketization would produce a middle class that could furnish the sturdy basis for civil associations, without directly antagonizing the state. The resulting civil society would then blossom into a democracy. These ideas were actually first developed by Taiwanese liberals in the eighties. My reaction was "but what kind of civil society do you want? What sort of social structure do you have in mind?".'

17. Lipset, S. M. 'Some social requisites of democracy: economic development and political legitimacy'; Lipset, S. M. *Political Man: The social bases of politics*, New York: Anchor Books, 1960; Huntington, S. *Political Order in Changing Societies*, New Haven, CT and London: Yale University Press, 2006; Inglehart, R. *Modernization and Post-Modernization: Cultural, Economic, and Political Change in 43 societies*; Inkeles, A. and Smith, D. H. *Becoming Modern: Individual change in six developing countries*, London: Heinemann Educational, 1975; Moore, B. *Social Origins of Dictatorship and Democracy: Lord and peasant in the making of the modern world*, Boston, MA: Beacon Press, 1966.

contribution of middle classes boosting domestic demand, raising the overall quality (*suzhi*) of the population,[18] introducing modern ways of life and playing the role of avant-garde of political change without threatening stability, democratic institutions cannot be successfully established in any country. Even liberals like Ren Jiantao, who believe that society is bound to eventually rise up in protest if the Party still refuses to share its power, consider that a democratic system cannot be introduced all at once without plunging China into chaos.

> I wish the Party, as the ruling party, could clearly acknowledge that it must reform institutions so as to share its power with other parties. There is no other way to avoid social violence compromising its authority. This is a matter of time. Because of the Soviet example, the Party rejects reform and stagnates, but there will be a historical backlash. A reform would make it go down in history, as the initiator of the reform process. This is the ideal situation I envisage. On the other hand, I sincerely hope that the Chinese people can remain patient. Of course, this is hard, especially when houses are brutally demolished and when resistance movements organised by citizens resort to violence. This shows that Chinese society has already lost patience. This is a major issue because it means that civil servants and citizens are totally opposed. As a result, I hope the Chinese can still wait for five to eight more years, so as to avoid widespread chaos and trouble.

China's democratisation is considered by the great majority of academics involved in the debate on political reform as inevitable and highly desirable. Democracy is indeed the paragon of essentially contested concepts, which Walter Bryce Gallie defines as concepts referring to different political perspectives and competing philosophical or anthropological conceptions,[19] which rely on diverging and competing political perspectives and philosophical and anthropological conceptions. This can help explain such a consensus on China's democratic horizon among intellectual elites. Chinese scholars, like those in other parts of the world, take part in controversies on the socio-political meaning of democracy and on the organisation of democratic action. They criticise liberal representative democracy and renew these debates in the light of the recent evolution of democratic theory debates in western universities.

The first of the seven criteria that Gallie puts forward to define whether a concept is an essentially contested concept is the appraisiveness, or evaluative dimension, that is attached to it. Gallie explains that 'many would urge that during

---

18. In Xiao Gongqin's work, Liang Qichao's resonates, especially his concept of 'political capacity' (*zhengzhi nengli*) and the idea of a necessary transfer of citizenship and the tasks of state modernising. *See* Xinmin shuo (*People's Renovation*), mentioned in Chevrier, Y., Roux, A. and Xiao-Planes X. (eds) *Citadins et citoyens dans la Chine du XXe siècle: Essais d'histoire sociale*, Paris: Maison des Sciences de l'Homme, 2010, p. 52. *See also* Ma, J. 'Liang Qichao, un intellectuel entre réformisme et conservatism', *SinoPolis*, June 2010, http://sinopolis.hypotheses.org/158 (last accessed 14 November 2014).

19. Gallie, W. B. 'Essentially contested concepts', *Proceedings of the Aristotelian Society* 56, 1956, pp. 167–98.

the last one hundred and fifty years it [democracy] has steadily established itself as the appraisive political concept *par excellence.*'[20] As a result, when Chinese academics agree on the democratic future of China, they simply agree on the fact that the Chinese political system must improve. 'Democracy' is understood in the broad sense of a system that is more open, fair and free. However, when we talk about democracy, we do not limit ourselves to the positive value of the concept of democracy. As William Connolly states, when we designate a political system as a democracy,[21] we 'ascribe a value to it' but we also, and above all, try to describe it. Pierre Rosanvallon explains that 'in it [the concept of democracy] the good and the vague have overlapped for a very long time.'[22]

Democracy = chaos?

Before investigating these diverging descriptions of the democratic system these academics mostly support, we should note that in China, as in Europe and in the United States in the nineteenth century, the values associated with a democratic regime are not seen as solely positive by everyone.[23] In China, in the official discourse inherited from communism, but also in the discourse of some academics, the best government is necessarily meritocratic and democracy amounts to chaos.

Pan Wei: The rule of law without a democracy

Pan Wei is a controversial figure. He is one of the most outspoken media intellectuals as far as condemning the promotion of an Anglo-American democratic regime – which he claims cannot be established in countries with radically different social conditions – is concerned. He believes China must find its own model. This academic, the director of the Centre for Chinese and Global Affairs of Peking University's International Relations department, criticises the 'sacralisation' of democracy and the missionary-like approach of western democratic-promotion. He rejects the introduction of competitive elections – which he refers to when he resorts to the word 'democracy' – under the pretext that they would be completely useless in China. Worse, Pan Wei associates democracy with chaos.[24] According to him, the

---

20. 'The concept of democracy which we are discussing is appraisive; indeed many would urge that during the last one hundred and fifty years it has steadily established itself as the appraisive political concept par excellence', Gallie, W. B. 'Essentially contested concepts', p. 184.

21. Connolly, W. E. 'Essentially contested concepts in politics', in *Terms of Political Discourse*, 2nd edition, Princeton, NJ: Princeton University Press, 1983 [1974], chapter 1, p. 22.

22. Rosanvallon, P. *La démocratie inachevée*, Paris: Folio histoire, Gallimard, 2000, p. 12.

23. Huntington, S. P. *The Third Wave: Democratisation in the late twentieth century*, Norman, OK: University of Colorado Press, 1991; Rosanvallon, P. 'Democratic universalism as a historical problem', *Books & Ideas*, 8 April 2008, available online at http://www.booksandideas.net/Democratic-Universalism-as-a.html (last accessed 14 November 2014).

24. Pan Wei, 'You talk about democracy as if it were a religion which needs to be spread around the world. But elections will not solve any of the problems facing China today.' quoted in Leonard, M. *What Does China Think?*, London: Fourth Estate, 2008.

Chinese equate democracy with three nightmarish visions: the collapse of the Soviet Union in the wake of Gorbachev's liberalisation; the so-called 'people's democracy' of the Cultural Revolution; and the risk of Taiwan becoming independent.[25]

Pan Wei's publication in 1999 of an article denouncing the 'myth of democracy' [electoral democracy being neither universal nor a panacea] and claiming that, unlike the rule of law and the independence of the judiciary, without which China could not solve its acute corruption and inequality issues, democratisation was no priority.[26] To his mind, the right approach was first to establish rule of law and introduce checks and balances on the use of political power, without hastening democratisation; that is, establishing competitive elections. Pan favours establishing a consultative rule of law based on five institutional pillars,[27] deemed the only efficient remedy against corruption, as well as the most urgent to implement and the easiest to realise. His comprehensive and sophisticated proposal for political reform, which was inspired by the Singapore and Hong Kong models, gained traction and Denver University's Centre for China-US Cooperation convened an academic conference in Summer 2000 to discuss Pan's article, in which he details a far-reaching political programme.[28] The regime he defends is based on rule by law rather than rule by men; fair laws abiding by the principle that all are equal before the law; strict law-enforcement; checks on the scope and functions of government; and pursuit of order and freedom in accordance with Chinese traditions. Pan Wei's elitism is explicitly professed. His experience of the Cultural Revolution and the misdeeds of an 'uncontrollable mob' have apparently convinced him that the people cannot be endowed with power. Hence his defence of a 'high-tech consultative dictatorship, where there are no elections but decisions made by a responsive government, bound by law and in touch with its citizens' aspirations'.[29]

Since 1999, Pan Wei has refined his definition of a Chinese model of development[30] and has seemed less radically opposed to China's democratisation. However, to his mind, the aim of political reform is not a procedural democracy but a 'genuine' democracy, which is meritocratic, where citizens live comfortably, express themselves freely and enjoy a wide array of instruments allowing them to participate in political decisions, so that they can do so on a daily basis and not only through the ballot box. As a result, the only voices which are now explicitly

25. Leonard, M. *What Does China Think?*, pp. 61–4.

26. Pan, W. 'Fazhi yu zhongguo weilai zhengti' ('Rule of law and the future Chinese political regime'), *Zhanlue yu Guanli (Stategy and Management)* 5, 1999, pp. 30–6.

27. A system of neutral civil servants; an independent judiciary; independent anti-corruption institutions; an extended social system of consulting national and provincial People's Congresses; the legal protection of the freedom of the press, speech, assembly and association.

28. Pan then revised the English version of his article and published it, with articles commenting on it, in *Journal of Contemporary China* 12(34), 2003. A book was also published: Zhao, S. (ed.) *Debating Political Reform in China: Rule of law vs Democratisation*, Armonk: New York: M. E. Sharpe, 2006.

29. Leonard, M. *What Does China Think?*, p. 66.

30. Pan, W. *Zhongguo moshi: Jiedu renmin gongheguo de liushinian (The China Model: Understanding 60 years of People's Republic)*, Beijing, Zhongyang Bianyi Chubanshe, 2009.

raised against China's democratisation, no matter how it is defined, are cultural nationalists such as Kang Xiaoguang and Jiang Qing, who oppose democratic reforms and advocate establishing a benevolent, elitist, Confucian regime, which would, allegedly, be better suited to China's political culture and needs.

Kang Xiaoguang and the critique of democracy

For ten years, Kang Xiaoguang has been developing a theory of political legitimacy and he defends a new kind of regime founded on the Confucian notion of *renzheng* (benevolent government).[31] An interdisciplinary researcher of People's University, he advocates the establishment of an elitist and meritocratic regime combining political authoritarianism, a liberal market economy, corporatism and a welfare state. This elaborate political programme is based on four principles:

1. autonomy (of power, capital, knowledge and labour);
2. co-operation (multi-party consultation and negotiation: citizens become members of official associations based on the organisation of professions and public policies are jointly decided by these associations and the government, which neutrally chairs negotiations between associations and classes so as to solve social conflicts);
3. balance of power; and
4. sharing (wealth and opportunities).

In the May 2010 interview he gave me, Kang explained the precise reasons which led him to reject the perspective of introducing liberal democracy in China: successive disillusions and shock at the consequences of the collapse of the Soviet Union and Yugoslavia's division; fear of chaos and implosion; and awareness that China's democratisation would not necessarily bring more economic development, social justice and power.

> I started reassessing all this with a critical mind. I wondered about the global strategy of full westernisation and pursuit of democratisation. Was it adapted to the interests of the Chinese people and China? Originally, it could not be a problem; it could only bring happiness and satisfaction, and solve all issues. But with a better understanding of foreign countries and after reading a lot and observing many different democratisation processes, I came to the following conclusion. The definition of democracy is limited to press freedom, freedom of association, independence of the judiciary, multi-partyism and competitive elections. We have had the opportunity to realise that, even though the Philippines, India, Bengal, Pakistan, Thailand, and some African countries

---

31. Kang, X. 'Renzheng: quanweizhuyi guojia de hefaxing lilun' ('Benevolent government: the legitimacy of the authoritarian state'), *Zhanlue yu Guanli* 2, pp. 108–117 2004; Kang, X. *Renzheng: Zhongguo zhengzhi fazhan (Renzheng: The third way for China's political development)*, Singapore, World Scientific Publishing Co., 2005. *See* Ji, Z. 'Confucius, les libéraux et le Parti: Le renouveau du confucianisme politique', *La Vie des Idées* 2, May 2005, pp. 9–20.

benefited from these breakthroughs, China's economic achievement was no match to theirs. China is corrupted, but so are these new democratic countries. This is how we finally gave up the idea that democratising would solve all our problems. In the 1980s, we thought we had found a transparent solution. Democratising would allow us to remedy all the issues China faced. But when this belief receded, we were left having to find a Chinese way and the means for China to solve its problems all by ourselves. This realisation is a personal watershed. I cannot say I was specifically influenced by such and such book or theory. I formed and changed my views mostly through observation and comparison, in particular of democratic transition in former socialist countries. I wondered what China was doing, in what aim and with which difficulties, but also what the way the former Soviet satellite countries evolved would teach us and what the democratisation of Third-World countries in South-East Asia, Latin America and Africa would lead to. The crucial point is to compare a wide array of experiences. It resulted in shattering my sense that China's democratisation would be instrumental.

Such detailed genealogy of the questioning of the benefits of democratising China is evidence that Kang Xiaoguang, like Pan Wei and many other intellectuals, has a completely utilitarian vision of democracy. Kang simply doubts the whole process will be useful in achieving China's 'real' goals. His work is, indeed, very consistently aimed at resolving the problems he has identified as the most urgent for China to solve (the leaders' legitimacy crisis; the absence of national sentiment and moral principles among the Chinese; the social justice deficit and so on). With the explicit intention of meeting these pressing needs, he offers to establish a paternalist authoritarian regime, the *renzheng*, whose legitimacy is founded on the benevolence or compassion or its leaders. According to Kang, only an innovating renaissance of political Confucianism can solve the legitimacy crisis the government is going through, thanks to the efficient management, continuous economic growth and reinforced national sentiment among the Chinese that would follow the establishment of Confucianism as the state religion.

As a result, he sees democracy as a form of superstition, comforting the Chinese in their passivity as regards political reflection, which he explains in thorough detail in a section of the preface to his book *Renzheng*[32] entitled 'Criticizing liberal democracy': 'They should simply get in line and wait for their time to come.' Democracy is no panacea since it eventually has little chance of solving or even reducing the problems of corruption, economic risk and social injustice which undermine China. 'On the contrary, we could even lose our recent achievements: economic prosperity, political stability, integrity of the state and national unity.' Kang anticipates possible objections: how could he be

---

32. Kang, X. 'Wo weishenme zhuzhang ruhua? guanyu zhongguo weilai zhengzhi fazhan de baoshouzhuyi sikao' ('Why I advocate Confucianism: conservative thoughts on China's future political development'), preface to *Renzheng: Zhongguo Fazhan De Disan Tiao Daolu*. For an English version *see* Kang, X. 'Confucianization: a future in the tradition', *Social Research* 73(1), 2006, pp. 77–120.

so certain of the consequences of democratising China? That's exactly what he is so concerned about. He insists that we cannot afford to play the part of the sorcerer's apprentice with the fate of the country. Kang refers to World Bank and Transparency International statistics to posit that there is no confirmed connection between the democratic level and the annual GDP growth of the last decade, and no statistical evidence could be established as regards democracy's capacity to boost growth, to reduce corruption, improve the Gini coefficient or reduce the poverty incidence. According to Kang, this teaches us that only the absolute level of economic development truly has an impact on the poverty and corruption levels of a country. These arguments could convince ordinary people, for whom the charms of the democratic regime rely on its supposed efficacy in putting an end to China's ills. However, liberals are attached to the values of democracy: individualism, the neutrality of society, a limited government. Kang discards these boldly, and perhaps rather too quickly. Why would these values be superior? He favours communitarianism and the defining of a set of values for Chinese society. The idea of a self-sufficient individual is contrary to man's nature and makes the virtuous government he holds dear impossible to establish. Besides, even if the values underlying liberal democracy were superior, in practice, it relies on a 'pack of lies'. Kang highlights democracy's contradictions, since, like any regime, it consecrates the rule of elites. Democracy relies on an essential social equality which is impossible in capitalist societies. Elections, as well as legislatures, the media, education and research institutions are controlled by money. Consequently, 'for China, western democracy is a useless tool and it is not efficient as a value.' Worse, it could well lead China to disaster (*huoguo yangmin*).[33]

Qing and political Confucianism

Jiang Qing is another anti-democratic cultural nationalist, whose most commented-on book is *Political Confucianism*.[34] Kang and Jiang indeed stand out from the majority of scholars advocating a Confucian revival since many among the latter believe that Confucianism is compatible with liberal democracy. This is exactly what Jiang Qing denies in his book. According to him, the neo-Confucianism of thinkers like Mou Zongsan,[35] who adheres to the Song-Ming tradition of 'lived Confucianism' (*shengming ruxue*), has proved incapable of providing a genuine Confucian political philosophy for modern China. However, Confucian values are most relevant to today and tomorrow's China, which the book aims at demonstrating. Jiang Qing's 'political Confucianism', is connected both to

---

33. *See* http://news.boxun.com/news/gb/pubvp/2005/01/200501010516.shtml (last accessed 14 November 2014).

34. Jiang, Q. *Zhengzhi ruxue: Dangdai ruxue de zhuanxiang, tezhi yu fazhan* (*Political Confucianism: New direction, characters and development of contemporary Confucianism*), Beijing: Sanlian Shudian, 2003; Jiang, Q. *A Confucian Constitutional Order*, Princeton, NJ: Princeton University Press, 2012.

35. *See* Thoraval, J. 'Idéal du sage, stratégie du philosophe, introduction à la pensée de Mou Zongsan', in Mou, Z. *Spécificités de la philosophie chinoise*, Paris: Editions du Cerf, 2003, pp. 7–60.

the Gongyang tradition of the Spring and Autumn Annals (*Chunqiu*) and to Han Confucianism; like them it is an 'institutional Confucianism' as it focuses on building and maintaining social and political institutions. However, Jiang makes a distinction between the Gongyang tradition and the 'politicised Confucianism' of the Old Text School (*guwen jingxue*), a Han-dynasty ideology which insisted on the holy and absolute authority of the emperor. In contrast, the Gongyang tradition not only served as an ideological justification of the imperial government but it also generated independent criteria for assessing how power was exercised.

The proposal to set up a regime based on institutions deriving from the Gongyang tradition is both an implicit criticism of the *status quo* – which explains why the book in which he most precisely details his alternative institutional propositions could not be published in mainland China[36] – and an explicit criticism of the universality of the democratic regime the West developed. Jiang is not opposed to democracy as such but he insists that it is not suited to China. Liberal democracy is only based on democratic legitimacy; that is, it corresponds to the will of the people or public opinion. This is, however, insufficient since democratic majorities tend to favour policies that are contrary to the interests of those who cannot hold political power – children, ancestors, future generations and animals.

The regime he devised should, he claims, be more suited to China in as far as it relies on two other forms of legitimacy. Jiang Qing indeed designed a tricameral system associating representatives of three sources of legitimacy: representatives of the people through the People's House (*shuminyuan*); Confucian elites selected thanks to an examination of their mastery of Confucian classics and their political experience through the House of Exemplary Persons (*tongruyuan*); and, finally, religious representatives (of Buddhism, Daoism, Islam and Christian churches) as well as descendants of great historical figures and scholars such as Confucius, whose role would consist in guaranteeing the cultural continuity of the regime through the House of Historical Continuity (*guotiyuan*). These three houses represent three different types of legitimacy: democratic or human legitimacy, stemming from the people's authorization of political power and giving leaders the will to obey; meritocratic and holy legitimacy, originating in the selective exam on the knowledge of sacred texts; and historical or terrestrial legitimacy, deriving from the historical continuity brought about by the presence of Confucius' descendants.[37]

The idea conveyed by Jiang Qing, Kang Xiaoguang and Pan Wei that democracy is not the most satisfactory regime for China is actually quite prevalent in the intellectual community, even if these three scholars stand out in the Chinese intellectual landscape. This can be explained by the widespread fears of social chaos, the country's division, Taiwan's secession and regression to the poverty and violence of the Cultural Revolution, and how these fears strongly condition the way political change is envisaged in China. These daring proposals

---

36. Jiang, Q. *Shengming Xinyang Yu Wangdao Zhengzhi: Rujia wenhua de xiandai jiazhi*, Taipei: Yang Zhengtang, 2004.

37. Jiang, Q. *Shengming Xinyang Yu Wangdao Zhengzhi: Rujia wenhua de xiandai jiazhi*, Taipei: Yang Zhengtang, 2004, pp. 293–4.

of meritocratic rather than democratic regimes nevertheless echo views widely shared among Chinese intellectuals. They have attracted considerable attention, because political analyses and criticisms rarely give rise to sophisticated proposals of new institutional arrangements.

My hypothesis is that these three scholars take pains to thoroughly expound their critical analysis of the democratic regime and conceive a new type of regime better suited to China because they are aware that their radical rejection of the democratic regime was not self-evidently justified and the idea of democracy deserved more constructive criticism. It is also interesting to note that the conservative rejection of democracy amounts *both* to a refusal to consider it the least imperfect existing regime or to describe it, like Churchill, as the 'worst form of government, except for all the other forms that have been tried from time to time', *and* to entertain the more optimistic idea that new institutional frameworks are possible.

Advocating a neo-conservative democratisation

Overall, therefore, the prospect of democratisation is welcomed by Chinese intellectual elites, despite various levels of impatience and a wide array of definitions of the democratic regime best suited to China. Democracy – in its twentieth-century definition, that is, as a regime that guarantees every adult citizen the right to vote – was widely accepted among the Chinese intellectual elites of the 1980s as the outcome of the process of political reform that would complete the ongoing economic reform. Since the 1990s and the 'neo-conservative' tidal wave that carried most of the intellectual elite in its wake, however,[38] this has no longer been the case.

The seething cultural and intellectual life and the vivacious intellectual debates of the 1980s were encouraged by the Open and Reform policy and the hope it triggered after the Cultural Revolution. It was a moment of liberalisation of society, thinking and publications. For most students and intellectuals, democracy then was a distant ideal, to reach out towards so as to leave the arbitrariness and violence of the Cultural Revolution behind. The main exception were neo-authoritarians, who emphasised the need for a relatively long authoritarian transition. This marginal tendency became more prevalent after the 1989 repression. In China, the 'neo-conservative' label is mainly used to designate the tendency to justify the need for a strong government, able to boost and maintain economic reform and social stability, which are the tenets of the gradual introduction of a sustainable democratic regime. This label inconveniently obscures the dissolving of the relative ideological consensus of the 1980s and the myriad of ways of thinking and types of intellectual engagement which succeeded it. It does, however, explain why, even if few intellectuals openly discard democracy, few of them advocate the direct and immediate importation of the western democratic model that the Party, sometimes vehemently, rejects. The theory of the 'Five Negations' (*wu bu gao*) promoted by

---

38. Wang, J. *Reverse Course.*

Wu Bangguo is an illustration: no multi-party elections, no ideological pluralism, no separation of powers, no federal system, and no privatisation.[39] However, some official publications implicitly show that the Party has understood that a total negation of the universality of democracy, freedom and human rights could harm its interests. Song Jiangang's article, which was published in the official *Guangming Daily (Guangming Ribao)* in July 2009 thus admitted that democracy and human rights were universal values but added that only socialism allowed their accomplishment.[40]

While Kang's radical rejection of the democratic regime is polemical, his analysis of the reasons why intellectual circles turned to neo-conservatism after 1989 is consensual. He identifies several factors: the legitimacy the Party gets from the good results of the reform policy; the uncertainty and complexity of the consequences of the collapse of the former Soviet Union; and a deeper understanding of democracy, which no longer appears as a cure-all.[41] As a result, after 1980 intellectuals tend to be less idealistic, more reality-driven. Comforted by the intensification of the Open and Reform policy after Deng Xiaoping conducted his landmark 'Southern tour' to Guangzhou, Shenzhen, Zhuhai and Shanghai – the four major cities that had been at the forefront of pro-market 'reform' in the previous decade, which became a key turning point in the process of capitalist restoration in China – they are also more circumspect. They are influenced by a swell of conservative opinion, which liberal analyses attribute to cowardice and compromising – which they both condemn and yet understand as due to the violent repression of the students' movement. It is no easy task to decide in this debate, all the more so as the neo-conservative turn includes intellectuals who have left the country and are entirely financially independent from the Chinese state.[42]

The neo-conservative praise of gradualism

Since the early 1990s, awareness that reformed China is undergoing a deep crisis has been particularly common among the intellectual elites. Whatever their convictions and disagreements, they all issue the same warning: the country could easily slip into chaos (*hunluan*) and disintegrate. Under a patriotic impulse, most intellectuals and researchers have willingly rallied to try to rise to the challenge of

---

39. *See* Jianmin, Q. 'The debate over "universal values" in China', *Journal of Contemporary China*, 20(72), 2011, pp. 881–890.

40. Song, J., Liang C. and Guo Z. 'Jianchi he wanshan shehuizhuyi minzhu, ziyou, renquan' ('Let us encourage and perfect socialist democracy and human rights'), *Guangming Ribao*, 22 July 2009.

41. Kang, X. 'Wo weishenme zhuzhang ruhua?'

42. A study conducted on Chinese-born academics in American, European, Australian, Singaporian and Hong-Kongese universities would probably show that neo-conservative ideas appeal to them as well. Wang Juntao concludes his PhD dissertation by saying that the spectacular loss of influence of dissidents and their defense of democratic transition from the 1990s on in China and among the Chinese community abroad is evidence of the popularity of neo-conservatism in China and among Chinese people abroad: Wang, J. *Reverse Course*, p. 426.

these times of emergency; but they have endorsed differing approaches to solving the crisis. The most extreme conservatives, such as He Xin, underline that order and stability are to be maintained at all cost (*wending yadao yiqie*), which justifies the 1989 repression. In the 1990s, more moderate ones, such as Xiao Gongqin, advocated a form of nationalism enriched with Confucianism so as to pursue political integration (*zhengzhi zhenhe*) and cohesion (*ningju*).

The very term 'neo-conservatism' (*xin baoshouzhuyi*) is problematic. Analysts often talk of a neo-conservative wave in China, even though Xiao Gongqin and He Xin are representatives of neo-conservatism in its most narrow sense, because the term actually gathers together a heterogeneous set of political ideologies and schools. As Wang Juntao explains, this makes things even more complex;

> [...] not all political neo-conservatives are really opposed to democratisation and liberal values; Some were worried about the possible consequences – a potential collapse due to insufficient preparation for reform. Others appeared to oppose democracy only because their understanding of democracy was different from that of the liberals. Most advocates of political neo-conservatism did not state explicitly to reject democratisation, but they wanted to postpone it until conditions in China had changed. However, because they oppose democracy, for the time being and they never ask the authority to schedule a democratic reform, I can still call them political neo-conservatives.[43]

Therefore, the best way to define the prevalence of neo-conservatism among Chinese intellectuals in the wake of the 1989 repression is to consider that this trend is not truly opposed to democratisation in China but rather advocates prudent reform that is not radical but gradual.

Elite consensus on the critique of 1990s radicalism

Different views about the timing and different necessary steps of the democratisation process are the critical distinguishing factors between the conceptions of political reform in China adhered to by the various ideological factions. The anti-radical defence of a progressive and careful reform has been globally consensual since the mid 1990s, as previously explained and as suggested by Li Zehou and Liu Zaifu's *Farewell to Revolution* and Xiao Gongqin's *Farewell to Political Romanticism*.[44] The concept of 'conservatism' and the counter-concept of 'radicalism' are used to describe the thought of diverse intellectuals such as Yü Yingshi, Xiao Gongqin, Chen Lai, Liu Junning and Wang Shaoguang; that is, to describe expatriate scholars as much as Beijing or Shanghai academics, a New Left representative

---

43. Wang, J. *Reverse Course*, pp. 11–12.
44. Li, Z. and Liu, Z. *Gaobie geming: Huiwang ershi shiji Zhongguo*, 1995, Hong Kong: Cosmos Books; Xiao Gongqin, *Yu zhengzhi langmanzhuyi gaobie*, Chansha: Hubei Press, 2001.

as well as a libertarian and a cultural nationalist.[45] What unites these scholars is their dismissal of sudden revolutionary change and their defense of historical continuity; this is first and foremost the promotion of the idea that accumulated tradition, wisdom and experience from past generations are still meaningful, and of an other conception of change: gradualism. The surprising parallel many analysts have identified between official ideology and intellectual debates after the Tiananmen Square massacre, especially as regards the discarding of radicalism, can be explained by both sides' will to solve the same issues and the fact that official ideology and intellectual discourse were built in exactly the same context; that is, as a response to the radicalism of the Cultural Revolution and to the collapse of the Soviet Union. The discussion intellectuals and political leaders launched on the criticism of radicalism were separate at first but their 'pragmatic convergence' is striking.[46] Wang Juntao explains that neo-conservative elites expressing themselves against immediate democratisation in the mid 1990s were independent from the authorities and the official ideology but they 'co-operated with the government propaganda, and imposed a radical label on their liberal competitors who could not defend themselves' because of the political repression.[47] In the 1990s, viewpoints converged to denounce the 'radicalism' of advocates of an immediate democratic transition (some students in June 1989), referring to the recent situation in the former Soviet Union. Xiao Gongqin thus evokes the *volte-face* reception of neo-authoritarianism/neo-conservatism in the 1980s and 1990s.

After the 1989 repression, Chinese intellectuals were led to reconsider their 'radical' attitude. After a few months, a great number of them were willing to making the 'compromise' which put an end to their radical opinions, mainly as concerns directly importing western institutions or a democratic regime. According to Xiao Gongqin, this 'systemic determinism' or 'institutional fetishism' is radical because it refuses to take into account the fact that any institution or political system results from a long social and historical development process and that such a transplant in an unprepared society is likely to lead directly to social instability.[48]

This discourse on the conditions for the successful introduction of democratic institutions is no novelty in China. Liang (1873–1929), one of the first Chinese thinkers to consider that democracy was the best political system, nevertheless claimed that establishing a constitutional monarchy was an indispensable first step. Indeed, according to him, a constitution, because it mobilises popular energies in the service of the state, allows strengthening of the leader's powers. Andrew Nathan explains that Liang Qichao, until 1903, was a radical democrat because

45. Van Dongen, E. *Goodbye Radicalism: Conceptions of radicalism among Chinese intellectuals during the early 1990s*, PhD dissertation, Leiden University, 2009; Liu, J. *Baoshou Zhuyi (Conservatism)*, Beijing: Zhongguo Shehui Kexue Chuban, 1998, pp. 255–7.

46. Wang, C. 'Introduction: minds of the nineties', in Wang, C. *One China, Many Paths*, pp. 16–17, quoted in Van Dongen, E. *Goodbye Radicalism*, p. 39.

47. Wang, J. *Reverse Course*, p. 275.

48. Xiao, G. 'Lishi jujue langman: Zhongguo gaige di'er sichao de jueqi', *Xiao Gongqin Ji*, p. 115, quoted in Van Dongen, E. *Goodbye Radicalism*, p. 60.

he was an 'optimistic Confucianist', convinced that institutional changes, in particular the establishment of democratic institutions, would lead to an immediate transformation of society.[49] After a trip to the United States, Liang Qichao lost his optimism and denounced the corruption of society, like 'pessimistic Confucians'.[50] He deemed that without a prolonged period of education and indoctrination, Chinese citizens would not understand that their ultimate individual interests and collective interests converged. Without this new citizenship, establishing a democratic republic would lead nowhere: 'My trip to America has made me feel that the republican form of government is not as good as constitutional monarchy, which has fewer flaws and functions more efficiently.'[51] American democracy disappointed him and his observation of the Chinese who lived in the United States, who, to his mind, should be more advanced than the Chinese in China, shattered his illusions. Before going back to China, Liang Qichao wrote these few remarks:

> Were we now to resort to rule by [freedom, constitutionalism, republicanism; the general terms which describe majority rule], it would be the same as committing national suicide. Freedom, constitutionalism, republicanism – this would be like wearing summer garb in winter, or furs in summer: beautiful, to be sure, but unsuitable. No more am I dizzy with vain imaginings; no longer will I tell a tale of pretty dreams. In a word, the Chinese people must for now accept authoritarian rule; they cannot enjoy freedom […] Those born in the thundering tempests of today, forged and molded by iron and fire – they will be my citizens, twenty or thirty, nay, fifty years hence. Then we will give them Rousseau to read, and speak to them of Washington.[52]

The Chinese neo-conservative elites' rhetoric of a return to realism and the end of idealism and fine words is strikingly reminiscent of Liang Qichao's discourse. In 1905, Liang Qichao elaborated, in 'On enlightened despotism' ('*Kaiming zhuanzhi lun*'), a defense of enlightened despotism, based on Napoleon I and Frederic II, whom he considered model rulers. He believed the individual should be subordinated to the needs of a modern state if it is underdeveloped. Liang Qichao laid the groundwork for the justification of authoritarianism: if the quality (*suzhi*) of the population is insufficient, the natural harmony of the political order cannot be achieved. The Chinese must first be transformed into citizens, otherwise the freedom which is granted to them will only lead to chaos.

---

49. Nathan, A. *Chinese Democracy*, Berkeley, CA: University of California Press, 1986.

50. According to Ma Jun, Chang Peng-yuan was the first to highlight this trend, in Chang Peng-yuan, 'Liang Qichao yu qingji geming' ('Liang Qichao and the revolution at the end of the Qing dynasty'), *Academia Sinica's Institute of Modern History* 11, special issue, Taipei, 1969, pp. 167–75. *See* Ma, J. 'Liang Qichao, un intellectuel entre réformisme et conservatism', *SinoPolis*, June 2010, available online at http://sinopolis.hypotheses.org/158 (last accessed 14 November 2014).

51. Quoted in Nathan, A. *Chinese Democracy*, p. 60.

52. *See* Nathan, A. *Chinese Democracy*, p. 60.

The argument of the insufficient development and 'civilisation' (*wenming*) of rural masses still seems to prevail among Chinese intellectuals, whether they live in China or abroad.[53]

Promoting 'piecemeal engineering'

Since the 1990s, the main feature of neo-conservative ideas on the reform policy is advocacy of progressive and reasonable change. To Xiao Gongqin, the democratic transition must imperatively follow a strict order so as not to lead to chaos. Neo-conservatism is epitomised by its wariness towards immediate, brutal, unreasonable change. As a result, Chinese neo-conservatives are not opposed to reforms or their radical objectives but they condemn the radicalism of their pace and strategy. This explains why scholars as different as Xiao Gongqin and Wang Shaoguang can be gathered under a common banner. The intellectual guarantees of such gradualist thinking are not limited to Burke. References to Karl Popper abound and focus on his distinction between 'piecemeal engineering' and 'utopian social engineering.' First in *The Open Society and Its Enemies* and in later works, Popper rejects the argument that experimentations must be conducted on a large scale so as to produce sufficient data. He favours social experiments conducted in laboratory-like conditions or in isolated villages, in line with the trial-and-error principle. These experiments are supposed to be more rational.

The prevalence of gradualist thinking among intellectual and political elites is patent in Chinese academics' theoretical justification of the realism and pragmatism of Deng Xiaoping's reform policy – the strategy summed up in the saying 'crossing the river by groping for stones' (*mozhe shitou guo he*) previously mentioned. In 1992, Xu Jilin went as far as stating that the Popperian concepts 'piecemeal social engineering' and 'utopian social engineering' were more relevant to the description of modern Chinese history than conservatism and radicalism.[54] Gradualism, a meeting point for academics and government after the 1989 repression, remains attractive: over the past few years, it has been a key feature of the growing literature devoted to defining a 'Chinese model' (*zhongguo moshi*) of development. Xiao Gongqin thus describes the trial-and-error method (*shicuoxingzhi*) as the key feature in the Sino-Vietnamese reform model.[55]

---

53. Bruce Gilley quotes an expatriate researcher saying that speaking about democracy in China right now is like playing the violin to an ox, because the concept is too sophisticated for so unsophisticated an audience: Yanan, J. *Understanding China: Center stage of the fourth power*, New York: State University of New York Press, 1996. p. 71, quoted in Gilley, B. *China's Democratic Future: How it will happen and where it will lead*, New York: Columbia University Press, 2005, p. 13.

54. Xu, J. 'Jijin yu baoshou de mihuo', *Ershiyi Shiji (21st Century)* 11, June 1992, pp. 137–40, quoted in Els Van Dongen, *Goodbye Radicalism*, p. 168.

55. Xiao, G. 'Zhuanxing zhengzhi shiye xia de zhongguo sanshinianz' ('30 years of reforms from the perspective of transition political science'), *Leaders* 21, April 2008. *See also* the interview of Yu, K. 'Zhongguo moshi yu sixiang jiefang' ('Chinese model and liberation of thought'), *Journal of the History and Construction of Shanghai's Party*, November 2008.

The approach is condemned by some liberal researchers, judging that the attempt to promote a Chinese 'model' is premature and aggressive. But those who indulge in the practice justify their endeavour as resulting from the desire to understand the Chinese path, thereby identifying the ingredients of China's success, at least as far as the economy is concerned.

Deng Zhenglai introduced the Chinese method as gradual and experimental, as a result of the size of the Chinese population and territory: trial and error was thus preferred to shock therapy and it was supposed to have already proven its efficiency:

> China is an immense country, and so is its population. One single policy cannot change things. The Chinese population is about 20 times that of France. When a policy addresses the rural population, and consists in giving 10 yuan to everyone, this affects 900 million people. This cannot happen in the blink of an eye. It is bound to be slow, progressive and step by step. It's got nothing to do with shock therapy. It does not mean that the government makes speeches which are not followed by facts. When new policies are announced, they are finally implemented. However their mode of action is to start small and expand it later on. This allows to correct possible mistakes. It's easier to amend a policy in such conditions. China's economic reform was not uniformly implemented on the whole territory at once. This is a form of Chinese wisdom. [...] We must be patient. When a policy is launched in this country, it is enforced step by step, in an empirical way. Small countries with a limited population can launch policies all at once but this is not possible on a scale like China's.

Wise development and modernisation could only be achieved through repeated and constantly amendable experiences. This slow and cautious method is also introduced by this scholar as a kind of wisdom which emerged from constraints specific to China, an element specific to the 'China model'. Li Qiang, who notably found fame with his book entitled *Liberalism*, manifestly masters western liberal theories and adheres to them. He subtly resorts to them to criticise the collusion between political and economic elites in China.[56] However, even for this liberal-minded academic, who rejects the idea that such a thing as a Chinese model of development could exist, political reform should follow a specific order and be conducted step by step:

> I think three main issues must be solved as regards political reform in China. First, a modern state should be built; that is, modern state–society relations must be established. The totalitarian state must be limited and transformed into a state with clearly defined boundaries. Theory on this issue is extensive. There should be a market economy, individual liberties and some space given to civil society. This is the first step. Once it is achieved, a way should be found to allow everyone to participate and build a modern legitimacy. Of course, this has

---

56. Li, Q. *Ziyou Zhuyi* (*Liberalism*), Beijing: China Social Sciences Press, 1998.

nothing to do with modern western democracy. Our traditions weigh against the realisation of such a kind of democracy. I am still currently studying this issue. How can a model for China be found where people can participate more? I focus on constitutionalism specifically. Individuals, society, government and state must all respect some rules. I always keep in mind the ideal political structure of course. It is Strauss' modern state structure: constitutional and liberal.

The statist reports of Hu Angang and Wang Shaoguang, which were first rejected by more liberal intellectuals in the early 1990s, seem part of the consensus nowadays. We may wonder what role the evolution of *democratisation studies* might have played in their *a posteriori* validation.[57] Explicitly in line with Thomas Carothers and Francis Fukuyama, and implicitly with New Left statists, Beijing scholars like Li Qiang and Yang Guangbin advocate a rational, step-by-step democratising process, since a well functioning state is seen as an indispensible condition of democratisation.[58] To establish a democratic regime, the relations between state and society should be modern and the state strong enough to enforce the rule of law and guarantee order and stability. This is Yang Guangbin's view:

I think democracy is currently spreading in China. Scholars talk about democracy all the time: intra-party democracy, popular democracy, etc. Moreover, each local government is implementing their own institutional innovations. This is hectic. I think China should first set up a representative assembly, then the rule of law, and finally establish a democratic regime.

The point is to set up a solid rule of law before introducing competitive elections so as to contain the representatives thus accessing power. Yang Guangbin refers to *Kicking Away the Ladder: Development Strategy in Historical Perspective*, a book which explicitly accuses Anglo-American democracy-promotion of undermining the development of southern countries by promoting a path to democratisation that simplistically omits important stages that industrialised countries passed through themselves and recommends a counter-productive path.[59] Korean economist Ha-Joon Chang also refers to Friedrich List's metaphor of 'kicking away the ladder', which List wrote about in 1841 in *The National System of Political Economy*. He explained that free trade never factually existed and was a myth invented by the British; that it is fairly common for someone who has achieved something to 'kick away the ladder' up which he or she climbed to success, so as

57. Guénard, F. 'Promoting democracy: a theoretical impasse?', *Books & Ideas*, 28 November 2007, available online at http://www.booksandideas.net/Promoting-democracy-a-theoretical.html (last accessed 14 November 2014).

58. Fukuyama, F. 'The imperative of state-building', *Journal of Democracy* 15(2), April 2004, pp. 17–31; Thomas Carothers, 'The "sequencing" fallacy', *Journal of Democracy* 18(1), January 2007, pp. 12–27.

59. Chang, H. -J. *Kicking Away the Ladder: Development strategy in historical perspective*, London: Anthem Press, 2002.

to prevent competitors from joining him or her at the top.[60] Yang Guangbin strives to stand out from the liberals, who, to his mind, have fallen into the trap of thinking that there cannot be a rule of law without a democracy, whereas in fact this had been the case in Britain, in the United States, in Canada and so on before these countries became democracies. The few countries which established a democratic system before ensuring their rule of law was solid went through serious trouble.

The ultimate aim is obvious for these academics: a constitutional democracy. The 'unrealistic' method of the immediate transition advocated by the democracy promotion is out of the question for the time being. Some conditions such as developing civil society and setting up the limits of the state have not been fulfilled yet. The parallel with global debates on democratisation is striking. The distinction between the neo-conservative sequentialism and the liberal gradualism which transition studies make applies.[61] Among observers of recent African democracies notably, there are some neo-conservatives who question the relevance of electoral practice, a technical feature of democracy, compared to a more substantive justice, in contexts where the political culture is not westernised. The sequentialist tendency promotes the idea that political reform should be delayed in the case of some southern and eastern countries that are not 'ready' for the establishment of a liberal government. Sequentialism is distinct from gradualism, which is more liberal and advocates the careful introduction of reforms which, without explicitly threatening the *status quo*, launch a process of change that will be self-reinforcing and transform the system in a diffuse and progressive manner.

However, it is worth distinguishing at least two instances of the neo-conservative tendency generally affecting Chinese elites: the sequentialism of self-assumed neo-conservatives like Xiao Gongqin, and the gradualism of more liberal scholars like Li Qiang or Yang Guangbin, or the New Left. The dividing lines are strikingly reminiscent of the debates on democratisation that are conducted on a world scale. The distinction between neo-conservative sequentialism and liberal gradualism used in transition studies also applies here.[62]

---

60. List, F. *The National System of Political Economy*, translated by Sampson S. Lloyd MP, Kitchener, Ontario: Batoche, 2001[1841].

61. What differentiates sequentialism from gradualism is the former's stress on preconditions for democratisation. Gradualism is defined as an alternative version of democratisation and democracy-promotion while sequentialism is conceived as a way to delay democratisation indefinitely. 'Democratic gradualism is different from sequencing. It does not entail putting off for decades or indefinitely the core element of democratisation – the development of fair and open processes of political competition and choice. It involves reaching for the core element now, but doing so in iterative and cumulative ways rather than all at once', Thomas Carothers, 'The "sequencing" fallacy', p. 25.

62. Among observers of recent African democracies, some neo-conservatives question the relevance of electoral practice, a technical form of democracy, compared to a more substantive justice, in contexts where political culture is not westernised. The sequentialist tendency advocates delaying political reform in some countries in the south and east that are not 'ready' for the introduction of a liberal government. Sequentialism is distinct from gradualism, which is more liberal and favours the careful introduction of reforms which, without explicitly challenging the *status quo*, ignite a process of change that seeps into the system, develops on its own and therefore diffusely and progressively transforms it.

Incrementalism and institutional innovations

The trial-and-error method, experimentation and localised innovation have proved efficient as regards the economy. China has for some years institutionalised its innovation policy and leaders from the bottom up to the top of the hierarchy regularly hold forth on the importance of innovation as the essential driver of China's economic and social development. Determined to counter the stereotypical complaint about the Chinese's lack of invention as they are stuck with the exact copying of foreign countries' best achievements, the Chinese government tries to create the necessary conditions for a strong initiative spirit – which matches its ambitions – to thrive in all fields.

Even if at the national level, resistance and obstacles to political reform are indomitable, at the local level, resorting to institutional innovations is quite commonplace and compatible with the conservative preference for gradual reform and 'piecemeal engineering'. Heberer and Schubert refer to the 'percolation model,' according to which political reform proceeds through legalising successful local practices.[63] Yu Keping, director of the Political Innovations Research Centre (*Zhongguo Zhengfu Chuangxin Yanjiu Zhongxin*), a think tank affiliated to the Translation and Compilation Bureau of the CCP's Central Committee of which he is the Vice-Director, developed a theory of incremental democracy (*zengliang minzhu*) according to which the political system is slowly pushed in the democratic direction. Concerned with the 'disaster' for the state and the people if democracy was implemented without the necessary conditions being met, he focuses on the importance of procedure, the role of civil society in building a socialist democracy, setting up the rule of law, advancing intra-party democracy and mass democracy. His think tank has set up a research programme awarding prizes for local government innovation and institutional excellence, combining academic research and policy-aimed expertise. Daunting inequalities have contributed to rising instability: cases of corruption or abuses of power, unfair evictions, police or judiciary mistakes and pollution constantly trigger protests and uprisings all over the country. The Ministry of Public Security estimated 87,000 popular uprisings (or 'mass incidents') had taken place in 2005, a 6.6 per cent rise compared to 2004 and a 50 per cent increase compared to 2003. Official data rose up to 180,000 uprisings in 2010.[64] Protestors do not have a monolithical conception of the Chinese state and their first action consists in lodging a complaint at higher levels. The central government is thus supposed to solve or settle the dispute with local authorities. As the local leaders risk losing all chance of promotion if social instability rises in their jurisdiction, (economic growth is no longer the paramount criterion) they look for institutional innovations designed to pacify social conflicts and guarantee their legitimacy.

---

63. Heberer, T. and Schubert, G. 'Political reform and regime legitimacy in contemporary China', *Asien* 99, 2006, pp. 9–28, p. 16.

64. Shirk, S. 'Ending secretive selection of China's top leaders doesn't guarantee peaceful rise', *Yale Global*, 20 April 2012.

172 | Conditional Democracy

The laureates of the political innovation award, such as Pingchang's district-level elections in 2006, come under the spotlight. In that case, 86 research teams consequently visited the place and studied the experience. However, county-level elections in Buyun (also in Sichuan), the first county to launch that experience in 1998, and renew it in 2001, did not gain so much traction, even after being awarded the prize in 2004. Even though the expansion of these experiments is blocked by a glass ceiling, according to the Political Innovations Research Centre, these low-level local elections should not be underestimated because local leaders are in charge of family planning, taxation and land acquisition. Besides, Yao Yang has shown that elections encouraged village committees to be more accountable to their constituents, helped limiting corruption, improving the quality of public services (raising expenditure and public investment while reducing the share of administrative expenses in the village budget), even though the greatest obstacle remains the Party's role in these elections.[65]

Yu Keping is one of the Chinese theoreticians of democracy with Chinese characteristics who is most widely read, both within and outside China. In 'Democracy is a good thing', an article published in December 2006, he stood out for his advocacy of democracy not for utilitarian reasons but for the sake of intrinsic values. Mark Leonard in *What Does China Think?*, associates Yu Keping's strategy with that of Zhang Weiying, an economist who conjures up an old Chinese story of horses disguised as zebras. He explains that though the 'zebras' of capitalism are nowadays seen as necessary to China's economic development, the Chinese state had, at first, been compelled to hide them from the population after years of fierce propaganda against 'zebras'. This led leaders to paint stripes on the coats of Chinese 'horses' (socialism), while explaining that they were hardly any different from the original horses, before gradually replacing the painted horses with genuine zebras (the market economy). It was, indeed, wiser to praise the benefits of zebras only when people had been convinced, after many years, that they were superior to horses. This is how, according to Zhang Weiying, the Chinese became capitalists without saying it loud.[66] Similarly, Yu Keping hopes that local democratic experiments will become the Shenzhen, or Trojan horse, of democratisation policy and that Chinese leaders will one day be faced with a *fait accompli* in the democratisation process that had been unfolding gradually for years.

Yu Keping and his colleague He Zengke are among the most vocal political scientists about (gradual and grassroots) electoral democracy. Their repeated, thorough field research and interviews with local cadres have fully convinced them that it is one of the key measures for giving political leaders the legitimacy and

65. *See* Charon, P. *Le vote contre la démocratie. Construction de l'État et processus de politisation dans la Chine rurale post-maoïste*, PhD dissertation, Paris: EHESS, December 2012; Yao, Y., 'Village elections, accountability and income distribution in rural China', *China & World Economy* 14(6), 2006, pp. 20–38; Shen, Y. and Yao, Y. 'Does grassroots democracy reduce income inequalities in China?', *Journal of Public Economics* 92, 2008, pp. 2182–98; Wang, S. and Yao, Y. 'Grassroots democracy and local governance: evidence from rural China', *World Development* 29(10–11), 2007, pp. 1635–49.

66. Leonard, M. *What Does China Think?* London: Fourth Estate, 2008.

motivation they need to rule properly. Their complementary proposals have the same aim: 'building a liberal socialism'. The incremental democracy Yu Keping has theorised focuses on the way to set up democracy in China. The complex democracy (*fuhe minzhu*) He Zengke has devised combines electoral democracy, deliberative democracy and constitutional democracy. It corresponds to the end result of the democratising process and these institutional innovations. He Zengke is nonetheless aware that the completion of this democratising process through expanding these innovations to the whole national territory ultimately depends on the Party's will:

> I think that this type of democratic regime is double since, as you know, we have already introduced electoral democracy for village committees and village heads. County-level direct election experiments have also taken place and the results are positive. They must be exported to other regions. As regards deliberative democracy, China can boast having allowed many experimental innovations and good practices to emerge. Many studies have been published as far as this issue is concerned. This is the reason why, if the central government has the political will to do it, it can expand these successful experiments to other parts of China. Finally the rule of law has become an official aim.

This is the reason why researchers affiliated to the Political Innovation Research Centre take pains to convince Party leaders of the benefits of electoral procedures. He Zengke and Yu Keping, thanks to their proximity to government, have had the opportunity to convey this message to Chinese leaders through telling them the stories of local Party secretaries who spontaneously wished to be elected so as to benefit from the same legitimacy as village committees – that is, no longer to draw their legitimacy solely from the Party but also from the people. He Zengke explains:

> In villages, village committees led by the committee's head, are elected by villagers. They rule along with the Party Secretary, who sometimes happens to feel the need to be himself elected by villagers so as to gain as much legitimacy as the village committee. He therefore organises elections, which give him the support of villagers and no longer some Party members only. This is how elections can be expanded. I consider it a major achievement that local leaders find benefits in the political legitimacy they acquire through the electoral game. These committees are more legitimate. We have told this story to top-level leaders.

In an article on government innovations and political legitimacy which he based on empirical investigation, He Zengke insists that local innovations, in the political realm especially, boost the political legitimacy of the regime in various ways.[67]

The other benefit of progressively introducing elections at the lowest level is the possibility of getting not only the leaders but also the Chinese people accustomed to electoral procedures and for them to seize what these can yield.

---

67. He, Z. 'Zhengzhi hefaxing yu zhongguo difang chuangxin – yixiang chubu de jingyan xing yanjiu', *Zhongguo Zhengfu Chuangxinwang*, 4 April 2007.

Teaching Chinese citizens electoral procedures gradually is comforting to Chinese elites who worry about the poor 'quality' (*suzhi di*) of China's voters-to-be and the potential risks the country could be confronted with. Xiao Gongqin thus claims:

> I think democratisation must first go through local constituencies' education to election. A constituency and the interests of voters are closely connected. They must learn how to use to vote so as to protect their interests. Elections cannot be directly organised. Direct elections are highly dangerous in my view. Only few countries have not failed as regards this issue.

He Zengke and Yu Keping's undertaking has its drawbacks, though. They work within the framework of an official think tank with limited leeway. Moreover, according to advocate of civic culture theory Xiao Gongqin, civil society must first be reasonably developed for a democratic transition to take place and get going, since it needs a minimum of support – as a result democracy cannot originate from the top but only from society.[68]

Can criticism of gradualism be heard?

The liberals who are the most distant from power and are the closest to dissidence consider that the strategy adopted by organic scholars is based on delusion. They scoff at the idea that the Party will eventually set up procedures and institutions whose main role would be to constrain its won power. They refuse to delay the country's democratisation under the pretext that rushing democratisation would plunge China into the same kind of chaos that caused the Soviet Union and Eastern European countries – especially Yugoslavia – to disintegrate. This is the case of Liu Xiaobo and Bao Tong. They are very few, which can easily be understood given the harsh repression they are subject to. Some former leaders, whose age and prestige protect, regularly express the pressing necessity of democratising. However, these voices receive greater attention abroad than in China, where even their closest friends and relatives remain careful. Such prudence is not necessarily only a matter of cowardice but of political efficacy, since becoming a Chinese dissident leads to marginalisation.[69] Dissidents lose their influence on public opinion, even online. Due to the repressive policy, the rise of nationalism and populism, and their ideological schisms over the issue of reform, dissidents have grown more and more marginalised. Their proposals for complete and immediate political reform as well as criticism of gradualism can hardly be heard in China.

Liberals who work in Chinese universities are necessarily more moderate. However, like dissidents, they do not share the optimism of advocates of gradualism, who patiently wait for leaders to accept to share their power. Their scepticism mainly

68. Almond, G. and Verba, S. *The Civic Culture: Political Attitudes and democracy in five nations*; Diamond, L. *Developing Democracy Toward Consolidation*; Inglehart, R. *Modernization and Postmodernization: Culture, economic, and political change in 43 societies.*

69. Tang, W. *Party Intellectuals' Demands for Reform in Contemporary China*, Stanford, CA: Hoover Press, 1999; Wang, J. *Reverse Course.*

originates from the idea that Fang Lizhi, among others, conveyed that a democracy granted by the top is no true democracy. It is simply a release of control.[70] Accused of being utopian, these liberal-minded scholars nevertheless define themselves as realistic and sensible observers of the situation. This is the reason why they emphasise their pessimism, the way Xu Youyu often does: there is nothing to expect from the Party, which will never accept sharing its power.

Ren Jiantao, a liberal academic from People's University believes this is idiosyncratic of power-holders in China:

When 'foreign powers' entered China, they forced us to modernise and to modernise our political institutions. As a matter of fact, Chinese leaders have never accepted to integrate the western system because it mainly consists in sharing power. Neither the emperor nor the Guomindang or the CCP have ever accepted to share their power.

For want of sharing power, the Party must accept sharing wealth, so as to avoid the people's wrath. It has no other choice but to make concessions:

Power is rational when it wants to monopolise everything but realises this is not possible and learns to share, which allows capping popular dissatisfaction. If Princelings [the offspring of top Party leaders] monopolise too many economic resources, how to transfer to other interest groups? If you spend lavishly to improve the country's image, with the opening ceremonies of the Olympic games or the World Expo, much money must conversely be allocated to assuage social conflicts through rising salaries and social benefits to the whole population, so as to temper its anger at realising that it does not benefit from the country's economic development at all. I hope leaders can share wealth more and people can remain patient. Given the current situation, it seems harder to achieve.

It is fascinating that Ren Jiantao, who claims to be a member of the liberal camp, expresses the same fears as more conservative and gradualist academics. Too brutal a change could destabilise China greatly. Like them, he refers to the spectre of the Soviet Union's collapse, which has haunted the CCP and Chinese intellectuals for years.[71] He hopes 'for change without wanting it too much' as the fear of instability and chaos compel him to encourage gradual reform. This is all the more the case as he explains that Chinese society, even though normally quite apathetic, would rise up in protest if inequalities become too great:

I hope for change without wanting it too much. Things must change, though. Brutal change could lead to collapse, as happened in the Soviet Union. But the scale of the Chinese population precludes comparisons. Russia's education

---

70. Fang Lizhi's speech at Jiaotong University, 15 November 1986, quoted in Liu, M. *Intellectual Dissidents in China*, Chinese Studies 17, Lewiston, NY: Edwin Mellen Press, 2001.

71. *See* Shambaugh, D. *China's Communist Party: Atrophy and adaptation*, Oakland, CA: University of California Press, 2009.

level is extremely high, but mafias are very powerful there. In China, the level of education is low. We have not had churches, social organisation or public interest groups for a long time. They can prove very useful though. In Russia, the Orthodox Church was strong enough to maintain some order. In China's case, it is obvious that a Soviet-like collapse would lead to social chaos of horrendous scale. Violent events could easily break out.

The fear of disorder thus conveyed shows that the conservative fear of losing control transcends ideological splits. We should also keep in mind that liberals take pains to qualify their discourse so as to anticipate typical accusations as to their supposed lack of realism and patriotism. Gradualist thinking can also be found in Chinese liberalism. In an article published in 1995 and which served as a manifesto, Zhu Xueqin described the then-reinvigorated liberalism as influenced by empirical philosophy, a refusal of historical determinism and a fallibilist theory of evolution.[72] Chinese liberalism was notably defined first by its rejection of the utopian desire to change reality for the sake of abstract ideas characteristic of radicalism and second by its thinking of evolution, which explains its preference for progress and gradual improvement. What ultimately marks out Chinese liberals from other tendencies is less the timing and sequentialising of reform than the way political reform is defined.

---

72. Zhu, X. '1998: ziyouzhuyi xueli de yanshuo' ('1998: the discourse of liberal theory'), *Nanfang Zhoumo* (*Southern Weekend*), 25 December 1998. Zhu also refers to this article in 'For a Chinese liberalism', in Wang, C. *One China, Many Paths*.

Chapter Six

Democratisation with Chinese Characteristics?

Is democratisation under way?

Analyses are divided on the question whether China's democratisation process has already started or not. Liberals view past reforms as administrative and not political reforms, since their goal is to allow the Party to keep its power. According to the libertarian Liu Junning, the only striking reform of the past few years is the institutionalisation of the succession process for political leaders.[1] Schumpeter's minimalist theory of democracy emphasises that one of the greatest benefits of a democratic regime is to ensure the peaceful competition and alternation of elites in power.[2] In a regime in which leaders are not elected, the emperor, or other dictator, is only replaced when he dies. In China, it was only in the 1980s that age limits were imposed, introducing a retirement age for top Party leaders.[3]

Officially, the democratisation process has undoubtedly started, since reforms since the Seventeenth Party Congress of 2007 are supposed to have introduced intra-Party democracy (*dangnei minzhu*);[4] these amount to a pursuit of transparency and accountability and to preventing an individual or a minority from making arbitrary decisions. As a result, Hu Jintao used political reform to encourage a more 'scientific' governance, notably by way of revising the assessment system for cadres in July 2009, to ensure that they focused more on co-ordinating economic priorities and social development (improving social stability and people's living standards). The performance of local governments has long been assessed on economic growth but Chinese society has become more and more 'fractured' (*duanlie*) – the concept sociologist Sun Liping's used when he raised the alarm[5] – and priorities have evolved. Foreign analysts tend to receive these evolutions positively. Guo Baogang explains that the Party is as powerful as

1. Interview with Liu Junning, December 2008.
2. Schumpeter, J. *Capitalism, Socialism and Democracy*, New York: Harper & Row, 1942. Karl Popper theorised this peaceful alternation in *The Open Society and its Enemies*: volume 1: *The High Tide of Prophecy*, 5th edn, London: Routledge Kegan Paul, 1966.
3. These regulations mainly set age limits for ministers, Party secretaries and provincial governors.
4. He, B. 'Intra-party democracy: a revisionist perspective from below', in Brødsgaard, K. E. and Zheng, Y. (eds), *The Chinese Communist Party in Reform*, London: Routledge, 2006.
5. Sun, L. *Duanlie (Division)*, Beijing: Shehui Kexui Wenbian Chubanshe, 2003.

it used to be but that China has improved in Transparency International's ranking of worldwide corruption.[6]

Answers to the question 'Is China's democratisation under way?' vary depending on the conceptions of democracy and political reform (defined as introducing competitive elections or not) of the scholars under scrutiny.

The tricky definition of political reform

Each ideological camp (liberals, New Left, cultural nationalists) revels in caricaturing its opponents' proposals. The following paragraph, in which Kang Xiaoguang blames liberals for their 'intellectual laziness', illustrates that point:

> How can these problems be solved? How to know, comprehend and assess the current Chinese political system? This is an essential matter. For liberal scholars, this is very simple. China is on the wrong track. One simply needs to compare China and the United States in all the domains where China has not followed the American example, and China is bound to be wrong. These issues are also very easy to solve. China should do like the United States. I would say liberal thinkers in China reflect on issues in a simplistic way. They display some intellectual laziness. I do not think things are as simple as that. If China followed all the American methods and the so-called 'Washington consensus' to the letter, the country would very quickly be divided into many parts. With Tibet, Xinjiang, Taiwan and Hong Kong, the situation of the central government, the stability and the unity of the country are seriously threatened. If we adopt a multi-party system, the country will be divided and it's already the case.

Kang Xiaoguang provides only a sketchy description of liberal thinking. All liberals do not want China 'to follow American methods and the so-called "Washington consensus" to the letter'. His attitude could be connected to his journey: Kang claims he was a liberal in the 1980s.

> After 1989 I started observing closely and systematically reflecting on politics. In the 1980s, things seemed to be clear. We wanted a political reform aiming at one very precise goal: adopting a US-like system.

He seems to discard liberal criticisms somewhat dismissively, associating them with the rash liberalism of his youth (he was 26 in 1989). He is, however, right on one point: what makes liberalism distinct from other Chinese currents of thought is that liberals are convinced that the best model to follow is that of western democracies. According to Wang Juntao, this dividing line has existed in China for over a hundred years:

> Although the liberals might not have always agreed about transplanting all elements from western democracies, they did not deny that a western democracy

---

6. He, B. 'Intra-party democracy: a revisionist perspective from below', p. 192.

is the model to be followed in China. In political theory, this point is not a criterion to distinguish democrats and non-democrats. However, in the Chinese context, it has been a critical point to divide the advocates of liberal democracy from proponents of other ideologies for more than one hundred years.[7]

As regards the debate on political reform in China, this is precisely the point. What sets liberals apart from others is that their definition of what Chinese political reform should be roughly corresponds to the introduction of the institutions of a 'western democracy', even though they don't typically want a complete and unqualified transplant of such institutions, as caricatures wrongly suggest. Xu Youyu thus explains:

I think that if China sets up a system, it is not impossible to establish an American-like or European-like regime. These are not ideals which should be copied exactly. I have had many opportunities to go to the United States, even though I spent more time in Europe, and my view is that the various democratic regimes all have some specific benefits. However, they have one thing in common, which China does not have. No matter what they say, they are all founded on the same basic elements: a basic constitution, constitutional democracy. This is what we need to learn from.

As seen in the previous chapter, what explicitly marks liberals off from the New Left is that liberals call for political reform to solve the social inequalities resulting from economic reforms. Indeed, 'twenty years of economic reforms have failed to establish the political checks necessary to control and balance it, and so problems of social justice have become steadily worse. These can only be resolved by reform of the political system to establish the rule of law in a constitutional democracy.'[8] While the New Left unremittingly criticises the 'invisible hand' of the market, liberals relentlessly condemn the 'visible foot' which stamps on it. Therefore, to liberals, reforms have been numerous over the past 30 years but none of them was political. They have not contributed to making the Chinese regime more democratic, that is, they have not encouraged its evolution towards electoral and constitutional democracy. Therefore, should political leaders lose public support, there is no peaceful way for the people to safely get rid of them.

When adopting an open definition of political reform, like Li Qiang, director of the Government Studies department of Peking University, answering whether reform is under way or not is less easy. Li Qiang does not actively take part in the debate opposing liberals to the New Left but, as a political scientist, he claims he approaches the issue of political reform more scientifically. According to him, political reform corresponds to two distinct steps.

7.　Wang, J. *Reverse Course: Political neo-conservatism and regime stability in post-Tiananmen China*, PhD dissertation, Columbia University, 2006, p. 151.

8.　Zhu, X. 'For a Chinese liberalism', in Chaohua, W. (ed.) *One China, Many Paths*, London: New York: Verso, 2003.

First of all, state-building. We must establish a market economy, a civil society and destroy the original totalitarian state structure. We must therefore first clearly define the state structure and the structure of companies. Only then can we set up a legal framework and a market economy. For the last thirty years, breakthroughs in that field have been significant. We are now half-way there. Even more. We are 70 per cent of the way, but there is another problem. Authorities must let individual consciences express themselves and develop, and find a new legitimation mode through tolerating some modern democratic elements. We have so much to work on in that field. We lack radical criticism. A feasible solution, an acceptable means must be found. Besides, we need a structure which is adapted for constitutionalism to develop and for power to become more democratic. Its reach should be limited. The problem is still unresolved.

Li Qiang therefore expands the definition of political reform in two different respects. As far as state-building is concerned, progress is significant (70 per cent). The Chinese state has shed its totalitarian clothes and has already become more functional, has allowed the development of a market economy and civil society. As to the other facet, transition to a democratic and constitutional regime, much remains to be done.

Li Qiang believes political reform is the cornerstone of all splits among Chinese elites. Three questions divide the various factions:

1. Should building a modern Chinese state and its relations with society come before democratic transition?
2. Concerning democracy itself, what are the rules that the government should abide by as regards social justice?
3. Where should the limits to state intervention be located?

When the first question arose, some, Deng Xiaoping included, thought that it should be a step-by-step process. Others were against delaying the democratic transition.

Another group, influenced by simplifications of western political science, thought that political reform was limited to democracy. If democracy was not the point, there was no such thing as political reform. This is how we came to stop talking about political reform.

Li Qiang considers exponents of this view as demagogues, since he cannot picture 'how to establish a democracy without clearly defining the state'. Li Qiang thus implicitly refers to the sequentialist and gradualist work of Thomas Carothers and Francis Fukuyama. To him, the second question encapsulates the debates between the New Left and liberals. The former encourage the state to shoulder its responsibilities, that is, organising the redistribution of wealth and providing for sufficient social security. Liberals encourage the government to further abide by the market and accept that state power over the market should be reduced. Li Qiang therefore explicitly asserts that this debate focuses on China's democratic reform. He also refers to an emerging third group: cultural nationalists, who deem that no democratic regime should be introduced in China. When Li

Qiang implicitly positions himself as an 'objective' critic, who can evaluate the claims and criticisms made by holders of various ideological positions, he seeks to invalidate liberal attempts to disqualify the New Left, on the grounds of its being anti-democratic.

According to Yang Guangbin, who advocates a gradual reform of the Chinese regime and Chinese society, China should be properly prepared before a democracy is established. After a long emphasis on economic rights, the priority should now be social rights, contrary to the order of events in western countries in which political revolutions occurred first and came to combine political, economic and social rights belatedly, in the wake of the two World Wars.

> China proceeds differently. For the last few years, the focus has been on social democracy, social rights. This can be explained by the political protest, which leads to social rights. Let us take the example of Chinese intellectuals. They now live comfortable lives. Their situation has greatly improved for a decade. Ten years ago, they were very dissatisfied. Their relationship with the government was very tense. The government then decided to invest a lot in education and intellectuals have gradually started supporting the government. Later on, demobilised soldiers, public companies, industry as a whole, have brought their support to the government which became richer and became able to improve their condition. The government then focused on the countryside. Starting in 1978, with Deng Xiaoping and Jiang Zemin, economic development came first. Obviously with economic development, society became more unequal and the issue of social rights (social security, health coverage and so on) had to be solved. I think that this aspect, for China, for the government and for the Chinese people, is more essential than democracy.

In other words, conceptions of political reform or democracy in China vary: it depends on whether one considers that it corresponds to a global, comprehensive reform of the Chinese regime and society, and whether it is independent from social and economic conditions and breakthroughs or not. What is more, liberals advocate that political reform should proceed independently from the advances of both economic and social reforms; in fact, it is a necessary condition of their success. Indeed, according to Qin Hui or Hu Ping, privatisation is conducted in China without the people's involvement or control. How could a Chinese welfare state even be conceived if no one can stop the sheer robbery of public goods?

> Everyone knows in China that those who became rich first, especially those who belong to spheres close to power, have enriched themselves through illegal shameful means. China's current problem cannot be solved by way of strengthening the fiscal system or improving social security. The wealth powerful lobbies have looted should, above all, be handed back to its legitimate owner, the people.[9]

---

9. He, P. *Chine: à quand la démocratie? Les illusions de la modernisation*, Paris: L'aube, 2007, 2nd edition, p. 40; Qin, H. 'Dividing the big family assets', *New Left Review* 20, 2003, pp. 83–110.

The Chinese liberal stance might be likened to the adherence to 'optimistic' principles spread by democratisation studies, at the time of the third wave of democratisation (roughly, from 1974 on).[10] For less liberal intellectuals, economic reform has made the reform of the state and social reform necessary and it is only when economic reforms bear fruit that an institutional reform as such will become truly necessary.

Various conceptions of democracy in China

Liberal and New Left conceptions of democracy are quite distinct. Liberals seem resigned to 'negative democracy', construed as the reverse of dictatorship and originating from the experience of the Mao era and the Cultural Revolution in particular, while in Europe it stemmed from the fear of totalitarianism before World War Two.[11] The democracy they call for is understood narrowly, as a procedural conception of 'a regime protecting liberties, distant from the older ambition of a commanding sovereignty of the people', and not in terms of an ethically substantive conception of the value of democracy. Distrust of the totalitarian state makes Hayek's work and his strict alternative between the market's spontaneous order and dictatorship attractive to Chinese liberals.

For the Chinese New Left, on the contrary, the definition of a minimal and negative democracy is unacceptable. Popular sovereignty cannot express itself only through the vote. Democracy must also defend positive values of substantive rather than formal equality. It therefore depends on building not only political but also social citizenship and on pluralising modes of participation in public life. These two conceptions of democracy lead to opposed assessments as regards the advancement of political reform in China.

As regards the first component of political reform, which liberals qualify as administrative, progress is slow but building the rule of law has improved efficiency, justice and stability, aiming at justifying the Party's hold on power. When official propaganda and the majority of the Chinese population refer to political reform, they mostly have in mind governance improvements, which the Party has introduced to progressively submit the system to the rule of law. The willingness of the new ruling team when it comes to fighting corruption is a new confirmation that the Party has understood that without instruments to cap corruption and solve conflicts procedurally and peacefully, social and political insecurity is destined to occur.[12] Therefore, China's major accomplishments in these last 30 years have been to have 'established a comprehensive, modern and sometimes innovative

---

10. Guénard, F. 'Promoting democracy: a theoretical impasse?', *Books & Ideas*, 28 November 2007, available at http://www.booksandideas.net/Promoting-democracy-a-theoretical.html (last accessed 14 November 2014).

11. Rosanvallon, P. *La démocratie inachevée*, Paris: Gallimard, 2000, p. 400.

12. Heberer, T. and Schubert, G. 'Political reform and regime legitimacy in contemporary China', *Asien* 99, 2006, pp. 9–23.

body of law'[13] and to have professionalised their legislative and enforcement institutions. The needs of the market economy, the demands of foreign investors and domestic industry, international pressure, the need to make the system more efficient and the desire to be legitimate in the eyes of the Chinese people and the international community have all driven legal reforms. A lot remains to be done as regards their enforcement and in regard to the independence of the judiciary, since the Party has not given up its monopoly. However, recurring references to all things legal in the official rhetoric and the significant development of law and legal institutions, administrative law constraining political power included,[14] contribute to constituting a new culture of legality and bode well for the advancement of the rule of law in China.

Formal democracy versus extended democracy

Proponents of the Chinese New Left have long criticised a lack of state intervention in market regulation while highlighting the need for the implementation of social welfare policies. To those of this mind, these not only provide necessary compensation for those who have been harmed by state reforms but are also a way of reducing various inequalities. Since the Hu–Wen government announced a far-reaching social policy on the road to its final goal of 'extended democracy' (*guangfan de minzhu*), which will give more power to the people and allow for a more equal society, they have seemed to be more optimistic about social policy in China.[15]

Indeed, the Hu–Wen government launched a wide-ranging plan of action along the lines of the hackneyed motto 'building a harmonious society' (*jianshe hexie shehui*). It involved a rather impressive list of social reforms aimed at rebuilding a social security system,[16] with higher pensions and fewer

13. Horsley, J. 'Rule of law: pushing the limits of Party rule', in Fewsmith, J. *China Today, China Tomorrow: Domestic politics, economy, and society*, Lanham, MD: Rowman & Littlefield, 2010; Peerenboom, J. (ed.), *China's Long March toward Rule of Law*, Cambridge: Cambridge University Press, 2002; Peerenboom, R. P. *Judicial Independence in China: Lessons for global rule of law promotion*, Cambridge: Cambridge University Press, 2010; Zhao, S. (ed.) *Debating Political Reform in China: Rule of law vs. democratisation*, Armonk, NY: Sharpe, M. E. 2006.

14. *Lifa fa*, the law on legislation passed in 2000, aimed at clarifying the hierarchy and competence of the statutory sources, enforcement procedures and legitimacy controls of laws and regulations. Legal education has also shifted its emphasis from teaching citizens to abide by the law to teaching cadres to do so as well. Besides, concepts such as *yimin weiban* (the source of political authority is the people), *yixian zhiguo* (ruling the country in respect of the constitution), *zhiqing quan* (right to information) and *zunzhong minyi* (respecting the popular will) have become popular.

15. Frenkiel, E. 'Political change and democracy in China. An interview with Wang Shaoguang', *Books & Ideas*, 15 July 2009, available online at http://www.booksandideas.net/Political-change-and-democracy-in.html (last accessed 14 November 2014).

16. Meng, Q. 'Reforming China's healthcare system: Beijing's strategy for establishing universal coverage', *China Brief*, the Jamestown Foundation 6(24), December 2006, available online at http://www.csrchina.net/page-857.html (last accessed 14 November 2014). Thompson, D. 'Healthcare reform in China: design by committee', *China Brief* 7(14), July 2007, available online at http://www.jamestown.org/chinabrief (last accessed 14 November 2014).

taxes on peasants.[17] These reforms were made possible by the reform and recentralisation of the fiscal system that preceded them. They were a reaction to growing social unrest caused by the blatant inequalities that the progress of economic reforms in the country has generated. These reforms were justified to the population not only in terms of the quest for economic growth but also of the will to advance socialism. They were meant to address feelings of insecurity (*meiyou anquan gan*) among the Chinese population, who save more than 50 per cent of their income to make up for the shortcomings of social welfare and the rising costs of education and housing.[18] Thus in October 2007, President Hu Jintao himself opened the Party's Seventeenth Congress by stating that without social reforms, notably in the domain of health, China would not continue to grow at its current rate, given that the majority of its population was currently forced to save vast sums of money which should be used for consumption or investment instead. This highlights the pragmatic motivations behind the Party's new social orientation: if Chinese leaders want to stay in power, they have to reduce social instability and boost China's national market, especially at a time when the USA and Europe are hard-hit by the global financial crisis. Ren Jiantao realistically considers the government is compelled to learn how to share wealth so as to reduce popular discontent. Let us recall that, to his mind, the unexpected awakening of the Chinese people – whom he considers to be naturally highly apathetic – originates in the unfair wealth distribution.

> Chinese society currently lacks energy. The only thing which can rid it of its torpor is the unfair distribution of wealth. People rebel when they compare the size of their apartment with others', or their salaries. This is the only thing which angers them and drives them to act.

For left-leaning scholars like Wang Shaoguang, who was one of the whistle-blowers pushing for the early 1990s fiscal reforms, this is not only due to pragmatism. These reforms fuel the hope that Chinese leaders will eventually question their neo-liberation orientation, which the scholar explicitly explains in an interview with Ma Ya.[19] Wang Shaoguang detects a confirmation of the leaders' ideological U-turn in the scale and swiftness of social reforms launched in the Hu-Wen era.[20]

---

17. 'La Chine débloque 2 milliards de dollars pour augmenter la pension de retraite cette année', *Beijing Information*, 17 January 2008; Hao, Y. 'Reforming China's pension programs to cope with an aging population', *IAE Brief* 654, 2 September 2011.

18. Chamon, M., Lu, K. and Prasad, E. 'The puzzle of China's rising household saving rate', *Vox*, 18 January 2011, http://www.voxeu.org/article/puzzle-china-s-rising-household-saving-rate (last accessed 14 November 2014).

19. Ma, Y. 'HuWen gaige: xin de gongshi xin de zouxiang' ('Hu Jintao and Wen Jiabao: new consensus, new direction'), *Fenghuang Zhoukan* (*Phoenix Review*), April 2007.

20. Li, C. 'The Chinese Communist Party: recruiting and controlling the new elites', *Journal of Current Chinese Affairs* 38(3), 2009, pp. 13–33; Li, C. 'Besieged by factions, China's leaders struggle with succession, reforms and worried foreign investors', *Yale Global*, 16 April 2012.

When investigating the history of social reforms in other countries, we realise it is an extremely slow process. In China, social policies have emerged when serious polarisation was surfacing and they developed at high speed and rapidly institutionalised. This is very uncommon. It cannot be simply explained by regime consolidation. Some condemn the pace of the Party's reforms. They consider the issue from the perspective of government strategy. From the point of view of the government's interests, a Machiavellian method of moderate but persistent effort should be adopted; that is, giving a little more every year or every second or third year. It is much easier this way. But the pace of social reform in China is extremely fast. Policies are launched one after the other. From a purely strategic point of view, it is absurd to go too fast.

According to Wang Shaoguang, a modern regime necessarily comprises a comprehensive distributive and regulatory policy, in charge of large-scale protection of individuals. In an article in which he praises recent achievements in that field, he introduces Karl Polanyi's theory that an unregulated market economy can lead to desperate situations.[21] The scholar's self-ordained task is to introduce, explain and apply to China other western theories than classical liberalism and the defense of an unregulated market economy, so as to go beyond interpretations which he deems simplistic, erroneous or insufficient, such as Friedrich Hayek's, which are extremely popular in China and which, the New Left believes, have caused many major problems.[22] His article 'Democracy and state effectiveness', which aims at defending a strong state through demonstrating that it is correlated to the quality and strengthening of democracies, is a perfect illustration of his approach.[23] Polanyi's *Great Transformation* provides the political scientist with a theoretical framework to think and justify the recent steering of reforms. He analyses it as a 'counter-movement' of social protectionism aiming at reducing inequality and providing a social security which was badly needed after twenty years of reforms introducing a market economy. He lists the various social policies which were introduced from 1999 to 2007 for that purpose.[24]

21. Wang, S. 'Dazhuanxing: 1980 niandai yilai zhongguo de shuangxiang yun', *Zhongguo Shehui Keshui* 1, 2008, published in English as 'The great transformation: the double movement in China', *Boundary 2* 35(2), summer 2008, pp. 15–47; Polanyi, K. *The Great Transformation: The political and economic origins of our time*, Boston, MA: Beacon Press, 1944.

22. Mishra, P. 'China's New Left calls for a social alternative', *International Herald Tribune*, 13 October 2006. Wang Shaoguang criticises, for instance, the concept of an autonomous civil society: *see* Wang, S. 'Jinqian ziyou: shimin shehui mianlin de liang nan jingdi', *Kaifang Shidai* 3, 2002, published in English as 'Money and autonomy: patterns of civil society finance and their implications', *Studies in Comparative International Development* (SCID) 40(4), 2006, pp. 3–29.

23. Wang, S. 'Democracy and state effectiveness implications', paper given at the international conference The Crisis of Democratic Governance in East Asia: Implications, National Chengchi University, Taipei, 12–13 March 2002. The article was also published in Dinello, N. and Popov, V. (eds), *Political Institutions and Development: Failed expectations and renewed hopes*, Cheltenham, UK: Edward Elgar, 2007. Out of 81 bibliographical references only two are Chinese.

24. Wang, S. 'The Great Transformation'.

1999   Go West policy.
2002   Urban minimum income guarantee programme.
2003   Rural fee-tax reform; re-establishment of rural Co-operative Medical Systems (CMS).
2004   Reduction in agricultural taxes; introduction of 3 types of rural subsidies.
2005   Partial abolition of agricultural taxes.
2006   Abolition of all agricultural taxes; introduction of comprehensive rural subsidies; free compulsory education in western and central rural areas; public housing for urban poor.
2007   Free compulsory education in all rural areas; basic health insurance for all urban residents; CMS for over 80 per cent of rural population; promotion of rural minimum income guarantee programme; pensions for migrant workers; public housing for urban poor.

Wang Shaoguang argues that the return of capitalism to China allows socialist reforms to be launched. This situation is specific to China, a country shaped by its socialist past as well as the Confucian ideal of *ren'ai* (goodness, love) and the idea of extending filial respect for a more equal society.[25] This recent change in the political direction of the country 'shows that the Chinese government has the political will and the fiscal capacity to feed a fairer market economy, even if this political will and this fiscal capacity still need strengthening'. However, these social reforms have been implemented unequally, leaving certain areas of the country worse off than others,[26] as Zheng Yongnian remarks:

> The mounting problems and dissatisfaction resulting from China's market-oriented development over the past three decades show that China's policy shifts are long overdue. But one should not read too much into the official rhetoric of a policy shift from growth to greater social service provision. On the one hand, China still depends on market-oriented development to deal with the socio-economic side effects of growth. On the other hand, China's current governance system has a built-in bias toward market growth, particularly below the central state level. This market-growth orientation discriminates against proposed goals, such as greater equality, improved quality of life, better environmental protection and so on.[27]

Peking University economist Yao Yang is also less optimistic than Wang Shaoguang on the scope of the social reforms announced by the government because the 'context is such that the government mainly focuses on economic issues'. China produces a lot but distributes little. A massive part of the budget

25.   'Building a strong democratic state: an interview with Wang Shaoguang', in Ma, Y. *Zhanlue Gaodu: Zhongguo sixiangjie fangtan lu*, Hong Kong: Sanlian Shudian, 2008

26.   *See* Huang, Y. 'The sick man of Asia: China's health crisis', *Foreign Affairs*, December 2011, pp. 119–36.

27.   Zheng, Y. 'Society must be defended: reform, openness, and social policy in China', *Journal of Contemporary China*, 19(67), pp. 799–818.

is devoted to dealing with the aftermath of the global financial crisis. This is the reason why the Chinese government mainly listens to what economists, rather than political scientists, suggest. This could also help explain how economic liberalism can be so influential in China while vocal advocates of political liberalism are severely repressed. The criticisms of the European welfare state by Chinese officials like Jin Liqin are vivid reminders of the influence of Friedrich Hayek and Milton Friedman's liberal ideas in the most powerful Chinese circles. In November 2013, Jin Liqin argued on Al Jazeera that the problems currently plaguing Europe were due to 'an exhausted welfare state. Labour law makes for sloth and idleness'.[28] The fact that most Chinese leaders believe in these theories does not bode well for a distributive revolution in the future. Yao Yang claims that local governments need incentives from the state to implement reforms aiming at reducing inequalities:

> Even though the government is concerned with inequalities, our political institutions are not sufficient to undertake this kind of social policy. When the government decides something, it does not have the means to set it up. It must first fight against the resisting local governments and decide once and for all the way power is distributed between different levels. The government lacks motivation to focus on other issues than economic growth. When local governments maintain a high economic growth and a relative stability, the central government has no motivation to act against them. This is the reason why I am not as optimistic as Wang.

Yang Guangbin has explained that the Hu-Wen government's reliance on the mottoes of the harmonious society (*hexie shehui*), of new socialist campaigns (*shehuizhuyi xin nongcun*) and of a scientific conception of development (*kexue fazhan guan*) pointed to a certain recognition on its part that 30 years of economic reforms have created problems that must now be dealt with. But it does not mean the problems have been solved yet:

> These are beautiful speeches, but without expanding the budget allocated to social policy, how can the poorest be assisted, and given a place to live? [...] To focus on social security, 12 per cent of the budget is allocated to it. To expand it to 18 per cent, or even 30 per cent, or more, like in western countries, we have to go through intense political debates. This is a matter of resources allocation, a decisive issue. China must however change. The country possesses too many resources. Primary and secondary resources are excessive. The country must evolve for the sake of development and prosperity. But what is the end goal of development? Western countries are overburdened with the welfare state, but this is precisely the role of states. Why should a state develop? Developing

---

28. Jin Liqin, former Deputy Finance Minister, is currently the President of China Investment Corporation (CIC); http://www.aljazeera.com/programmes/talktojazeera/ (last accessed 14 November 2014).

quickly cannot be its ultimate aim. I think the way the Chinese state functions should be transformed. Of course, our slogans have already changed, but the state system hasn't changed yet.

While the central government's financial extractive capacity has considerably improved, redistribution has not yet taken place because there have not yet been any true changes in the system. The famous liberal Qin Hui, who teaches history at Tsinghua University in Beijing, compares the debates between the liberal and the social-democratic conceptions of the state to the ways in which horses can be treated. While liberals don't want to feed their horse much but wouldn't ask for much in return, social-democrats are ready to feed the horse well but would also expect a lot in return. However, nobody wants a well fed horse that refuses to walk.[29]

As a result, the political direction of the Chinese government evolved considerably under Hu and Wen. The rhetoric changed: economic growth was no longer characterised as the sole priority, which satisfies the New Left, even though results are mixed. This changing of priorities corresponds to the first element of the New Left's definition of a maximalist democracy. The evolving discourse of the New Left has uncovered the hopes brought about by this new social orientation of public policies, which the new administration now has to pursue. Since the issues of state capacity and wealth distribution are now high in the agenda, the New Left's new hobby horse is promoting new forms of popular participation, the second element of a maximalist definition of democracy.

For twenty years, Wang Shaoguang has argued that establishing a stable democracy is only to be contemplated if the state is strong and efficient. The ingredients of democratic construction are therefore 'an extended democracy, a fair liberty and a strong state'. This extended democracy is more participative, thanks to the multiplication of participation modes (direct participation and decision, sortition and vote) but, most of all, more egalitarian than a democracy à l'américaine.[30]

The critics of electoral democracy

For Chinese academics from the New Left, economic democracy and social justice should take precedence over political democracy.[31] They do not take western democracies, where the gap between these two elements has increased

---

29. Qin, H. 'La crise économique mondiale et l'avenir du "modèle chinois"', conference organised by Jean-Philippe Béja at Science Po CERI, Paris 7 November 2011.

30. Wang Shaoguang defends the idea of a pragmatic democracy where issues are concretely debated, for instance, when a polluting factory is to be built or not. 'Jianli yi ge qiang youlide minzhu guojia: yu Wang Shaoguang de duihua' ('Building a strong democratic state: a dialogue with Wang Shaoguang'), in Ma, Y. *Zhanlue Gaodu: Zhongguo sixiangjie fangtan lu*, Hong Kong: Sanlian Shudian, 2008.

31. Gan, Y. 'Zhongguo ziyou zuopai de youlai', in Zuwei, C. and Wentao, L. (eds), *Zhengzhi Lilun Zai Zhongguo*, Oxford: Oxford University Press, 2001.

so dramatically, as examples but rather as counter-examples for the building of a Chinese type of democracy that would not make the same mistakes. This is Pierre Rosanvallon's starting point in his *Société des Egaux*: 'Democracy as a regime has never been more alive than now, when it is dying as a form of society.'[32]

New Left scholars have questioned, for instance, the importance of elections, which they see as an abstract method that does not truly contribute to reducing social inequalities. A good government, under which citizens can take an active part in decision-making, cannot come into being through elections alone. Their ideas are similar to Kang Xiaoguang's, who denounces the gap between the democratic ideal and its practice, where 'the bourgeoisie uses democracy to dissimulate an oligarchic policy while depriving the masses of their democratic rights. [...] Elections are controlled by money. So is the Parliament.'[33] Wang Shaoguang has for the last few years advanced potent and telling arguments in favour of making a distinction between electoral democracy and democracy in general. In a 2008 interview, he told me that 'Democracy means that it is the people who are in power. Electoral democracy merely means that a selection has taken place, as in Supergirl [*chaoji nusheng*], the famous Hunan TV reality TV singing contest.' Along with Gan Yang, he thus promotes the idea of 'substantial democracy'.

The latter explains that it could seem to contradict his advocacy of a quality – elitist – education and culture but he believes that, in practice, a balance can be found between cultural elitism and great economic egalitarianism:

> Citizens must first be good people. If in a given society or civilisation, the basic concept of good people, or moral men, does not exist, if nobody knows of this concept and everyone is considered to be good, this is impossible. It leads to formal democracy, which is absolutely unavailing in China.

In this quote, Gan Yang evokes the limits of formal equality in countries where inequalities are very intense. His distinction between formal and real democracy reminds us of the Communist criticism of the bourgeois democratic 'fiction' and, in particular, of the distinction between democracy's purely formal equality and the true equality of the proletarian democracy. Beside objecting to the abstraction of the vote and reminding us of the irreducible economic inequalities, Gan Yang adds that if voters are barely educated – another occurrence of the quality (*suzhi*) argument, the insufficient education of Chinese citizens – voters will only vote so as to get a substantial return. They are bound to be 'bad citizens' and this kind of democracy is not desirable; to Gan Yang, it is even worse than a democracy in which citizen participation in political decision-making is limited to going to the ballot box every five or ten years.

---

32. Rosanvallon, P. *La société des égaux*, Paris: Le Seuil, 2011, p. 11.

33. Kang, X. 'Why I advocate Confucianism', preface to Kang, X. *Renzheng: Zhongguo zhengzhi fazhan* (*Renzheng: The third way for China's political development*), Singapore: World Scientific, 2005.

Economic inequalities have long overpassed the limits that a country can tolerate. In these conditions of intolerable inequality, discussions on the necessity of a democratic regime appear meaningless. A meaningless solution cannot be found to solve such a dramatic problem. This is ridiculous and non realistic. [...] What matters in China is that the majority of the population is interested in what a substantial democracy would be, rather than a formal democracy. They think that they should get something. If they vote for you, you should achieve something. This has nothing to do with elections in western countries [... where] you vote for somebody every five or ten years and do nothing else in the meantime. It seems to me that, to the Chinese population, this is totally unacceptable. I believe this is one way or another connected to Chinese traditions and above all to the socialism of the Mao era. Mao insisted on substantial change, not formal change. [...] Encouraging formal voting equality cannot be sufficient. This formal equality as regards the vote is in itself made impossible by the problem of economic inequality.

The relevance of elections in China's democratisation process is often downplayed by academics – not only from the New Left – as exemplified in the following excerpt from an interview with a Renmin University political scientist, Yang Guangbin, who is, supposedly, more neutral, ideologically speaking. He explains that the 'philosophy of democracy' is as not prevalent in China as in western countries:

Local elections have been organised for over 20 years in villages. But even today, voters still do not frame elections as electing the best leaders. They do not have this philosophy of democracy that you have in western countries. Even now, villagers do not see the point of voting. They only make the effort to vote if they get something in exchange: money, cigarettes and so on. That's the situation after a 20-year practice of village elections. This means that culture matters. To understand a country's regime, one is compelled to take its cultural legacy into account. If I had to hierarchise political, economic and social issues, I'd rank economy first, then social and political matters, the right to vote and so on.

These arguments echo the official discourse, according to which China does not need to replicate western democratic processes to reach political modernity and enjoy the support of its citizens. Andrew Nathan reminds us that 'it is essential not to misconstrue these Chinese actors' views of democracy. Persons of influence in China who call for democracy are not advocating competitive elections for top posts.'[34] While this causes despair among dissidents and foreign commentators alike, academics from the New Left find a justification for it in the fact that democracy means much more than a mere electoral process. New Left scholars indeed oppose what Gan Yang calls a 'politically-correct strait-jacket' according to which political reform can only mean introducing direct elections. This is all the more so as they all

---

34. Nathan, A. 'China's political trajectory', in Li, C. (ed.), *China's Changing Political Landscape: Prospects for democracy*, Washington, DC: Brookings Institutions Press, 2008.

reject the systematic association between democracy and elections, and point out that the latter were considered far more aristocratic than random selection for office for a very long time after their introduction. Indeed, with random selection (*chouxuan*), everyone has the same chance of getting picked, regardless of their capital, their charisma or their oratorical skills. To make his point, Wang Shaoguang refers to the role that celebrity and money played in the election of Arnold Schwarzenegger as governor of California and argues that random selection would guard against this kind of democratic abuse.[35] The academic often talks about his first visit to Russia in 1990 with his colleagues from Yale, and how it made him realise the importance of building 'a *strong* democracy rather than just *a* democracy':

> Only when I arrived in Russia did I realise how wrong I was. The situation in Moscow when we arrived was the worst situation I had ever seen anywhere anytime, even compared with the 1960s in China. Moscow was much worse, because all the shops were absolutely empty. Even during the worst time during the Cultural Revolution or the Great Leap Forward, there was still something on store for sale. So I began to realise some big ideas – free market, democratic elections – may not be so helpful for them. That's why I talk about a strong democracy and not about a regular democracy, and about the state capacity. Fukuyama didn't pick up this idea until a few years ago. When he wrote a book about rebuilding the state.[36] I developed the idea probably twelve years earlier than him.

Note, however, that the New Left claims it is not anti-liberal. It rather defines itself as liberal, in that it does not oppose a market economy or the defence of human rights. In Pierre Rosanvallon's terms, as opposed to those who claim to be Chinese liberals, the New Left does not uphold the two doctrines of political liberalism at the same time. The New Left does not oppose the market economy but does not adhere to utopian liberalism, that is, the democratic anarchism corresponding to extending Adam Smith's principles to politics.[37] It purports to defend a positive brand of liberalism, which adherents present as crucial to limit social instability; that is, the protection of human rights, which they claim to extend to economic and social rights. Gan Yang also protests against what he calls 'political correctness'.

> The framework we discuss politics in seems particularly narrow. It can only be democratic western politics – and more particularly in the American sense of competitive elections between two parties. This framework is very limited. We pretend to discuss freely, but everything is already set. [...] We are limited to a shrunk context everyone is enthusiastic about. I am tired of this. In this confined framework, the possibility to discuss Chinese politics has been completely eradicated.

---

35. Wang, S. 'Jianli yi ge qiang youlide minzhu guojia'.

36. Fukuyama, F. *State-Building: Governance and world order in the 21st century*, Ithaca, NY: Cornell University Press, 2004; this book was derived from lectures he gave in 2003 at Cornell.

37. Rosanvallon, P. *Le libéralisme économique: histoire de l'idée de marché*, Paris: Le Seuil, 1989, p. xxx.

Gan Yang's next quotation should be interpreted against the backdrop of his rejection of a general depoliticisation and a consensual liberal neutrality:

> I think politics is the ultimate issue. However, our policy is not taking this direction. On the contrary, our political systems, especially the democratic electoral system, is but a kind of governance [*xingzheng zhuyi*]. Substantial issues are never at stake. We are not interested in them and we don't dare mention them. According to liberalism, the state should be neutral. There cannot be a moral aim. This is a mistake! But most of us already accept it. This is the reason why I refer to nineteenth-century England and the conservative thinking of that time. It was a political line of thought advocating a cultural direction devoted to understanding man and culture. Man must transcend himself and material considerations. [...] Nobody dares to say what is good. Nobody dares to say what a good leader is any longer. Besides, this leads to hypocrisy. Nobody tells the truth and this is very worrying.

These two quotes illustrate the New Left's taking up of the concept of 'liberation of thought', which is usually resorted to as a reference to the free debates younger generations were encouraged to organise during the Cultural Revolution and in the more open environment of the 1980s. This is also Cui Zhiyuan's point in *Politics: The Central Texts, Theory Against Fate*, a book in which he introduced and edited Roberto Unger's writings in order to '*reinterpret* and generalize the *liberal and leftist* endeavor by freeing it from unjustifiably restrictive assumptions about the practical institutional forms that representative democracies, market economies and the social control of economic accumulation can and should assume'.[38] The political thinkers of this ideological trend are in line with the analyses conducted by Weber, Bryce, Michels, Ostogorski and Pareto on the 'aristocratic' elements introduced with elections in democracy.[39] They echo arguments about the crisis of representation often put forward in western democracies and the criticism of what is known as 'electocracy' (*xuanzhu*).[40]

Wang Shaoguang denounces the plutocratic mistakes of elections – especially in the United States – and attempts to demonstrate that the connection between electoral procedure and democracy is not self-evident and was introduced quite late in world history.

> Elections may not be that important in my idea. Rather all forms of participation are equally important. In my little book *Four Lectures on Democracy* (a booklet

---

38. Unger, R. M. and Cui, Z. (eds) *Politics: The central texts, theory against fate*, New York: Verso, 1997.

39. *See* Rosanvallon, P. *La démocratie inachevée*, Paris: Gallimard, Folio histoire, 2000, p. 401.

40. Guinier, L. 'Beyond electoral democracy: rethinking the political representative as powerful stranger', *Modern Law Review* 71(4), pp. 1–35, quoted in Gao, M. 'Netizenship and its implications for democratisation in China', in Cheng, J. Y. S. (ed.) *Whither China's Democracy? Democratisation in China since the Tiananmen Incident*, Hong Kong: City University of Hong Kong Press, 2011, pp. 151–176.

very easy to read and just published), I point out that before the nineteenth century, elections had never been associated with democracy. Rather, it was random lots that had been associated with democracy. Now, again, there are some experiments in Britain, in Canada, in Australia and New Zealand. Because they talk about a democratic deficit. They begin to try to use randomness to resolve the problems associated with elections. My idea is that elections are now for people with resources to occupy positions of power. Which is unfair, undemocratic. Only when everyone has the opportunity not only to vote, but to be elected, it is democratic. In particular, I criticise the American democracy. Because if you don't have hundreds of millions of dollars in your possession, you cannot participate in the game of the elections.

He refers to the connection the Greeks made between democracy and another procedure than elections (which were perceived as aristocratic) – sortition (random selection). Wang explains that this procedure allows for a true equality between citizens and he proposes to replace elections by sortition, which would allow a perfect equality of all and to be rid of some – notably financial – factors which weigh upon elections.[41] Cui Zhiyuan is among the most influential representatives of the theory of institutional innovation in China. He initiated the debate on that issue in the mid 1990s in a series of publications.[42] In the preface to Cui's book on innovations, Tang Tsou, a political science professor at the University of Chicago, wrote about the idea of Chinese exceptionalism, which, similarly to American exceptionalism, may explain why China could develop a unique political system: a goal to which Cui Zhiyuan tries to contribute. It is because he thinks that China's institutional future is open that Cui, who used to teach at MIT, came back to China, which seems to him to be a particularly favourable terrain for institutional innovations to develop. According to him, sortition should be more systematically introduced around the world, China included.

Elections is about electing someone with distinctive features: not an average person, but richer, with more qualities, or looking better. No average people are elected. It is logically impossible. Aristotle and Machiavelli also thought that elections only belonged to the aristocracy. So democracy demands random selection. This argument appears crazy now in large states. We have to understand now why today we no longer use random selection.

---

41. Wang, S. *Minzhu Si Jiang* (*Four Lessons on Democracy*), Beijing: Sanlian Shudian, 2008, p. 246. Some books and articles devoted to sortition were translated into Chinese and published, mainly thanks to Wang and He Baogang's efforts. There is also a Chinese version of Sintomer, Y., Traub-Merz, R. and Zhang, J. (eds), *Participatory Budgeting in Asia and Europe. Key challenges of deliberative democracy*, Hong Kong: Palgrave, 2012, published by Shanghai People's Publishing House, Shanghai, 2011.

42. Cui, Z. 'Zhidu chuangxin yu di'erci sixiang jiefang' ('Institutional innovations and the second liberation of thought'), *Ershiyi Shiji*, 8 August 1994, pp. 5–16; Cui, Z. *Zhidu Chuangxin Yu Dierci Sixiang Jiefang* (*Institutional Innovations and the Second Liberation of Thought*), Hong Kong: Oxford University Press, 1997.

These Chinese academics are interested in institutional innovations and, having studied and taught at famous American universities for extended periods of time, they have a good command of western debates on the 'crisis of democracy' and its essential contradictions. But they also have in-depth knowledge of theories questioning the single-handed effectiveness of elections as an expression of the will of the people. It seems that when proponents of the New Left criticise the vote as equality in the abstract and highlight its aristocratic connotations, it is also because they are trying to open up the debate to a 'more complex' definition of democracy than that of the liberals, one that would bring about an order of things 'more fitting' for China, with more social justice. Liberals use their rejection of China's revolutionary past to justify their settling for a restricted definition of democracy as the opposite of dictatorship. They remain suspicious of any positive definition of democracy; while the Chinese New Left purports to liberate minds and open up possibilities for China, which *prima facie*, is nothing to be concerned about. What is more worrying, however, is certain considerations which are neglected in the New Left's questioning of the importance of the vote. For instance, they never make any reference to the retrospective function of elections. As a matter of fact, many theories claim that elections are not sufficient but they never question their absolute necessity. What New Leftists and liberals alike tend to underplay is that elections still ensure that all the citizens who could not play a part in the decision-making process get to exercise a certain degree of control after the fact. Universal suffrage would also amount to public recognition of the dignity of all responsible Chinese adults, by giving all equal right to take part in the political decision-making process of the country. The end of CCP rule and the implementation of competitive elections for the highest government jobs still count among the most 'sensitive' topics in China, which may help explain such a troubling ambiguity on the part of the New Left, whose academics have decided to argue for a realistic and gradual reform of the regime and which sometimes seems to voice official discourse on democracy with Chinese characteristics.

Interestingly, the critics of electoral democracy do not question the advantages of that system (participation, accountability, responsibility, receptivity, legitimacy, and so on). They prefer to focus on its downsides in order to demonstrate that the same results can be arrived at by way of other processes or institutions, and that these may even allow a better outcome with fewer problems (limited representation and participation; difficulty of long-term decision-making and so on). They also rely on the analyses of researchers like Bernard Manin, who argue that representativeness in government actually combines democratic and non-democratic elements.[43] This allows them not only to invalidate those theories that reduce democracy to the vote, but also to open up the debate and give legitimacy to their plan for the creation of a mixed Chinese regime. Like many scholars in western universities, such as Yves Sintomer, they refuse to settle for an equivalence between democracy and elections, or between political freedom and the will of the government. As a

---

43. Manin, B. *Les principes du gouvernement représentatif*, Paris: Calmann-Lévy, 1995.

consequence, their position in the eyes of the Party – until the dismissal of Bo Xilai in March 2012 – remained rather comfortable. Their strategy consists in the realistic analysis of western democracies as imperfect mixed democracies, so that they can justify a Chinese type of democracy that would include non-democratic elements, such as the preservation of single-Party rule, as well as the democratic elements such as guaranteeing individual freedoms, social and economic rights, and the political expression and participation of Chinese citizens.

Let us remark that the arguments the New Left puts forward hardly answer the liberals' objection that, without competitive elections ensuring that power is shared and elites peacefully alternate in ruling, the stability the regime's defenders cherish so can only dwindle, with rising levels of corruption and injustice. Ren Jiantao, for instance, worries about the consequences of the political frustration of a great part of the Chinese elites: the new rich striving for power and constrained to resort to corruption; leaders marginalised by the Party's nomination system, such as Bo Xilai; or the religious elite.

Is the 'extended' democratisation of China under way?

From a strictly liberal point of view, no democratisation is taking place in China. Liberals who live and work in mainland China cannot express themselves as freely on that point as intellectuals who live abroad like Hu Ping. They reject the idea that a gradual reform is taking place as regards freedom of expression, for instance, despite the explosion in the number of publications, the improvement of freedom of the press and the vivacity of political discussions on internet forums.

> Once a government has killed enough people to guarantee its authority, they can reduce the number of people killed. That's the reason why we cannot consider that the least quantitative reduction of repression mechanically amounts to a breakthrough in the progressive evolution towards democracy.[44]

Crusading against the 'politically correct' discourse of Chinese liberals and foreigners on democratisation, New Left scholars echo the more or less recent calls throughout the world for a more complex democracy and a multiplication of modes of citizen involvement. They thus praise institutional reforms and innovations that allow the Chinese population to take part in the control, oversight and assessment of leaders at all levels.

However, if, as the New Left wishes, the definition of democracy is extended, all institutional reform or experimentation aiming at enhancing 'real equality' and Chinese citizens' political participation is a contribution to the political reform of the country. From Cui Zhiyuan's perspective, Rousseau invented the modern theory of democracy because he emphasised that 'people's sovereignty depends on making and revising and obeying the law of their own making', even though Rousseau's admiration for the great law-givers of the Greek

---

44. Hu, P. *Chine: à quand la démocratie? Les illusions de la modernisation*, Paris: L'aube, 2007.

city-states is ambivalent.[45] As regards people's participation, 'China has made some achievements but still has a long way to go.' The institutional innovations that have taken place in China nonetheless signal the regime is steering toward more popular participation in decision-making, in his view:

> The Chinese political system needs some new perspectives to be properly described. Because many categories and conceptualisation are not suitable to describe what is going on. For example, this definition of random selection as democracy from Aristotle to Manin can be found in a twisted manner in China. For example, now, in the selection of leaders at the city level or even for university school deans. For instance if you try to select the leader of a city or a province, there are now experiments to send a survey or hire a polling company to do a survey of the citizens. If this opinion survey gives a bad opinion about the mayor for two years continuously, then the provincial leader will change the mayor. In a way, it is a little bit similar to the principle of random selection.

The optimism of New Left scholars stems from their conviction that leaders have become aware that only transparency, openness and responsiveness can solve the governance crisis China now faces. Based on Bernard Manin, Machiavelli and Gramsci, Cui Zhiyuan, for whom leaders' responsiveness is one of the pivotal aspects of democratisation, finds interest in a mixed-constitution system, combining government by one (the king in the worst case; a benevolent leader in the best scenario); government by a minority (or aristocracy); and government by the majority (the people).[46] Transplanted to China, this constitution would manage interactions between the central government, the elites (local governments and capitalists) and the whole population, for the benefit of all. Such a system is deemed democratic, since it is designed to turn popular demands into national policy and to prevent a new aristocracy and/or an alliance between the state and powerful interest groups from emerging.[47]

> This CCP becomes one and many at the same time and in recent years, there have been important internal innovations. For example, before, there used to be a 5-year interval between the Party congresses and members of

---

45. Cui Zhiyuan was probably inspired by the way Sun Yat-sen and revolutionaries read Rousseau. Wary of individualism, they praised Rousseau for substituting collectivism for individualism, which they interpreted from the idea of a general will prevailing over individuals, who sometimes must be constrained to abide by the social will: Bergère, M. -C. *Sun Yat-sen*, Paris: Fayard, 1994, p. 186.

46. Cui, Z. '"Eryuan lianbang zhuyi" de xiaowang', *Dushu* 9, 1996 and Cui, Z. '"Hunhe fanfa" yu dui zhongguo zhengzhi de sanceng fenxi', *Zhanlue Yu Guanli* 3, 1998.

47. Famously, Kang Xiaoguang has theorised this 'alliance of elites' (*jingying lianmeng*). Kang, X. *Renzheng: zhongguo fazhan de disan tiao daolu*, Singapore, Shijie Keji Shubanshe (World Scientific Press), 2005, pp. 234–8.

the congress had nothing to do in between. Now they have this new rule that when the congress is in session, the delegates at all levels should have day-to-day responsibilities to monitor the government officials at the same level (provincial or city leaders). This involves 70 million people and those people are mostly common people from all walks of life. They do not have some particular privilege. Of course, there are many problems that need to be reformed in the political regime, but how to conceptualise this is an interesting challenge. Because if we have a predetermined idea about the direction where the political reform must go, we may overlook what is really happening.

Cui also attempts to analyse the Chinese political system with the help of the theoretical framework of Albert Otto Hirschman, in *Exit, Voice, and Loyalty*.[48] He is convinced that this theory can apply to the CCP and explain why it is constrained to become more receptive to social aspirations and therefore to democratise. He even goes as far as saying that in the Chinese context, where exit is impossible (people cannot vote the CCP out and select another party) and where the Party is convinced that it is not legitimate – mostly due to pressure from the international community – the Party feels compelled to listen to criticisms and to improve.

If there is too much exit, many potential improvements of quality will not be reached, and without threat of exit at all, the voice may be useless. But how to think about this notion of threat in China, assuming there is only one party? If it is only voice, no threat of exit, it won't be effective. So, paradoxically, I think that CCP leaders, because they are influenced by this worldwide call for multi-party competitive elections, think that they are not legitimate. Because they are not elected in multi-party competitive elections, they feel they have to be very responsive to the people's complaints. Paradoxically, in many other states, for instance India, the ruling party thinks they are legitimate because they were elected in competitive elections and do not worry too much about people's demands, especially in-between elections. [...] I am not saying China is a perfect paradise, I try to understand the mechanism (Jon Elster always uses this term, mechanism, not laws) at stake in exit and voice. Chinese leaders do not feel legitimate so they have to be responsive. But responsive in a way is paradoxically a more important feature of democracy, because leaders have to respond to people's demands in their policies.

As a result, New Left scholars tend to reject the radical incompatibility between one-party rule and democratisation. Even though much remains to be done, political

---

48. Hirschman, A. O. *Exit, Voice, and Loyalty: Responses to decline in firms, organizations, and states*, Boston, MA: Harvard University Press, 1970.

reform is undoubtedly underway for the Chinese New Left,[49] who optimistically accept the idea that the Party is democratising. As a result, they somehow echo the official discourse on inner-party democratisation (*dangnei minzhu*). They also publicise the idea that institutional innovations take place in China and that various experiences of participative, deliberative or direct democracy reveal a growing responsiveness to the diverse demands and interests expressed in Chinese society.

Democracy is also defined as information transparency, without which no political participation is possible. Wang Shaoguang states that no true democracy can exist without budgetary transparency, because otherwise there can be no supervision of the functioning of the state. The first step in any political reform, therefore, consists in making the budget more transparent.[50] The Vice-Premier and the Minister of Finance noticed an article he devoted to the lessons to be drawn from the American Progressive era and he was invited to edit a book on the issue exactly when the central government, various administrations and ministries started presenting their detailed budgets. His point was that political reform starts with creating budget forecasts through a more transparent and open process. In certain provinces, the budget is now accessible online. Anyone can check how public money is allocated and spent. In other provinces, such as Hubei, representatives are given permanent access to data relative to budget performance and they can assess budget propositions. Zhejiang and Heilongjiang were the first provinces in which participatory budgeting experiments took place.[51]

New Left scholars are optimistic because, to their minds, leaders are now aware that transparency, openness and responsiveness are the only solutions to the governance crisis China is currently going through. They are convinced that leaders have grasped that only through showing that they can make the Chinese regime as transparent, open and responsive as a democratic regime can they make the Party legitimate enough to keep its hold on power. Access to information certainly is an essential democratic aspect but it must be associated with the freedom of expression of all citizens. Despite regularly publicised cases of censorship – especially since 2008 and the Olympics – Wang Shaoguang thinks the freedom of expression situation is improving.[52]

---

49. *See* Wang Hui's interview 'Fire at the castle gate', in Mulhern, F. *Lives On the Left*, London, New York: Verso, 2012, p. 314. He explains his views are closer to liberals like Qin Hui than to Liu Junning, but that he cannot accept their claim that China is still a socialist country and that the Chinese state has not changed. 'There are much more radical figures like Qin Hui, who continue to insist on the importance of social justice and – still more – political democracy. He argues that the Chinese regime basically remains Mao's old socialist state, which we need to replace with a liberal democracy. To some extent I agree with this, because it is true that we need political democracy to solve virtually all other problems. But I don't believe the current state is just a continuation of the old one. The country cannot be described as socialist, and the state itself has changed a lot.' Heberer and Schubert also defend this idea in Heberer, T. and Schubert, G. 'Political reform and regime legitimacy in contemporary China', *Asien* 99, 2006, pp. 9–23.

50. Wang, S. *Meiguo 'Jinbushidai' De Qishi*, Beijing: Public Finance Press, 2002.

51. He, B. 'Civic engagement through participatory budgeting in China: three different logics at work', *Public Administration and Development* 1(2), April 2011, pp. 122–33; Fewsmith, J. 'Participatory budgeting: development and limitations', *China Leadership Monitor* 29, August 2009, available online at http://media.hoover.org/sites/default/files/documents/CLM29JF.pdf (last accessed 14 November 2014).

There used to be no way to express ourselves. It was extremely difficult. But with wider access to the internet, each social stratum has suddenly found a medium, they can all express their desires. We can criticise the *hukou* policy,[53] express ourselves on a series of issues such as the way migrants are treated, the health system, education and so on.[54]

The development of the internet has had a definite impact on public opinion, the traditional press and public policies. In an article focusing on the evolution of the means to make an impact on the Chinese government's political agenda, Wang states that with the explosion in the number of internet users in China (in July 2013, 591 million people had broadband access) and the lively exchanges on discussion forums, Chinese leaders have been forced to pay more attention to the activity and opinion of internet users. As a result, the Information Section of the First Secretariat Bureau under the General Office of the State Council began to edit and submit excerpts of online information to the State Council leaders on a daily basis.[55] Young, educated urban-dwellers, who are the great majority of Chinese internet users, feel concerned by political and social issues. And, without other official channels than the *xinfang*[56] to absorb and channel citizen expression and participation, the internet and mobile phones have become natural outlets. In general, cases of flagrant injustice trigger vivid reactions among internet users. Such was the case after Sun Zhigang's death in March 2003 or the different car accidents involving the offspring of official cadres, among many other cases.[57] These virtual

---

52. Let us note that the situation has far from improved with the 2011 pro-democracy protests (sometimes called the 'Jasmine Revolution') and Xi Jinping's takeover. The China Media Project monitors the Chinese media and occurrences of censorship: *see* http://cmp.hku.hk (last accessed 14 November 2014).

53. The *hukou* is a family residential permit delivered by the Chinese government. All the Chinese have a *hukou* attached to their residence. Even though it is less crucial than it used to be, it still determines access to education, healthcare and public services.

54. Ma, Y. 'HuWen gaige: xin de gongshi xin de zouxiang' ('Hu Jintao and Wen Jiabao: new consensus, new direction'), *Fenghuang Zhoukan* (*Phoenix Review*), April 2007.

55. Wang, S. 'Changing models of China's policy agenda setting', *Modern China* 34(1), January 2008, pp. 56–87.Wang also uses this argument in 'Lishi de luoji yu zhishifenzi mingyun de bianqian' ('The logic of history and the evolution of the condition of intellectuals'), an interview published in *Nanfengchuan*, 5 December 2011.

56. The *xinfang*, literally 'letters and visits', is a system of administrative petitioning that receives more than 13 million requests a year. *See* Thireau, I. and Hua, L. *Les ruses de la démocratie: Protester en Chine*, Paris: Le Seuil, 2010.

57. Sun Zhigang, a student from Hubei Province, was arrested on the streets of Guangzhou in March 2003 for not carrying the required registration permit. Police brought him to a 'custody and repatriation' centre, one of the hundreds of detention facilities run by local governments to control migrant populations. Three days later, Sun was dead. After the newspaper *Nanfang Dushi Bao* broke the story on April 25, 2003, newspapers and Web sites throughout China republished the account, chat rooms and bulletin boards exploded with outrage and legal experts intensified calls for the abolition of the abuse-ridden 'custody and repatriation' centres. As a result, in June 2003, the central government announced that all of the more than 800 centres would be closed. Six police officers and officials were eventually jailed for their role in Sun's death. Thireau, I. and Hua, L. 'De l'épreuve publique à la reconnaissance d'un public: le scandale Sun Zhigang', *Politix* 71(3), pp. 137–64; Beach, S. 'The rise of rights?', *China Digital Times*, 27 May 2005, available online at http://chinadigitaltimes.net/2005/05/rise-of-right (last accessed 14 November 2014). *see also* an excellent documentary on citizen journalists: Maing, S. 'High tech, low life', 2013.

convulsions of public opinion are not systematically targeted by censorship as they are not necessarily directed against the system.[58] On the contrary, these citizen manifestations undoubtedly help the central government understand public expectations better and supervise government agencies and local authorities,[59] in a process that has been described by Isabelle Thireau and Hua Linshan regarding the *xinfang*.[60] To go back to Wang Shaoguang's study of the six models of impacting agenda-setting,[61] it ends with the claim that the popular-pressure model is now the most influential in China. This explains why interviewed academics declare they now find writing in internal journals less useful for influencing decision-makers. They have realised that they are more likely to make an impact on the direction of government policy through diffusing ideas or research results in public opinion.[62]

Yang Guangbin explains that with 'age and further research', his conception of politics and political reform have considerably evolved:

Political reform used to be a matter of freedom of expression, association, multi-party system and so on. Now, I believe it is more than that. I have gradually understood that adjusting the relations between diverse interest groups was also political. In that sense, political reform in China is already under way and transformations are massive. From an institutional perspective, the CCP has also reformed itself, and the relations between central and local governments too. Not to mention state-society relations and relations between the government and companies. The evolution is significant.

This academic believes that the growing influence of public opinion and interest groups on decision-making is evidence of China's current democratisation process. His current research actually focuses on interest groups, which have

---

58. *See* Arsène, S. 'De l'autocensure aux mobilisations: prendre la parole en ligne en contexte autoritaire', *Revue française de science politique* 61(5), 2011, pp. 893–915.

59. While reading Wang Shaoguang and Isabelle Thireau, we have the impression that, for Chinese authorities like for French *doctrinaires*, the logic of extending liberties is related to conceptions of them as 'means of government' rather than as extensions of individual liberties in the traditional liberal sense. Freedom of the press and protest mechanisms are conceived as means to make society and government interpenetrate each other and as communication means that serve both society and government. *See also* Rosanvallon, P. *Le moment Guizot*, Paris: Gallimard, 1985, pp. 65–9.

60. Thireau, I. and Hua, L. *Les ruses de la démocratie*.

61. Wang, S. 'Changing models of China's policy agenda setting', *Modern China* 34(1), 2008, pp. 56–87.

62. Wang, S. 'Changing models of China's policy agenda setting', p. 56: 'This study suggests that today the public is not an ignored bystander but is seriously involved in the agenda-setting process and that there is an impressive congruence between the priorities of the public and the priorities of the Chinese government. In the ruling party's terminology, agenda setting "is becoming a more and more scientific and democratic process"; or in Wen Jiabao's words, agenda setting "emphasizes solutions to major problems, either relevant to the grand strategy of the country's social-economic development or of deep concern to the mass public". Although the political process in China has yet to become as scientific and democratic as desired, the logic of Chinese politics has nevertheless been undergoing fundamental change.'

become extremely powerful.[63] 'Ministries, economic authorities, the real-estate sector all have their say when there are economic returns. Public companies and the couple of two or three largest companies in each industry sector also have a formidable impact on decision-making.'

Consequently, outside the most liberal circles, the idea that China is now slowly democratising prevails. It means that, to the scholars who are involved in the debate on political reform, progress has been made in terms of political participation, transparency, leaders' responsiveness and the protection of Chinese citizens' interests. The concepts usually framing the discussions on democratic transition, such as the dichotomy between democracy and authoritarianism, are deemed too limited.[64] Calls for renewed concepts for a more appropriate description of the evolving Chinese regime and society are now commonplace. Cui Zhiyuan, for instance, claims that 'the Chinese political system needs some new perspectives to be properly described because many categories and conceptualisations are not suitable to describe what is going on.' Xiao Gongqin, although radically opposed to Cui Zhiyuan's analysis, agrees that focusing only on China's democratic status is a flawed approach as it conceals the concrete evolution of the regime. According to him, different political elites already successively rule the country:

How can China be so skilful? This is not a democracy and yet it looks exactly as if two parties ruled alternately!

The view that, despite the absence of multi-party politics and the implementation of competitive elections, all the different political tendencies can be found in China, and that power alternates between them, is quite widespread. A recent *Christian Monitor* article reads: 'Since the party established the People's Republic in 1949, under the leadership of a single political party, changes in China's government policies and political environment have covered the widest possible spectrum.'[65]

However, with resilient autocratic institutions, practices and reflex actions related to the existence of only one party, it is still impossible to talk of a Chinese democracy; but we could say that the country is slowly heading towards a 'democracy with Chinese characteristics' adapted to Chinese conditions

63. Li, C. 'Besieged by factions, China's leaders struggle with succession, reforms and worried foreign investors', *Yale Global*, 16 April 2012.

64. *See* Wang, S. 'Changing models of China's policy agenda setting' and Pan, W. 'Vous, Occidentaux, ne comprenez rien à la Chine', *Libération*, 8 July 2008. *See also* Heberer and Schubert, 'Political reform and regime legitimacy in contemporary China'. This argument can also be found in democratisation studies and the concept of 'grey zones'.

65. Li, E. L. 'China's political system is more flexible than US democracy', *Christian Science Monitor*, 17 October 2011: 'Since the party established the People's Republic in 1949, under the leadership of a single political party, changes in China's government policies and political environment have covered the widest possible spectrum.'

(*guoqing*).[66] The nationalist leaning of some scholars, notably New Leftists, has led them to question the universality of the democratic ideal. For instance, Chen Kuiyuan, then the head of the Academy of Social Sciences, declared in July 2008 that it was high time China recovered its self-esteem and self-confidence: 'We shouldn't blindly believe in western values and consider them as universal. We shouldn't consider that the values of the Party and of our nation are "inferior".'[67] The scholars under study do not go as far as Chen when criticising democracy but their approach is not so far away when they claim that a slow democratising process is currently under way in China and that, instead of underestimating it under the pretext that it does not correspond to the agenda of American-style democracy activists, it should be encouraged.

A self-evident democracy with Chinese characteristics

A unique regime for a unique culture

To get round the inadequacies of total and unadapted westernisation, a nativist trend has emerged. The least democratic among intellectuals, such as Pan Wei, explain that 'We couldn't plant giant dragon seeds from the West and then harvest it in China.' Many new publications and newly opened university China Studies departments signal the rise of sinology and the renaissance of Confucian tradition(s), which is of great variety – with elitist, populist, authoritarian and democratic branches. The point is, above all, to moderate the anti-traditionalist – sometimes even iconoclastic tendencies that prevailed in early nationalist movements for a strong China. This new focus on Chinese 'tradition' (*chuantong*) and 'culture' (*wenhua*), even as regards the need for political change, crosses the whole political spectrum.

Deng Zhenglai, a philosophy professor at Fudan University well known for his translations of Hayek and his systematic introduction of twentieth-century liberal thinkers to China, devoted the end of his career to writing a book on Chinese popular wisdom. These liberal thinkers did not provide sufficient tools for him to answer what he considered the core issue of political philosophy: how to found a just order. This led him to focus on the Chinese experience and its legacy in his later years.

> We cannot dispense with finding the Chinese political wisdom again, instead of copying the western model. Many people only talk of democracy, constitutionalism and rule of law. These western contributions are very

---

66. *See* Bell, D. A. *Beyond Liberal Democracy: Political thinking for an East Asian context*, Princeton, NJ: Princeton University Press, 2006, p. 9: 'If human rights, democracy and capitalism are to take root and produce beneficial outcomes in East Asia, they must be adjusted to contemporary East Asian political and economic realities and to the values of nonliberal East Asian political traditions such as Confucianism and Legalism.'

67. *See* Chen's speech published in *Academy of Social Sciences Journal*, 2 September 2008.

valuable but the Chinese cannot limit themselves to learning from the western experience. They must also rediscover their own country's wisdom instead of emulating the western model. The Chinese have looked at their country from a western perspective for 150 years. This is a very poor method.

This passage is evidence that efforts at 'decentring the world' have also appeared in China. The point is to get over viewing European political modernity as the end of the development process. Some scholars try to go beyond the 'not yet' rhetoric of 'the antechamber of history where non-western people who haven't completed their political maturity patiently wait'.[68] After two decades of gorging on and digesting theories and concepts produced in the West, in which Chinese scholars expected to find the answers to understanding and solving China's problems, they eventually undertook to 'get their hands dirty' by creating new concepts and paradigms. Li Qiang therefore reaches the following two-fold assessment, already quoted in the first chapter: American political science is over-specialised while Chinese political science is underdeveloped. Li currently searches for a model allowing more political participation by the Chinese people. He relies on the liberal and constitutional structure developed by Leo Strauss and focuses on constitutionalism in particular:

Individuals, society, the government and the state must all abide by some rules. […] These democratic elements cannot be found in the Chinese tradition. Some elements of our tradition are under attack in our contemporary society, such as family. In traditional China, the focus is not on individuals but on families. Family is the most basic unit. Each actor must abide by some rules, it is an absolute imperative. Each one holds the position of someone's father, son, or brother, and his individual duties derive from this.

[…] The idea that the individual is the most basic unit of society is not ingrained in China's society, which is a major obstacle to overcome. I am no extremist: I don't think Chinese society should completely give up its past traditions and become individualistic. Individuals must obviously be given rights. This is a theoretical issue. Men and women should be given rights – civic rights – without making society necessarily individualistic in a country with different traditions. This is my ideal.

What appears as the main obstacle to setting up a constitutional democracy, according to Li Qiang, therefore, is that individualism is alien to Chinese 'culture', which is based on harmony. Yang Guangbin also wonders about this issue.

---

68. Guilhamon, L. 'Le décentrement du monde', *La Vie des Idées*, 4 November 2010, available online at http://www.laviedesidees.fr/Le-decentrement-du-monde.html (last accessed 14 November 2014). Chakrabarty, D. *Provincializing Europe: Postcolonial thought and historical difference*, Princeton, NJ: Princeton University Press, 2000.

China's future will undoubtedly be democratic. We will adopt a democratic regime for sure, but it is impossible to know what kind exactly. [...] Democracy emerged in a culture based on individualism. This necessarily triggers a clash of cultures. I think that the democratic regime and competitive elections in particular do not only raise a cultural problem. What is more worrying is how, when competitive elections are organised in China, this political system based on an individualistic culture will be implanted in a country with a collective culture of harmony. It does not mean it is an impossible thing to do. We simply cannot foretell its outcome, which is worrying. Men are always scared when they have no idea of what could come next. They cannot make up their minds. The democratic regime emerged in the mid nineteenth century, in 1848. The United States followed. It imposed itself like an inevitable wave. The onset of the internet is a comparable phenomenon. No country can miss out on these tendencies. However, the precise type of democracy is not predetermined. What kind of democracy do we need?

The certainty that a democratic regime will be established in China does not prevent this academic from insisting upon the indeterminacy of the precise type of democracy and the concrete institutional arrangements which will finally be adopted so as to closely fit with the contours of its culture.

For other scholars, like Yao Yang, far from being obstacles, Chinese history and culture will, on the contrary, guide China's democratisation process: 'I have recently focused on the idea that China must draw on its own history and tradition to find its path toward democracy.' The economist explains that Fudan University's Bai Tongdong's book *Jiubang xinming*,[69] which aims at bringing some elements of Confucian culture to contemporary society, strongly impressed him.

For a long time, China was not more despotic than Europe. But the European society started modernising first. China is still in the middle of a transition which has ended in Europe. That is all. I don't think it is easy to determine how these two cultures differ concretely. As to liberal democracy, I don't think we can claim that the Chinese tradition is so different from the western tradition that China is incompatible with liberal democracy. Our Chinese tradition can lead to tyranny, but so can the ideas of great western thinkers. The western tradition also provides justification for autocratic regimes. Many books defend the virtues of these regimes, from Plato to Machiavelli. The watershed is when two hundred years ago democratic thought started to develop.

As Pierre-Etienne Will showed, 'sprouts of democracy' can be found in the history of China.[70] Taiwan's democratisation is also a powerful case against culturalist arguments justifying the incompatibility of democracy with Chinese conditions.

69. Bai, T. *Jiubang Xinming* (*A New Mission of an Old State: The contemporary and comparative relevance of classical Confucian political philosophy*), Beijing: Peking University Press, 2009.

70. Will, P. -E. 'Sprouts of democracy in Chinese history', *Books & Ideas*, 30 May 2011.

The successful establishment of a democratic regime in Taiwan also allows liberals and neo-conservatives like Xiao Gongqin to criticise the analyses of the New Left or Pan Wei that downplay the impact of introducing competitive elections.

Democratic disillusionment from a Chinese perspective

What prompts some scholars to promote a non-minimalist democracy in China is the urge to set up a different sort of politics, which the establishment of democracy in Taiwan or South Korea has not allowed. They are driven by their disappointment as regards existing democratic regimes. This is Gan Yang's case, who has been greatly influenced by the Straussian critique of the political apathy and mass culture which characterise current democratic regimes.[71]

> I cannot identify any good political regime throughout the world today. The best regime dates back to the Song dynasty and the literati. At that time, there was such a thing as a cultural ideal. Everything was done to entice people to raise difficult questions. [...] Politics today comes down to distributing pork meat – distribution and redistribution. And these issues are far from being solved. They are absolutely horrendous. Neither the United States nor France have solved them. Inequalities are extreme. [...] To be frank, all these alleged elections and democratic politics are hardly attractive at all, especially from an Asian perspective. Who can say that Taiwan, Thailand or the Philippines are democratic or not? These countries also organise elections, but it leads to nothing. [...] According to me, a good polity must be founded on a cultural ideal, a higher aim and a conception of the good. But we never tackle these issues. [...] I really doubt modern times have any aim. In other words, my political philosophy derives from Leo Strauss's.

Gan Yang has therefore become, like Strauss, a staunch advocate of a revival of classical political philosophy as a starting point for assessing political action. The best model for China's political regime is the Song dynasty. It is remarkable that he explains Strauss's popularity in China (Strauss is intensely studied in political philosophy courses) as due to the 'lassitude' many people feel towards

---

71. Strauss, L. *Liberalism Ancient and Modern*, Chicago, IL: University of Chicago Press, 2nd edn., 1989, p. 5: 'There exists a whole science – the science which I among thousands profess to teach, political science – which so to speak has no other theme than the contrast between the original conception of democracy, or what one may call the ideal of democracy, and democracy as it is. According to an extreme view which is the predominant view in the profession, the ideal of democracy was a sheer delusion and the only thing which matters is the behavior of democracies and the behavior of men in democracies. Modem democracy, so far from being universal aristocracy, would be mass rule were it not for the fact that the mass cannot rule but is ruled by elites, i.e., groupings of men who for whatever reason are on top or have a fair chance to arrive at the top; one of the most important virtues required for the smooth working of democracy, as far as the mass is concerned, is said to be electoral apathy, i.e., lack of public spirit; not indeed the salt of the earth but the salt of modern democracy are those citizens who read nothing except the sports page and the comic section. Democracy is then not indeed mass rule but mass culture.'

the discourse of democracy-promotion. In most of the interviews, the lack of enthusiasm towards existing democracies was manifest, and China's economic achievements add grist to the mill. It can be found in the way Yang Guangbin and Kang Xiaoguang assess the so-called Chinese governance and its economic achievement in comparison with India, Pakistan or Thailand. In a similar fashion, Liu Dong acknowledges that Chinese leaders' advantage is that they can bridle the horse and gallop it, without falling off, which allows China to become prosperous rapidly. Even though 'they are corrupted and out of control', the point is to control the economy while leaders of western countries and in Taiwan 'only focus on elections.' To Xiao Gongqin as well, no democratic model could better suit China than its current system, in order to maintain the direction of the *fuqiang* (the hope, at the turn of the twentieth century, for a wealthy and powerful China).[72] The undemocratic Singaporean regime is presented as the most attractive for him as well as for Pan Wei or Zhu Guanglei:

> I am more and more convinced that it is extremely hard for us to directly copy the western model of democratic regime. If we look at Pakistan, Thailand, South Korea or Taiwan today, they have not succeeded in doing it. This is the reason why the question must be thoroughly pondered. China will probably have to develop a democratic model of its own and that suits it better. In this democratic regime, the role of authority will still be great, and a little paternalistic – quite similar to Singapore. China can learn directly from regimes such as Singapore, more than any other.

What justifies the rejection of ready-made democratic models is therefore both the disappointment stemming from a more thorough understanding of existing regimes abroad and a strong feeling of actual crisis (or the conviction that China is facing such massive problems that the worst could occur), and the hope brought about by thirty years of successful economic reforms 'with Chinese characteristics'.

The future is wide open

> The examples of the United States, France, Japan or Taiwan cannot be of help here. In that sense, I think that China's future is wide open. For the time being we have no ready-made answers. Here is my state of mind (Kang Xiaoguang).

It is hard to determine whether the New Left's defense of a 'mind liberation' has won hearts or if it reflected a tendency prevailing in the Chinese intelligentsia. In any case, the idea that the precise form the Chinese regime to come will take is absolutely undefined and that everything is possible is undeniably the consensus.[73]

---

72. Kuhn, P. A. *Les origines de l'État chinois moderne*, Paris: Colin, A. 1999; Bergère, M. -C. *Sun Yat-sen*, 'Les problèmes de la transition: tutelle et dictature', Paris: Fayard, 1994.

73. Bell, D. chose to introduce *China's New Confucianism* with this idea: *see* Bell, D. A. *China's New Confucianism*, p. 3.

Even liberal intellectuals fully convinced of the assets of 'western democracy', such as Xu Youyu, stick to general principles (a market economy with a minimum of regulation; limits on the use of political power) which allow for quite a wide array of institutional possibilities.

Less pro-democratic scholars such as Kang Xiaoguang (as in the epigraph to this sub-section) and Pan Wei have promoted the idea of a 'Chinese way' since the early 2000s. As the convoluted and pragmatic Open and Reform policy bore fruit and brought China closer to its centennial *fuqiang* objective, attempts at outlining a Chinese model have multiplied in their wake. Striving to spearhead this trend, in 2008 Pan Wei initiated a large project aiming at defining the Chinese economic, social and political model. He indeed identified a pattern in Chinese contemporary history: every thirty years, China finds itself at a crossroads and must make a choice of direction. The years 1919, 1949 and 1979 were all landmarks: everything was possible, 'nothing was decided yet':

> Now 30 years later, China is again at a crossroads. The reform is now exhausted. Just like the command economy was exhausted in 1979. The Reform and Open policy? Now we see the casualties. No one blindly believes in the market any longer. Education, infrastructures, social security marketised. We no longer believe in that, with the widening gap between rich and poor, corruption. We have to realise that the reforms after 30 years encountered difficulties. As well as the mainstream belief in liberal democracy, believing that the United States today, or western Europe today is China tomorrow – whether liberal or social democracy. Now we are at a crossroads.

Pan Wei explicitly joins forces with the New Left to make this assessment. He refers to the redirection of reforms which Wang Shaoguang associates with the 'great transformation' Polanyi described.[74] He also echoes Gan Yang's following call for greater freedom to think China's political horizon:

> What is stimulating with China, is that there are many possibilities. Nothing is predefined. China is still undecided. Nobody knows where we are heading. This is one of China's advantages: everything is under discussion, nothing is decided. In a way, the current Chinese thinking is way more open than thinking in western countries. Here, we can discuss everything and we all have opportunities to express ourselves. This uncertainty, the fact that nothing is decided, is very stimulating. Once things are set, which is for instance Hong Kong's case, with its very normal society, it is much harder to imagine or invent something else.

Gan Yang resigned from his job at the excellent University of Hong Kong and went back to mainland China, where 'everything is under discussion', which is a rare opportunity. More liberal scholars like Deng Zhenglai draw similar

---

74. Polanyi, K. *The Great Transformation: The political and economic origins of our time*, Boston, MA: Beacon Press, 1944.

conclusions, which are, however, more explicit and rigorous. If China's future is open, the minimum framework is clear: the single Party is to be upheld, corruption is to be fought against and growth and stability maintained:

> We cannot guess the direction China will take. China ceaselessly changes and adapts without having a predefined and steady direction. It experiments, makes mistakes and tries something else. Chinese people are quite satisfied. The government needs their support. It cannot follow a theoretical direction to the end. The only certainties are the upholding of the Party, the fight against corruption and the guarantee of a stable economic development, security and order. This is already quite a lot for Chinese people. We wish the advances of political philosophy in China can bear long-term fruit if leaders read our publications.

In China too, opinion polls matter a great deal. Scholars such as Deng Zhenglai in this quotation regularly refer to studies measuring the legitimacy of the incumbent authorities. These polls reinforce the feeling that the Chinese development path has proved effective and justifies the rejection of a democratic transition based on the theoretical models put forward by democratic-promotion. Kang Xiaoguang's claims are particularly explicit in that matter:

> I could observe the continuous development of the country over the last 20–30 years: the Chinese economy has thrived, living conditions improved and infrastructures densified. Many problems have concomitantly mushroomed and the Chinese have confronted them one after the other. For instance, when Deng Xiaoping and Jiang Zemin were in power, inequalities became more obvious. The living conditions of the poorest strata remained dreadful. But during Hu Jintao and Wen Jiabao's two mandates, significant progress was achieved. This led me to scrutinise the connection between the achievements of the Chinese development and the country's political institutions. Weren't we told that without a democracy, no country's economy could thrive? That without it, corruption could only spread further, inequalities worsen, the country split and the government's popularity plummet? All this did not prove right. If we compare the current situation with that of the 1990s, the Chinese government's popularity has constantly improved and Chinese politics has stabilised.

China's dramatic comeback on to the world stage, the dizzying changes in the lives of Chinese urbanites – the prodigious improvement of living conditions for intellectual professions, in particular – added to the picture of a regime largely supported by its population, all tend to give economic, political and intellectual elites the feeling that the Chinese way of development is a success. Most academics involved in the debate on political reform reject the idea of a democratic transition modelled on the theories put forward by democracy promotion.

The contours of a 'democracy with Chinese characteristics'

While these scholars claim the future is wide open, the outline of such a 'democracy with Chinese characteristics' is taking shape. They are indeed convinced that they have enough insight to accurately discern the problems which have emerged and are to be solved. One of the main identified issue is the implementation of public policy. As mentioned above, the implementation of the large-scale social policy the Hu–Wen government launched was limited by the prior objective of economic development and by resistance from powerful interest groups. A historian such as, who is miles away from the defence of state capacity that is dear to the New Left, also singles out the impossible implementation of public policies as a major problem urgently to be solved:

> The aim of a general policy (that of the Hu–Wen government is to focus on the least privileged so as to strike a balance) is one thing, but enforcing it is another issue. Achieving that goal depends on existing policies and on the interests of every one. I would like to add that the Chinese elites have now monopolised too many resources and they do not wish to transmit them to the rest of the population. As a result, policies are considerably sold off when they are implemented.

Grand official statements of the will to reduce inequality come down to nothing nowadays when ideology carries so little weight compared to the resistance and power of the interests at stake. This is the great challenge the Party must face. These interests are expressed more or less directly, according to their political efficacy; but Kang Xiaoguang believes they do not bring into question the legitimacy of the Party directly:

> The conflicts we currently witness are not political but social conflicts – conflicts of interests. For instance, when the land is unfairly seized; when one's pension is too limited; when I am too poor to get quality healthcare and so on. Political stability is not at stake in these cases. No one says the government should be toppled or a democratic regime should be established. On the contrary, protesters recognise the legitimacy of the government and demand that it solves their problems. This is social, not political, instability.

'Rightful resistance' studies confirm Kang's point: protesters and rioters do not conceive the state as a monolith and they instinctively turn to the central government to solve or arbitrate disputes.[75] The legitimacy of the Party can be challenged if it proves unable to fulfil that role of arbiter. This is a colossal challenge as Chinese society is waking up and its voice can no longer be silenced.

---

75. O'Brien, K. J. and Li, L. *Rightful Resistance in Rural China*, New York and Cambridge: Cambridge University Press, 2006; Thireau, I. and Wang, H. (eds) *Disputes au village chinois. Formes du juste et recompositions locales des espaces normatifs*, Paris: Editions de la Maison des sciences de l'homme, Paris, 2001.

Yao Yang attributes China's economic achievement and political stability to 'its disinterested government' (*zhongxing zhengfu*) – as it plays the role of a detached arbiter of the conflicts of interests opposing various social and political groups – and to the legitimacy it gained through constantly improving the Chinese's living conditions. Yao Yang based his disinterested government model on Mancur Olson's theory of 'encompassing organizations', whose interests converge with the nation's.[76] A disinterested government refuses to favour the interests of any particular section of society, which would be detrimental to long-term growth. As a result, the disinterested government, contrary to a partial government, tends to adopt policies favouring national economic growth even if these go against its own interests.

> [The concept of disinterested government] allows to explain why the Chinese government has focused so much on economic growth for the last thirty years. As a disinterested government, it is confronted with various interest groups and adopts a neutral position. It does not mean that it is indifferent to the outcome of these conflicts. When two groups conflict, the government does not take sides. It all depends on the circumstances. The government favours one group and grants it more resources only when it is convinced that it will benefit overall growth. In that sense, it can be said to be disinterested. This idea of a disinterested government also allows to explain why the gap between the rich and the poor is getting worse. The government represents no one else than itself. It is aware of the situation but does not necessarily react. If it still were a Communist government, as it initially used to be, it would have acted against these income inequalities long ago. It used to be its role to protect the interests of the popular strata. It has given up its communist government role and become a government without any ideology. Only economic growth matters. This is its new ideology.

To corroborate this theory, Yao Yang provides three examples. First, the consensus on growth: the objective of economic growth has allowed the government to federate potentially opposed forces. Second, the convergence of the double-track price system – transitional coexistence of market price system and centrally determined administrative prices – with the market has proven the Party's will to end the privilege of its own members. It has indeed put a stop to this system, which was incredibly profitable to the elites, and has adopted a policy benefitting society as a whole. Last of all, the privatisation of public companies showed that the Party could resist populist protest and adopt a more efficient structure, to the detriment of its support base: workers.

Disinterested governments can be found in democratic and non-democratic countries alike, which explains why the democratic criterion is insufficient to properly analyse the 30-year achievement and legitimacy of Chinese policy. However, Yao Yang thinks that China's progressive adoption of neo-classical

---

76. Olson, M. *The Rise and Decline of Nations*, New Haven and London: Yale University Press, 1982.

principles of economics has considerably reinforced inequalities. But the Chinese central government can no longer respond to popular demands with social measures (countryside reforms, healthcare reforms and so on) whose scale and scope are limited by the intense lobbying of local governments and private companies – which the Beijing economist believes only democratic procedures can rein in. In other words, if the Chinese regime eventually launches a veritable democratisation, it will be in response to internal pressures rather than to pressures from the international community.

Consequently, apart among official spheres and the most conservative intellectuals, the idea that China will necessarily become a democracy prevails. When Yao Yang claims that 'even if history leads to liberal democracy, it can take on different forms [...] China will most certainly follow its own path towards liberal democracy', he manifestly speaks for the great majority of Chinese intellectuals. Let us not misrepresent that as a call for multi-partyism,[77] which remains one of the main taboos in reflection on China's democratisation. The Party still violently represses any attempt to create an opposition party; all the diverse social interests in China are supposed to be represented within the Party. There is a consensus, therefore, that the best means to achieve the democratic ideal of equal information and participation for all is to multiply the channels leading to it. In that sense, the Party's resilience and its rejection of a multi-party system are both a major obstacle to and a remarkable incentive for institutional innovation; officials at all administrative levels are compelled to resort to such innovations, in the absence of direct elections, to boost their legitimacy and prove that the Party can respond to the expectations of a more complex and diversified society.

Conclusions

Several views clash. Cultural nationalists, influential but isolated, unequivocally reject the possibility of China's democratisation and lobby for establishing a meritocratic regime. Neo-conservatives do not oppose liberal democracy but advocate delaying democratisation as long as the Chinese economy and society have not reached a sufficient level of development. One part of the Chinese intelligentsia, including dissidents, considers that the New Left and intellectuals who reject the liberal critique of the regime just lack the courage to confront the Party-emperor directly, which conditions and therefore invalidates their proposals. Qin Hui, who offers to synthesise the two approaches,[78] thinks that the debates between the New Left and liberals have deferred political reform, that their demands are not contradictory and that the two camps should unite instead of tripping each other up. To him, it is high

---

77. He, B. 'Intra-party democracy: a revisionist perspective from below', pp. 205–6.
78. Xu Jilin also claims to reconcile the New Left and liberals, since their respective conceptions of democracy are equally necessary. *See* Cheek, T. 'Xu Jilin and the thought work of China's public intellectuals', *China Quarterly* 186, June 2006, pp. 401–20, p. 416.

time that power was simultaneously limited and made to fulfil its (distributive) functions. However, Qin Hui is himself subject to criticisms for his unfailing adherence to economic liberalism. Last of all, members of the New Left, who defend a maximalist version of democracy and downplay the importance of competitive elections in China's political reform, congratulate themselves on the gradual introduction of large-scale social reforms and institutional innovations.

Chapter Seven

Conclusion

This investigation stemmed from the desire to understand how democracy is conceived in China from the perspective not only of ideology but also of sociology. It therefore introduced the complex situation of Chinese intellectual elites and described their turning from an activist elite into an academic elite, adopting different positions as regards political power. Some scholars strive to keep as much distance as possible from power so as to ensure their independence. This, however, is not the most widespread scenario in the research field; all the more so as it is no longer forbidden for Chinese scholars to focus on political issues. The government and various other organisations actually ask academics to do so (and they are decently paid for it when they are well known). Is it possible to speak of freedom of opinion and thought in the Chinese academia? It is, but academic freedom is still relative and freedom of publication limited, as academic research and commitment are still bridled by the Party and resilient censorship. Academics endeavour to make an impact on political decisions but this does not mean they are simply bound hand and foot to power, with which, one way or another they are always associated. In China, a veritable market of ideas exists: the technocratic and pragmatic nature of the Chinese regime and the great diversity of viewpoints within political elites make it possible to voice criticisms and suggestions, and to experiment with reform proposals – including for institutional reform – at different levels. Besides, the variety of interests and political opinions within political elites guarantees powerful sponsors for any kind of proposal coming from academics, if it is legitimised by their cultural capital and expertise.

Even though when Chinese academics are involved in the public sphere, like academics worldwide they have to take into account the standards of rigour, disinterestness and open-mindedness that characterise their profession, the patriotism of the scholars under scrutiny stands out. They indeed address a public which is not spoken to in France or in the United States: the country at large. And they are still searching for state recognition. Academics who do not fear losing their independence or are convinced that their proximity to power brings them a legitimacy and political influence which counterbalance any disruption to their lives as researchers often accept official functions. Within Chinese think tanks, official researchers, specific intellectuals playing the part of experts advising power, as well as political intellectuals like Hu Angang, Kang Xiaoguang and Wang Shaoguang, who are intellectual originators of policy proposals resembling what Gérard Noiriel describes as 'government intellectuals' (*intellectuels de gouvernement*). They are willing to actively but occasionally collaborate with authorities but have retained some leeway since their political proposals derive from criticising the *status quo* and some policies. As to liberals, their criticism of the regime is less compatible with official discourse and they are restricted to the last two strategies in Chapter Three's typology of intellectuals: the media intellectual and the politically committed professor, whose political influence is indirect. The growing importance of public opinion in the decision-making process nonetheless contributes to erasing the distinctions between these various strategies, which some scholars do not hesitate to take in turn or combine.

This study has investigated the fragmentation and pluralisation (*duoyuanhua*) of the Chinese intellectual field. The convenient but simplistic labels of 'liberalism', 'New Left', and 'cultural nationalism' do not suffice to account for its diversity. From the most anarchist libertarianism of Liu Junning to the authoritarian and elitist Confucianism of Jiang Qing, to the variants of social democracy – whether liberal as championed by Qin Hui, or statist as defended by Wang Shaoguang – the most diverse trends of thought can be found in Chinese academia. Ren Jiantao attributes this transformation of the intellectual field to the Open and Reform policy, which 'split it into many contending kingdoms with their respective sphere of influence' (*zhuhou fenqi gequ yi di*). This fragmenting of political trends is partly due to academics' increased professionalism and deeper mastery of both western theories and Chinese traditional thinking, which was quite limited until the 1990s. Chen Yan's thesis is worth mentioning here:

> [...] to circumvent censorship, all sorts of actions are possible: criticizing the current policy, claiming for individual rights, analysing social phenomena and describing things as they truly are. They must nonetheless all borrow the words of westerners or hide behind quotes from thinkers of the past.[1]

This could explain the recurrent but often partial and superficial references to classic or foreign authors, theories and concepts, even though, as already explained, censorship is much less debilitating than it used to be. Liu Dong's theory of theoretical patchwork or *bricolage* is more convincing, and it describes a tendency prevailing among all the scholars under study. Their rejection of dogmatism and universal theories has led to a propensity to glean ideas, concepts and fragments of theories which form the pieces of a puzzle – the puzzle of China's development and greatness, a project which each Chinese individual, even if expatriate, is proud of and which contributes to his or her self-realisation. The remoteness of these fragments, whether because of their geographical or historical origins, seems to render the discourse of the intellectuals who deploy them more innocuous. This is not the only reason for their usefulness, however. They are also instrumental as authoritative arguments, attesting to the cultural capital of the intellectual and the legitimacy of his or her involvement in public and political debate. Last of all, the legitimacy of expressing oneself on major issues and national problems is all the greater as the intellectual displays independence and a fine sense of Chinese

---

1.   Chen, Y. *L'éveil de la Chine: les bouleversements intellectuels après Mao, 1976–2002*, Paris: Editions de l'Aube, 2002.

realities. He or she must be able to take things into consideration with realism and pragmatism, to patiently select the necessary ingredients to solve problems and set up the right regime for China. The principal driving force of intellectual production, expression and commitment is patriotism, a desire to defend the national interest and awareness of and concern about the problems that remain unsolved.[2] In the name of the general interest, despite the harsh criticisms the opposing intellectual factions make of each other, the overall debate is perceived as constructive and each camp is seen to be contributing in its own way. Liu Dong recognises all the protagonists have a role to play but he believes the process can be perverted by private interests and recognition-seeking:

> I think that the New Left theory is very useful to criticise western hegemony and the fact that westerners promote spectacular ideas while having a hidden agenda. The New Left is indispensible from an intellectual perspective and the liberals from a domestic perspective, to fight against all sorts of hegemony and criticise unfair situations. Most wealthy capitalists are the offspring of cadres. But China is unique in as much as liberalism here is externally oriented. The *New York Times* and the *Washington Post* are most interested in Chinese liberalism while the New Left is domestically oriented. This is our main problem. But this criticism has been used for political reasons and criticising has become dangerous, and exhausting. As a result, intellectuals are less critical and they take less pains. What is an intellectual? To be a Zola. We have many problems to solve but China must first grow. It must first seize the unique opportunity currently offered to impose itself more on the international stage.

Liu Dong therefore describes the lassitude of intellectuals, which he attributes to the exceptional circumstances of China's achieving world-power status without a democratic transition, contrary to 150 years of belief within China that only the pursuit of science and democracy would lead China to wealth and power and the conventional wisdom that tells poor countries that democracy is the route to prosperity. This relegates democratisation to a position of secondary importance. Many studies show that pressure from the thriving middle classes will not necessarily lead to more democratic claims because elites and those benefitting from the reforms do not fundamentally put the Party or the regime into question for the time being.[3] On the contrary, the Party's policy has considerably improved their condition and they still hold that only the Party can maintain the order and growth which are their main priority. It is tricky to generalise about Chinese elites but, as they are the main beneficiaries of the reforms, they tend to defend the *status*

---

2. The titles of two different books explicitly refer to this concern: Davies, G. *Worrying About China: The language of Chinese critical inquiry*, Boston, MA: Harvard University Press, 2007; Davies, G. *Voicing Concerns: Contemporary Chinese critical inquiry*, Lanham, MD: Rowman & Littlefield, 2001.

3. *See* Jean-Louis Rocca's publications on the middle classes as well as Li, C. *China's Emerging Middle Class: Beyond economic transformation*, Washington, DC: Brookings Institution Press, 2010.

quo and prefer the Party to stay in power to further their interests and guarantee economic growth and social stability. Besides, the economic and political elites are tightly connected and cannot be easily distinguished.[4] As already mentioned, intellectual elites also tend to share common interests with them.

The group of intellectuals under scrutiny, because of its political commitment, contrasts with the majority of Chinese society, which is depoliticised due to its relatively comfortable life, its fear of losing its newly gotten gains and its wariness of populism. This study has confirmed the prevalence of elitism even among progressive intellectuals, who hardly stand out from political and economic elites for that matter. The idea that the majority of the Chinese do not know their own interests and are not ready to elect their leaders is ubiquitous.[5] Similarly, the promotion of meritocracy and the quest for good leaders who are well advised come prior to establishing a regime that is stable and efficient independently of the moral and political qualities of its leaders,[6] who are seen as responsible for the general public interest. The resilient idea that such a thing as a single public interest exists is evidence that old objections against political pluralism are still alive and kicking. The selfish competition between different political parties is presented as unacceptable as it can only undermine the public interest.[7] Let us note, however, that the multi-party system has, nevertheless, not always been scorned in the history of China. In the 1930s, party and minority group elites were indeed in favour of multi-partyism, especially pro-democracy activists.[8] What separates today's intellectuals and their early-twentieth-century elders is the greater trust on the part of the former in the Party today. It indeed gives the impression of tackling Chinese society and its problems more efficiently, thanks to greater technological mastery of power. Despite its mistakes and weaknesses, the Party gives the impression of being – at least partly – capable of overseeing China's transition.

Since conflicts and tensions are conceived as having to be harmonised rather than institutionalised, and since a good regime is defined from a technocratic perspective, politics can be said to be circumvented.[9] However, this depends on the way politics is defined. Many issues are debated in China, even though the debate often does not exactly meet our expectations. Besides, divergences and conflicts do exist and proliferate. Each stage of the regime's development triggers intense struggle and various consultations and negotiations, as was the case in 2007 with

---

4.   Domenach, J. -L. speaks of a pluto-bureaucratic class: *see* Domenach, J. -L. *La Chine m'inquiète*, Paris: Librairie Académique Perrin, 2008.

5.   Cui Zhiyuan: 'In times of high uncertainty and very rapid development, the people do not know what their interests are. And that's another reason why I increasingly dislike Marxism. Marxism assumes people know their own interests, their class interests.'

6.   Will, P. -E. 'China: back to the imperial sense of the state', *Books & Ideas*, 17 February 2012, available online at http://www.booksandideas.net/China-Back-to-the-Imperial-Sense.html (last accessed 14 November 2014).

7.   Kuhn, P. A. *Les origines de l'État chinois moderne*, Paris: Armand Colin, 1999.

8.   Fung, E. S. K. *In Search of Chinese Democracy: Civil opposition in Nationalist China, 1929–1949*, Cambridge: Cambridge University Press, 2000, pp. 10–11.

9.   Chevrier, Y. 'Les réformes en Chine ou la stratégie du contournement', *Politique étrangère* 50(1), 1985, pp. 119–38.

the law on private property and more recently with the criminal law. State and society, in China like in the rest of the world, are permeable and interdependent and interact constantly[10] – as our inquiry on the connections between scholars and power has indicated. The authorities' co-optation of elites and responsiveness to both intellectual and popular demands are put forward to legitimise the Party's monopoly of power and the regime's delayed democratisation. As the focus of Chinese political science on large issues such as the nature of a good regime and state-building suggests, Chinese priorities are different from other countries'. From a Chinese perspective, it seems less urgent to debate the necessity of electing leaders than to define what can be expected from the government; the main values it should defend (order and wealth *versus* equality and justice); and its role (limited/ extended). The debate focuses on the way the government functions (opaque *versus* transparent; participative *versus* closed; centralised or not; technocratic and scientific *versus* arbitrary); the best means to solve the main problems China faces (inequalities, corruption, inflation and so on) and therefore to make it more legitimate. The discourse of the New Left – praising advancing social reform and experimentation, diversifying consultation and deliberation procedures – should be understood from that perspective. This study has, nonetheless, shown that, despite diverging points of view, standards of propriety govern the intellectual field. What brings intellectual elites closer – no matter how fragmented they are – is their pragmatism, elitism, patriotism, hedging and moderation.

This investigation has underscored that the scholarly debate combines 'pre-democratic' earnestness and reticence towards regime democratisation – such as the argument on voters' capacity, which justifies a limited franchise on account of the low 'quality' (*suzhi*) or educational level of voters – that are specific to debates preceding the introduction of democratic institutions and procedures and up-to-the-minute 'post-democratic' deliberation, doubts and criticisms, which correspond to more recent calls for a more complex form of democracy.[11] It has also described how a nationalist and gradualist conservative thinking emerged, advocating a Chinese modernisation which does not go against its 'tradition' but, on the contrary, draws its resources from tradition as much as from western theories. This reflection goes beyond ideological splits and the back-to-tradition paradigm spans the whole Chinese intelligentsia, beginning in the 1990s, so much so that it has become common to consider the traditional legacy as a whole as an asset for China's future. We have observed the tensions between the Chinese exceptionalism thesis – which opens the range of possibilities and offers greater freedom to innovate politically – and the irreducible constraints that one-party rule and the rejection of multi-partyism constitute. It is quite remarkable that a great many of the intellectuals under scrutiny accept the rules of the game and attempt

---

10. *See* Yves Chevrier's introduction in Chevrier, Y. Roux, A. Xiao-Planes, X. *et al.* (eds), *Citadins et citoyens dans la Chine du XXe siècle: Essais d'histoire sociale*, Paris: Maison des Sciences de l'Homme, 2010, p. 28 and Rocca, J. -L. *La Condition chinoise: Capitalisme, mise au travail et résistances dans la Chine des réformes*, Paris: Karthala, 2006, pp. 214–15 and p. 286.

11. Rosanvallon, P. *La contre-démocratie, la politique à l'âge de la défiance*, Paris: Le Seuil, 2006.

to define this 'democracy with Chinese characteristics' as inseparably connected to the 'good regime' China could adopt.

Intellectuals who distance themselves from so-called western democracy do not justify their stance by an absolute rejection of its values and principles. They rather criticise its emphasis on electoral procedure, without explicitly questioning its assets (participation, accountability, responsibility, responsiveness, legitimacy and so on). They underscore its drawbacks and try to demonstrate that other procedures and institutions can lead to similar results with less inconvenience (limited representation and participation, neglect of the long-term perspective and so on). Besides, they endeavour to show that representative government combines democratic and non-democratic elements, so as to invalidate simplifying theories that reduce democracy to elections and, probably, to open up the scope of possibilities. They do not resign themselves to reducing the democratic idea to the vote and political freedom to the choice of rulers. Their strategy consists in identifying western democratic regimes realistically as imperfect mixed democracies so as to justify establishing a democracy with Chinese characteristics which would conflate democratic and non-democratic elements too – that is, keeping the single-party rule but introducing diverse democratic elements. This results in the accumulation of complex institutional arrangements such as the ones designed by Jiang Qing, He Zengke, Cui Zhiyuan or Pan Wei.

Rejecting the unconditional adoption of democratic institutions is therefore presented as the outcome of a comprehensive reflection on the constraints and issues specific to the Chinese case and of the will to follow a suitable and reasonable path to solve them. In that sense, it can be said that a conditional thinking about democracy, whose definition is therefore distorted, prevails in China nowadays. In that perspective, even though a new generation of leaders is now in power who are likely to be even more attentive to the scholars under study and their reform propositions, a rapid and clear-cut democratic change is quite unlikely. The current leaders could rather bring about a strengthening of the elitist rationalist consensus justifying the complex and moderate launch of another type of political modernisation 'with Chinese characteristics'.

Appendix A – Primary Sources

Transcribed and translated interviews

Cui Zhiyuan 1: February 2009
Cui Zhiyuan 2: May 2010
Deng Zhenglai: April 2010
Gan Yang: May 2010
He Zengke: November 2008
Kang Xiaoguang: May 2010
Li Qiang 3: May 2010
Liu Dong 2: May 2010
Pan Wei: November 2008
Ren Jiantao: April 2010
Wang Shaoguang 1: August 2008
Xiao Gongqin: November 2008
Xu Jilin: November 2008
Xu Youyu 1: November 2008
Yang Guangbin: April 2010
Yao Yang: May 2010
Zhu Guanglei: April 2010

Other interviews

Daniel A. Bell 1, 2 and 3: 2004–10
Han Shuifa 1, 2 and 3: 2004–5
Li Qiang 1: 2008
Liu Dong 1 and 2: 2004–5
Liu Junning: December 2008
Pan Wei 2 and 3: May 2012 and January 2013
Wan Junren: 2005
Wang Shaoguang 2 and 3: February 2009 and January 2013 February 2009
Xu Youyu 2: May 2010
Zheng Yongnian: February 2009

Appendix B – Secondary Sources

Books and articles written by scholars under study

Cui, Zhiyuan, 'Anshan xianfa he hou Futezhuyi' ('Angang constitution and post-Fordism'), *Dushu* 1, 1996.

— 'Eryuan lianbang zhuyi de xiaowang' ('Disappearance of dual feudalism'), *Dushu* 9, 1996.

— '"Hunhe fanfa" yu dui zhongguo zhengzhi de sanceng fenxi' ('An analysis of the "mixed constitution" and the three political levels'), *Zhanlue Yu Guanli* 3, 1998.

— 'Liberal socialism and the future of China: a petty bourgeois manifesto', in Cao, T. (ed.), *China's Model for Modern Development*, London, Routledge, 2005.

— 'Partial intimations of the coming whole', *Modern China* 37(6), November 2011, pp. 646–60.

Deng, Zhenglai, 'The state of the field: political science and Chinese political studies', *Journal of Chinese Political Science* 14, 2009, pp. 331–4.

— *Guojia Yu Shehui: Zhongguo shiminshehui yanjiu de yanjiu* (*State and Society: A study of Chinese civil society studies*), Chengdu: Sichuan Renmin Chubanshe, 1997.

— *Yanjiu Yu Fansi: Zhongguo shehui kexue zizhuxing de sikao* (*Research and Reflection: The autonomy of the Chinese social sciences*), Shenyang: Liaoning Daxue Chubanshe, 1998.

— *Ziyou Yu Zhixu: Hayeke shehui lilun de yanjiu* (*Liberty and order: Hayekian social theories*), Nanchang: Jiangxi Jiaoyu Chubanshe, 1998.

— *Hayeke Falu Zhixue De Yanjiu* (*Hayek's Legal Philosophy*), Beijing: Falu Chubanshe, 2002.

— *Zhongguo Faxue Ciang Hechu Qu* (*Where Are Law Studies Going in China?*), Beijing: Shangwu Yinshuguan, 2006.

Gan, Yang, 'Chuantong, shijianxing yu weilai' ('Tradition, temporality and future'), *Dushu* 2, 1986.

— 'Fanminzhu de ziyou zhuyi haishi minzhu de ziyou zhuyi?' ('Anti-democratic liberalism or democratic liberalism?'), *Ershiyi Shiji* 39, 1997.

— 'Huaren daxue linian yu beida gaige' ('The founding of Chinese universities and the Beida reform'), *Business China*, 3 May 2003.

— 'Zhongguo ziyou zuopai de youlai' ('The origin of Chinese left-wing liberalism'), in Zuwei, C. and Wentao, L. (eds), *Zhengzhi Lilun Zai Zhongguo* (*Political Theory in China*), Hong Kong: Oxford University Press, 2001.

—   'Zhongguo ziyou zuopai de youlai' ('Origins of the Chinese New Left'), paper given at University of Hong Kong conference, 28–9 September 2000, available online at http://www.douban.com/group/topic/1601360.

—   'Zhongguo daolu, sanshi nian yu liushi nian'('The Chinese way, 30 years and 60 years), *Dushu* 6, 2007.

Gan, Yang and Zhang, X., 'A critique of Chinese conservatism in the 1990s', *Social Text* 55, 1 July 1998, pp. 45–66, available online at http://www.jstor.org/stable/466685.

He, Zengke, *Fanfu Xinlu: Zhuanxingqi Zhongguo Fubai Wenti Yanjiu* (*New Ways of Fighting Corruption: Corruption in Chinese tradition*), Beijing: Zhongyang Bianyi Chubanshe, 2002.

—   *Jiceng Minzhu He Difang Zhili Chuangxin* (*Grassroots Democracy and Innovations in Local Governance*), Beijing: Zhongyang Bianyi Chubanshe, 2004.

—   *Gong Min She Hui Yu Min Zhu Zhi Li* (*Civil Society and Democratic Governance*), Beijing: Zhongyang Bianyi Chubanshe, 2007.

—   'Zhengzhi hefaxing yu zhongguo difang chuangxin — yixiang chubu de jingyan xing yanjiu' (Political legitimacy and Chinese local innovations), *Zhongguo Zhengfu Chuangxinwang*, 4 April 2007.

—   'Democratisation: the Chinese model and course of political development', in Yu, K. (ed.), *Democracy and Rule of Law in China*, Leiden: Brill Academic Publishers, 2010, pp. 49–76.

Hu, Angang, *Zhongguo Fazhan Qianjing* (*The Future of Chinese Development*), Zhejiang Renmin Chubanshe, 1999.

—   'Yigeguojia sigeshijie fendiqu fazhanchaju' ('One country, four worlds'), *Zhongguo Jingjishibao* (*China Economic Times*), 4 April 2001.

—   *Diqu yu fazhan: xibu kaifa xinzhanlüe* (Locality and development: new strategy for developing the West), Beijing: Zhongguo Jihua Chubanshe, 2001.

—   *Toushi SARS: jiankang yu fazhan* (*Perspective on SARS: Health and development*), Beijing: Qinghua Daxue Chubanshe, 2003.

—   'Equality and efficiency', in Chaohua, W. (ed.), *One China, Many Paths*, London: Verso, 2003, pp. 219–24.

—   'Shishi lüse fazhan zhanlüe shi zhongguo de bixuan zhi lu'('Green development, the inevitable choice for China'), *Lü ye* (*Green Leaf*) 6(15), 2003, available online at http://www.chinadialogue.net/article/show/single/en/134-Green-development-the-inevitable-choice-for-China-part-one.

—   'Zhongguo renlei buanquan de zuida tiaozhan–jiankang buanquan'('Insecurity in health: China's safety's greatest challenge'), *Guoqing Baogao* 653(10), December 2004.

—   'Zhongguo: lüse fazhan yu lüse GDP (1970–2001)'('China: green development and green GDP (1970–2001)'), *Zhongguo Kexue Jijin* 2, 2005.

—   *China in 2020: A new type of superpower*, Washington, DC: Brookings Institution Press, 2011.

Hu, A., Wang, S. and Zhou, J. (eds), *Dierci Zhuanxing: Guojia zhidu jianshe* (*The Second Transformation: Construction of the state*), Beijing: Tsinghua University Press, 2009.

Jiang, Qing, *Shengming xinyang yu wangdao zhengzhi: rujia wenhua de xiandai jiazhi*, (*Lived Faith and the Royal Way in Politics: The modern values of Confucian culture*), Taipei: Yang Zhengtang, 2004.

— *Zhengzhi Ruxue: Dangdai ruxue de zhuanxiang, tezhi yu fazhan* (*Political Confucianism: Redirection, characteristics and development of contemporary Confucianism*), Beijing: Sanlian Shudian, 2003.

Kang, Xiaoguang, 'Falungong wenti de zhengzhi xiaoying'('The political impact of the Falun Gong problem'), *Zhongguo Shehui Daokan* 33, 2000.

— 'Wenhua minzu zhuyi suixiang'('Essay on cultural nationalism'), *Zhanlüe Yu Guanli* 2, 2003.

— 'Renzheng: quanwei zhuyi guojia de hefaxing lilun'('Renzheng: a theory of the legitimacy of the authoritarian state'), *Zhanlüe Yu Guanli* 2, 2004.

— Shi nian bu bian: shichang jingji, jinying lianmeng, quanwei zhengzhi'('Market economy, elite alliance and authoritarianism'), interview published by Haiying, L. in *Xueshu Zhongguo*, April 2004.

— 'Zhongguo teshulun' ('Chinese exceptionalism'), *Zhanlüe Yu Guangli* 4, 2004.

— 'Wo shi ruhe zouxiang rujia' ('How I became a Confucian'), interview conducted by Dasan, W., *Zhexue Zhuanye Wangzhan*, 2004, http://phi.ruc.edu.cn/pol/html/03/t-14903.html.

— 'Wo weishenme zhuzhang ruhua? guanyu zhongguo weilai zhengzhi fazhan de baoshouzhuyi sikao' ('Why I advocate Confucianism: conservative reflections on China's future political development'), preface of *Renzheng: Zhongguo fazhan de disan tiao daolu*, Singapore: Shijie Keji Shubanshe (World Scientific), 2005; published in English as 'Confucianization: a future in the tradition', *Social Research* 73(1), 2006, pp. 77–120.

— *Renzheng: Zhongguo zhengzhi fazhan* (*Renzheng: The third way for China's political development*), Singapore: World Scientific, 2005.

— 'Hezuozhuyiguojia: ziyouzhuyi, shehuizhuyi zhiwaide disandaolu' ('Co-operationnism: liberalism, socialism and the third way'), *aisixiang.com*, 2006, http://www.aisixiang.com/data/11511.html.

— 'Jianshe minzhu fazhi: chongjian hefaxing jichu de changqi xingdong'('Building a democratic rule of law: the slow process of reconstruction on legitimate foundations'), *aisixiang.com*, October 2006.

— 'Confucianization: a future in the tradition', *Social Research* 73(1), 2006, pp. 77–120.

Li, Qiang, *Ziyou Zhuyi* (*Liberalism*), Beijing: China Social Sciences Press, 1998.

— *Xianzheng Ziyou Zhuyi Yu Guojia Goujian* (*Constitutional Liberalism and State-Building*), Beijing: Sanlian Shudian, 2003.

—   'Chaoyue dazhong mingzhu yu quanwei zhuyi: gonghe zhuyi dui zhongguo zhengzhi zhuanxing de qidi' ('Beyond people's democracy and authoritarianism: lessons from European Republicanism for China's political reform'), *Daguo (Power)* 2, 2005.

Liu, Dong, 'Jingti renweide "yangjingbang xuefeng"', *Ershiyi Sjiji* 32, 1995; revised English version translated by Davies, G. and Kaiyu, L. as: 'Revisiting the perils of "designer pidgin scholarship"', in Davies, G., *Voicing Concerns: Contemporary Chinese critical inquiry*, Lanham, MD: Rowman & Littlefield, 2001.

—   'Daguo zhi "da"– yi wangdao haizhi badao?' ('The Meaning of "great" in a great power: Benevolent rule or rule by force?'), (first published in *Zhongguo Qingnian Bao* (China Youth Daily)) in Liu, D., *Daoshu Yu Tianxia*, Beijing: Peking University Press, 2011.

Liu, Junning, (ed.), *Ziyouzhuyi De Xiansheng: Beida chuantong yu jindai Zhongguo (The origins of liberalism: Beida's tradition and modern China)*, Beijing: Zhongguo Renshi Chubanshe, 1998.

—   *Baoshou Zhuyi (Conservatism)*, Beijing: Zhongguo Shehui Kexue Chuban, 1998.

—   *Minzhu, Gonghe, Xianzheng: Ziyou zhuyi sixiang yanjiu (Democracy, Republicanism and Constitutional Government: A study of liberalism)*, Shanghai: Sanlian, 1998.

—   'Ziyou zhuyi: jiushu niandai "buzuzhike"' ('Liberalism: a surprised guest in the 1990s'), *Nanfang Zhoumo*, 29 May 1999.

—   'Classical liberalism catches on in China', *Journal of Democracy* 11(3), 2000, pp. 48–57.

Pan, Wei, 'Fazhi yu zhongguo weilai zhengti' ('Rule of law and the future Chinese political regime'), *Zhanlue Yu Guanli* 5, 1999, pp. 30–6.

—   *Politics of Marketization in Rural China: State and society in East Asia*, Lanham, MD: Rowman & Littlefield, 2001.

—   *Nonming Yu Shichang: Zhongguo jiceng zhengquan yu xiangzhen qiye (Farmers and Market: China's grass-roots government and rural enterprises)*, Beijing: Zhongguo Tongji Chubanshe, 2003.

—   *Fazhi Yu Minzhu Minxin (The Rule of Law and the Myth of Democracy)*, Hong Kong: Hong Kong Press for Social Sciences, 2003.

—   'Toward a consultative rule of law in China', in Zhao, S. (ed.) *Debating Political Reform in China: Rule of law vs. democratisation*, Armonk, New York: M. E. Sharpe, 2006.

—   'Reflections on the "consultative rule of law regime": a response to my critics', in Zhao, S. (ed.), *Debating Political Reform in China: Rule of Law vs. Democratisation*, Armonk, New York: M. E. Sharpe, 2006.

—   'Vous, Occidentaux, ne comprenez rien à la Chine', *Libération*, 8 July 2008.

—   *Zhongguo Moshi: Jiedu renmin gongheguo de liushinian (The Chinese Model: Understanding 60 years of the People's Republic)*, Beijing: Zhongyang Bianyi Chubanshe, 2009.

Qin, Hui, (writing as Wu, B.) 'Gongzheng zhishang lun' ('On the supremacy of justice'), *Dongfang* 6, 1994.

— (Wu, B.) 'Zailun gongzheng zhishang: qidian gongzheng ruhe keneng' ('Second essay on the supremacy of justice: possibility of justice from the start'), *Dongfang* 2, 1995.

— (Wu, B.) 'Gongzheng, jiashi lixing yu fan fubai: sanlun gongzheng zhishang' ('Justice, rationality of values and anti-corruption: third essay on the supremacy of justice'), *Dongfang* 6, 1995.

— (Wu, B.). 'Gongzheng wei daode zhiji' ('Justice, foundation of morality: fourth essay on the supremacy of justice'), *Dongfang* 6, 1995.

— *Wenti Yu Zhuyi* (*Problems and –isms*), Changchun: Changchun Chubanshe, 1999.

— 'Dividing the big family assets', *New Left Review*, April 2003, sect. 3., available online at http://www.newleftreview.org/?view=2441.

— 'La culture traditionnelle aujourd'hui: un devoir d'inventaire pour penser le politique', in Billioud, S. and Thoraval, J. (eds), 'Regards sur le politique en Chine aujourd'hui', special issue, *Extrême-Orient, Extrême-Occident* 31, 2009; first published as 'Xiru huirong, jiegou fadao hubu', in *Chuantong Shilun* (*Ten Essays on Tradition*), Shanghai: Fudan Daxue Chubanshe, 2003.

— 'China's economic development performance under the prereform system', *The Chinese Economy* 38(4), July–August 2005, pp. 61–85.

— 'Command vs. planned economy 'dispensability'of the economic systems of Central and Eastern Europe and of prereform China', *The Chinese Economy* 38(4), July–August 2005, pp. 23–60.

— 'Justice in the economics of market transition what is "transition economics"?', *The Chinese Economy* 38(5), September–October 2005, pp. 70–95.

— 'The dialectic of"downsizing" and"prioritizing employment": techniques for how to subtract value from state-owned assets', *The Chinese Economy* 38(5), September–October 2005, pp. 66–69.

— '"MBOs", yes; "year of the MBO", no: some basic issues in property rights reform', *The Chinese Economy* 38(5), September–October 2005, pp. 55–65.

Ren, Jiantao, 'Jiedu xin zuopai' ('Deciphering the New Left'), *Tianya*, February 1999, pp. 35–46.

— *Lilun Zhengzhi Yanjiu: Cong zaoqi ruxue shijiao de lilun toushi* (*Inquiry into Ethical Politics: The perspective of early Confucianism*), Guangzhou: Zhongshan Daxue Chubanshe, 1999.

— *Zhengzhi Zhexue De Lilun Shijie* (*Theoretical Perspective on Political Philosophy*) Guangzhou: Zhongshan Daxue Chubanshe, 2003.

— *Zhongguo Xiandai Sixiang Mailuo Zhong De Ziyouzhuyi* (*Liberalism in the Mainstream of Contemporary Chinese Thought*), Beijing: Beijing Daxue Chubanshe, 2004.

— 'Shehui pitai xia de baoli weihan yu minzhu jiuzhi' ('The devastation of violence against an apathetic society and the democratic remedy'), *Tansuo* 2, 2009.

—   'Ideology, its role in reform and opening', in Fewsmith, J. (ed.), *China Today, China Tomorrow: Domestic politics, economy, and society*, Lanham, MD, Rowman & Littlefield, 2010.

Wang, Hui, 'Humanism as the theme of Chinese modernity', *Surfaces* 5(202), November 1995, available online at http://www.pum.umontreal.ca/revues/surfaces/vol5/hui.html.

—   'Fire at the castle gate', in Mulhern, F. (ed.), *Lives on the Left*, New York: Verso, 2012.

—   *The End of the Revolution: China and the limits of modernity*, New York: Verso, 2009.

—   *China's New Order: Society, politics, and economy in transition*, Cambridge, MA: Harvard University Press, 2003.

Wang, Hui and Huters, T., *The Politics of Imagining Asia*, Cambridge, MA: Harvard University Press, 2011.

Wang, Haoguang and Hu, A., *Zhongguo Guojia Nengli Yanjiu Baogao* (*Report on State Capacity*), Hong Kong: Oxford University Press, 1994.

—   *The Political Economy of Uneven Development: The case of China*, Armonk, New York: M. E. Sharpe, 1999.

—   *Bupingdeng Fazhan De Zhengzhijingjixue* (*The Political Economy of Uneven Development: The case of China*), Beijing: Beijing Jihua Chubanshe, 2000.

—   *The Chinese Economy in Crisis: State capacity and tax reform*, New York: East Gate Books, M. E. Sharpe, 2001.

Wang, Shaoguang, 'Qunzhong yu Wenhua dageming' ('Masses and the Great Cultural Revolution'), in Shaomin, L. (ed.), *Dalu Zhishifenzi Lun Zhengzhi, Shehui, Jingji* (*Mainland China Intellectuals Discuss Politics, Society and Economy*), Taipei: Guiguan Tushu Gufen Youxian Gongsi, 1991, pp. 90–4.

—   'Jianli yige qiang youli de minzhu guojia–taolun "zhengquan xingshi" yu "guojia nengli" de qubie' ('Building a strong democratic state: regime type and state capacity'), *Publications of the Contemporary China Research Centre* 4, February 1991.

—   'Meiguo "jinbushidai" de qishi' ('Lessons from the progressive era in the United States'), *Dushu* 8, 2001.

—   'Democracy and state effectiveness implications', paper given at the international conference on The Crisis of Democratic Governance in East Asia: Implications, National Chengchi University, Taipei, 12–13 March 2002, published in Dinello, N. and Popov, V. (eds), *Political Institutions and Development: Failed expectations and renewed hopes*, Edward Elgar 2007.

—   'Jinqian ziyou: shimin shehui mianlin de liang nan jingdi', *Kaifang Shidai* 3, 2002, published in English as 'Money and autonomy: patterns of civil society finance and their implications', *Studies in Comparative International Development (SCID)*, 40(4), 2006, pp. 3–29.

—   *Meiguo 'Jinbushidai' de Qishi* (*Lessons From the Progressive Era In the United States*), Beijing, Public Finance Press, 2002.

— 'Zhongguo gonggong weisheng de weiji yu zhuanji', *Bijiao* 7, 2003 published in English as 'China's health system: from crisis to opportunity', *Yale China Health Journal* 3, Autumn 2004, pp. 1–47.

— 'Meikuang anquan shengchan jianguan: zhongguo zhili moshi de zhuanbian', *Bijiao* 13 July 2004, published in English as 'Regulating death at coalmines: changing mode of governance in China', *Journal of Contemporary China* 15(46), 2006, pp. 1–30.

— 'Zhongguo gonggong zhengce yicheng shezhi de moshi', *Chinese Social Sciences* 5, 2006, published in English as 'Changing models of China's policy agenda setting', *Modern China* 34(1), 2008, pp. 56–87.

— *Anbangzhidao: Guojia Zhuanliede Mubiao Yu Tujing*, 2007, Beijing: Sanlian Shudian.

— 'HuWen gaige: xin de gongshi xin de zouxiang' ('The reform of Hu Jintao and Wen Jiabao: new consensus, new direction'), interview by Ma, Y., *Fenghuang Zhoukan (Phoenix)*, April 2007.

— 'Dazhuanxing: 1980 niandai yilai zhongguo de shuangxiang yun', *Zhongguo Shehui Keshui* 1, 2008, published in English as 'The great transformation: the double movement in China', *Boundary 2* 35(2), Summer 2008.

— 'Jianli yi ge qiang youlide minzhu guojia: yu Wang Shaoguang de duihua' ('Building a strong democratic state: a dialogue with Wang Shaoguang'), in Ma, Y. (ed.), *Zhanlue Gaodu: Zhongguo Sixiangjie Fangtan Lu*, Sanlian Shudian, 2008.

— 'Xuexi jizhi yu sheying nengli: zhongguo nongcun hezuo yiliao tizhi bianqian de qishi', *Zhongguo shehui kexue* 6, 2008, published in English as 'Adapting by learning: the evolution of China's rural health care financing', *Modern China*, 35(4), 2009, pp. 370–404.

— 'Dakai zhengzhixue yanjiu de kongjian' ('Opening the scope of political science research: interview with professor Wang Shaoguang by Sun Hui'), *Zhongguo Shehui Kexue*, 13 January 2009.

— '"Jiegui" haishi "nalai": zhengzhixue bentuhua de sikao' (Harmonising or bringing in; reflections on indigenising political science', in Wang, S., *Qumei Yu Chaoyue: Fansiminzhu, Ziyou, Pindeng, Gongminshehui* (*Desacralising and Transcending: Rethinking democracy, freedom, equality and civil society*), Beijing: Zhongxing Chubanshe, 2009.

— 'Lishi de luoji yu zhishifenzi mingyun de bianqian' ('The logic of history and the evolution of the condition of intellectuals'), *Nanfengchuan*, 5 December 2011.

Xiao, Gongqin, *Xiao Gongqin Ji* (*The Works of Xiao Gongqin*), Harbin: Heilongjiang Jiaoyu Chubanshe, 1995.

— 'Yan Fu's reflections on China's modernisation and Enlightenment', paper given at the conference on Chinese Tradition and Socialism organised by the *Zhongguo Qingnianbao* (*Youth Daily*), December 1990; published in Xiao, G. (ed.), *Fansi de niandai* (*The Era of Reflection*), Shanghai: Fudan University Press, 2010.

—   'Gongchang zaofanpaide liangzhong leixing' ('Two types of factory'),
       China News Digest, August 8, 2000.
—   *Yu Zhengzhi Langmanzhuyi Gaobie* (*Farewell to Political Romanticism*),
       Hubei Press, 2001.
—   'China's changing of the guard: the rise of the technocrats', *Journal of
       Democracy* 14(1), 2003, pp. 60–65.
—   'Zhuanxing zhengzhi shiye xia de zhongguo sanshinian' ('30 years of
       reform through the looking glass of transition political science'), *Leaders*
       21, April 2008.
—   *Fansi De Niandai* (*The Era of Reflection*), Shanghai: Fudan University
       Press, 2010.
Xu, J. *et al.*, *Qimeng De Ziwo Wajie* (*The Self-Destruction of the Enlightenment*),
       Changchun: Jilin Chuban Jituan, 1994.
Xu, Jilin, 'Qimeng de mingyun: ershi nian lai de Zhongguo sixiang jie' ('The fate
       of the Enlightenment: the Chinese intelligentsia for the past 20 years'),
       Ershiyi Shiji 50, Hong Kong, December 1998.
—   'Ershi zhongguo shiji liu dai zhishifenzi' ('Six generations of Chinese
       intellectuals in the twentieth century'), available online at http://
       zaiyezhimin.bokee.com/1395843.html and in Xu Jilin, *Xu Jilin Xuanji
       (Selected Works)*, Guangxi Normal University Press, 1999.
—   'Lun liang zhong ziyou he minzhu: dui "ziyou zhuyi" yu "xin zuopai"
       lunzhan de fansi' ('Commentary on two forms of liberty and democracy:
       reflections on the theoretical argument between liberalism and the New
       Left'), *Dongya Lunwen* 31, 2001.
—   *Gonggongxing Yu Gonggong Zhishifenzi* (*The Public and Public
       Intellectuals*), Jiangsu Renmin Chubanshe, 2003.
—   'What future for public intellectuals?', *China Perspectives* 52,
       March–April 2004, available online at http://chinaperspectives.
       revues.org/799.
—   'The fate of an Enlightenment: twenty years in the Chinese intellectual
       sphere (1978–1998)', in Gu, E. and Goldman, M. (eds), *Chinese
       Intellectuals Between State and Market*, London and New York:
       RoutledgeCurzon, 2004.
—   'Valeurs universelles ou valeurs chinoises? Le courant de pensée
       de l'historicisme dans la Chine contemporaine', *Rue Descartes* 72,
       2011/2012, available online at http://www.ruedescartes.org/articles/2011-
       2-valeurs-universelles-ou-valeurs-chinoises-le-courant-de-pensee-de-l-
       historicisme-dans-la-chine-contemporaine/.
Xu, Youyu., 'Ziyouzhuyi yu dangdai zhongguo' ('Liberalism and contemporary
       China'), *Kaifang Shidai* 3, 1999, pp. 43–51.
—   *Zhimian Lishi* (*Confronting History*), Beijing: Zhongguo Wenlian
       Chubanshe, 1999.
—   *Ziyoude Yanshuo* (*The Liberal Discourse*), Changchun: Changchun
       Chubanshe, 1999.

—   'The debates between liberalism and the New Left in China since the 1990s', *Contemporary Chinese Thought* 34(3), 2003, pp. 6–17, available online at http://philpapers.org/rec/YOUTDB.

Yang, Guangbin, 'Xifang guoji guanxi lilun yu "zhongguo weixie lun"' ('The Western theory of international relations and the theory of the Chinese threat'), *Shijie Jingji Yu Zhengzhi* 4, 1999.

—   *Zhengzhixue Daolun (An Introduction to Political Science)*, Beijing: Peking University Press, 2007.

—   *Interest Groups in China's Politics and Governance*, Singapore: East Asian Institute, 2007.

Yang, Guangbin and Miao, L., 'Western political science theories and the development of political theories in China', *Journal of Chinese Political Science* 14, 1999, pp. 275–97.

Yao, Yang, 'Village elections, accountability and income distribution in rural China', *China & World Economy* 14(6), 2006, pp. 20–38.

—   'Zhongxing zhengfu yu shehui pingdeng shi zhongguo jingji zengzhang de yuanyin' ('Disinterested government and social equality are the two reasons for economic growth'), *Zhongguo Jingji*, 16 October 2009.

—   'The end of Beijing Consensus', *Foreign Affairs*, 2 February 2010.

Yao, Yang and Wang, S., 'Grassroots democracy and local governance: evidence from rural China', *World Development* 35(10), 2007, pp. 1635–49.

Yao, Yang and Wu, H.-M., *Reform and Development in China: What can China offer the developing world*, Oxford: Routledge, 2011.

Yao, Yang and Yan, S., 'Does grassroots democracy reduce income inequalities in China?', *Journal of Public Economics* 92, 2008, pp. 2182–98.

Yu, Keping., 'Democracy is a good thing', *Beijing News*, 23 October 2006.

—   'Zhongguo moshi yu sixiang jiefang' ('The Chinese model and the liberation of thought'), *Shanghai Journal of Party History and Building*, November 2008.

—   'Zhongguo zhengzhixue bainian huimou' ('Reflecting on a hundred years of Chinese political science'), *Bureau of Tranlations and Compilations*, 15 January 2009, available online at www.chinaelections.com/newsinfo. asp?newsid=101404.

—   'Political science and public administration: an overview', in Yu, K., *Democracy Is a Good Thing*, 2009, below.

—   *Democracy Is a Good Thing: Essays on politics, society, and culture in contemporary China*, Washington, DC: Brookings Institution Press, 2009.

—   *Democracy and Rule of Law in China*, Leiden: Brill, 2010.

Zhu, Guanglei, *Dangshai Zhongguo Zhengfu Guocheng (Government Processes in Contemporary China)*, Tianjin: Tianjin Renmin Chubanshe, 1997.

—   *Dangdai Zhongguo Shehui Gejiecengjenxi (Analysis of Social Strata In China)*, Tianjin: Tianjin Renmin Chubanshe, 1998.

—   *Xiandai Zhengfu Lilun (Modern Theories of Government)* Beijing: Gaodeng Jiaoyu Chubanshe, 2006.

Zhu, Xueqin, '1998, Ziyouzhuyi de yanshuo' ('1998: the discourse of liberalism'), *Nanfang Zhoumo*, 25 December 1998.

— *Shuzai Li De Geming* (*The Revolution of Study*), Changchun, Changchu Chubanshe, 1999.

— 'Zhu Xueqin, male, college professor', interview in Jiang, Y. and David, A. (eds), *Mao's Children in the new China: Voices from the Red Guard generation*, London and New York: Routledge, 2000.

— *Daode Lixiang Guo De Fumie* (*The End of Moral Utopia*), Shanghai: Sanlian, 2004.

— 'For a Chinese liberalism', in Chaohua, W. (ed.), *One China, Many Paths*, London: Verso, 2003.

Appendix C – Biographies of Scholars Interviewed

Cui Zhiyuan 崔之元, b. 1963

Cui Zhiyuan is a professor at Tsinghua University's School of Public Policy and Management, Beijing. He is a leading member of the Chinese New Left through his work on alternatives to neo-liberal capitalism. Cui is an admirer of the work of James Meade (the 1977 British Nobel Economics Prize winner) on liberal socialism. His PhD on soft budget constraint was supervised by Jon Elster, Adam Przeworski and Lester Telser at the University of Chicago. He taught political science for six years at MIT and met Roberto Unger at Harvard Law School. His research focuses on economic democracy and political innovations. To his mind, China constitutes a unique terrain for worldwide institutional and theoretical innovations. His articles have triggered controversy and fierce criticism from liberals like Xu Youyu and Qin Hui as he has dared praise some elements of the Maoist past, which he identified as potential foundations for institutional innovations. More recently, Cui has become known for his work on and as a proponent of the 'Chongqing experience' as a model for development. He is close to Chongqing's mayor, Huang Qifan, and to the city's now-disgraced Party Secretary, Bo Xilai, prior to his political downfall. He worked for a year as an official at the municipal government's public goods commission (*guoziwei*).

Deng Zhenglai 邓正来, 1956–2013

Deng Zhenglai was a Distinguished Professor (*Tepin Jiaoshou*) at Fudan University, Dean of the Institute for Advanced Study in Social Sciences and head of the Contemporary China Studies Centre. He was the editor in chief of the *Fudan China Social Studies Journal* (*Zhongguo Shehui Kexue Jikan*) and the *Fudan Humanities And Social Studies Journal* (*Fudan Renwen Shehui Kexue Luncong*). Deng was a leading scholar in several academic fields, including law, political philosophy and academic translations, as he introduced to the Chinese scholarly circle such important thinkers as Frederick von Hayek and many other liberal thinkers. Liberalism had brought him only partial answers to questions the Cultural Revolution had raised so he dedicated his later years to Chinese popular wisdom and launched the *Fudan Political Philosophy Journal* (*Zhengzhi Zhexue*).

Gan Yang 甘阳, b. 1952

Gan Yang used to be a political philosophy professor at the Chinese University of Hong Kong. He is now Sun Yat-sen University Professor, Director of the Advanced Studies in Humanities of the Liberal Arts College and Head of General Education in Sun Yat-sen University. His main research field is in political philosophy and his recent interests include the work of Leo Strauss. He was sent to Heilongjiang for eight years during the Cultural Revolution. After his Master's degree in western philosophy at Beida, he studied at the University of Chicago for nine years. Gan Yang's intellectual journey can seem convoluted. He used to be one of the main members of the editorial board of the journal *Culture: China and the World* – vocal advocates in the 1980s of the introduction of liberalism in China and critics of China's tradition – before he joined the New Left in the 1990s. From 2000 on, he has devoted himself to the Confucian renaissance and advocated establishing a Confucian socialist republic.

He Zengke 何增科, b. 1965

He Zengke is a Doctor of Politics from Beida; President of the Contemporary Marxism Research Institute, Central Compilation and Translation Bureau and Member of the Academy Committee of Central Compilation and Translation Bureau; Vice-Director of the Centre for China Government Innovations, Peking University; part-time researcher at the Anti-corruption Research Centre, Tsinghua University; Council Member of the Chinese Association of Political Science; and former Consultation Expert of the United Nations Development Program. His research directions include contemporary Chinese politics; corruption and anti-corruption; citizen, society and the third sector; grass-roots democracy and local governance; social construction; and social-system reform. He has taken part in significant research works organised by the central government and led and participated in over 30 national-level, provincial/ministerial-level and overseas-funded projects.

Hu Angang 胡鞍鋼, b. 1953

Hu Angang is a very influential economist. He is the Director of the Centre for China Studies (*Guoqing Yanjiusuo*), a Chinese Academy of Sciences and Tsinghua University think tank, and a Professor of the School of Public Policy and Management, Tsinghua University. After being sent to a farm in Heilongjiang for seven years, he got his PhD in engineering at the Chinese Academy of Sciences. He did postdoctoral study at Department of Economics, Yale University, where he met Wang Shaoguang. He has been a visiting professor or fellow at MIT, Keio University, Harvard University, the World Bank, and Colombia University. His main research focus is on economic development, social transition and public policy.

Jiang Qing 蒋庆, b. 1953

Jiang Qing is a cultural nationalist, a *daru* (Great Confucian). A former law professor in Shenzhen, he quit in 2001 to withdraw to a Guizhou mountain village where he established a private Confucian academy (*Yangming Jingshe*). A staunch defender of political Confucianism, Jiang Qing attempts to devise a Confucian political philosophy suiting modern times as an alternative to liberal democracy. He developed the idea that the legitimacy of political power relies on three sources: Heaven, Hearth and Man. As a result, a proper institutional arrangement should balance these three types of legitimacy, contrary to democracy, which only focuses on popular sovereignty.

Kang Xiaoguang 康晓光, b. 1963

Kang Xiaoguang is a Professor of Regional Economics and Politics at People's University and also affiliated to the Centre for China Studies, (*Guoqing Yanjiusuo*), the Academy of Sciences and Tsinghua University. His research focuses on poverty and anti-poverty strategies; the relationship between state and society (especially social-structure change and NGOs); political development and political stability as well as the international grain trade and food security; land-reform in Chinese villages; and environmental-protection policies. He is a cultural nationalist close to China's neo-conservative movement, who has written extensively on the Chinese political system. Concerned with the lack of values, he considers that nationalism can be instrumental in reinforcing the political cohesion and legitimacy needed in times of transition. He claims to be among the first scholars to have theorised the China model with his 2005 book, (*Renzheng*).[1] To his mind, the pragmatic Chinese reform has been positive from an economic point of view but not from a social and cultural perspective. Confucianism must fill the ideological void and become a state religion.

Li Qiang 李强, b. 1953

Li Qiang is a political science professor at Peking University. He is Director of the Development Planning Department of Peking University and of the Centre for European Studies. His 1998 book *Liberalism* revealed his great mastery of and adhesion to western liberal theories, while subtly criticising the collusion between political and economic elites in China. He is no active participant in the liberals *versus* New Left debate but endeavours to approach the issue of political reform scientifically. An undergraduate student in international politics at Beida, he studied for eight years in Great Britain (London School of Economics and University College London). He has also been invited to many US, Canadian and German universities.

---

1.   This book is mainly known under the title: Kang Xiaoguang, *Renzheng: Zhongguo zhengzhi fazhan* (*Renzheng: The third way for China's political development*), Singapore, World Scientific, 2005 but was also edited under the title *Zhongguo de daolu* (*the Chinese way*).

Liu Dong 刘东, b. 1955

Liu Dong has actively contributed to the renewal of China studies as an editor and a professor. A former professor in Peking University's Chinese literature department, he has transferred to Tsinghua's China studies department, which had reopened in November 2009 with Chen Lai as its head. A philosophy graduate from Nanjing University, a former student of Li Zehou, with a doctorate from the Academy of Social Sciences in the aesthetic culture of the Song dynasty, he was one of the members of the editorial board of *Culture: China and the World* (Gan Yang was the chief editor). Liu Dong was an invited scholar at the universities of Harvard, Hawaii, Stanford, Berkeley, NYU, Columbia, and the New School, among others. He invited Charles Taylor, Rudolf G. Wagner, Joseph W. Esherick, Haun Saussy, Prasenjit Duara, Arif Dirlik, Dudley Andrew, Torbjorn Loden and Alan Macfarlane to speak in his department. Liu Dong is the editor of several book series: Overseas Chinese Studies Series; Humanity and Society Translation Series; Chinese Scholarship; Concerns of University; Japanese Studies in the West; Chinese Learning Digest and so on.

Liu Junning 刘军宁, b. 1961

A political scientist trained by Zhao Baoxu with Yu Keping and He Zengke in Beida, Liu Junning is libertarian thinker. Even though he was very young during the Cultural Revolution, he was deeply marked by it as his grandfather, a Party member in charge of the village shop, was attacked and accused of being a 'capitalist roader' (*zou zipai*). During the repression which took place in the wake of the hundreth anniversary of Beida's foundation, an occasion which Liu had seized to edit a collection of liberal texts, publish many articles and give conferences on liberalism and calling for free and competitive elections, he was ejected from the Academy of Social Sciences. After spending a short time at Harvard, he became a researcher at the Chinese Culture Institute of the Ministry of Culture. Blacklisted, Liu Junning can only publish on the web. A freelance writer, he lanched *Res Publica* (*Gonggong Luncong*) in 1995, an unregistered journal promoting liberal democracy in China.

Pan Wei 潘维, b. 1964

Pan Wei is a professor and Director of the Centre for Chinese and Global Affairs of Peking University's International Relations department. He criticises the 'sacralisation' of democracy and the missionary-like approach of democracy-promotion. He rejects the introduction of competitive elections – which is what he means when he refers to 'democracy' – in the belief that they are completely useless in China. According to him, the Chinese equate democracy with three nightmarish visions: the collapse of the Society Union in the wake of Gorbachev's liberalisation; the alleged 'people's democracy' of the Cultural Revolution and the risk of Taiwan becoming permanently independent. A IR student at Beida and the

Academy of Social Sciences, he was a student of Pu Shan and Chen Han-seng, who encouraged him to study rural China, to which he devoted his PhD at Berkeley, under the supervision of Elizabeth Perry. Pan is a conservative figure close to the New Left and one of the theoreticians of the China model.

Qin Hui 秦晖, b. 1953

Qin Hui is Professor of History at the Institute of Humanities and Social Sciences, Tsinghua University. After the Cultural Revolution and a long stay in the countryside, he started a Master's degree in Lanzhou University. He is Director of the China Federation of Economic History; the Institute of China Farmer History; and the China Youth Development Foundation; and an advisor of the academic journals *Method*, *Open Times*, *China Scholar* and *China Social Sciences Quarterly*. He is one of the most famous liberal intellectuals and critics of the China model.

Ren Jiantao 任剑涛, b. 1963

A political philosophy professor at People's University, International Studies department, this liberal taught for a long time at Sun Yat-sen University in Guangzhou. After a philosophy doctorate devoted to the political aspects of Confucian thinking, he focused on more contemporary politics. Invited to Harvard, he has studied China's recent political evolution.

Wang Hui 汪晖, b. 1959

Wang Hui is a professor in the department of Chinese Language and Literature, Tsinghua University. His research focuses on contemporary Chinese literature and intellectual history. He was the executive editor, with Huang Ping, of the influential magazine *Dushu*, from May 1996 to July 2007. The US magazine *Foreign Policy* named him as one of the top 100 public intellectuals in the world in May 2008. Wang Hui has been Visiting Professor at Harvard, Edinburgh, Bologna, Stanford, UCLA, Berkeley, and the University of Washington, among other universities. His academic research focuses on modern literature (he was accused of plagiarism a few years ago as regarded his work on Lu Xun), but he is famous for his political publications as an active member of the New Left, criticising liberalism, consumerism, globalisation and imperialism.

Wang Shaoguang 王绍光, b. 1954

A PhD in Political Science from Cornell University in 1990, Wang Shaoguang is a professor in the Department of Government and Public Administration at the Chinese University of Hong Kong, and a non-official member of the Hong Kong Special Administrative Region (HKSAR) Commission on Strategic Development. He taught at Tijiao High School in Wuhan, China from 1972 to 1977 and at Yale University in the United States from 1990 to 2000. His research interests include political economy, comparative politics, fiscal politics, democratisation and economic and political development in former socialist countries and East-Asian countries. This influential member of the New Left is mostly known for his research on state capacity and state-building. He was a consultant for the Chinese government, the UN, the World Bank and so on. He is the chief editor of the *China Review* (CUHK), and member of the editorial board of *Modern China* (US), *Mainland China Studies* (Taiwan), *Public Economic Research* (China), *University Review of Political Science* (China), *Chinese Public Administration Review* (US), *Journal of Contemporary China* (UK), *Chinese Journal of Political Science* (US), *China Public Administration Review* (US), *Chinese Public Policy Review* (China), *Volunteer Service Journal* (China).

Xiao Gongqin 萧功秦, b. 1946

Xiao Gongqin is a history Professor at Shanghai Normal University. He is the main theoretician of the neo-authoritarian movement in the 1980s and neo-conservatism in the early 1990s. A protégé of the official ideologue Yuan Mu for some time, he considers that liberal democracy is the best regime for China. For China's democratisation to succeed and last, a number of conditions must apply, namely a relatively high level of economic development, a dynamic civil society and a strong civic culture. The authoritarian transition he advocates is only a temporary, necessary evil. Xiao belongs to the generation of scholars who directly experienced the Cultural Revolution. He wrote extensively on the rising nationalism.

Xu Jilin 许纪霖, b. 1957

Xu Jilin is a distinguished professor of East China Normal University, executive vice dean of the Si-mian Institute for Advanced Studies in Humanities, and executive vice director of the Institute of Modern Chinese Thought and Culture. He is a historian of 20th Century Chinese thought and culture. Xu serves on the editorial board of the journal *Twenty-First Century*. Well known for disavowing political extremes of the right and the left, he is a moderate liberal, a leading exponent of the third way in intellectual discussions about China's present and future.

Xu Youyu 徐友渔, b. 1947

Xu Youyu is a retired philosophy researcher at the Chinese Academy of Social Sciences (CASS). He is one of the main representatives of the liberal movement in China. Known for his focus on memory of the Cultural Revolution (when he was a rebel and later sent to a north-Sichuan village for three years and to work in a factory in Chengdu for six years) and the June Fourth movement. He first studied mathematics but studied Anglo-American philosophy at the CASS. He also studied language philosophy with Michael Dummet at Oxford. He was a member of the editorial board of the journal *Culture: China and the World*. From May 6 to June

5, 2014, public security officials in Beijing municipality criminally detained him on suspicion of 'picking quarrels and provoking trouble', because he had attended a seminar with other scholars, lawyers, and family members of victims of the 1989 Tiananmen protests. Participants reportedly discussed the impact of the 1989 protests and called for an investigation into the violent suppression of protesters. He was released on bail.

Yang Guangbin 杨光斌, b. 1963

Yang Guangbin is a professor of political science, Director of the Institute of Comparative Politics and Chairman of the Department of Political Science, School of International Studies at Renmin University. After completing a political science degree at Henan University and a Master's in international politics at Beida, he studied international public policy at George Washington University, where he was also a Fulbright professor. He was also an invited scholar at Sussex University and Denver University. He is a professor at the Jinggangshan Party School, academic advisor of *Political Science Monthly* and a member of the editorial board of the journals *Asian Politics & Policy* (US) and *Studies of East Asia* (Taiwan). Yang Guangbin does not officially take sides in the ideological debate. His research interests are comparative institutional analysis; China's political economy; institutions of governance; the regulatory state; democratic politics; and political development.

Yao Yang 姚洋, b. 1964

Yao Yang is a professor at the China Centre for Economic Research (CCER) and the National School of Development (NSD), Peking University. He currently serves as the director of CCER and deputy dean of NSD in charge of academic affairs and the editor of the centre's house journal, *China Economic Quarterly*. His research interests include economic transition and development in China. He is an associate editor of *Agricultural Economics* and serves in the editorial boards of several domestic and international journals, such as *China Journal of Finance*, *Fudan Economic Papers*, *Journal of Rural Cooperatives* and *Public Policy Review*. A graduate in geography and economics, both from Peking University, he completed his PhD in agricultural and applied economics from the University of Wisconsin, Madison. Yao Yang is also a prolific writer for magazines and newspapers and has elaborated the concept of 'disinterested government'.

Yu Keping 俞可平, b. 1959

Yu Keping is the Director of the Centre for China Government Innovations at Peking University. One of the first trained political scientists in China (taught by Zhao Baoxu, in Beida) after the Cultural Revolution, he is a prominent scholar, promoting an incremental democratisation of China and having produced many well known books, including the widely noted *Democracy is a Good Thing*.

In addition to his academic work he has also acted as an advisor on political reforms to the Chinese government: he is the Deputy Director of the Central Compilation and Translation Bureau of the Central Committee of the Chinese Communist Party. Yu is also the New World Senior Fellow in the Ash Centre for Democratic Governance and Innovation in the John F. Kennedy School of Government, Harvard University. *Foreign Affairs* considered him as one of the most influential thinkers in the world in 2011. He is a member of the editorial board of many journals, such as *Bijiao, Fudan Political Philosophy Journal, New Political Science* (US) and *Global Studies* (UK).

Zheng Yongnian 郑永年, b. 1962

Zheng Yongnian is a professor and the Director of the East Asian Institute, National University of Singapore. A Bachelor's and Master's graduate in political science at Peking University, he later studied at Princeton University, where he obtained a PhD in political science. After a two-year stint at Harvard as SSRC-MacArthur Fellow in International Peace and Security, he was a research fellow at the newly founded East Asian Institute in Singapore before his appointment as a full professor and founding Research Director of the China Policy Institute at the University of Nottingham. Since July 2008, he has served as Director of the East Asian Institute, a Singapore think tank under a statute of the National University of Singapore. Zheng is a co-editor of *China: An International Journal, East Asian Policy* and the Series on Contemporary China published by World Scientific in Singapore; he is editor of the China Policy Series published by Routledge. His research interests include nationalism; China's foreign policy; the transforming Chinese state; the relationship between local and central governments; social movements; and China's technological and democratic development. Zheng has been a consultant for the United Nations Development Program and the Chinese government. His research has been funded by the MacArthur Foundation and the Ford Foundation.

Zhu Xueqin 朱学勤, b. 1952

This Professor in the department of History, Academy of Letters, Shanghai University was one of the most famous liberal intellectuals in the 1990s. A factory worker during the Cultural Revolution, he graduated in history at Jiangxi Normal University and Fudan. He is a famous critic of nationalism and cultural determinism, taking part in many controversies, including one on history manuals he helped design for Shanghai schools. According to him, only political reform can lead to greater social justice and prevent the regime from becoming a Latin-American-style dictatorship. Blacklisted for a long time because of his explicit advocacy of a constitutional and representative regime, Zhu Xueqin's publications have been more limited in the past few years.

Zhu Guanglei 朱光磊, b. 1959

Zhu Guanglei is Provost at Nankai University as well as a professor in the Zhou Enlai School of Government and Management. He also has political responsibilities: he is a member of the Chinese Communist Party centre's Project on Marxist Theory Research and Construction and Director of the Tianjin Political Science Association. His main areas of research are Chinese government and politics; issues in China's stratification; and contemporary political theory and policy. He is a philosophy and economics graduate. He has been invited to Ohio State University and York University and is now a leading political scientist and specialist in government studies. His report on social stratification was quite influential.

Bibliography

Abélès, M., *Pékin 798*, Paris: Stock, 2011.

Arsène, S., 'La satire ou la ringardisation de la censure sur le web chinois', *Kiosque*, CERI-Science Po, April 2010, available online at http://www.ceri-sciencespo. com/archive/2010/April/dossier/art_sa.pdf (last accessed 14 November 2014).

— 'De l'autocensure aux mobilisations', *Revue française de science politique* 61(5): 2011, pp. 893–915.

— *Internet et politique en Chine*, Paris: Karthala, 2011.

Bell, D. A., *Beyond Liberal Democracy: Political thinking for an East Asian context*, Princeton, NJ: Princeton University Press, 2006.

— *China's New Confucianism: Politics and everyday life in a changing society*, Princeton, NJ: Princeton University Press, 2010.

— 'What China can teach Europe', *New York Times*, 7 January 2012.

Bender, T., *Intellect and Public Life: Essays on the social history of academic intellectuals in the United States*, Baltimore, MD: Johns Hopkins University Press, 1997.

Bennett, G. A. and Montaperto, R. M. (eds), *Red Guard: The political biography of Dai Hsiao-Ai*, Anchor Books, 1972.

Bergère, M. -C., *Sun Yat-sen*, Paris: Fayard, 1994.

Billioud, S. and Thoraval, J., 'Jiaohua: le renouveau confucéen en Chine comme projet éducatif', *Perspectives chinoises* 2007/4.

— 'Regards sur le politique en Chine aujourd'hui', *Extrême-Orient, Extrême-Occident* 31, 2009.

— 'La Chine et son passé', *Perspectives chinoises* 2007/4, December 2007, available online at http://perspectiveschinoises.revues.org/2453 (last accessed 14 November 2014).

— 'Reconfigurations religieuses en République populaire de Chine', *Perspectives chinoises* 2009/4, available online at http://perspectives chinoises.revues.org/5367 (last accessed 14 November 2014).

Billioud, S., '"Confucianisme", "tradition culturelle" et discours officiels dans la Chine des années 2000', *Perspectives chinoises* 2007/3, available online at http://perspectiveschinoises.revues.org/3133 (last accessed 14 November 2014).

Bonnin, M., *Génération perdue: le mouvement d'envoi des jeunes instruits à la campagne en Chine, 1968–1980*, Editions de l'Ecole des hautes études en sciences sociales, 2004.

Boudon, R., 'L'intellectuel et ses publics: les singularités françaises', in Grafmeyer, J. D. and Reynaud, Y. *Français qui êtes-vous? Des essais et des chiffres*, Paris: La Documentation Française, 1981.

Brødsgaard, K. E. and Zheng, Y., *The Chinese Communist Party in Reform*, Oxford: Routledge, 2006.

Brouwer, D. C. and Squires, C. R., 'Public intellectuals, public life and the university', *Argumentation and Advocacy* 39(3): 2003, pp. 201–13.

Cabestan, J. -P., review of Chu, Y. -H., Diamond, L., Nathan, A. J. and Shin, D. C. (eds.), *How East Asians View Democracy*, Perspectives chinoises, 2009/3, available online at http://perspectiveschinoises.revues.org/5326.

Carothers, T., 'The "sequencing" fallacy', *Journal of Democracy* 18(1): 2007, pp. 12–27.

Cheek, T., 'Historians as public intellectuals', in Gu, E. X. and Goldman, M. (eds), *Chinese Intellectuals Between State and Market*, Oxford: Routledge, 2004.

—   *Living With Reform: China Since 1989*, New York: Zed Books, 2006.

—   'Xu Jilin and the thought work of China's public intellectuals', *China Quarterly* 186, June 2006, pp. 401–20, available online at http://www.jstor.org/stable/20192619 (last accessed 14 November 2014).

Chen, A. H. Y., 'Socio-legal thought and legal modernization in contemporary China: a case study of the jurisprudence of Zhu Suli', in Doeker-Mach, G. and Ziegert, K. A., *Law, Legal Culture and Politics in the Twenty First Century*, Wiesbaden: Franz Steiner Verlag, 2004, pp. 227–49.

Chen, F. -C. and Jin, G. (eds), *From Youthful Manuscripts to River Elegy: The Chinese popular cultural movement and political transformation 1979–1989*, Hong Kong: Chinese University of Hong Kong Press, 1997.

Cheng, J. Y. S., *Whither China's Democracy? Democratisation in China since the Tiananmen Incident*, Hong Kong: City University of Hong Kong Press, 2011.

Chen, L., 'Ershi shiji wenhua yundong zhong de jijin zhuyi' ('The radicalism of cultural movements in the twentieth century'), *Dongfang* 1, 1993.

—   *Tradition and Modernity: A humanist view*, translated by Ryden, E., Leiden and Boston, MA: Brill, 2009.

—   'Le débat entre libéralisme et nouvelle gauche au tournant du siècle', *Perspectives chinoises* 84, 2004, available online at http://perspectiveschinoises.revues.org/673.

Chen, P., 'Xueshu shi yanjiu suixiang' ('Throughout research on the history of academic life'), *Xueren* 1, Jiangsu Wenyi Chubanshe, 1991.

—   'Scholarship, ideas, politics', in Wang, C. (ed.), *One China, Many Paths*, London: Verso, 2003.

Chen, S., 'Jiu 95 "renwen jingshen" zhenglun zhi riben xuezhe' '(Letters to a Japanese researcher concerning the debates on humanist spirit in 1995'), *Tianya* 1, 1996, pp. 19–25.

Chen, Y., *L'éveil de la Chine: les bouleversements intellectuels après Mao, 1976–2002*, Paris: Editions de l'Aube, 2002.

—   'Liberalism in contemporary China: ten years after its "resurface"', *Journal of Contemporary China* 17(55), May 2008, pp. 383–400.

Cheng, Y., *Dégel de l'intelligence en Chine: 1976–1989: quatorze témoignages*, Paris: Gallimard, 2004.

Cherrington, R., *Deng's Generation: Young intellectuals in 1980s China*, Basingstoke: Macmillan, 1997.

Chevrier, Y., 'Chine, "fin de règne" du lettré? Politique et culture à l'époque de l'occidentalisation', *Extrême-Orient, Extrême-Occident* 4(4): 1984, pp. 81–139.

— 'De l'occidentalisme à la solitude: Chen Duxiu et l'invention de la modernité chinoise', *Études Chinoises* 3, 1984, pp. 7–34.

— 'Les réformes en Chine ou la stratégie du contournement', *Politique étrangère*, 50(1): 1985, pp. 119–38.

Chevrier, Y. Alain, R. and Xiao-Planes, X. (eds), *Citadins et citoyens dans la Chine du XXe siècle: Essais d'histoire sociale*, Paris: Maison des Sciences de l'Homme, 2010.

Chong, W. L., *China's Great Proletarian Cultural Revolution: Master narratives and post-Mao counternarratives*, Lanham, MD: Rowman & Littlefield, 2002.

Chow, G. C., *China's Economic Transformation*, Malden, MA and Oxford: Blackwell, 2002.

Collini, S., *Absent Minds: Intellectuals in Britain*, Oxford and New York: Oxford University Press, 2006.

Connolly, W. E., 'Essentially contested concepts in politics', in *Terms of Political Discourse*, 2nd edition, Princeton, NJ: Princeton University Press, 1983 [1974] ch.1.

Davies, G., *Voicing Concerns: Contemporary Chinese critical inquiry*, Lanham, MD: Rowman & Littlefield, 2001.

— *Worrying About China: The language of Chinese critical inquiry*, Cambridge, MA: Harvard University Press, 2007.

Delmas-Marty, M. and Pierre-Etienne, W., *La Chine et la démocratie*, Paris: Fayard, 2007.

Deng, X., *Selected Works of Deng Xiaoping (1975–1982)*, Beijing: Foreign Language Press, 1983.

Diamond, L., *Developing Democracy Toward Consolidation*, Baltimore, MD: Johns Hopkins University Press, 1999.

Dittmer, L., 'Rethinking China's Cultural Revolution amid reform', in Chong, W. L. (ed.), *China's Great Proletarian Cultural Revolution: Master narratives and post-Mao counternarratives*, Lanham, MD: Rowman & Littlefield, 2002, pp. 3–26.

Dittmer, L. and Liu, G. (eds), *China's Deep Reform: Domestic politics in transition*, Lanham, MD: Rowman & Littlefield, 2006.

Domenach, J. -L., *La Chine m'inquiète*, Paris: Librairie Académique Perrin, 2008.

Domenach, J. -L. and Richer, P., *La Chine*, 2 vols., *Chine 1 1949–1971; Chine 2 De 1971 à nos jours*, Paris: Le Seuil, 1995.

Easton, D., Gunnell, J. G. and Graziano, L., *The Development of Political Science: A comparative survey*, New York: Routledge, 1990.

Elman, B. A., 'Political, social, and cultural reproduction via civil service examinations in late imperial China', *Journal of Asian Studies* 50(1): 1991, pp. 7–28.

Etzioni, A., and Bowditch, A., *Public Intellectuals: An endangered species?* Lanham, MD: Rowman & Littlefield, 2006.

Fairbank, J., and Goldman, M., *An Intellectual History of Modern China*, New York: Cambridge University Press, 2002.

Feng, C., 'The Chinese liberal camp in post-June 4th China', *China Perpectives* 2009/2, available online at http://chinaperspectives.revues.org/4803.

Fewsmith, J., *Dilemmas of Reform in China: Political conflict and economic debate*, Armonk, New York: M. E. Sharpe, 1994.

— *China Since Tiananmen: The politics of transition*, New York: Cambridge University Press, 2001.

— *China Today, China Tomorrow: Domestic politics, economy, and society*, Lanham, MD: Rowman & Littlefield, 2010.

Foucault, M., 'La fonction politique de l'intellectuel', in *Dits et écrits II, 1976–1988*, Paris: Gallimard, 2001.

Frenkiel, E., *Perfect Freedom: A study of the evolution and representation of contemporary Anglo-American political philosophy in China*, Master 2 ENS-LSH, September 2005.

— 'Political change and democracy in China. An interview with Wang Shaoguang', *La vie des idées*, 15 July 2009, available online at http://laviedesidees.fr/Political-change-and-democracy-in.html

— 'From scholar to official. Cui Zhiyuan and Chongqing City's local experimental policy', *Books & Ideas*, 6 December 2010, available online at http://www.booksandideas.net/IMG/pdf/20101206_Cui_Zhiyuan_EN.pdf (last accessed 14 November 2014).

Froissart, C., 'Xu Youyu, or how to write the history of the Cultural Revolution so as to set China on the right future path', *China Perspectives* 42, July–August 2002, pp. 15–23, available online at http://www.cefc.com.hk/issue/issue-2002-07-01/ (last accessed 14 November 2014).

Fung, E. K., *In Search of Chinese Democracy: Civil opposition in Nationalist China, 1929–1949*, Cambridge: Cambridge University Press, 2000.

Gallie, W. B., 'Essentially contested concepts', *Proceedings of the Aristotelian Society* 56, 1956, pp. 167–198.

Gao, R. *et al.*, 'Renwen jingshen xunzong' ('Looking for the humanist spirit'), *Dushu* 4, 1994.

Gao, M. C. F., *The Battle for China's Past: Mao and the Cultural Revolution*, London: Pluto Press, 2008.

Gilley, B., *China's Democratic Future: How it will happen and where it will lead*, New York: Columbia University Press, 2005.

Goldman, M., 'Hu Yaobang's intellectual network and the theory conference of 1979', *China Quarterly*, June 1991, pp. 219–42.

— *Sowing the Seeds of Democracy in China: Political reform in the Deng Xiaoping era*, Cambridge, MA: Harvard University Press, 1994.

— 'A new relationship between the intellectuals and the state in the post-Mao period', in Fairbank, J. and Goldman, M., (eds), *An Intellectual History of Modern China*, New York: Cambridge University Press, 2002.

— *From Comrade to Citizen: The struggle for political rights in China*, Cambridge, MA: Harvard University Press, 2005.

Goldman, M., Cheek, T. and Hamrin, C. L. (eds), *China's Intellectuals and the State: In search of a new relationship*, Cambridge, MA: Harvard University Press, 1987.

Gu, E. X. and Goldman, M., *Chinese Intellectuals Between State and Market*. Oxford: Routledge, 2004.

Gunnell, J., 'The founding of the American Political Science Association: Discipline, profession, political theory, and politics', *American Political Science Review* 100(4), 2006, pp. 479–86.

Guo, B., 'From conflict to convergence: modernity and the changing Chinese political culture', in Hua, S. and Yang, Z., *Political Civilization and Modernization in China*, Singapore, World Scientific, 2006, also available at http://www.academia.edu/165452/From_Conflicts_to_Convergence_Modernity_and_the_Changing_Chinese_Political_Culture (last accessed 14 November 2014).

Hamrin, C. L. and Cheek, T., *China's Establishment Intellectuals*, Armonk, New York: M. E. Sharpe, 1986.

Hao, Z., *Intellectuals at a Crossroads: The changing politics of China's knowledge workers*, Albany, NY: State University of New York Press, 2003.

— *Whither Taiwan and Mainland China: National identity, the state, and intellectuals*, Hong Kong: Hong Kong University Press, 2010.

Hayhoe, R., *China's Universities, 1895–1995: A century of cultural conflict*, New York and London: Garland Publishers, 1996.

Hays Gries, P. and Rosen, S. (eds), *State and Society in 21st Century China: Crisis, contention, and legitimation*, New York and London: Routledge, 2004.

He, B., 'Intra-party democracy: a revisionist perspective from below', in Brødsgaard, K. E. and Zheng, Y. (eds), *The Chinese Communist Party in Reform*, Oxford: Routledge, 2006.

— 'Civic engagement through participatory budgeting in China: three different logics at work', *Public Administration and Development* 31(2): 2011, pp. 122–33.

He, J. '"Women laizi hechu yu you quwang nali": dangqian "zhongguo wenti yanjiu" de sanzhong jinlu' ('Where are we from and where will we go? Three roads of China's problem research today'), *Tribune of Social Sciences* 4, 2003.

He, H. Y., *Dictionary of the Political Thought of the People's Republic of China*, Armonk, NY, M. E. Sharpe, 2001.

Heberer, T. and Schubert, G., 'Political reform and regime legitimacy in contemporary China', *Asien* 99, 2006, pp. 9–28.

Heilmann, S., 'From local experiments to national policy: the origins of China's distinctive policy process', *China Journal* 59, January 2008, pp. 1–30.

Hu, P., *Chine: à quand la démocratie ? Les illusions de la modernisation*, Paris: Editions de l'Aube, 2nd edition 2007.

Hua, L., *Les années rouges*, Paris: Le Seuil, 1987.

Hua, S., *Scientism and Humanism: Two cultures in post-Mao China (1978–1989)*, Albany, NY: State University of New York Press, 1995.

Huang, P., Yang, T. and Liumei, C., *Womendeshidai, Xianshizhongguo Congnalilai, Wangnaliqu? (Our Times, Where Today's China Comes From and Which Direction to Take?)*, Beijing: Central Compilation & Translation Press, 2006.

Jacoby, R., *The Last Intellectuals: American culture in the age of academe*, New York, Basic Books, 1987.

Ji, Z., 'Chine: L'amorce d'une "sphère de délibération publique"? Le débat sur la réforme de l'Université de Pékin', *La Vie des Idées*, November 2004, pp. 16–20.

— 'Confucius, les libéraux et le Parti: Le renouveau du confucianisme politique', *La Vie des Idées*, May 2005, pp. 9–20.

Jiang, Y. and David, A., *Mao's Children in the New China: Voices from the Red Guard generation*, London and New York: Routledge, 2000.

Jie, C., *Popular Political Support in Urban China*, Stanford, CA: Stanford University Press, 2004.

Jing, Y. and Guoqin, W., 'Western political research approaches and the development of political science methodology in China', *Journal of Chinese Political Science* 14, 1999, pp. 299–315.

Kalathil, S. and Boas, T. C., *Open Networks, Closed Regimes: The impact of the Internet on authoritarian rule*, Washington D.C., Carnegie Endowment for International Peace, 2002.

Kipnis, A., 'Suzhi: a keyword approach', *China Quarterly* 186(1), 2006, pp. 295–313.

Kuhn, P. A., *Les origines de l'État chinois moderne*, Paris: Armand Colin, 1999.

Kuhn, R. L., *How China's Leaders Think: The inside story of China's reform and what this means for the future*, Hoboken, NJ: John Wiley & Sons, 2009.

Lam, W. W. -L., *Chinese Politics in the Hu Jintao Era: New leaders, new challenges*, Armonk, New York: M. E. Sharpe, 2006.

Leonard, M., *What Does China Think?* London: Fourth Estate, 2008.

Li, C. (ed.), *China's Emerging Middle Class: Beyond economic transformation*, Washington, DC: Brookings Institution Press, 2010.

— 'The Chinese Communist Party: recruiting and controlling the new elites', *Journal of Current Chinese Affairs* 38(3): 2009, pp. 13–33.

— *China's Changing Political Landscape: Prospects for democracy*, Washington, DC: Brookings Institution Press, 2008.

— 'China's new think tanks: where officials, entrepreneurs, and scholars interact', *China Leadership Monitor* 31, 2008, available online at http://media.hoover.org/sites/default/files/documents/CLM29CL.pdf.

— 'Introduction', in Hu, A., *China in 2020*, Washington, DC: Brookings Institution Press, 2011.

Link, P., *Evening Chats in Beijing*, New York and London: Norton, 1992.

— 'China: the anaconda in the chandelier', *New York Review of Books*, 11 April 2002.

Manin, B., *Les principes du gouvernement représentatif*, Paris: Calmann-Lévy, 1995.

Mannheim, K., 'The problem of generations', [1923], in Mannheim, K. and Wolff, K. H. (eds), *From Karl Mannheim*, New Brunswick: Transaction Publishers, 1993.

Melzer, A. M., Weinberger, J. and Zinman, M. R., *The Public Intellectual: Between philosophy and politics*, Lanham, MD: Rowman & Littlefield, 2003.

Merle, A., 'Towards a Chinese sociology for "communist civilisation": in Peking, a group of sociologists at Tsinghua University are proposing a new course of research', *China Perspectives* 52, March–April, 2004, available online at http://www.cefc.com.hk/article/towards-a-chinese-sociology-for-communist-civilisationin-peking-a-group-of-sociologists-at-tsinghua-university-are-proposing-a-new-course-of-research/ (last accessed 14 November 2014).

Metzger, T. A., 'Did Sun Yat-sen understand the idea of democracy? The conceptualization of democracy in Three Principles of the People and in John Stuart Mill's On Liberty', *American Asian Review* 10(1): 1992, pp. 1–41.

Mok, K. H., *Intellectuals and the State in Post-Mao China*, London: Macmillan, 1998.

Nathan, A. J., *Chinese Democracy*, Berkeley: University of California Press, 1986.

— 'China's constitutionalist option', *Journal of Democracy* 4(7): 1996, pp. 43–57.

— 'Authoritarian resilience', *Journal of Democracy* 14(1), 2003, pp. 6–17.

O'Brien, K. J. (ed.), *Popular Protest in China*, Cambridge, MA: Harvard University Press, 2008.

O'Brien, K. J. and Li, L., *Rightful Resistance in Rural China*, New York and Cambridge: Cambridge University Press, 2006.

Ownby, D., 'Kang Xiaoguang: social science, civil society, and Confucian religion', *China Perspectives*, 2009/4, available online at http://chinaperspectives. revues.org/4928.

Pan, Z., 'Bounded innovations in the media', in Lee, C. K. (ed.), *Reclaiming Chinese Society: The new social activism*, New York: Routledge, 2009.

Peerenboom, R. P., *China's Long March Toward Rule of Law*, Cambridge: Cambridge University Press, 2002.

— *Judicial Independence in China: Lessons for global rule of law promotion*, Cambridge : Cambridge University Press, 2010.

Perry, E. J., 'Trends in the study of Chinese politics: state–society relations', *China Quarterly* 139, September 1994, pp. 704–13.

— *Challenging the Mandate of Heaven: Social protest and state power in China*. Armonk, New York: M. E. Sharpe, 2002.

Popper, K., *The Open Society and its Enemies*, vol. II, *The High Tide of Prophecy*, London: Routledge & Kegan Paul, 5th edition, 1966.

Posner, R., *Public Intellectuals: A study of decline*, Cambridge, MA: Harvard University Press, 2001.

Pye, L., 'Political science and the crisis of authoritarianism', *American Political Science Review* 84(1): 1990, pp. 3–19.

Qi, J., 'The debate over "universal values" in China', *Journal of Contemporary China*, 20(72): 2011, pp. 881–90.

Qian, G., 'Guidance/supervision/reform/freedom: looking at Chinese media through the media buzzword', *China Media Project*, 13 July 2005, available online at http://cmp.hku.hk/2005/07/13/33/.

Rai, S., *Resistance and Reaction: University politics in post-Mao China*, Hemel Hempstead, Herts: Harvester Wheatsheaf and New York: St Martin's Press, 1991.

Rocca, J. -L. (ed.), *La société chinoise vue par ses sociologues. Villes et mobilité, classes moyennes, travail, éducation*, Paris: Presses de Sciences Po, 2008.

— *Une sociologie de la Chine*, Paris: La Découverte, Collection Repères, 2010.

— 'The conflicting formation of the Chinese middle classes', paper given at the conference Power in the Making: Governing And 'Being Governed' in Contemporary China, Oxford, 30 March 2012.

Rosanvallon, P., *Le moment Guizot*, Paris: Gallimard, 1985.

— *La démocratie inachevée*, Paris: Gallimard, 2000.

— *La contre-démocratie: La politique à l'âge de la défiance*, Paris: Le Seuil, 2006.

— *La légitimité démocratique: Impartialité, reflexivité, proximité*, Paris: Le Seuil, 2008.

Rudolf, H., *Social Movements*, New York: Appleton-Century Crofts, 1951.

Ryan, J., *China's Higher Education Reform and Internationalisation*, Oxford: Routledge, 2011.

Sausmikat, N., 'Generations, legitimacy, and political ideas in China: the end of polarization or the end of ideology?', *Asian Survey* 43(2): 2003, pp. 352–84.

Schubert, G., 'Stability through more participation? Local direct elections and their impact on communist rule in present-day China', *Asien* 84, 2002, pp. 47–55.

— 'Democracy under one-party rule', *China Perpectives* 46, 2003, available online at http://chinaperspectives.revues.org/256.

Schwarcz, V., 'Behind a partially-open door: Chinese intellectuals and the post-Mao reform process', *Pacific Affairs* 59(4), December 1986, pp. 577–604, available online at http://www.jstor.org/stable/2758537 (last accessed 14 November 2014).

Schwartz, B., *In Search of Wealth and Power: Yen Fu and the West*, Cambridge, MA: Belknap Press of Harvard University Press, 1964.

— *China and Other Matters*, Cambridge, MA: Harvard University Press, 1996.

Shambaugh, D., *China's Communist Party: Atrophy and adaptation*, Berkeley: University of California Press, 2009.

Sleeboom-Faulkner, M., *The Chinese Academy of Social Sciences (CASS): Shaping the reforms, academia and China (1977–2003)*, Leiden: Brill, 2007.

Snyder, C., 'Should political science have a civic mission? An overview of the historical evidence', *PS: Political Science and Politics* 34(2): 2001, pp. 301–5.

Strauss, L., *Persecution and the Art of Writing*, Chicago, IL: University of Chicago Press, 8th edition, 2010[1954].

Sun, L., 'Women zai kaishi miandui yige duanlie de shehui?' ('Are we facing a fractured society?'), *Zhanlue Yu Guanli* 2, 2002.

— *Duanlie (The Fracture)*, Beijing: Shehui Kexui Wenbian Chubanshe, 2003.

Tan, H. and Jian, S. (eds), 'Wenhua dageming'de shi nian' ('The ten years of the Cultural Revolution'), in Tan, H. and Jian, S. (eds), *1895–1995 Shiji dang'an (The Archives of the Century)*, Beijing: Dang'an Zhongguo Chubanshe, 1995, pp. 571–8.

Tang, W., *Party Intellectuals' Demands for Reform in Contemporary China*, Stanford, CA: Hoover Press, 1999.

— *Public Opinion and Political Change*, Stanford, CA: Stanford University Press, 2005.

Terence, B., *L'Empereur jaune*, Paris: Les Indes savantes, 2007.

Thireau, I. and Hua, L., 'De l'épreuve publique à la reconnaissance d'un public: le scandale Sun Zhigang', *Politix* 71(3): 2005, pp. 137–64.

Thireau, I. and Wang, H. (eds), *Disputes au village chinois. Formes du juste et recompositions locales des espaces normatifs*, Paris: Editions de la Maison des Sciences de l'Homme, 2001.

— *Les ruses de la démocratie: Protester en Chine*, Paris: Le Seuil, 2010.

Trebitsch, M. and Granjon, M. -C. (eds), *Pour une histoire comparée des intellectuels*, Brussels: Editions Complexe/IHTP-CNRS, 1998.

Trilling, L., *Beyond Culture: Essays on literature and learning*, New York: Viking Press, 1965.

Tsou, T., *The Cultural Revolution and Post-Mao Reforms: A Historical Perspective*, Chicago, IL: University of Chicago Press, 1986.

Tu, W. (ed.), *Confucian Traditions in East Asian Modernity: Moral education and economic culture in Japan and the four mini-dragons*, Cambridge, MA: Harvard University Press, 1996.

— 'Intellectuals in a world made of knowledge', *Canadian Journal of Sociology* 30(2): 2005, pp. 219–26.

Van Dongen, E., *Goodbye Radicalism, Conceptions of radicalism among Chinese intellectuals during the early 1990s*, PhD dissertation, Leiden University, 2009.

Vandermeersch, L., *Wangdao ou la voie royale. Recherche sur l'esprit des institutions de la Chine archaïque*, Paris: Publication de l'École française d'Extrême-Orient, 1977 and 1980.

Vidal, C., *À l'épreuve du politique: les intellectuels non communiste chinois et l'émergence du pouvoir maoïste dans la première moitié du XXe siècle*, 2 vols, PhD dissertation, EHESS, 2006.

Wang, C. (ed.), *One China, Many Paths*, London: Verso, 2003.

Wang, J., *Reverse Course: Political neo-conservatism and regime stability in post-Tiananmen China*, PhD dissertation, Columbia University, 2006.

Weatherley, R., *The Discourse on Human Rights in China: Historical and ideological perspectives*, London: Macmillan, 1999.

—   'Human rights in China: between Marx and Confucius', *CRISPP* 3(4): 2000, pp. 101–25.

White III, L. T., 'Thought workers in Deng's time', in Goldman, M., Cheek, T. and Hamrin, C. L. (eds), *China's Intellectuals and the State: In search of a new relationship*, Cambridge, MA: Harvard University Asia Center, 1987.

Will, P. -E., 'Sprouts of democracy in Chinese History', *Books & Ideas*, 30 May 2011, available online at http://www.booksandideas.net/Sprouts-of-Democracy-in-Chinese.html (last accessed 14 November 2014).

Wong, Y. -C., *From Deng Xiaoping to Jiang Zemin: Two decades of political reform in the People's Republic of China*, Lanham, Md: University Press of America, 2005.

Xu, X., 'Mianxiang 21 shiji de zhongguo zhengce kexue' ('Chinese political science and the twenty-first century challenge'), *Peking University Academic Review* (philosophy and social sciences) 37(4): 2000, pp. 108–20.

Xu, B., *Disenchanted Democracy: Chinese cultural criticism after 1989*, Ann Arbor: University of Michigan Press, 1999.

Yahuda, M., 'Political generations in China', *China Quarterly* 80, 1979, pp. 793–805.

Yan, X., *Ancient Chinese Thought, Modern Chinese Power*, Princeton, NJ: Princeton University Press, 2011.

Yang, G., 'Days of old are not puffs of smoke: three hypotheses on collective memories of the Cultural Revolution', *China Review*, 5(2), Fall 2005, pp. 13–41, available online at http://www.academia.edu/4321185/_2005_Days_of_Old_Are_Not_Puffs_of_Smoke_Three_Hypotheses_on_Collective_Memories_of_the_Cultural_Revolution (last accessed 14 November 2014).

Yu, J., 'Baozhu shehuiwending de dixian' ('Maintaining a reference level in social stability'), paper given at a conference of Beijing lawyers, 26 December 2009, available online at http://www.chinaelections.org/Newsinfo.asp?NewsID=169507 (last accessed 14 November 2014).

—   'Zhengzhixue fazhan de ziwo fansi yu zhongguo zhengzhixue de jiangou' (Reflection on the development of political science and the construction of Chinese political science), *Jiaoxue yu Yanjiu* (Teaching and Researching) 5(21): 2005.

Zhang, L., 'La crise de la recherche fondamentale: recherche académique, logique du marché et intervention étatique', in Rocca, J. -L. (ed.), *La société chinoise vue par ses sociologues*, Paris: Presses de Sciences Po, 2008.

Zhang, W., *Daxue De Luoji* (*The Logic of the University*), Beijing: Daxue Chubanshe, 2004.

Zhang, Y., 'Politics, culture, and scholarly responsibility in China: toward a culturally sensitive analytical approach', *Asian Perspective* 31(3), 2007, pp. 103–24.

—   'No forbidden zone in reading?', *New Left Review* 49, January–February 2008, available online at http://www.newleftreview.org/?view=2704 (last accessed 14 November 2014).

Zhao, B., *In Pursuit of Harmony: An academic anthology*, Foreign Languages Press, 2008.

Zhao, S. (ed.), *Debating Political Reform in China: Rule of law vs. democratisation*, Armonk, New York: M. E. Sharpe, 2006.

Zhao, Y. and Sun, W., 'Public opinion supervision: the role of the media in constraining local officials', in Perry, E. and Goldman, M. (eds), *Grassroots Political Reform in China*, Cambridge, MA: Harvard University Press, 2007.

Zheng, Y., *Technological Empowerment: The internet, state, and society in China*, Stanford, CA: Stanford University Press, 2008.

— *Shijiehua Yu Zhongguo Guojia Zhuanxing (Globalization and the Transition of the Chinese State)*, Hangzhou: Zhejiang People's Press, 2009.

— 'Society must be defended', *East Asian Institute Working Paper* 152, July 9 2009.

— *The Chinese Communist Party as Organizational Emperor: Culture, reproduction and transformation*, New York: Routledge, 2010.

Zheng, Y., and John, W., *The Nanxun Legacy and China's Development in the post-Deng Era*, Singapore: World Scientific, 2001.

Zhu, X., 'Government advisors or public advocates? Roles of think tanks in China from the perspective of regional variations', *China Quarterly* 207, September 2011, pp. 668–86.

Zins, M. -J., 'L'intellectuel occidentalisé indien: de l'intellectuel syncrétique à l'intellectuel organique', in Trebitsch, M. and Granjon, M. -C. (eds), Pour une histoire comparée des intellectuels, Paris/Bruxelles: Editions Complexe/IHTP-CNRS, 1998, pp. 141–76.

Glossary of Names, Institutions and Terms

Names of persons

Bai Tongdong	白彤东
Bao Tong	鲍彤
Bei Dao	北岛
Bo Xilai	薄熙来
Bo Yibo	薄一波
Cai Yuanpei	蔡元培
Cao Siyuan	曹思源
Chen Han-seng (Chen Hangsheng)	陈翰笙
Chen Lai	陈来
Chen Ming	陈明
Chen Sihe	陈思和
Chen Yinke	陈寅恪
Chen Yizi	陈一咨
Chen Yun	陈云
Chen Zimin	陈子民
Cixi	慈禧太后
Confucius	孔子
Cui Zhiyuan	崔之元
Deng Pufang	邓朴方
Deng Xiaoping	邓小平
Deng Zhenglai	邓正来
Dong Furen	董辅礽
Dufu	杜甫
Fang Lizhi	方励之
Fang Ning	房宁
Fei Xiaotong	费孝通
Gan Yang	甘阳
Gao Quanxi	高全喜
Gu Zhun	顾准
Han Han	韩寒
Han Shuifa	韩水法
He Huaihong	何怀宏
He Jiaodong	何家栋
He Weifang	贺卫方
He Xin	何新
He Zengke	何增科
Hu Angang	胡鞍钢
Hu Jintao	胡锦涛
Hu Jiwei	胡绩伟
Hu Ping	胡平
Hu Qiaomu	胡乔木
Hu Shi	胡适
Hu Yaobang	胡耀邦
Huang Qifan	黄奇帆

Huang Zongliang	黄宗良
Jiang Qing	蒋庆
Jiang Zemin	江泽民
Jiang Zhaolin	降兆林
Jiao Guobiao	焦国标
Jin Guantao	金观涛
Jin Liqun	金立群
Kang Xiaoguang	康晓光
Lao Tseu (Laozi)	老子
Liang Qichao	梁启超
Li Changchun	李长春
Li Keqiang	李克强
Li Peng	李鹏
Li Qiang	李强
Li Rui	李锐
Li Shenzhi	李慎之
Li Xiannian	李先念
Li Zehou	李泽厚
Liang Shuming	梁漱溟
Lin Biao	林彪
Liu Dong	刘东
Liu Junning	刘军宁
Liu Qingfeng	刘青锋
Liu Shaoqi	刘少奇
Liu Xiaobo	刘晓波
Liu Xiaofeng	刘小枫
Liu Yingsheng	刘迎胜
Liu Zaifu	刘再复
Lu Xun	鲁迅
Ma Jun	马军
Mao Zedong	毛泽东
Mao Yushi	茅于轼
Pan Gongkai	潘功凯
Pan Tianshou	潘天寿
Pan Wei	潘维
Pu Shan	浦山
Pu Songling	蒲松龄
Qian Mu	钱穆
Qin Hui	秦晖
Rao Zongyi	饶宗颐
Ren Jiantao	任剑涛
Su Shaozhi	苏绍智
Sun Liping	孙立平
Sun Yat-sen (Sun Zhongshan)	孙中山
Tang Tsou (Zou Dang)	邹谠
Tu Weiming (Du Weiming)	杜维明
Wan Junren	万俊人
Wan Runnan	万润南
Wang Dingding	汪丁丁
Wang Gang	王刚

Wang Guixiu	王贵秀
Wang Guowei	王国维
Wang Hui	汪晖
Wang Huning	王沪宁
Wang Jisi	王缉思
Wang Juntao	王军涛
Wang Li	王力
Wang Shaoguang	王绍光
Wang Xiaoming	王晓明
Wang Yang	汪洋
Wang Yuanhua	王元化
Wei Jianhang	尉健行
Wei Jingsheng	魏京生
Wen Jiabao	温家宝
Wen Tiejun	温铁军
Wu Bangguo	吴邦国
Wu Guoguang	吴国光
Wu Jinglian	吴敬琏
Xi Jinping	习近平
Xia Yong	夏勇
Xiao Gongqin	萧功秦
Xie Fei	谢非
Xu Jilin	许纪霖
Xu Xianglin	徐湘林
Xu Yong	徐勇
Xu Youyu	徐友渔
Yan Fu	严复
Yan Jiaqi	严加其
Yan Xuetong	阎学通
Yang Guangbin	杨光斌
Yao Dali	姚大力
Yao Yang	姚洋
Ye Gongchao	叶公超
Yu Dan	于丹
Yu Jianrong	于建嵘
Yu Keping	俞可平
Yü Ying-shih (Yu Yingshi)	余英时
Yu Yongding	余永定
Yuan Shikai	袁世凯
Zhang Chunqiao	张春桥
Zhang Guangda	张广达
Zhang Jingfu	张景福
Zhang Weiying	张维迎
Zhang Wuchang	张五常
Zhang Xudong	张旭东
Zhang Zhihong	张志红
Zhao Baoxu	赵宝煦
Zhao Ziyang	赵紫阳
Zheng Bijian	郑必坚
Zheng Yongnian	郑永年

Zhou Enlai	周恩来
Zhou Tianyong	周天勇
Zhu De	朱德
Zhu Guanglei	朱光磊
Zhu Houze	朱厚泽
Zhu Rongji	朱镕基
Zhu Xueqin	朱学勤
Zhang Xuan	张轩

Names of institutions, organisations, provinces and cities

Academy of Social Sciences (China)	*zhongguo shehuikexueyuan*	中国社会科学院
Beida (*see* Peking University)		
Central Compilation and Translation Bureau of the Central Committee of the Chinese Communist Party	*zhonggong zhongyang bianyi ju bijiao zhengzhi yu jingji yanjiu zhongxin*	中共中央编译局比较政治与经济研究中心
Central Party School	*zhonggong zhongyang dangxiao*	中共中央党校
Centre for China Government Innovations	*zhongguo zhengfu chuangxin yanjiu zhongxin*	中国政府创新研究中心
Centre for China Studies	*Guoqing yanjiusuo*	国情研究所
Chongqing		重庆
Cultural Revolution	*Wenhua dageming*	文化大革命
Guangdong		广东
Letters and Visits Bureau	*Xinfang*	信访
Red Guards	*hong wei bing*	红卫兵
Little Red Guards	*hong xiao bing*	红小兵
Universities		
Fudan University	*Fudan daxue*	复旦大学
Nankai University	*Nankai daxue*	南开大学
Peking University	*Beijing daxue*	北京大学
People's University	*Renmin daxue*	人民大学
Sun Yat-sen University	*Zhongshan daxue*	中山大学

Terms, concepts and phrases

benevolent, humane government	*renzheng*	仁政
'building a harmonious society'– Hu-Wen era slogan	*jianshe hexie shehui*	建设
cat (no matter if the cat is white or black as long as it catches mice)	*buguan baimao heimao zhuazhao laoshu jiushi haomao*	不管白猫黑猫抓着老鼠就是好猫
censorship	*shencha zhidu*	审查制度
chaos	*hunluan*	混乱
China model	*zhongguo moshi*	中国模式
China studies	*guoxue*	国学
Chinese conditions	*guoqing*	国情
Chinese essence, Western means	*zhongti xiyong, zhongxue weiti, xixue weiyong*	中体西用, 中学为体, 西学为用
Chongqing experience	*Chongqing jingyan*	重庆经验
Confucianism	*ruxue*	儒学
Democracy	*minzhu*	民主
big democracy	*da minzhu*	大民主
complex democracy	*fuhe minzhu*	复合民主
deliberative democracy	*shenyishi minzhu; shangyishi minzhu; xieshang minzhu*	审议式民主; 商议式民主; 协商民主
extended democracy	*guangfan de minzhu*	广泛的民主
gradual democracy/incremental democracy	*zengliang minzhu*	增量民主
inner-party democracy	*dangnei minzhu*	党内民主
elections	*xuanju*	选举
generation	*dai*	代
government		
benevolent government/enlightened government	*wangdao*	王道
disinterested government	*zhongxing zhengfu*	中性政府
Go West policy	*xibu da kaifa*	西部大开发
indigenization	*bentuhua*	本土化
innovations introduced in the political system	*zhidu chuangxin*	制度创新
intellectuals	*zhishifenzi*	知识分子
Let some people get rich first	*rang yibufen ren xian fuqilai*	让一部分人先富起来
liberalism	*ziyouzhuyi*	自由主义

liberation of thought	*sixiang jiefang*	思想解放
moderate prosperity	*xiaokang*	小康
neo-authoritarianism	*xin quanweizhuyi*	新权威主义
neo-conservatism	*xin baoshouzhuyi*	新保守主义
New Left	*xin zuo pai*	新左派
Open and Reform policy	*gaige kaifang*	改革开放
people-centered growth	*yirenweiben*	以人为本
priority to order and stability	*wending yadao yiqie*	稳定压倒一切
priority to the welfare of the people	*minsheng*	民生
protest	*kangyi*	抗议
quality (of the population)	*suzhi*	素质
quest for power and wealth	*fuqiang*	富强
rise of China	*zhongguo jueqi*	中国崛起
peaceful rise	*heping jueqi*	和平崛起
scientific development	*kexue fazhanguan*	科学发展观
sent-down policy; down to the countryside movement	*shangshan xiaxiang yundong*	上山下乡运动
socialist countryside	*shehuizhuyi xin nongcun*	社会主义新农村
socialist harmonious society	*shehuizhuyi hexie shehui*	社会主义和谐社会
stability, maintaining of	*weiwen, weichi wending*	维稳, 维持稳定
think tank	*zhiku*	智库
tradition	*chuantong*	传统
university entrance examination	*gaokao*	高考
winning people's hearts and minds (through considering them as the root of the country)	*minben*	民本

Index